HOME RUN ON WHEELS

by Ron Clements

DORRANCE
PUBLISHING CO
EST. 1920
PITTSBURGH, PENNSYLVANIA 15238

Dorrance Publishing Co
585 Alpha Drive
Pittsburgh, PA 15238
Visit our website at *www.dorrancebookstore.com*

ISBN: 978-1-6453-0122-6
eISBN: 978-1-6453-0949-9

INTRODUCTION

What began as a bucket-list trip turned into something so much more. My wife Patti and I never set out to do anything magnanimous or philanthropic. We initially just wanted to take advantage of being able to work remotely by traveling in an RV to all 30 Major League Baseball stadiums during a single season.

A dinner on July 28th, 2017 changed everything as our journey suddenly had a mission. Things were set into motion two months earlier when Patti began a new job with a bank that was 100-percent remote. Then one July afternoon, she stepped out of the office at our home in Charlotte and said, "You know, I could do this anywhere."

We then started to kick around travel ideas and a baseball trip came up. It didn't take very long before we just said, "Why not? Let's do it. We'll get an RV and go."

The proverbial wheels were starting to roll. We recorded and watched *Going RV* on the DIY Network to get ideas of what we wanted in an RV. Neither of us had ever owned or driven an RV before, and the show was the first step in our research process. We also read quite a bit online and began to formulate some ideas of features and layouts we desired. Patti, ever the project manager, created a spreadsheet ranking must-have and nice-to-have elements.

It wasn't until February that we purchased our RV and by then we had partnered with Children's Hope Alliance — a foster care advocacy organization in North Carolina. That partnership was spawned during the aforementioned dinner.

After moving from St. Louis to Charlotte in December of 2014, Patti joined a gym and met a woman named Celeste Dominguez. The two bonded during their workouts and quickly became friends. Celeste was an executive with Children's Hope Alliance and traveled quite a bit with her job. The summer of 2018 was unusually busy for her, roving in-state to fundraising events and out of state to conferences. She also made time to visit her two college-aged children. Her travel schedule slowed down by late July, and she reached out to ask us if we wanted to join her for dinner.

We set a date — the day after my birthday — and met at a Cajun place near the Concord Mills Mall north of Charlotte. I joked that I had two dates for a birthday dinner. This was simply meeting with a friend to catch up. But when Celeste asked if anything was new, that dinner became the foundation of our 2018 plans. We told Celeste of our intent to buy an RV and travel to all 30 MLB stadiums.

The lightbulb went on.

"Wouldn't it be cool if we could take a kid to a game," Patti said half-jokingly.

"What if you could take multiple kids to games?" Celeste responded.

What followed was about a 30-minute conversation about how that might work. Children's Hope Alliance operates solely in North Carolina, where there are no Major League Baseball teams. Patti and I also did not know what the legalities were of trying to get kids to games, and we weren't even sure how to go about requesting tickets from teams. These were all questions to which we eventually found answers over the next few months.

After dinner, Celeste said she would run our idea past the Children's Hope Alliance board. Another event occurred a month later that helped the plan come to fruition. Celeste got promoted to chief executive officer of Children's Hope Alliance. Now we felt confident things were going to happen and we'd be able to get children to professional baseball games.

"It's an experience that most of our children here don't have," Celeste told us as we discussed our mission before we left. "They can't afford them; they don't have access to them. It's a treat that they just don't get to experience unless somebody helps them get there."

"That is exactly what we are trying to do," I replied.

What we didn't know at the time is we'd receive some terrible health news before our journey ended. Holmes, our 11-year-old border collie/black lab mix, was diagnosed with lymphoma on September 20th, 2018. We feared this was the last road trip we'd ever take with him. Thankfully it was not. He was our "Barketing Manager," after all.

By the time we completed our trip in September of 2018, we had acquired 220 total tickets for games at six different MLB stadiums – and 80 from two minor-league clubs – for foster families to join us at some baseball games. We wish we could have done more, but that was never the mission Celeste laid out for us. Getting kids to a game was a bonus. Her primary objective for us was to drive around a giant Children's Hope Alliance "billboard" to get people talking about foster care.

"Our heart is getting the word out about children," she told us. "Every state you're going to be in, every city center that you're going to be in, there are agencies like ours that serve and support children that have needs and have experienced trauma – trauma like abuse or neglect or some sort of life experience that has just really hurt them. In every one of these towns, people can volunteer. They can help with this initiative by just bringing awareness by helping with the tickets, helping to celebrate what we're doing, helping to pass the word. Putting us on their Facebook page or Instagram. Taking a picture of your RV as you're traveling by and helping us get the word out."

Before we left Charlotte for good on March 12th, 2018, I needed to figure out what I was going to do with my job. Patti could work remotely, but I had an office I went into almost every day. I did have the option to work from home, on occasion, but spending seven months on the road probably wasn't going to work.

I was the lead NFL reporter for the United States Omnisport news desk in Charlotte. The parent company is England-based Perform Media, which also owns Sporting News in the U.S. Just about everything I wrote was published at Sporting News while some content was picked up by international outlets. I occasionally did short news videos in the Sporting News studio.

We ran our trip by the Perform brass in England but were told writing about an RV tour to all 30 MLB stadiums did not "fit the model" of Omnisport or Sporting News. I knew then I had to leave my job to take this trip. It wasn't an easy decision, leaving the security of a regular paycheck, but it was a leap of faith Patti and I made together. I had grown frustrated by being asked to cover NFL games from an office instead of being on-site at a stadium, especially since Bank of America Stadium (home of the Carolina Panthers) was just a few blocks away. My frustration made the decision to leave easier.

We sought sponsors for the venture and I began in October, reaching out to just about every company that sponsors Major League Baseball. I had this grand idea of multiple companies getting involved to help get some foster kids to games. We didn't care if the RV looked like a NASCAR car with company logos decorating the rig from the hood to the tow hitch. Any sponsorship money would go toward fuel and tickets to get some children in the foster system to MLB games.

Most of my emails to companies did not prompt a response. But I did at least hear back from a couple: Scott's Miracle-Gro and Starwood hotels.

Scott's Miracle-Gro said it couldn't sponsor the trip monetarily but did send an indoor gardening kit I had hoped to use in the RV to grow some herbs and vegetables. When the kit arrived, I realized that would not be feasible. The thing was huge and came in two large boxes. One box contained the actual indoor gardening unit while the other had the lighting unit. We wanted to make it work somehow, but once we started to pack up the RV to live in permanently, we knew there would be no room for the AeroGarden. We were thankful for the gift, but along with several other things we wanted to keep from our Charlotte home, it went into our storage unit in St. Louis.

A representative from Starwood, which operates the Marriott and Sheraton hotel chains, told me his company also did not have it in its 2018 budget to sponsor the trip but offered to comp us a "night or two" at one of its hotels. That offer never came to fruition.

Children's Hope Alliance, a non-profit foster care organization in North Carolina, would be our only sponsor. Other than that, we knew by Christmas we would be on our own.

After Celeste's promotion to CEO, we met with her again in Huntersville, N.C. This time she was joined by Abigail Lord-Ramsey, who is the chief development officer for Children's Hope Alliance and handled most of the organization's outreach events.

Soon after, Celeste got approval from the Children's Hope Alliance board to sponsor the trip and they had a modest budget to pay for a vehicle wrap with their logo, as well as a logo we had yet to create. Heck, we didn't even know at that point what we were going to call the trip.

Our first thought centered around the stitching of a baseball and I was very proud of "Stitches Be Tripping." Then I remembered we were working with a children's advocacy organization and that probably didn't have the proper connotation. Patti and I tried to brainstorm ideas as I interrupted her one weekday afternoon as she sat in the wheeled chair at her home office desk. We knew "Stitches Be Tripping" was out (That big hutch-style desk and accompanying wooden wheeled chair were two of the items we donated to the Salvation Army).

"This is going to be our home for at least seven months," I told her at one point.

"It's a baseball trip," Patti added. "What about Home Run On Wheels?" We had a winner.

"We could have an RV as our logo with baseballs for wheels," Patti continued.

It was a great idea and one we quickly moved to implement. Home Run On Wheels would become our brand. We decided we would have a website, do a podcast twice a week, and create Facebook and Instagram accounts, all of which would be Home Run On Wheels. But we needed that logo.

Fortunately for us, I was still working at Perform and Sporting News employs a few graphic designers who are open to freelance work. The first person I asked was Paul Howe, a British expatriate who does a terrific job for Sporting News, and I knew he could design a fantastic logo. Unfortunately, he was traveling to England to visit family and then was moving from Charlotte to Washington, D.C. He referred me to his co-worker, Riley Meek. I knew Riley also has a creative mind and we told her our idea. After a couple weeks, she sent us some options for Home Run on Wheels and even designed a logo for my website, RonClementsSports.com. After a couple of tweaks, we had what we wanted, a red and white RV with baseballs for wheels and a bat running along the side of the vehicle with the hashtag #HomeRunOnWheels under the rig.

As for the route, we'd take, well, that was one of the easiest things to figure out once the 2018 MLB schedule was released in September of 2017. Within two hours, I had the trip plotted out with most of March spent in Florida for Spring Training before we took in Opening Day in Miami. From there, it would be up the East Coast and into Canada before heading west across the northern U.S. Denver would be our last stop before the All-Star break, and Coors Field would be our 19th stadium. We'd see a game at Seattle's Safeco Field, following the All-Star Game, before heading south down the West Coast and then back east from San Diego to Phoenix before heading to Texas. The trip would end in St. Louis in September. We knew the route and just needed places to stay, which we figured out during the trip.

There were so many moving parts to launching Home Run On Wheels, and by the time the calendar turned to 2018, we still didn't know what kind of RV we were going to purchase. We had an idea of what we wanted and things started to become clearer after we attended an RV show in Charlotte in mid-January.

We saw some high-end RVs we loved but knew would not afford something priced at $400,000 and higher. We had a budget about a quarter of that and that definitely limited our options. We had to find a layout we liked. Patti grabbed every floorplan pamphlet she could get her hands on. I walked into just about every RV at the convention center to see the assorted designs. It didn't take long to figure out that we did not want a fifth-wheel or a trailer because we would have to purchase a truck to tow it. Patti had a 2009 Infiniti G37S and I had a 2011 Scion xD. We decided Patti would sell her car and we would tow mine, which got significantly better gas mileage.

We also knew we wanted a Class A motor coach as opposed to a Class B or C. A Class A gave us more room, though we had to be sure we weren't getting something so large that it would be cumbersome to drive.

After visiting a few RV dealerships and attending that RV show, we test-drove two RVs — a 2015 Fleetwood Bounder and a 2018 Thor Windsport. We liked the way the Windsport handled and loved the layout, so that is the one we selected. What we didn't know is that we would have multiple issues with the Thor. The slideout topper — a piece of rolling vinyl that is meant to protect the top of the slideout from debris like leaves and branches — snapped twice within the first five months, the water heater didn't work properly for the first two months, the awning wind sensor was faulty over the first month, and the radio dash display — which includes the rear-view and side-view cameras — was out for about three weeks in July before we were able to get the fuse replaced. Fortunately, none of these issues delayed our trip during the regular season — though it did push back our ultimate departure from Charlotte by a couple of days. We second-guessed our decision of purchasing a

Thor multiple times during our trip but spoke with many people who paid significantly more for their motor coaches and every RV has issues – especially over the first year. It's an accepted fact in the RV industry, even though it shouldn't be. Lemon laws may exist for cars, but they don't exist for RVs.

It didn't help that the Camping World in Concord, North Carolina was habitually unresponsive. We'd send several emails and leave multiple voice-mails without getting a reply. When we showed up on March 10th to pick up the RV, assuming all the repairs had been made, the service representative seemed surprised to see us, despite our numerous messages. It wasn't ready.

Before the RV was officially ours, we rented a U-Haul to take some of the things we wanted to keep to St. Louis. Patti had owned a house there and rented it out using Airbnb shortly after we had moved to Charlotte in December of 2014 until it finally sold in July of 2017. The closing date on the house was September 1st. Because the house was furnished, that furniture went into a storage unit in St. Louis. It's also the unit into which we placed our things from the Charlotte house we had been renting.

While we did take those things to St. Louis, we still had a lot of items to get rid of. We sold some items and donated several things to Goodwill and then had a Salvation Army truck come out to the house. We also threw away a bunch of stuff. You have no idea what a trash truck can do to a sofa until you see that couch snapped in half before it's devoured by the hydraulic packers.

We put in our notice to the property management office that February 28th would be our final day in the house. By the time that date rolled around, the house was empty and we were almost ready to go. I had informed Perform I would work through the NFL Scouting Combine, but my last day would be March 6th. We left Charlotte for good six days later.

Where did we stay for those 12 days? Our sweet neighbor, Maryalyce Bedenbaugh, let us stay with her for those nearly two weeks. She and our other neighbors helped us out with another dilemma we faced.

We had too much food to fit in the RV. We had subscribed to a butcher service to deliver fresh, flash-frozen meat and vegetables to us. We placed our final order in October of 2017, knowing we'd be leaving in in March. We figured a four-month order would be perfect. The problem is I was not home when Patti placed the order and she was not there when the food was delivered. We received the wrong order. There was some overlap in what we received, but what we ordered and didn't receive was sent to us about a week later. But what was delivered could not legally be returned, so we had an excess of food.

By the time we took our chest freezer to St. Louis, we didn't have room to put everything in the smaller freezer in the house refrigerator. So, there I was in our garage, loading a bunch of frozen food into a laundry basket. I took the basketful of meat and vegetables over to Maryalyce's house after she said we could keep it in her freezer. Her freezer was now full. There was still a lot left. So, I knocked on our neighbor's house on the other side belonging to Craig and Keri. Another laundry basket of food, mostly fish, went to their place. There was still more. Enter Eddie and Janet across the street and their garage freezer was packed with mostly beef. Our freezer was finally empty, and I told them we'd pick up that food when we came back through Charlotte in early April on our way from Atlanta to Washington, D.C. In the meantime, we told them to eat as much as they wanted.

"I see you through the window and you're carrying a laundry basket full of food across our yard," Patti said while unsuccessfully trying to stifle a laugh.

When we came through in April, we did not cut into our food supply as much as we thought we would and the RV freezer was still rather full. We also found out our neighbors had barely touched any of the food we stored in their freezers, so we faced a similar problem of too much food and not enough space. I ended up filling a large cooler we had stored under the RV with ice and packed it full of the frozen food our former neighbors were holding. The food remained cold and frozen for a few days as I replaced the ice, but it eventually began to thaw. A week after passing through Charlotte, I spent the better part of two days grilling at an RV park in College Park, Maryland. Patti later said our stay in College Park was the first time we had a "camping experience" because we used our on-site grill to cook and sit by a fire.

· · · · ·

We took a weekend trip to Jupiter, Florida shortly after purchasing the RV to check out the first weekend of Spring Training and give our new home a test run. The first time we put out the main slideout to fill up the RV for its maiden voyage was the first time that slideout topper broke. It was February 20th. The brackets on either side of the roller snapped as we tried to extend the slideout.

The technician said the manufacturer didn't attach a necessary spacer. This, we later found out, was not exactly the cause of the problem. We had the topper removed and put it in our garage so our trip wouldn't be delayed.

Not only did that maiden voyage weekend provide us an opportunity to become more familiar with our new home, it also gave us the chance to record some interviews for our upcoming podcast. We had our first three interviews recorded — Children's Hope Alliance CEO Celeste Dominguez was our first guest and helped explain how this whole venture began; my former boss, Marc Lancaster, who used to work as a Cincinnati Reds and Tampa Bay Rays beat reporter, gave us some food pointers and discussed his favorite and least favorite stadiums and Sporting News national baseball writer Ryan Fagan offered some travel advice while explaining why he had never been to Yankee Stadium. The fourth episode would be Patti and I talking about our first few weeks in the RV and the issues we inevitably faced trying to downsize from our three-bedroom house to a 36-foot home on wheels.

After that, however, I wanted to fill the podcast by speaking with multiple MLB players. The first three came courtesy of the St. Louis Cardinals after they agreed to provide me with a media credential for that opening weekend. Jordan Schafer, who did not make the 2018 big-league roster, Marcell Ozuna and Luke Gregerson were three of our first MLB player guests. Schafer told me an inspirational story that led to the creation of his foundation to benefit the Boys & Girls Club in his hometown of Winterhaven, Florida.

"There's a kid I met while I was in Atlanta who was battling cancer. I didn't know this at the time," Schafer began. "I was running off the field and I just threw my wrist band (into the stands). A couple weeks later, I get a letter in the mail at the field. It was from his mom. His mom told me that he was battling cancer and I didn't know it, obviously didn't know who the kid was, but he would sleep with it on every night. She wanted to know how big of a difference that made and how that brightened his day. Every single night he'd wear it.

"That's kind of when it clicked. I have a greater purpose than just playing baseball. I can affect kids' lives.

"When you go to the Children's Hospital and you see the kids' faces, you see these kids are fighting for their lives, but they have the biggest smiles on their faces when you walk through the door. They're just happy to see you. That puts life into perspective."

After the Cardinals allowed me access over that weekend in late February, we were able to get other teams to fall in line when we returned to Florida in mid-March. We interviewed Detroit Tigers pitcher Daniel Norris, Rays ace Chris Archer, Martin Prado, and Cameron Maybin of the Miami Marlins, and Pittsburgh Pirates pitchers Jameson Taillon and Chad Kuhl and first baseman Josh Bell. I also interviewed Rays first baseman Jake Bauers in early April while he was still with the Durham Bulls.

Unfortunately, I did not have the same access during the regular season and my grand idea of having a big-league player on our podcast in each MLB city did not come to fruition.

A high school classmate of mine named Jason Stevens, who lives in Chicago, told me the podcast episodes he liked the best were the ones with Patti and I discussing life in the RV and traveling to new sites.

"I can get baseball player interviews anywhere," he told me on June 20th as we sat in Crestwood, Illinois to see a minor-league baseball game between the Windy City Thunderbolts and Joliet Slammers of the independent Frontier League.

"What you guys are doing is unique and I want to hear more of that," he continued. "It's fun when you guys have that banter going back and forth."

Patti does remind me her maiden name is Wright and sometimes says, "I may not always been correct, but I am always Wright."

I no longer felt disappointed I couldn't land more MLB players for the podcast. We did have a few teases with Pirates manager Clint Hurdle and Reds second baseman Scooter Gennett as brief options before they ultimately passed on my interview request. The Philadelphia Phillies and Washington Nationals, both of whom credentialed me during Spring Training, wouldn't do the same once the calendar turned to April. I didn't take it personally and Jason's advice stuck. This was an RV baseball trip and that's what the podcast would chronicle.

That didn't mean we wouldn't have guests. We spoke with representatives from the organizations that received tickets from MLB teams. Michael Williams of Our Kids of Miami/Dade-Monroe, Gordon Wykes of the Student Advocacy Center of Michigan, Matt Roesler of Any Family Services in Wisconsin, Mary Lennick of Family Alternatives in Minnesota, and Cindi Noah, Dona Dalton, and Nicole Vail of Lutheran Services Rocky Mountains all spoke about their respective organizations and what it meant to receive a donation of tickets from their local MLB team.

Cardinals beat reporter Derrick Goold of the St. Louis Post-Dispatch helped me preview the 2018 season with an interview in March. Derrick even accurately predicted that Cardinals manager Mike Matheny could get fired, which happened July 14th.

St. Louis film critic Dan Buffa, who is an avid Cardinals fan, came on to discuss his favorite baseball movies. We all agreed that Kevin Costner has been in three of the best. We also learned that Patti does not like *The Natural*. That was quite the stunning revelation.

Israel National Baseball Team General Manager Peter Kurz was on the podcast to talk about Project Baseball, an initiative we learned of while at Roger Dean Stadium in Jupiter, Florida. With support of the Jewish National Fund in the United States, youth baseball fields are being built in Israel, so kids there can learn the game, and played Little League just like their counterparts in the U.S. Celeste told us as long as people are helping children, she didn't care if we had someone on our podcast who wasn't involved with foster care. The needs of children go beyond foster care and are not exclusive to the United States.

We had Pittsburgh band Nevada Color and Dallas-based country singer Charlie Barrale, a St. Louis native and another diehard Cardinals fan, on to talk music and baseball. Another fun interview was with Steve Melia and Marybeth Longona, a pair of Yankees fans who attended all 162 Yankees games in 2018. Steve also attended every Yankees game in 2011 and has been dubbed "The 162 Guy."

I later interviewed best-selling sports author Jeff Pearlman, who used to cover MLB for Sports Illustrated, and former MLB umpire Gary Darling about Umps Care. Darling is the board president of the Umps Care, which is a charity foundation that works with children's hospitals and foster care organizations to get kids out to games. The umpires also visit hospitals to talk baseball with kids. It is an organization that popped up on my radar in late August and I wish I had known about it sooner. Should we decide to do another MLB trip, a relationship with Umps Care would help us get more kids to games.

"Some of these kids haven't had the chance to really develop a love for a sport. They're in a bad place," Gary told me. "They're foster home to foster home. Baseball isn't their first choice for a day. But you never know, one of these kids who comes through there might end up being a coach or a player or umpire. We just want to introduce them to the game a little bit."

We had Celeste on again when we ended our journey in St. Louis. Celeste made the trip from Charlotte and attended the September 16th game against the Los Angeles Dodgers. We had a group of 26 people at Busch Stadium for that game. We also partnered with the Foster & Adoptive Care Coalition in St. Louis and were able to acquire 50 tickets for two other Cardinals games to get some kids out to Busch Stadium and end the trip on a high note.

"This was more about North Carolina. We jumped into this because we care about children in the foster care system, but not just our children — all children," Celeste said in September. "What you guys have done was to help spread the message across the nation, and that is the difference that was made on your trip.

"It takes four years or more for a seed to grow," Celeste added. "You tell someone about foster care and it's really years and years later before that seed you planted initially about what this is and how you can make a difference, again, whether it's donating luggage or parenting somebody who needs a for-ever home. This is going to pay off years from now. You don't even recognize yet the impact you've had for children."

While we didn't have the astronomical podcast numbers we would have liked, our listenership steadily grew and it was a venture that we plan on continuing. I had these grand ideas of media coverage, but we didn't get nearly the exposure for which I had hoped.

There was one radio interview that led directly to a donation of gifts from a North Carolina man named Richard Beeson. Children's Hope Alliance communications director Adam Hicks and I were in the studio at Statesville, North Carolina country station, WAME, about a week before we left Charlotte. Richard, who works for Allstate, heard the interview and emailed Children's Hope Alliance gifts coordinator Barbara Carlson on March 29th to ask what sort of items were needed and how he could help. A donation was then made through the Allstate Helping Hands program.

My hometown newspaper in Wisconsin, the La Crosse Tribune, did something on us for its April 1st edition. Tribune reporter Zach James reached out to me via Twitter, and a few days later, Patti and I spoke with him while sitting in RV in Bradenton, Florida. The Tribune also ran an article on October 7th to recap the trip. That was an in-person interview conducted when Patti and I went to La Crosse to visit my family the last weekend in September.

Additionally, I was interviewed by Sports Radio America in April and did spots with Fox Sports Radio in June; July interviews with Mile High Sports in

Denver; Pirate Radio 1250 in Greenville, North Carolina; and the Greenville-based Sports Objective podcast. I also did an interview on August 29th with A2D radio in Philadelphia. We had a couple of television nibbles in Cincinnati, Seattle, and Phoenix, but none of those came to fruition. The Talk of the Town radio program in St. Louis interviewed me following the conclusion of our trip. East Carolina University, my alma mater, also featured us in its October alumni magazine. We got our first, and only, television coverage in Houston when KHOU came out to the RV park to profile us. I reached out to MLB Network, the Today Show, Good Morning America, and radio and television stations across the country but most of my emails went unanswered.

It was frustrating, but we pressed on in the hopes that the message was still being received as we drove across the country. We did the podcast twice a week and posted reviews of all 30 stadiums. Patti also wanted to blog about the trip in general, living in the RV, trying to eat right and exercise, but as I found with this book – finding the time to write this was difficult while driving from place to place. The entire trip was one huge learning experience – not just about traveling, but an education on the tribulations of children in the foster system.

You won't get a city-by-city chronology but rather a story separated into categories of the highlights — and a few low-lights of the trip.

We are going to start with Spring Training and Opening Day, however.

CHAPTER 1:

SPRING TRAINING

March 10th was the target date to leave Charlotte and head to Florida to see the Cardinals play the Nationals in West Palm Beach the next day. Unfortunately, the issue with the slideout topper pushed our Charlotte departure back to March 12th.

We couldn't even leave early in the day because the water heater wasn't properly fixed. The work flow at the Concord Camping World was clogged and we were unsuspecting hostages. We had to wait hours, even though we had a 10 a.m. appointment to pick up the RV. No real explanation was given, other than it wasn't ready. The propane tank had also been drained and we asked them to fill that up at no charge before we left. They did. We were also missing the spare set of keys and the remote control for the Blu-ray player. By the time we hit the road, without those missing items, it was 6 p.m. and we were going to see the Rays and Phillies at 1 p.m. the next day. I had a media credential and was hoping to get a Philadelphia player or two for the podcast.

We drove through the night and arrived in Clearwater around 9 a.m. We parked right at Spectrum Field and I rushed over to the stadium to pick up my credential. It took me a few minutes to find the media center, but I finally did and then hustled to the interview room where the Phillies were holding an introductory press conference for newly acquired pitcher Jake Arrieta. I just missed it. Arrieta was gone, though his agent, Scott Boras, was still holding court with a small group of reporters.

After literally running from place to place to try to get some audio, I was panting and sweating by the time I reached the Spectrum Field interview room. I must have looked out of sorts, too, because Chris Ware of the Phillies media relations department walked up to me to ask what I needed. I had forgotten a lanyard for my credential, which I had clutched in my hand, along with a notebook and our TASCAM DR-40 recorder. Chris brought me a lanyard for the credential and told me where I could find a bottle of water. I was then introduced to Kenny Ayres, who handles credentials for the club, and he asked with whom I'd like to speak.

Because Cameron Rupp had done a lot in the Philadelphia community, specifically with the SPCA, I asked for him. I was told to wait for Rupp to get done with batting practice and then he'd be available. The Phillies never took batting practice that day and I instead waited over three hours for the afternoon game to begin. The day was sort of a dud. Patti had been back in the RV working, but she later joined me to watch the Phillies beat the Rays. We were both impressed by the quaint Spectrum Field with its 360-degree boardwalk and excellent concessions.

While I didn't know at the time how well a Delco Philly cheesesteak compared to the real thing in Philadelphia, what I can say is that it was very good. Delco is short for Delaware County, which is adjacent to Philadelphia. We later tried to eat our way through the City of Brotherly Love by sampling multiple cheesesteaks. For the record, Pat's is far superior to Geno's, but Jim's is better than both of them.

The boardwalk at Spectrum Field allows you to watch the game on the move, stopping here and there to chat or grab something from the concessions. Like most of the Florida venues, there really is not a bad vantage point.

Spectrum Field was the third Grapefruit League stadium we saw – after Roger Dean Stadium, shared by the Cardinals and Marlins, and First Data Field in Port St. Lucie, the Spring Training home of the Mets. The Phillies' home in Clearwater was the first stadium where we were able to walk all the way around the stadium thanks to that aforementioned boardwalk.

Remember our test run in late February? We went to three games that weekend, all Cardinals games. Two were at Roger Dean while the other was at First Data Field. I was surprised by how large First Data Field is but disappointed your outfield walk stopped in center field. What we did love about that stadium, however, was the atmosphere. Mets fans are a passionate group, especially the 7 Line Army. They were there in full force on February 24th, taking over the right-field lawn area.

We had a blast hanging out with that group while watching the Cardinals' 10-5 win. There were four people in particular who stood out.

As we walked out to the lawn area, we got stopped by a pair of Latino men on the ramp near the right-field foul pole.

"Hey, man, help us settle an argument," one of the men, who was wearing a Mets jersey and New York Knicks cap, asked.

"OK," I responded, sort of confused by what was happening.

"Carmelo Anthony, first-ballot Hall of Famer or not?"

"Dude, he is definitely a first-ballot Hall of Famer," his friend interjected before I could answer. His friend had longer hair than his counterpart, who kept his hair cut short. The interrupting friend had his dark hair in a braided pony tail.

"I think it depends on who else is in that class," I ultimately responded. "I think he's easily a Hall of Famer because of what he did in college and the Olympics."

"That's what I've been saying," the first man shouted.

"I just don't know if he'll get in on the first ballot," I finished.

Patti, who wasn't sure who Carmelo Anthony is, had no opinion on the topic. We exchanged a few more pleasantries before we both continued our stroll in opposite directions. The funny thing about that conversation is that it came up on my Twitter timeline in mid-July. I stated the exact same opinion and was told by Knicks fans to stick to football. C'est la vie.

When we did make it to the right-field lawn, we were fully immersed in the rowdy 7 Line Army. They were shouting at players; some shouts were negative but most were positive.

"This is a fun group," I said to Patti. My comment was overheard by a woman standing in front of us.

"Oh, we love coming down here," she said after turning around. She was a Puerto Rican woman who was there with her husband, a comedian who told us to look him up when we were in New York. We gave him my contact info and told him to email me his own information. We never did hear from that guy, but we did learn a lot about his life in the 20 minutes or so that we spoke. He is a lifelong Mets fan who tries to come down to Spring Training every year. He had spent some time in prison but was now married and had a child and was trying to launch a stand-up career. I wish I would have remembered his name, but sadly I had forgotten by the time we returned to the RV park that weekend in Jupiter. If only he would have emailed me like he said. We found that to be a common theme on our trip, people not following through with what they say they are going to do.

Spectrum Field was my second-favorite Grapefruit League stadium of the ten we visited. We did not see the Braves at Disney in Orlando, the Blue Jays in Dunedin or the Twins in Fort Myers – although we did drive by the Twins stadium.

One unique quirk at Spectrum Field were signs of Pennsylvania locations with the mileage to various Gulf Coast League venues. There is a marsh behind the stadium's right-field wall and we saw Jesmuel Valentin's walk-off homer land there. The ball left the stadium and Patti and I tried to locate the ball but couldn't see it through the thick grass. We just assume an alligator kept it as a souvenir.

"The gator got it," Patti commented. "He's out there playing catch with his baby gators."

"Here, son," I added as we both shared a laugh. I jokingly told a few kids to go ahead and jump in to find the ball. Thankfully and not surprisingly, there were no takers.

The very next day, we saw the Rays play again – this time in Bradenton against the Pirates at LECOM Park. This was easily my favorite Grapefruit League stadium.

It just felt like a Florida venue with palm trees encircling the small airy stadium with an open design. There are no walls behind the last row of seats, allowing the breeze to blow through the grandstand unencumbered. LECOM, known to locals and longtime Pirates fans as McKechnie Stadium, is the oldest Grapefruit League stadium and has been dubbed Florida's Fenway Park. It opened in 1923 and renovated in 2013.

"You could tell it's old, but it doesn't feel dated," Patti said of the LECOM Park.

Most of the seats in the grandstand – with a white stucco, mission-style design adorning the press box roof – are covered to provide fans some shade.

The outfield concourse, however, is where I made the first encounter that affected our regular-season trip.

I was able to interview Pirates players Jameson Taillon, Chad Kuhl and Josh Bell before the game. Despite jettisoning All-Stars Andrew McCutchen and Gerrit Cole, the Pirates entered the 2018 season with a ton of confidence. Their 13-10 win over the Detroit Tigers began an 8-2 start, but the Pirates finished the year 82-79 and in fourth place in the National League Central.

Taillon overcame Tommy John surgery in 2014, a sports hernia in 2015, and testicular cancer in 2017 but knew he'd be nervous when he took the mound at Comerica Park. That paled in comparison to when he took the field for the first time in June 2017 five weeks after successful testicular cancer surgery.

"I just told myself, 'Take a step back, soak it all in, good or bad. I get to play baseball tonight. I'm back doing what I love,'" Taillon said before a 2018 Spring Training game. "I got a little emotional there, internally. I might not show it, but pitching Opening Day, I'll have butterflies. The challenge is how can I positively get those butterflies to help me."

Taillon's bout with cancer in 2017 put things in a new perspective for him.

"If I used to talk to a kid that's affected by cancer, it's like, 'What the heck do you say?' But now I've realized it's important to just have a conversation with somebody," Taillon told me as part of the Home Run On Wheels podcast. "You can touch them on a personal level. You don't have to talk about cancer. I try to not even go there with kids or other people I talk to. But how can I make them feel important? How can I make a difference in their life? I don't have a script or anything. I'm definitely a lot more comfortable talking to anybody about any situation now. I say something like, try to celebrate the successes, the good days you have," Taillon added. "Hitting a milestone, try to celebrate that. If you have a bad day, don't judge yourself. It's OK to get down a little bit but really try to focus on stringing good days together, whether that be with doctors, whether that be with your family, whatever you need to do. If you put a good day in today, you won that day. Go into tomorrow, how can I put in another good day? And you just string them together and you'll be in a lot better of a spot."

Taillon said baseball is a great game that has helped teach him to deal with adversity.

"A lot of it's mental," Taillon said in front of his locker. "Baseball is a game of failure. A 3.00 ERA gets you to an All-Star Game potentially. Hitting .300 can get you to the Hall of Fame, so that's failing seven out of ten times. You have to deal with failure really well.

"As a starting pitcher, you have four days off between when you pitch and if you have a bad game, you have to sit on a bad game for four days. That's not the easiest thing in life. Imagine having a tough day at work and not being able to go out and prove yourself the next day. You have to sit there for four and let it marinate a little bit. It's tough what we do."

· · · · ·

When I returned to the stadium, it was to enjoy the game as a fan and explore LECOM Park. My walk took me to the outfield bar area in center field. I grabbed a beer and then noticed a man wearing a Wisconsin Badgers cap.

I approached him and asked, "Where in Wisconsin are you from?"

"Menomonie," he said.

"Cool. I'm from La Crosse," I told him and his group of five other Wisconsinites.

The six Cheeseheads had made their way to Florida for Spring Training. They had previously seen the Brewers in Arizona's Cactus League and wanted to see what the Grapefruit League was all about. Included in the sextet was a woman named Cheryl Larson. As I spoke with the Badgers fan and Cheryl, I learned Cheryl worked for a foster care organization in Wisconsin called Anu Family Services. She also had with her a 9-year-old boy named Kenny, who had been adopted out of the foster system. I just about leapt out of my skin.

I had to tell them about our trip and mission. This was a serendipitous encounter.

I laid out the plan and told her we would be in Milwaukee between June 21st and July 5th.

"We want to get kids out to Major League Baseball games and hopefully we can work with Anu to get some kids to a Brewers game," I said.

"Wow. That would be great," she said. "Do you have a card?"

Of course, I did. I quickly pulled a card from my back pocket and handed it to her. She said she would pass my contact information along to people at Anu who handle community outreach projects. Now, when you meet someone at a baseball game, or any sporting event, and they tell you they're going to call you or email you, chances are you are never going to hear from them.

I handed out a lot of business cards while on our trip.

People told me, "It's so cool what you guys are doing. I'll definitely check out your website and podcast," or, "I know people with a foster care organization. I'll pass your information along," or, "I'll email you a name and number of someone." We heard those phrases or something similar more times than I can remember. Cheryl was among the very few people who actually followed through with what she said she was going to do. A few weeks later, I received a phone call from a man from Anu named Matt Roesler. We'll cover that later.

Patti had joined me at the park after finishing up some work. She took an Uber from the RV park in Bradenton and would have been there sooner had the Uber driver known where he was going. He was confused when she told him LECOM Park and took her to a strip mall. Patti knew she was in the wrong spot and corrected her driver to get her to the correct location.

"I put 'McKechnie' into the Uber app and Uber found a place. I don't know where I'm going, so I'm not going to dispute what the app says," Patti explained. "My driver comes and he did not speak English, which is fine unless there's a problem. Unless you end up at a strip mall in front of a nail place and he's all like, 'OK, get out.' I was like, 'What? This is not it.' He pointed to his map on the Uber app with the pin and I said, 'This is not right.' But I ended up getting there. My driver was laughing, and as he pulled up, he goes, 'Oh, ballpark.' He was very nice, but he couldn't help me figure it out because of the language barrier."

Just after her arrival, the Rays used a five-run seventh inning to leave LECOM Park that day with a 9-3 victory, but the game was secondary. It's Spring Training, after all.

We glanced at the field when we heard cheering, but I was still riding a high from my meeting with Cheryl and the Cheeseheads. We then met some other people who eventually enhanced our trip. Tony and Joann Grieco are Pittsburgh residents and diehard Pirates fans. Tony was nearing retirement after spending decades working for the Pirates as a stadium usher in Pittsburgh. Tony, a diminutive man who stands about 5 feet, 5 inches with a full head of white hair, and

Joann, with her dark hair and tan skin, struck up a conversation with us after they overheard me telling two other people about our trip. We had been speaking with a man named Steve and his adult son, Matt Burt. Steve lives in the Tampa area and Matt was in town visiting from Pennsylvania. Matt was fascinated by our trip and said he was big into podcasts. While Matt did recommend a very nice restaurant in Bradenton, we never heard from Matt again.

Joann, however, did email me to tell me that Pirates manager Clint Hurdle is very philanthropic. He has a relationship with the Children's Institute in Pittsburgh. The Children's Institute has a variety of programs, including adoption and foster care services. It was one of the organizations with which I spoke to try to get kids to games. After a couple of conversations with the Children's Institute, however, we weren't able to get any kids to a game in Pittsburgh over Memorial Day weekend.

Hurdle does not work with the foster care side of The Children's Institute, which also operates a children's hospital. Hurdle became involved with The Children's Institute after his daughter, Maddie, was diagnosed with Prader-Willi Syndrome — a genetic disorder that causes weak muscles and slow development because of a loss of function of specific genes. As his daughter became "the face" of the rare disorder, Hurdle organized several fundraisers to help combat the disease. We later requested to have Hurdle on our podcast to discuss his "Wins for Kids" campaign and his work with the Children's Institute, but he passed.

. . . . .

Joann told me to contact her when we got to Pittsburgh. I nearly forgot, but Patti reminded me after we arrived at PNC Park. We sat in the seats in Section 316 that I purchased for $17 apiece. I then texted Joann, apologizing for not contacting her earlier to take her up on her spring offer of a pregame meal. Joann texted back and told me she was sitting in Section 214. Patti then spotted her and I texted, "Turn around."

She turned and waved and then met us in the concourse. What happened next was phenomenal. Sections 207-228 at PNC Park comprise the Pittsburgh Baseball Club Level, which includes a pair of full-service bars and multiple pool tables while providing a wonderful view of the field and Pittsburgh skyline. The two bars inside the club are what you'd find at your neighborhood bar: guys wearing jerseys playing pool and drinking beer while keeping tabs on the game thanks to the multiple televisions dotting the walls.

Joann led us through the club level and to her favorite PNC Park bartender. She ordered a trio of drinks, all on her tab, and then gave us a guided tour of the stadium. We made our way down to the main concourse and began to circumnavigate the stadium.

As we approached the area behind home plate, Joann asked, "Do you want to go see Tony?"

"Of course," we replied in stereo.

As a longtime Pirates usher, Tony has one of the premium spots at PNC Park. He works at the Lexus Club directly behind home plate. Sections 14-20 are just 12 rows deep and included access to the all-inclusive club with a buffet and non-alcoholic drinks. Food and drinks could also be ordered from your seats thanks to servers roaming the sections.

When we sat down to watch the first inning, we were in Section 316. By the time the sixth inning had started, those $17 seats had been upgraded to tenth row seats in Section 17. We saw the Pirates cruise to an 8-1 victory over the Cardinals that day, but the experience at PNC Park was enhanced thanks to that Italian couple we met in Bradenton two months earlier.

· · · · ·

While PNC Park was my favorite MLB stadium, LECOM Park was my favorite Grapefruit League stadium. It is open, spacious, historic, and sits in a neighborhood chock full of bars and restaurants. The concession prices were also about a dollar lower than every other Grapefruit League stadium. We visited Patti's favorite spring venue a week later when we saw the Boston Red Sox take on the Baltimore Orioles in Sarasota.

Patti was impressed with the green initiatives at Ed Smith Stadium, as well as "The Orioles Health and Fitness Challenge" — a campaign that promotes healthy lifestyles, especially for middle-school children who want to "eat, train and live like the pros." LECOM Park is also a very green stadium with recycling bins at every entry way.

While the Red Sox went on to tally 108 regular-season victories to win the American League East and reach the World Series and the Orioles sputtered to a 47-115 campaign, we saw the Orioles hold off the Red Sox for a 10-7 victory on March 22nd.

Almost every Grapefruit League venue provides an intimate setting to see a baseball game. The stadiums are quaint with excellent access to players for fans seeking autographs or selfies. There are a couple of exceptions, however, and they are the two exceptions you'd expect. JetBlue Park in Fort Myers, which is Boston's "Fenway South," and George Steinbrenner Field, the spring home of the New York Yankees in Tampa.

George Stienbrenner Field is a miniature Yankee Stadium and feels sterile and corporate. It lacks the charm of the other Grapefruit League stadiums. They essentially took a mini Yankee Stadium and plopped it down in Tampa next to Raymond James Stadium, where the NFL's Buccaneers play. It's also ridiculously expensive. We saw the Yankees play the Houston Astros, and the Yankees definitely took advantage of having the defending World Series champions in Tampa. We purchased a pair of standing-room only tickets for $68 apiece. Let me repeat that: two standing-room only tickets for a Spring Training game were $68 apiece. That is $136 just to enter the stadium for an exhibition game in March. Most of the major stars didn't even play. The Yankees held out slugger Aaron Judge and shortstop Didi Gregorious. The Astros rested reigning American League MVP Jose Altuve and All-Star outfielders Alex Bregman and George Springer. New Yankees slugger, Giancarlo Stanton, went 0 for 3 in Houston's 2-0 victory.

Patti did notice an inspirational quote at George Steinbrenner Field, however.

"You hit home runs, not by chance, but by preparation," it said.

"That's a great message for anybody but especially for kids," she said.

We did meet a woman there named Patricia Morrisey, a New Yorker and life-long Mets fan. She was at a Yankees game because she was trying to see every Grapefruit League park. We bonded over our disgust of the Yankees and their outrageously expensive tickets. Patricia told us to hit her up when we were in New York and she would join us for a Mets game at Citi Field. She is a season-ticket holder, and as someone in her 40s, fondly remembers the 1986 Mets who won the World Series.

· · · · ·

We met up with Patricia at Citi Field, which was our least favorite MLB stadium. We were also joined by Eric Small, a former high school classmate of Patti's. Eric and Patti both attended Limestone High School in Bartonville, Illinois, outside of Peoria. They were a year behind Hall of Fame slugger Jim Thome at Limestone. We listened to Thome's Hall of Fame induction speech later that summer while driving through California on our way from the San Francisco Bay area to Los Angeles. Patti had tears in her eyes as a fellow Limestone Rocket talked about growing up in Peoria.

Eric, Patti and I sat in Section 130 next to a pair of very friendly Mets fans named Howard and Lee. Patricia's season tickets were in the 500 level, but after a couple of innings, she made her way down to see us. The problem is we weren't there and my phone died. We had a hell of a time trying to find a place to charge my phone.

We had spent the day visiting the Ellis Island and the Statue of Liberty. It was my first time ever seeing the Statue of Liberty. We weren't able to go inside the pedestal or the statue itself because ticket reservations for those excursions are booked months in advance. We weren't aware such advanced booking was required but still took several photos and posted them to my social media accounts. I wasn't worried about my battery power because we saw multiple charging stations that were easily accessible at the previous stadiums we visited.

After spending a few hours at Ellis Island and with Lady Liberty, we took the ferry to Battery Park in Manhattan and walked to the 9/11 Memorial and Museum. A couple hours later, we rode the subway to Central Park. We wanted to see the Metropolitan Museum of Art before heading to Queens. I had to see The Met before The Mets because I am the kind of dork who thinks that's cute and funny.

Being neophytes to the New York subway system, we knew we had to get off at the 79th Street stop. The problem is there are two 79th Street stops and we got off at the wrong one. We were on the other side of Central Park and essentially ran through the park and past the Central Park Zoo to get to the museum before it closed. We made it with less than 20 minutes to spare and did not even need to get a ticket to roam around. We saw as much as we could before security ushered everyone out of the building. As we exited, workers were setting up for a private event that night. I tried to talk my way into getting a few extra minutes at the Met but to no avail.

From there, it was onto Queens, where we would see Eric and Patricia. We figured we'd eat something before the game and then charge our phones at the stadium. We were dead wrong. There is absolutely nothing around Citi Field. As much as something can be in the middle of nowhere in New York City, Citi Field is in the middle of nowhere. The stadium is surrounded by multiple parking lots, with tailgating prohibited, and multiple chop shops beyond the right-field lots. We got off the subway and our only option was to stand in line to enter the stadium. I did snap a picture of the old Shea Stadium apple that is in front of the main entrance. My phone's battery power was at five percent. Patti's was at 17.

As soon as we made our way through security and past the beautifully decorated Jackie Robinson Rotunda, we asked around about a charging stations. We found most MLB stadiums had charging stations near each of the main concourse gates. That is not the case at Citi Field, and worse, most of the ushers were unable to tell us where to find a spot to charge our phones.

After my phone died sometime during the second inning, I finally spoke with someone who told us there was a charging station on the 300-club level by the Effen Vodka Bar, but we needed a special ticket to access the area. Fortunately for us, our tickets in Section 130 allowed us access. Patricia's 500-level tickets did not, but I found a way for her to join us by the Effen bar. I took Patti's ticket with me while she and Eric sat at the table where our phones were charging. Before I left, I messaged Patricia to tell us where to meet me. Once we met up and hugged, the two of us took the elevator back up to the third-base side of the restricted-access Excelsior level. I showed the tickets and we were allowed in. We sat and chatted while taking in Atlanta's 3-2 victory as the home teams dropped to 2-7 early in our regular-season journey.

The number one rule of real estate is location (location, location) and Citi Field fails in every aspect there. Its proximity to LaGuardia Airport is far from ideal and the constant — and deafening — air traffic was the most annoying thing we encountered while on our trip.

"We had great seats and the views of the field were good, but it's a huge distraction having all those airplanes going over," Patti recalled. "That was a big detriment."

"It is. You're trying to have a conversation with somebody and it's like, 'Hang on a second, let this plane go by.' You've been to stadiums, football, baseball, soccer, whatever, where they do flyovers. Imagine that every 20 seconds," I replied.

"That may be a slight an exaggeration, but there were a lot of them," Patti added.

The lone highlight of our visit to Citi Field was the ceremonial first pitch, which was thrown out by the "Karate Kid" himself, Ralph Macchio. Patti had a Ralph Macchio poster on her bedroom wall when she was younger. Making that first pitch even better was that it was caught not by a Mets player or coach, but by William Zabka, who played Daniel LaRusso's antagonist, Johnny Lawrence, in the first *Karate Kid* movie. The two were promoting the YouTube original series, *Cobra Kai*, which we said we were going to start watching and then never did.

It was fun hanging out with Eric, whom I had never met and Patti hadn't seen in 20 years, and Patricia.

We didn't hate Citi Field; the Shea Bridge in right-center field is a nice touch, but it was an enormous letdown.

· · · · ·

We saw the Yankees again in Florida at Publix Field at Joker Marchant Stadium in Lakeland, where the Tigers play their Spring Training games. We visited Lakeland on March 17th and interviewed Tigers pitcher Daniel Norris for the podcast. The Tigers were very accommodating, especially media relations coordinator Ben Fidelman. I reached out to Ben about interviewing

Norris, who spends his offseason living in a 1978 Volkswagen Westfalia van he calls "Shaggy." The *Scooby-Doo* allusion was not lost on us. Norris, who received a $2 million signing bonus after he was drafted out of high school in 2011, lives off $800 per month in the offseason. He said he's comfortable "being poor" and enjoys the simple life.

"It's really helped me simplify my life as far as material items. Shredding that down was a good call, for sure," Norris told me before explaining how his faith helped him get through a tumultuous 2015 season. Norris underwent treatment for thyroid cancer and was also traded from the Toronto Blue Jays to the Tigers in the same year.

"It was a whirlwind, that's for sure," Norris said. "There was a lot going on. But for me, it helped me grow my faith and that's something that's always been the most important thing to me. It seems like when you have a lot of things taken from you, that's when the only thing you have left is your faith. Sometimes God uses those circumstances that we think are pretty gnarly or not something we would have planned; he uses those to help us grow. That was a huge growing year for me. There is always a light at the end of the tunnel," he added. "A lot of times, you're going through something tough and think, 'I don't see the end of this.' It's tough and you start questioning your path in life, but there's always a light at the end of the tunnel and you'll be better for it. That's one thing I like to portray for kids. You're guaranteed to have struggles and unfortunate circumstances, but you've just got to find your way through it to get to the other end. Then you'll be stronger for it."

Ben even issued a photographer credential to Patti, who snapped a few shots of me interviewing Daniel in the tunnel outside of the Tiger clubhouse.

"There is a lot to be said for that simple life and we learned a lot about that," Patti said.

As I did in Bradenton, once the interview was over, I went back to the car to stow my equipment and we then enjoyed Detroit's 9-3 win over the Yankees as fans.

Publix Field at Joker Marchant Stadium is one of the oldest Grapefruit League venues but looks great following a recent renovation. The open concourse is nice and wide to easily accommodate foot traffic and there is myriad outfield viewing options. A new HD video board was erected beyond the left-field wall. It sits atop a rectangular building that houses bathrooms, concessions stands, and a good-sized bar. A picnic seating area is to the left of the structure and a popular home-run berm between the building and the field. Patti and I watched the Tigers hit batting practice before our Norris interview and then took advantage of our press credentials to watch the Yankees' BP on the field behind home plate. I spoke with a Yankees media-relations staff member about our trip and hoped it would lead to getting some kids to a Yankees game. I had a follow-up phone call with the Yankees, who said they already do a lot in the community and didn't have any tickets available for the April 25th game against the Twins. They wished me luck on our endeavor and that was that. The Angels told me the same thing a month later.

After we saw the Tigers in Lakeland, we drove my car back to Bradenton to get the RV and headed to Orlando, not to see the Braves, but to celebrate our one-year wedding anniversary like a Super Bowl-winning quarterback. We went to Disney World!

Patti wasn't too keen on the idea initially, but we had a blast during our two-day trip to Disney. It helped that we were comped a pair of two-day park-hopper passes thanks to a friend of mine who works at Disney World. That saved us $600 right off the bat, which added to the positive experience at Disney. We went to Italy for our honeymoon, so part of our anniversary celebration was dinner at "Italy" at Epcot Center.

With our two-day anniversary break over, it was back to Jupiter and the same RV resort we had stayed in February. We had more Cardinals games to see in Jupiter, but we weren't done with the Florida Gulf Coast.

· · · · ·

Patti's favorite feature of the minor-league parks of the Grapefruit League were the bullpens.

She loves how you can get so close to the field and even interact with some of the pitchers and catchers. Players and coaches often sign autographs for fans who congregate near the bullpens, especially at Roger Dean Stadium in Jupiter.

"It's that accessibility and being right there with the players," Patti said. "Anywhere else you go, I mean the dugouts aren't really accessible, just like at a Major League ballpark. That's why I have 'a thing' for dugouts."

While the Spring Training home of the Cardinals and Marlins lacks atmosphere in a rather sterile environment, it does have a certain intimacy. The wall, if you want to call it that, between the seats and the field is only about two feet high. You can walk right up to the field by the bullpens and we saw several fans clamoring to get autographs from Cardinals catcher Yadier Molina and 1985 NL MVP Willie McGee, who was a Cardinals coach in 2018.

We even got a little head nod from Cardinals bullpen catcher Jeremy Martinez as Patti was taking a picture during the first inning of the game on March 21st.

"Hey, Martinez, say cheese," I yelled from the fifth row down the first base line.

He turned and gave the universal body language of, "What's up?" with a raising and lowering of his chin.

While Roger Dean provides an intimate setting for fans to get up close and personal with players before a game, it does not offer opportunities for home run balls. There is no outfield seating at Roger Dean Stadium because the Marlins and Cardinals clubhouses — located down the third and first-base lines, respectively — block fans from walking around the 6,900-seat stadium.

There also isn't much "fun" for fans without the between-inning games we saw at other Grapefruit League venues. One stadium worker told me the Cardinals and Marlins prefer to "keep the focus on the game and the players."

That's understandable, but you also want the fans engaged. Even Busch Stadium has fun contests between innings with Todd Thomas serving as the entertaining MC.

I was able to land a couple more interviews for our podcast before the Cardinals cruised to a 13-6 victory. The Marlins granted me access to their clubhouse and I spoke with third baseman Martin Prado about his "Very Prado You" initiative to reward kids for good grades in school. I also chatted with North Carolina native Cameron Maybin, who was in his first season with the Marlins after helping the Astros win the 2017 World Series. Maybin, whose foundation is called the Maybin Mission and focuses on enriching the lives of inner-city youth, was sent to Seattle before the July 31st trade deadline.

Seattle was Maybin's seventh team in 11 years, and while moving from place to place is tough on his family, he said the silver lining is that he and his wife, Courtney, are able to take the mission to a new city.

"My thing was how can we use this baseball platform to touch and inspire the communities that we're in. That's where the Maybin Mission started with my hometown being the foundation," said Maybin, who grew up in Asheville, N.C. "It's taken off from there. It just started as how I can use my platform because I got tired of being defined as just a baseball player. I wanted to be known as the baseball player who really gives back and takes time to connect with kids in the community, wherever that community may be. I've clearly done something right to continue to be able to find a job and go into a locker room and impact whatever locker room I've been in," Maybin added. "And off the field, I look at it as a positive to be able to touch different communities. I started in Atlanta and then it was in Detroit and now it's continued to progress. I think that was the goal of the mission, how can we grow this thing to let people around the world know we care. It's gratifying to get messages from people, not about how you play baseball, but how much they miss what you've done for the community. That means a lot."

When I told him about our mission, Maybin gave me a response I was not quite expecting.

"Oh, man, that gives me goosebumps," Maybin said. "I think that's awesome what you guys are doing. Truly, man. Do you know how amazing it was, I met this little girl here. She was one of ten kids we have here, and she was so in awe to tell me, 'We're your VIP guests. We're your special guests. We got to come out on the field.'

"You'd be surprised at how far that goes for those kids, to be able to come down on the field, get those (batting practice) passes, get those tickets, and to see how much joy it brings to them. That's what it's about."

While we left the RV in Jupiter, we hopped in my Scion the next day and headed to Sarasota and saw the Orioles beat the Red Sox. We even found a restaurant in Sarasota that served crab cakes, though not the authentic lump cakes we ate in Baltimore a few weeks later. After dinner, we drove back across the state to Jupiter. But the morning, it was back on the road but just me, as Patti needed to remain with the Wi-Fi for a few meetings on this Friday. She was frustrated a day earlier as she kept losing her signal as we drove through Southern Florida's cattle country. We had no idea Florida had so many cattle ranches.

Friday's game was between the Blue Jays and Rays in Port Charlotte, and I had hoped to interview Rays pitcher Chris Archer, who checked every box we wanted for a podcast guest. He is a recognizable name and would be Tampa Bay's Opening-Day starter for the fourth straight season. He is also a North

Carolina native who was adopted by his grandparents at a young age. He also does a lot of charitable work and I wanted to ask him what his inspiration was for creating his Archway Foundation. If there would have only been one MLB player, we could get on our podcast, we wanted that player to be Chris Archer. While I wasn't able to get him for a one-on-one interview that Friday, we did get him the next day.

I headed back to Port Charlotte on Saturday, a day after seeing the Rays get a wild and improbable 6-5 walk-off win. The Blue Jays exploded for five runs in the top of the ninth to grab a 5-4 lead. Blue Jays reliever Conor Fisk retired the first two batters he faced before walking third baseman Matt Duffy. Center fielder Kevin Kiermaier then singled to center to give the Rays runners at the corners. First baseman C.J. Cron swung at the first pitch he saw from Fisk, slapping a blooper to left-center. The ball landed in the perfect spot for Cron and the Rays, striking the turf right between outfielders D.J. Davis and Reggie Pruitt and infielders Yeltsin Gudino and Andrew Guillotte. Duffy easily scored from third and Kiermaier hustled all the way from first to give the Rays the win. It was one of the wildest walk-offs I had ever seen and I just happened to be standing next to a unicorn while it happened. We'll get to that later.

With Patti joining me this time, we left Jupiter Saturday morning to see the Red Sox host the Astros at JetBlue Park, affectionately nicknamed "Fenway South," thanks to its own version of the Green Monster.

It's about a two-and-a-half-hour drive from Jupiter to Fort Myers, but we left about 8 a.m., something about which Patti was not happy. We had to make a detour before getting to Fenway South. Archer agreed to speak with me for the podcast in Port Charlotte at 11. After driving back through cattle country, which is also dotted with sod farms, we arrived at the Charlotte Sports Park just before 11. I called Rays media relations coordinator Karly Fisher to let her know we were there. She met us and directed us to the stadium's media lobby, which was a small white room with a Rays logo on the wall above the reception desk. Rays media relations director Dave Haller met us and said Archer was working out and would be out when he was done. We set up in the adjacent interview room and waited… and waited… and waited. It was almost an hour before Archer finally came to meet us. I was getting upset because we still had a 40-minute drive to get to Fort Myers and I wanted to get there on time.

Archer was apologetic, telling us he had family in town and was trying to co-ordinate meeting up with them later on his off-day. As Patti snapped a couple photos of me sitting with Archer, I asked him what the Archway Foundation does and what his inspiration was for starting it.

"We were doing a broad stroke of things, but we've narrowed our focus to youth homelessness," Archer explained. "There is such a huge need and I've been fortunate to partner with an organization in Tampa called Starting Right Now. They target teenage high schoolers that are considered unaccom-panied youth, which means they don't have a parent; they don't have a family member to stay with. They are literally on their own at 15, 16, 17 years old. They have a house, they take them in; they have different programs for them, leadership courses. They get them mentors. They help them get jobs, help them get scholarships, and they've had a 99-percent success rate of kids going to college, a trade school, or the military. I got an award while I was in the minor leagues for philanthropy and it was a $500 donation to the foundation of my choice. I said, 'You know what, this is a perfect time for me to start my own so that I can raise money to go to the specific causes that I want as op-posed to giving it to an organization and it going to keeping the lights on. I can give it to my own program, which has (in 2018) zero employees. We're going to hire somebody eventually, but I have zero employees, so money goes straight to the kids. It goes toward helping to feed them, with school supplies, holiday gifts, holiday parties.

There is a responsibility with my platform to help people, help put smiles on people's faces, and help encourage people to be the best person they can be. As an athlete, I have a voice and a platform and I love using mine."

I only had about five minutes to chat with Archer but had to ask him about his maternal grandparents, Donna and Ron Archer, whom he simply calls his parents. They adopted him when he was 2 years old and they helped shaped the man who wants to give back to his community.

"I had two very selfless parents and I definitely think my giving nature comes from them, certainly," Archer said. "Me and you would not be sitting here right now if it was not for them. Every day when I leave the house, I know what I'm representing. I'm representing them and the sacrifices they made to take me in and change my life, definitely for the better. I'm extremely grateful, extremely thankful. Having the Archer name on my back is more than just me. It's those two and representing what they stand for as well."

When the Rays hosted the Red Sox on March 29th at Tropicana Field, Archer — the subject of several offseason trade rumors — allowed four runs in six innings while taking a no-decision in Tampa's 6-4 victory. He became the first Rays pitcher in the franchise's 20-year history to be the Opening-Day starter in four straight seasons. While he was eventually traded to Pittsburgh on July 31st, Archer never expected to be dealt before the 2018 season began.

"I really didn't look into it that much," said Archer, who finished 2018 with a 6-8 record and 4.31 earned-run average to go with 162 strikeouts in 148-and-a-third innings pitched. "I was definitely aware, but it was people's opinions. It wasn't like the general manager, owner, or front office were saying those things. It was really opinions and hypotheticals and in life, you can't get too caught up in those things that are out of your control. I had great dialogue with our front office and they told me I should be confident about staying with Tampa."

Archer made his Pirates debut on August 3rd, taking a no-decision in a 7-6 win over the Cardinals.

· · · · ·

The Red Sox put a lot of effort into transforming JetBlue Park into a miniature Fenway Park. The dimensions are exactly the same as Fenway — 310 feet down the left-field line; 379 feet to the left-center gap; 420 feet to straight-away center field; 380 to the right-field alley; and 302 feet down the right-field line to a replica of "Pesky's Pole." But the one feature that stands out is the 37-foot wall in left field. The difference between Boston's "Green Monster" and the one in Fort Myers is that you can sit inside the wall at Jet-Blue Park.

Fenway Park has seating atop its "Monster" and that is also true of the wall at JetBlue Park. But there are also three rows of pavilion-style seating inside the Southern "Monster." Patti and I were able to sit inside the wall, thanks to a pair of fans who were leaving and asked us during the seventh inning if we wanted their tickets. These were high-demand tickets and we jumped at the chance to gain access to such an exclusive area. The 258 seats inside the wall are behind tightly woven protective netting. Because the netting is part of the wall, if a ball hits the net, the ball is still in play.

JetBlue Park may have features seen at Fenway Park, but it also stands alone as a unique venue. The wavy roof over the grandstand is meant to resemble the cypress trees indigenous to the area. While the park has a manual scoreboard, like that of Fenway, the concessions stands are far from standard. Most of the concessions are sold in large tents adjacent to the stadium along what is known as Fenway South Drive. Florida's version of Yawkey Way is where one goes to find a lobster roll, which is sort of a must for Red Sox games.

It was in this area where Patti and I ran into the same unicorn I met a day earlier. The Detroit native named Gordie Wykes was wearing a different outfit but was still dressed as a unicorn. We developed a special relationship with Gordie and he helped us get some kids out to a Tigers game at Comerica Park. That is covered in detail later in this book.

Following the game at JetBlue Park, we didn't immediately head back to Jupiter. Though the Twins were in Sarasota that day, we still wanted to see their Spring Training home. We made the short drive across Fort Myers to Hammond Stadium and discovered a ballpark with an off-white façade that resembled a condominium complex.

The three-tiered building has several apartment-style doors that lead to suites on the second level. Each level has an open causeway with white railing. The center of the grandstand façade is triangle-shaped and is adorned with a sign that identifies the venue as the CenturyLink Sports Complex. On the right-field side of the grandstand is a stairwell tower while the third-base side houses the team store and a giant TC Twins logo. Also adoring the stadium's exterior above Gate 3 were giant posters of Minnesota's standout players like outfielder Keon Broxton, pitcher Ervin Santana and 2009 American League MVP Joe Mauer.

The parking lot area does a respectable job of paying homage to Twins' greats with various avenues named for past players and managers. The Twins' training facility has a giant mural of Hall of Famer Kirby Puckett catching a ball over the fence.

After our self-guided exterior tour of Hammond Stadium, we got dinner along the Fort Myers waterfront at a place called Steve B. Waterfront Café. What drew us there was a Jamaican man singing and dancing in the outdoor seating area. We saw the live entertainment and decided to pop in for a burger. When he asked for requests, he was surprised when I suggested Buju Banton. I know more than just Bob Marley when it comes to reggae.

We returned to Jupiter that night with just one Spring Training game remaining on our itinerary and Opening Day just five days away.

We made our first and only visit to West Palm Beach on Sunday to see the Cardinals and Nationals play. The Nats share FitTeam Ballpark of the Palm Beaches with the Astros. Giant logos of each team are on display outside the stadium. Once inside, you find neither team "owns" any one part of the stadium, as both teams are well-represented throughout. The Astros do have a large sign commemorating their 2017 World Series championship hangs on the wall by the picnic patio area in left field. It was a very well-balanced stadium, differing from Roger Dean Stadium, which is essentially split in half between the Cardinals and Marlins.

Suites and party decks are found on the second level down both the first and third-base side. The outfield seating is an open berm with several first-come, first-served Adirondack chairs. The only shade out there is under the scoreboard, which has signs for both teams as well as Palm Beach County. Flags of each team flank the center-field batter's eye.

It was a windy day when we were there to see the Nationals hold off the Cardinals for a 4-2 win. The strong breeze did help us realize how good the customer service is at FitTeam Ballpark. We had just ordered some drinks at the picnic area craft beer stand and walked over to a high-top table with an umbrella. There were three men already there and they allowed us to join them. As we introduced ourselves and I began telling them about our trip and mission, a gust of wind caught the umbrella and flipped the table. I had taken just one drink from my cup before its contents were now being soaked into the concourse concrete. Within seconds a stadium employee rushed over to us and offered to get us new drinks at no charge. While he walked us over to the beer stand, another employee set the table back up and removed the umbrella to prevent further incidents. We were impressed by the swift reaction.

The complex around FitTeam Ballpark is huge with 160 acres that contain eight additional baseball fields that are used as practice fields by both teams during training and host youth tournaments during other times of the year. There are also five other fields that are used for local soccer, lacrosse, football, and rugby games.

The city of West Palm Beach put a minor-league ballpark and additional fields in the middle of Lincoln Park, which is surrounded by several office buildings and shopping centers. Palm Beach Lakes Community High School is also right across the street and Rams teams use the adjacent facilities. Unlike the Yankees facility in Tampa, the spring home of the Nationals and Astros was woven into the community and that was something we loved about the two-year-old stadium.

We used the next few days to relax following a grueling Spring Training schedule. As Marc Lancaster told me before we began our trip, Spring Training in Florida is difficult because the teams are spread across the state. He wasn't wrong, but Spring Training was over and it was time for Opening Day. We were ready for the traveling to really begin.

CHAPTER 2:

OPENING DAY

We could not have asked for a better day on March 29th. The weather was perfect and the roof at Marlins Park was open. We were also grateful that our trip was getting off to a marvelous start because the Marlins donated 40 tickets to Our Kids of Miami-Dade/Monroe for their Opening-Day game against the Chicago Cubs.

The efforts to get kids out to Opening Day began in November when I started to contact foster care organizations in Miami. After not hearing anything for weeks, I finally got a call from Alejandro Alamo, the director of communications for Our Kids. Alejandro, whose last name you should always remember, called me on February 25th as we were returning to Charlotte following our maiden RV voyage. He explained that he is a big baseball fan and some of his fondest memories were going to a game with his dad when he was a kid. If he could help create similar memories for kids in the Miami area, he wanted to partner with us.

Alejandro put me in contact with Flora Beal, who is the community relations manager for Our Kids. Flora submitted the request to the Marlins and then we had to play the waiting game. It had been a month since my conversation with Alejandro, and we were just days away from Opening Day. I was beginning to think this wasn't going to happen.

Then we got some inside help.

As I waited in the media room at Roger Dean Stadium on March 21st before conducting my interviews with Martin Prado and Cameron Maybin, I had a conversation with Marlins play-by-play announcer Glenn Geffner. He had heard me tell another media member about our trip and was interested. He asked several questions about our route, how long the trip would take, where we'd stay, and how we got involved with Children's Hope Alliance. He also offered some advice on places to eat and shared his takes on various stadiums he had visited as a broadcaster. Glenn and I exchanged cards, and after we were told the clubhouse was open, I told him thank you and left the media room while he continued his preparation for that day's broadcast.

I interviewed Prado almost immediately after entering the clubhouse. He could not have been nicer and spoke enthusiastically about his "Very Prado You" initiative. Prado and the Marlins provide autographed certificates of achievement, four game tickets for each student, food and beverage, parking, and "Very Prado You" T-shirts.

"Growing up in my family, the priority was school and second on the list was baseball," Prado told me. "It's important to play sports, but the main priority for all those families is to be good at school, not missing classes. My emphasis is to be passionate about school and the sports you play. I was helped by teachers, baseball coaches, and my mom. How I was raised was important to understand how I can impact people around me," the 2010 All-Star continued. "I know I have to give back to my community in the same way my community gave me all the information and knowledge that helped me in school, playing baseball, and I also played volleyball. People influenced my career in a positive way, so the least I can do is to influence people in a positive way. I use my career as a platform for people understanding how important it is to have discipline and be smart and how to socially interact with people. That's my main focus with this project."

As I waited for Maybin to get to his locker, a young man in his 20s with dark hair and wearing an all-access media credential asked if I was Ron. I told him I was and he introduced himself as Kyle Sielaff, another member of the Marlins radio broadcast team. Glenn had asked Kyle to interview me for the

Marlins pregame show. Of course, I said yes. This was our first media coverage and I was stoked. Though I was worried about missing Maybin, we stepped out of the clubhouse for a five-minute interview. After returning to the clubhouse, I was pleased Maybin was not yet at his locker. I stood near his locker and began telling Jason Latimer, Miami's director of communications, about our 2018 mission and that we wanted to start on a high note.

As the wheels were turning, Glenn wasn't done with the surprises.

I had told him that Our Kids had submitted a ticket request, but we were still waiting to hear back from the team. Glenn said he "mentioned our conversation to a couple of people," and on March 26th, three days before Opening Day, Flora told me we got the tickets. Five days earlier, Jamal Knibbs, the team's community outreach manager, told Flora tickets for Opening Day were "very limited." Five days earlier was March 21st, the same day I spoke with Glenn and Jason.

Now that we had the tickets, the next step was setting up an interview with someone from Our Kids. Flora informed me that we would speak with Our Kids chief operating officer Michael Williams before the game. She provided an outline of talking points, like the organization's mission to strengthen families and assist with kinship care, facilitate adoptions, and how people can get involved.

We wanted to make sure we arrived early so we could enjoy the Opening Day festivities and ensure Flora and Michael would not have to wait for us. We didn't mind waiting for them to fight Thursday afternoon traffic on their short ride over from the Our Kids office. Wearing our orange Children's Hope Alliance T-shirts, that helped us blend in well with orange-clad Marlins fans. Patti and I parked in an adjacent garage and then explored the exterior of Marlins Park. A giant "Opening Day" banner hung outside and we watched as the roof opened under clear skies. A large inflatable Marlins "M" was popular for selfies and we asked a couple to snap a photo of us in front of it. Around the corner near the team store, a DJ was blasting hip-hop music as a middle-school dance troupe entertained the spectators who had gathered.

We joined the group and watched the kids dance for one song before we headed inside the team store. We had decided to buy a lapel pin from each MLB stadium. The small souvenirs were items that were inexpensive and would not take up much room in the RV. Once we got our Marlins Park Opening Day pin, we continued our walk around the stadium's exterior to soak in the Opening-Day vibe. I initiated a Facebook Live session as we walked past active-duty military members who were waiting to go inside with a giant American flag to unfurl over the field during the playing of the national anthem. We eventually returned to the main entrance, where we would meet Flora, Michael, and another woman from Our Kids named Dudly, who was handing out the tickets to the families attending.

We interviewed Michael outside of Marlins Park about 15 minutes before the first pitch of the 2018 season was thrown at 12:40 p.m. Eastern Time. Just as we began, our chat was interrupted by a Navy jet flyover. I could have left it out of the podcast because it was an interview we published three days later, but it was a funny moment I left in. Michael, Patti, Flora and I all had a good laugh before the interview resumed. Michael, a greying black man, about 6 feet tall, then explained why Our Kids was so grateful to Marlins for donating tickets to give children an opportunity to attend Opening Day.

"It gives them opportunities to do things that for a lot of our families, they wouldn't have the opportunity to do. Quite honestly, the cost associated with an event like this whereas before, when I grew up, you could sneak under a fence to see a game. But now the cost with not only the admission, but food, most of our families can't afford it," Michael said, wearing a white Our Kids T-shirt. "To give them this opportunity, these memories go a long way for a child, who can say, 'I remember when my mom or my dad, my uncle took me to a Marlins game.' They don't have to know how it happened, just the fact that it happened. It's Opening Day of a sport that for a century has symbolized family and family unity and family values. It's a great opportunity to highlight and promote the work that we do," he added. "The fact that when children and families are really facing the some of the most difficult times of their lives, what is needed is an intervention from organizations that have the values of, first and foremost, how to keep them together. In times past, it was a different set of values in child welfare where the intervention was with judgment. If something happened, if you hurt your child, we're going to take your child. Now it's different. We've realized over the years the worst thing to do, particularly for the psychological development of a child, is to remove them from their biological families. If they are not unsafe, obviously safety is the paramount issue, and the other issues that are there can be addressed with support, then children should stay in their family units. Our role should be to strengthen those family units as much as we can; that's a great investment of time and resources because in the end, it pays off with healthy kids who can then become healthy adults. At the end of the day, it's not just one child, it's families and the whole system that benefits from this."

When our interview with Michael was over, Patti and I headed inside and found our seats in Section 323. We did miss the first pitch, which Cubs leadoff hitter Ian Happ smashed over the right field wall. Happ's blast of Marlins starter José Ureña excited the Cubs fans in attendance. Many Chicagoans were already in Florida for the winter and decided to stay. The Cubs, whose Spring Training home is in Arizona, closed their Spring Training slate in Florida on March 26th with an exhibition slate against the Red Sox in Fort Myers. Cubs supporters definitely comprised the majority of the 32,151 fans in attendance.

We didn't quite know what to expect from the Our Kids families who sat near us. As Michael said, the kids there didn't have to know why or how they were able to attend Opening Day, just that they were. We didn't have any interaction with those families, which was fine with us because we didn't undertake this venture with any expectation of overt gratitude. We left our seats after the third inning to explore and get something to eat. Thankfully for us, Marlins Park has some outstanding food, especially in the Taste of Miami behind Section 27. Several local eateries have spots in the small, congested food court. Given our penchant for going local, this was perfect for us. While the lines were long, the wait was worth it. Patti had a media noche sandwich while Ron tried Mama's lechon nachos. Both were delicious and we washed them down with sodas in the first of many stadium souvenir cups we acquired.

Once our bellies were content, we tried to see as much of Marlins Park as we could. We left a video message inside the Dímelo (Tell Me) kiosk thanking the Marlins for their donation of tickets. We took several photos of the Bobblehead Museum located on the main concourse and spoke with anyone who would listen to us about our trip. We were in the right-field corner by Section 21 when one conversation was interrupted between the seventh and eighth innings by the Marlins Pachanga Band. The two-minute musical interlude began with a strong percussion beat before a quartet of trumpet and trombone players joined in. The Marlins may not get a lot of fans to their stadium, but they sure do try to create a fun atmosphere. We were also glad we got to see a game at Marlins Park while the famous (or infamous) Home Run Sculpture was still located behind the left-center wall.

The Marlins decided following the 2018 season that the colorful structure would be moved outside in the stadium's plaza.

The Clevelander night club located inside the stadium is also a fun spot and it was packed following the game. We weren't the only ones who decided to hang out for a bit to allow traffic to subside before heading to the car. The club has a pool, though jumping in fully clothed is not advised as a couple people found out after they were ejected by the bouncers.

When we did finally leave Marlins Park, we wanted to find the best Cuban sandwich in town and to explore South Beach. So, on recommendation from Flora of Our Kids, we went to David's Café. The sandwich was good, but we both agreed that the homemade empanada was the best one either of us had ever tasted. We hope to return and spend more time in Miami and would definitely go back to David's for an empanada and to try another dish.

After our early dinner, we walked to the beach and strolled along the Art Deco district. The architecture lives up to the name and the place is hopping. As seen in movies and T.V., there are guys working out at the park next to the beach and people running and biking. The beach itself is very wide, but the weather was a bit chilly in late March, so it wasn't in its full glory, we suspect. We could tell it wasn't the best beach we've ever seen, though. Yes, there is white sand, but it's a bit rough.

We enjoyed tasty, though rather pricey, drinks at Down N Dirty Taco. We were paying for drinks and a show, as it was prime people-watching territory along South Beach's Ocean Drive. And, well, it's Miami. Patti's mojito was delish and the experience was worth it in her opinion.

As we walked back to the car, we passed the Carlyle, where the movie *The Birdcage* was filmed. Of course, we got many photos of that and other parts of the Art Deco district. We also walked through a residential area and Flamingo Park. We were wowed by the park's amenities and size. We first passed people playing soccer and softball, then saw basketball courts, racquetball courts, and a pool. It is clear why people love this area and there is indeed much to see and do. People were out taking advantage of it on this lovely Thursday night.

We can't wait to go back and spend more time there. We'd love to experience this area like a local… and maybe treat ourselves a bit as well.

But from Miami, it was onto St. Petersburg for Tampa Bay's series-ending game against the Red Sox. We had reached out to Eckerd Youth in Clearwater to get some kids out to that game. Eckerd was on board but then could not get enough families to commit to going to a baseball game on Easter Sunday. We were disappointed, but given the holiday and Tampa's reputation for baseball apathy, we understood. Eckerd, which has a national footprint, told us they were committed to getting some kids out to a game in Arlington. All was not lost, or so we thought.

We got off to a great start in Miami, but the Tampa disappointment was compounded by news from Atlanta and Philadelphia. We would be in Atlanta on April 2nd, the day after Easter, and I had spoken with two organizations that were initially very excited to work with us. Lutheran Services of Georgia and Families First of Georgia both wanted to get kids out to a Braves game. Then they looked at the date and realized it was the first day of spring break in Georgia and they already had several things planned for their kids with beach trips and camps. It wasn't going to work out in Atlanta.

Another scheduling conflict prevented us from getting kids to a Phillies game. Turning Points for Children in Philadelphia had also shown interest in partnering with us. I had several conversations with Turning Point's director of development Eartha Holland. I really enjoyed speaking with her until she said the organization's brass asked if we could plan something in May to coincide with Foster Care Awareness Month. Our visit to the City of Brotherly Love was planned for April 19-22 with a travel day to New York City on the 23rd. I told her we couldn't really alter our schedule and still hit every stadium. I then suggested we could do a tour of Citizens Bank Park on April 23rd, an off-day for the Phillies, and at the end of the tour, the organization could be presented with tickets for a May game. It was a no-go. Things fell through in Baltimore and Pittsburgh as well. We weren't able to get any kids out to any more games until we got to Detroit, thanks to that wonderful unicorn.

We did get our four-legged boy out to his first-ever game in Washington, D.C., the first of three games on the season for Holmes.

CHAPTER 3:

DOG DAYS

We knew Holmes wouldn't be bothered by the crowd or noise of a Major League Baseball game. He has such a calm demeanor, and once I noticed we had three opportunities to get Holmes out to a game, I knew we had to take advantage of it.

When I planned our trip following the MLB schedule release, I did so by looking at the series from city to city. Each series would give us a three-day window to see a game. Once I had the series identified, I then tried to settle on a game. The Nationals were hosting the Mets from April 5-8. That was a Thursday-to-Sunday series and Sunday's contest was a night game televised nationally on ESPN. It was also the first of six Pups in the Park games the Nationals hosted in 2018. I knew that was the one.

Though Holmes is a St. Louis dog, he had never been to a Major League Baseball game in his 10-plus years. This would be his first.

There is free street parking on Sundays in the nation's capital. We took advantage of this and left our RV park in College Park, Maryland around 11 a.m. to spend the day in the city. We had both traveled to Washington, D.C. before, and Nationals Park was the first stadium where we had already seen a game. It was one of only five stadiums we had each previously visited. Both of us had seen games at Busch Stadium, Wrigley Field, Miller Park and Nationals Park. I had also been to Angel Stadium, but back in 1993, while Patti had seen a couple of games at Kauffman Stadium in Kansas City. That was it. Every other stadium was new to us, making the trip even more exciting.

While we had some familiarity with D.C., there was still so much we had never seen. The first stop on our April 8th itinerary was the Marine Corps War Memorial in Arlington Ridge Park. The Marine Corps memorial is a massive sculpture recreating the iconic World War II photo of six Marines raising the American flag atop Iwo Jima's Mount Suribachi on February 23rd, 1945.

I spent eight and a half years in the Marine Corps but never saw combat during my service between 1992 and 2001. Marine Corps history is a huge part of boot camp and training throughout a Marine's active-duty service. I was very familiar with the story of Iwo Jima and seeing the 32-foot-tall figures raising the large billowing flag struck me with awe. I was unexpectedly overcome with emotion and left speechless, which, if you know me, is a big deal.

The park in which the Marine Corps War Memorial is located also contains the Netherlands Carillon, a 127-foot-tall bell tower that was a gift from the people of the Netherlands to the people of the United States in 1954. The Carillon was made to thank the U.S. for its aid to the Netherlands during World War II. The Carillon, which is about 500 feet from the Marine Corps War Memorial, is "guarded" by a pair of bronze lions who overlook a large field of tulips. While I walked Holmes around the park, Patti spent several minutes taking photos of the tulips from every angle she could think of.

The park wasn't crowded, but there were a lot of people taking advantage of a sunny day despite temperatures hovering around 50 degrees. The gametime temperature that night's contest between the Mets and Nats was 47 and dropping. A brisk 11-miles-per-hour wind only made it feel colder. It was near 70 degrees a day earlier.

Fortunately, we packed enough long-sleeve shirts and coats to make us comfortable while we toured the city. Holmes, a shaggy border collie/black lab mix, is equipped with his own coat. Once Patti was done with her tulip photo shoot and Holmes sniffed just about every blade of grass, we walked back to my car — which was parked on a street atop one of Arlington's many steep hills.

The Georgetown neighborhood was the next stop on our pup's day out. It took awhile to find street parking, but we grabbed a spot near Volta Park — a neighborhood green not far from the Duke Ellington School of the Arts. The school was on my list of sites to see, not because I thought it would be open to the public on a Sunday (It's not). But because of the giant green Adirondack chair that is situated in front of the sprawling, three-story building which is on the National Register of Historic Places.

The "Big Green Chair" is supposed to inspire students to think big. It's also a popular attraction for people who want to get their photo taken while sitting on the 14-foot wooden chair. We were no exception but had to wait our turn. We bided our time by taking Holmes on a walk around the school grounds. The same young couple sitting on the chair when we began our lap was still there on our return. We asked if they wanted their photo taken. Of course, they did. We then got the reciprocal response for which we had hoped. The tricky thing was getting Holmes on the chair. He's a 60-pound dog of an advanced age and hates to be picked up. But after Patti climbed onto the chair, I hoisted Holmes up and his paws nearly slipped through the gaps between the slats of the chair. He wasn't comfortable, but he was up there. I followed and the young couple snapped a few pictures with our phones. Those pictures were quickly posted to social media and later added to the photo gallery we had on our website. By the time our trip ended, the Home Run On Wheels photo gallery included over 650 pictures.

After climbing down from the chair, I carefully placed Holmes back on solid ground and we ventured into the neighborhood. I had another spot in mind, but lunch had to come first.

As we tried to figure out what to have and where to go, going through the typical married couple back-and-forth of, "What do you want?" "I don't know, what do you want?", we stumbled upon a coffee shop. I popped inside Saxby's to grab a couple of hot beverages while Patti walked across the street with Holmes and started to look up lunch spots. She found one near Georgetown Waterfront Park, or so we thought. The Key Bridge Boathouse does have food but is also a member-only establishment.

We took Holmes for a brief stroll through the park, which is situated alongside the Potomac River, but we were getting "hangry," Patti, especially. I got a brief distraction when my sister Danielle called. While I chatted with Danielle, we made our second pass by the Francis Scott Key Memorial and walked back up the hill. We were near Georgetown University and I told Patti our lunch had to be delayed a bit longer. I had to see and climb *The Exorcist* steps.

The 75 steps on the Georgetown campus are an official Washington, D.C. cinematic landmark. The steep and narrow stone stairway is almost hidden, sandwiched between a university building with ivy-covered brick walls and a gas station. The steps that provide a shortcut of sorts between Prospect Street NW above and Canal Road NW below are also where the death of Father Damien Karras was filmed for the classic 1973 horror film.

I jogged down and then back up the stairs, with Patti taking pictures from above. A placard directing visitors to other D.C. film locations is nearby, but one was enough for this day. It was past time to eat. We thought we could find a spot near the Georgetown University campus, but many were either closed at 2 in the afternoon or did not have outdoor seating. We had to find a place where we could eat outside with Holmes. To the Google machine!

After searching for restaurants that were open and had outdoor seating, we called ahead to ensure we could bring Holmes. We walked back to the car and headed toward Logan Tavern on P Street. Of course, there was one more detour. The drive from Volta Park to Logan Tavern took us over Wisconsin Avenue. Instead of crossing Wisconsin, I hung a left as we agreed to visit the National Cathedral. It was about a mile out of the way, but the deviation was worth it. The colossal Episcopal church is stunning. Officially named the Cathedral Church of Saint Peter and Saint Paul in the City and Diocese of

Washington, the National Cathedral is a towering Gothic-style structure. It's the second largest church in the United States — behind only Cathedral of Saint John the Divine in New York City — and fourth-tallest building in Washington, D.C.

The east-facing nave, one of nine high-arching naves inside the church, is lined with flags from every state in the union. State seals are embedded into the marble floor. The beautiful stain-glassed windows depict biblical figures and significant events from U.S. history. Statues of George Washington and Abraham Lincoln reside in vestibules inside the church. The long, rectangular building is intersected by a six-bay transept. At over 300 feet tall and sitting on an impeccably landscaped 57-acre plot atop a hill, the cathedral's bell tower is the highest point in Washington. Several gargoyles and grotesques, including one of Darth Vader, and flying buttresses adorn the exterior.

The National Cathedral is also the final resting place of several prominent Americans, including President Woodrow Wilson, Helen Keller, Leo Sowerby and John Burgess.

We didn't spend a lot of time at the cathedral because we were hungry and Holmes had to stay in the car, but we were glad we took some time to see it.

We finally made it to Logan Tavern about 4:45. We basically skipped lunch and were now about to eat dinner. Two hours later, we parked on the street directly in front of the U.S. capitol and walked the 1.3 miles to Nationals Park. Parking closer to the stadium is very difficult and expensive, so we didn't mind the walk.

Most night games begin either at 7 or 7:30, but because this was ESPN's "Sunday Night Baseball," the first pitch was scheduled for 8:09. We arrived at the stadium around 7:15 and didn't exactly want to take Holmes in yet. We ducked into the adjacent "Bullpen" at the Half Street Fairgrounds and got a couple of beverages while taking in some live music. The five-member bluegrass band was comprised of a guitar, stand-up bass, violin — or in this case, a fiddle — ukulele and banjo. Holmes wasn't the only dog there because we weren't exactly the only people who wanted to get a $5 beer before going inside the stadium.

Fans bringing dogs to games are required to provide proof vaccinations are current and sign a waiver. Dogs also need their own tickets and those with dogs are restricted to designated sections in the stadium. Those sections at Nationals Park were 140 through 143 in the outfield reserved area. We had a great view of Nationals right fielder Bryce Harper from our seats in Section 140 that cost a total of $87.

Because we entered at the right-field gate, we didn't get a chance to see the statues of Walter Johnson, Frank Howard, and Josh Gibson that line the walkway to the home plate entrance at Nationals Park.

Holmes didn't exactly get a proper dinner earlier, so we treated him to his first-ever hot dog. It wasn't just any hot dog, it was a $7 Nathan's Famous hot dog — minus the bun or condiments. We broke it up into pieces, which he scarfed down with enthusiasm. Holmes also got Nathan's hot dogs at his two other MLB games in Cincinnati and Houston.

The price of the hot dog is on the high end compared to other MLB stadiums. That was true of other concessions options at Nationals Park. The Nationals should be ashamed to charge $15 for a beer or $10 for a soda. Ticket prices for Nationals games aren't that bad, but the concessions prices were among the highest we encountered.

The Nationals do at least try to make the game fun with silly sound effects following a strikeout by a Washington pitcher or walk issued to a Nationals batter. While we could hear the between-innings games, we couldn't see any of it. We did not have a good vantage point of the scoreboard and Jumbotron because our view was obstructed by the deck above us. When the stadium speakers blasted "Who Let the Dogs Out" in the second inning, the dogs were presumably shown on the Jumbotron, but we don't know if we made it on the screen.

We put a lot of miles under our feet during the day, so Holmes didn't have much energy at the stadium. He pretty much just laid at our feet before we finally called it a night during the seventh-inning stretch. It was a good thing we didn't try to stick it out because it didn't end until after midnight. The Mets held a 5-4 lead when we left, but the Nationals tied things up in the bottom of the seventh on a Michael Taylor RBI single. The tie remained until the 12th inning when Mets outfielder Yoenis Céspedes singled to drive in Juan Lagares. Jacob Rhame was able to close out the Mets victory in the bottom of the 12th.

· · · · ·

The second game for Holmes came in Cincinnati when the Reds were hosting the Rockies for a three-game set in June. The team's second of four

Bark in the Park games was Tuesday, June 5th. I got our tickets in Section 136 for $90.50. The problem with special tickets, like Bark in the Park, is you must purchase them directly from the team because they're not available at third-party outlets like StubHub or VividSeats.

Because Cincinnati's Bark in the Park was on a Tuesday and not a Sunday like in Washington, we weren't able to go on a city-wide exploration prior to the game. We did spend a week in Cincinnati and tried to see as much as we could, just not on this day.

Cincinnati was the first city in which we saw multiple games. The Cardinals were coming to town the following weekend, and we couldn't pass up the opportunity to see Patti's favorite team. Our friends, Kirsten and Tricia Pohlman, and their 8-year-old son, Finnegan, were traveling up from Murfreesboro, Tennessee to join us. They would be the first guests we had spend the night in the RV.

Great American Ball Park sits on the banks of the Ohio River. Those sitting in the upper levels behind home plate and along the third-base side have a great view of the river and into Kentucky.

We were fortunate enough to find free street parking a block from the stadium, in front of the row of bars and restaurants along Freedom Way. The street leads to the Reds Hall of Fame entrance on the first-base side.

As soon as we got out of our car, we met a family of four who had parked directly in front of us and were exiting their vehicle as well. I had brought with us some Children's Hope Alliance cups, lanyards, and sunglasses. I noticed neither of the two kids had sunglasses and asked if they would like a pair. The parents said, "Sure," and told their children to say thank you. The kids politely obliged and I handed the family four of the orange cups, two lanyards, and the sunglasses. This was a common occurrence for us as Children's Hope Alliance gave us a couple of boxes full of T-shirts, sunglasses, cups, and lanyards to distribute along our journey.

The designated entrance for those with dogs was in right field, so we walked down Joe Nuxhall Way past the Pete Rose Garden toward Mehring Way. The Pete Rose Garden features a white rose, where his record-breaking hit landed at the old Riverfront Stadium. We showed the required paperwork at the registration tables in front of Gate 1 and then made our way inside. A small set of stairs leads to the main concourse and the first thing we saw was a small Wiffle ball field full of kids playing a game. The Kroger

Fan Zone also has a playground for kids, a stage for live music, and various carnival games.

We made our way to our seats and then remembered the Reds had a dog parade around the warning track. We jumped to our feet and led Holmes back to the kids' area, where the parade would begin. We missed it by about five minutes. Disappointed, we stopped for some drinks and hot dogs before going back to our seats in Section 138. Those with dogs were restricted to the Kroger Fan Zone and sections 136 through 139.

As we watched the pet parade near its completion, Holmes scarfed down his Nathan's hot dog while Patti and I tried a stadium dog topped with Cincinnati chili. We were very disappointed. The tiny Coney hot dog was served on an oversized bun and topped with so much shredded cheese, that's pretty much all you taste, cold shredded cheese and bun. While we were in Cincinnati, I felt like we had to try some authentic Cincinnati chili. We went to the famous Skyline chili on our last day in Ohio's Queen City and each got a bowl. It was just as disappointing as the Great American Ball Park hot dog. Cincinnati chili isn't chili. It's spaghetti with a weird sauce.

Though disappointed with our concessions choices, we got two new beverages and returned to our seats to watch Colorado hold off the Reds for a 9-6 victory. The Reds trailed 9-1 entering the seventh-inning stretch but scored twice in the bottom of the seventh and three times in the ninth before the rally fell short. Reds catcher Tucker Barnhart and first baseman Joey Votto had three hits apiece as the Reds tallied 17 hits. The Rockies had 12 hits, led by three each from center fielder Charlie Blackmon and right fielder Carlos Gonzalez. CarGo had one of three homers in the game with Rockies catcher Chris Iannetta and Cincinnati center fielder Scott Schebler blasting the other two.

When Great American Ball Park was first opened in 2003, one Cincinnati sports columnist wrote, "Maybe they should have called it 'Kind of Good Ball Park.'" But following 2009 renovations, the stadium named for Great American Insurance Company, is one of the better MLB venues. The aforementioned view of the Ohio River bank is nice, but other features of the stadium stand out, like the 14 bats atop the faux steamboat smokestacks in center field. The bats atop the "Power Stacks" celebrate the career of Pete Rose, baseball's all-time hits leader who spent 19 years of his 24-year playing career with the Reds and later managed the team.

The stacks are adjacent to the center-field riverboat that sits above the batter's eye and serves as a venue for large groups to watch the game. The riverboat serves as a party group area and provides 7,500 square feet of deck space to accommodate groups of up to 150 people.

The Reds are the oldest franchise in Major League Baseball and a mural in the main concourse depicts the original 1869 team. That mural features the starting nine in 1869 and the "Great Eight" of Cincinnati's "Big Red Machine" World Series team of 1975. The Great American Insurance Company building towers over the stadium, providing the centerpiece of the city's skyline views.

A statue of Hall of Fame catcher Johnny Bench, a stalwart on Cincinnati's "Big Red Machine" of the 1970s, welcomes fans to Great American Ball Park. His bronze likeness is behind a plate inscribed with his achievements as a 14-time All-Star and two-time NL MVP. A plaque on the pedestal refers to Bench as "Baseball's Greatest Catcher."

That claim is supported by a quote from former Reds and Tigers manager Sparky Anderson: "I don't want to embarrass any other catcher by comparing him to Johnny Bench."

We were fortunate enough to sit next to a couple named Patrick and Christine and learned a lot from the 25-year-old Patrick, who used to work at the stadium. The Xavier University graduate provided several tidbits of the stadium. One piece of information was where charging stations for phones were located. The answer was a large bar area with huge television screens, accessible to anyone, in the left-field corner.

When the game was over, we took Holmes on a stroll through Smale Riverfront Park. It's a picturesque park, especially at night, with several lighted water features and the John A. Roebling Suspension Bridge illuminating the span across the river into Kentucky. There are porch swings, several walking and biking trails, and even a small brush maze.

"You were like a little kid running around that maze, trying to figure it out," Patti told me after I successfully made my way through after only one try.

While I navigated the circular maze, Patti waited nearby with Holmes, who was struck by a young girl who had lost control of her bicycle. Fortunately, neither Holmes nor the girl was injured.

· · · · ·

Our entire schedule was available for anyone to see on our website. I had the series dates listed and updated it throughout the season as we identified the games we would attend. I also included a line at the bottom of the page: * Dates subject to change.

This became a necessary addendum once I looked closer at the Astros' schedule. I had originally planned on heading to the Dallas area to see my mom and sister the Saturday of Labor Day weekend. I had August 27th to August 30th listed on our schedule as our Houston dates. The Dallas dates were August 31st to September 8th. Once I saw that the Astros had a Dog Day scheduled for Sunday, September 2nd, I knew our stay in Houston had to be extended.

We saw the Angels four times in four cities across four weeks. We first saw the Angels beat the Tigers at Angel Stadium on August 6th. We saw the Angels again in Arizona, where the Diamondbacks got a 5-4 walk-off win on August 21st. Our inadvertent Angels tour continued in Houston, but this was the first time we were able to see star center fielder Mike Trout. The two-time American League MVP had been on the disabled list with an injured wrist. He returned for the series against the Astros and we saw him live on September 2nd. We saw Trout and the Angels for the fourth and final time in 2018 two days later in Arlington. The Angels lost both of those Texas games and we were joined by my family members for each.

We'll cover the Rangers' 4-2 win over the Angels in detail later, but my brother Ben joined us in Houston to see the Astros shut down the Angels in a 4-2 victory. Ben brought along his girlfriend, Bailey, and this was the first time we met her. My brother has two dogs and when Bailey told us she loves dogs, we knew they'd both enjoy Dog Day at Minute Maid Park.

Tickets for Dog Day were downright expensive.

Because you have to get those special section tickets from the Astros, you pay a premium. I had to call the Astros to purchase tickets because the team only accepts credit card purchases from Louisiana and Texas on its website. That geographical restriction was something we did not encounter anywhere else. Those three tickets — two for us humans and the other for Holmes — in Section 105 set us back $186. Ben got a pair of tickets in the same section a couple rows ahead of us.

It was nice, however, to be able to walk with Holmes — and many other dogs — around the warning track at Minute Maid Park. It was an experience we missed in both Washington and Cincinnati. We were instructed to head to plaza outside Home Run Alley by the left-field gate around 5:30. There was a costume contest for the dogs. We had no dog in this fight, so Holmes went in his shaggy, all-black birthday suit. Other canine costumes were quite good and the winner was a labradoodle named Barkley, whose coat had been dyed neon green. His human parents put him in an Astros jersey, and on his head, he wore a cap with orange antennas capped with tiny baseballs. He was dressed as Orbit, the Astros mascot, and Barkley easily won the costume contest. We didn't realize we would end up sitting directly in front of Barkley and his family. He became a bit of a celebrity as people walking through Home Run Alley stopped his family to ask for photos.

The line for the pet parade was quite long, but we were able to tell the people around us about our trip and mission while Holmes enjoyed the reciprocal sniffing of the dogs around us. The Astros staff guided us through the plaza outside of the stadium and into the tunnel under the concourse. We were in a holding pattern for a bit before the line started moving and we walked onto the warning track in right field. The line moved rather slowly as people stopped to take photos of themselves and their dogs on the field. We were among those trying to get our dog to look at the camera. I snapped a few pictures of Patti and Holmes but had to be quick about it because Astros staff members were trying to hustle people around the track to ensure everyone was off the field and into their seats before the first pitch at 7:05 Central Time. This was another ESPN Sunday Night Baseball game.

The Angels were starting rookie Shohei Ohtani, the two-way phenom from Japan. When we saw the Angels play in Arizona, a Japanese couple was sitting behind us wearing Diamondbacks attire. They cheered quite loudly when Diamondbacks pitcher Yoshihisa Hirano entered the game in the seventh inning and retired the only two batters he faced. But when Ohtani came up to bat as a pinch-hitter in the top of the eighth, the man behind us replaced his Diamondbacks cap with an Angels cap. I noticed it and gave him a hard time for switching teams. We laughed and he said he had to support his countrymen on both teams.

Ohtani was on the mound for the Sunday night contest against the Astros and he got tagged. The 'Stros chased him after just two-and-a-third innings, tagging him for a pair of runs on two hits with a couple of walks. Both runs came via George Springer's two-run homer in the bottom of the third inning.

Holmes was unimpressed by the home run because in true Holmes fashion, he simply laid at our feet for most of the game. As was the case in Washington, we took Holmes out prior to the game. Ben, Bailey, Patti and I all went to a bar and grill for a late lunch. It had a covered, yet dog-friendly outdoor patio and we hung out for a few hours and chatted while watching other patrons utilize the sand volleyball courts. While we were trying to order our food and drinks, my dad called. I told him I was with Ben, who has a frustrating reputation of not returning phone calls. Because our dad had been trying to get ahold of Ben, he asked if I could hand him my phone.

Ben proceeded to repeat the same information he had shared with me about how busy he was at work because while one co-worker was on vacation, another had a father who was placed in hospice. This meant Ben had to do the work of three people until the guy on vacation returned. Ben, who lives in San Antonio and works for Halliburton, had hoped to meet us on our two-day visit to the Alamo City but couldn't get away from his computer long enough to connect. I was very happy when he told me he could go to a Sunday game in Houston. An Alex Bregman home run even caromed off the Halliburton sign in left field, adding to the sign's collection of dents. Of the dozen sponsor signs in left field, Ben pointed out that nine of them were of oil companies.

"I guess that makes sense, considering where we are," Patti replied.

The game was a sellout, and because they had the dog sections sealed off with steel gates, the concourses were extremely congested. It didn't help that there are escalators in the middle of the concourse. One of the escalators was not operating and that added to the cluster.

"The flow was not good," Patti observed.

"Who puts escalators right in the middle of the concourse? Horrible design," I added. "That's one of the bigger flaws in what was otherwise a really nice stadium."

As people walked down long Home Run Alley arcade, they needed to watch where they stepped because there were some land mines left by a few dogs. I prevented a couple of people from stepping on some dog poop that was left in the concourse.

"Anyone who can't pick up after their dog should be kicked out of the stadium," I remarked to Patti and anyone else within earshot.

· · · · ·

We first noticed the lethargy in Orange County, California. We took Holmes on a long walk up Cactus Hill near the city of Orange. It was about 90 degrees when we hit the trailhead around 11:30 a.m. We scaled the small mountain, which provided little to no shade, and by the time we made our way to the bottom the hill on the other side, Holmes was beat. His back legs were shaking. He found some shade under a bush and laid down. We had water with us and gave him another drink before we made him get up to walk to our car about 200 yards away.

He got some more water at the car and then we drove him over to a dog park in Orange. Each one of the dozen or so dogs at the park stayed under the shade of the trees. The dogs had plenty of water, thanks to several bowls placed near the trees. Holmes ran around for a few minutes with some of the dogs, but he was exhausted and we took him back to the Orangeland RV Resort.

We attributed his lack of energy to the heat. We had no idea how serious things really were.

Holmes had a veterinarian appointment in Phoenix because he was due for some vaccinations boosters. Our friends Chris and Katie Harris, who live in the Phoenix area and have pets, recommended a vet near their home in Peoria. Thanks to the two Harris beagles and their two cats, with whom Holmes was obsessed, Holmes quickly regained his energy while in Arizona. The summer heat prevented us from taking him on many walks; a city ordinance prohibits dog walking if the temperature exceeds 100 degrees.

Holmes received his shots and the vet performed a quick, routine physical. She noticed that his lymph nodes were prominent.

"It might not be anything to be concerned about, but you should him checked out soon," she advised.

We knew we were going to be in St. Louis in a month and his old vet could take a look. As our trip was nearing its conclusion in the Gateway City, Patti made an appointment for Holmes at the Webster Groves Animal Hospital.

The cancer diagnosis was confirmed on September 20th. Holmes had Stage 4 lymphoma. The doctor said the cancerous cells had likely spread to his spleen and liver. We were devastated and did not know what to expect. Holmes had been our "Barketing Manager" and now we did not know how much longer we had with him.

"It was definitely taking a toll on him," Patti said before Holmes began treatment on September 24th.

Holmes had gone from about 70 pounds when we started the trip, to 54 pounds when he was weighed by the vet tech in St. Louis. Some of that weight he lost because of more regular walks, we no longer had a fenced in back yard to just let him outside to do his business. Probably half of the weight he lost was because he had lost his appetite. When we could coax him with chicken or other "people food" to eat, he often vomited. He had gone from a dog who is social with both people and dogs to a dog who didn't even want to stand. It was tough to see. Holmes is, by most counts, a perfect dog. He's sweet, loving and kind, and best of all, quiet. He rarely barks and he's been like that his entire life. We describe him as "chill" and anyone who meets him is usually quick to agree. Holmes is the type of dog you can have off-leash and he won't run off. When you pull the leash out for a walk, he would get excited like other dogs, but when you open the door, he waits for you. But now we were waiting on him to get better.

We had originally intended on taking about a month off from traveling and then heading to Chicago to see the Bears and New York Jets play at Soldier Field on October 28th. Though she's a Bears fan who grew up in Illinois, Patti had never seen a game at Soldier Field. We were then going to begin a journey from Chicago down historic Route 66 to Los Angeles. This had been a longtime dream of mine, but it got put on hold because of the six-month chemotherapy protocol required for Holmes. Because he needed weekly or bi-weekly appointments, traveling and taking him from vet to vet would not be conducive for effective treatment.

"He's my baby, and it's rough," Patti said at the time. "But we'll figure it out. We have a lot of support and people sending their prayers, and we appreciate that. We'll just keep loving him and hope he gets to feeling better."

We had to determine where we'd be for those six months. The RV had multiple things to repair, meaning our home on wheels wasn't an option for the 17 weeks it took to complete the work.

We had friends in St. Louis with whom we could stay for a night or two. We ventured north to Peoria and settled in at Patti's parents' place. That was not a long-term solution, so we moved into the home of her sister, Veronica. Holmes was comfortable there and Roni's house is just a couple of blocks from an animal hospital. Whenever Holmes needed a blood draw to check his white blood cell count, we could walk him the short distance. Roni also has a cat named Bootzi, with whom Holmes was infatuated (just like the Harris kitties).

Following his first chemo treatment, Holmes was put on a steroid, anti-vomiting and anti-diarrheal medication, and an antibiotic for about two weeks. We were also given four oral chemotherapy pills to give him over the course of the six-month protocol. After the first week, Holmes began to improve dramatically. He was eating again and getting the bounce back in his step. Three weeks into his treatment, his lymph nodes were back to the normal. A week later, he was acting like his old self, getting excited for walks, running with a deer-like prance at the park, and eating everything we put in his bowl. It didn't take long for Holmes to reclaim his "spot" on the left side of the couch. Because he lost strength in his back legs and had joint pain, Holmes had stopped jumping on the bed in the RV when we were gone and would no longer even get on the sofa. He wouldn't even get on the couch at Patti's parents' home. But while staying with our friends, Pete and Maria Shuleski, in St. Louis during the final leg of the trip, Holmes was caught relaxing on their basement sofa.

Patti had given him the nickname "Shel-Dog" after *The Big Bang Theory* character, Sheldon Cooper, when we lived in Charlotte. Sheldon had his "spot" on the couch and so did Holmes. He would nudge people out of the way or simply stand and stare until the person in his spot moved. When we cleared everything out of the house in Charlotte, his favorite green sofa was taken to the curb. But we had one last night in the house and nowhere for Holmes to lie. So, Patti went to get the cushion from his side of the couch. When she walked through the door with "his" cushion, he started jumping up and down, tail wagging; he even tried to hump the cushion, which was something completely out of his character. His excitement level was through the roof.

Eight months later, we had that excitable boy back and were delighted.

CHAPTER 4:

STATUES, STATUES, AND MORE STATUES

When Oriole Park at Camden Yards opened in 1992, it laid the foundation for every new stadium that followed.

It's easy to see aspects of Oriole Park throughout Major League Baseball.

Stadiums became more than just a place to eat some hot dogs and popcorn while watching a baseball game. They became museums, allowing visitors to take a journey through the history of the franchises by commemorating their best players.

The statue garden beyond the left-center field wall at Camden Yards has been emulated across baseball. The statue garden depicts Hall of Fame manager Earl Weaver overseeing fellow Orioles greats Cal Ripken, Jr., Eddie Murray, Frank Robinson, Brooks Robinson and Jim Palmer — all cast in bronze.

Weaver stands with his hands on his back pockets and back to the field watching Frank Robinson follow through on what we assume was a home run swing. Brooks Robinson, with his knees bent, leans in with a glove on his left hand, ready for a grounder to be hit to his third-base position. Murray, a switch-hitter who hit 504 home runs, is shown in his signature left-handed batting stance. Murray joined Hank Aaron and Willie Mays as the third player to have at least 3,000 hits and 500 home runs. Across the plaza, Ripken is depicted with his glove outstretched to receive a throw and get a force out at second base. The Hall-of-Fame shortstop recorded 3,651 put-outs and helped turn 1,565 double players during his career, in addition to slugging 431 homers at the plate. Then there's the high leg kick of Palmer, whose right arm is cocked to hurl one of his hard-breaking curveballs. Palmer was baseball's winningest pitcher in the 1970s and retired in 1984 with 268 victories.

Even as you enter Camden Yards, you're greeted by another baseball icon. The likeness of Baltimore native Babe Ruth stands near the Eutaw Street gate at the B&O Warehouse. The retired numbers of Ripken, Weaver, Palmer, Murray and the Robinsons stand on pedestals surrounding the statue, which is called "Babe's Dream." The bronze Ruth, standing 16 feet high, is shown standing with one foot crossed in front of the other and his left hand on a bat. His right hand rests on his hip as he holds a glove by a couple of fingers sticking through the opening for the palm. The Babe Ruth Birthplace and Museum is located just a couple of blocks from the statue.

Baltimore made it trendy to construct a new stadium while including elements that hark back to an older era. The Orioles incorporated the elongated eight-story B&O Railroad Warehouse to serve as the right-field backdrop. The vintage building was gutted and renovated and now houses the team offices, the official team store, and the popular Dempsey's Brew Pub & Restaurant.

The retro-modern ballparks were the new thing and it isn't a coincidence that Cleveland's Progressive Field has many of the same elements. Opening as Jacobs Field in 1994, construction on the new park began just as Camden Yards was preparing to open.

The architectural firm HOK designed Oriole Park, what is now called Guaranteed Rate Field in Chicago, Progressive Field, Coors Field in Denver, Comerica Park in Detroit, San Francisco's AT&T Park, Petco Park in San Diego, PNC Park in Pittsburgh, Great American Ball Park, Philadelphia's Citizens Bank Park, Busch Stadium in St. Louis, the new Yankee Stadium, Citi Field, Nationals Park, Target Field in Minneapolis, Marlins Park and SunTrust Park in Atlanta. The firm also oversaw the renovations of Angel Stadium and Kansas City's Kauffman Stadium. Each new stadium opened after 1991.

Before entering Progressive Field via the right field gate, you encounter statues of Bob Feller, Lou Boudreau and Larry Doby. Once inside the park, you find Heritage Park, which pays homage to former players whose placards surround a center statue of Frank Robinson — the first African-American manager in MLB history. There is also a player statue whose likeness Patti immediately recognized as Hall of Famer Jim Thome. Patti said I told everyone in the stadium that she went to high school with Jim Thome.

The 2018 Hall of Fame inductee played for six different teams, but spent 13 years in Cleveland. Thome's statue, which is located in the center-field concourse, depicts the left-handed hitting slugger with his bat outstretched as he steps into the batter's box. A shin guard is on his right leg. An inscription on the statue's plinth reads:

> "Jim Thome's journey to become a member of the elite 600-home run club is a story built on consistency, dependability, professionalism, power, and character. The Indians' all-time career HR king and single-season leader spent 13 seasons in an Indians uniform, earning three All-Star appearances, ranks in the top ten in nine offensive categories – HR and walks, RBI, slugging percentage, on-base percentage and OPS, total bases, runs, doubles."

Boudreau, the 1948 American League MVP, is captured with his left leg raised as he rears back to swing. Feller is shown in midstride as he delivers a pitch to the plate. His left glove hand is high above his head with a baseball in his right hand. Known for his dominating fastball, "Bullet Bob" led the AL in wins six times and led the Indians to a World Series championship in 1948, the last time the Tribe won it all. Doby, who was the first black player in the American League, follows through on a swing from the left side of the plate and is on his way to first. Doby was also a member of that 1948 championship team and was a seven-time All-Star during his 13-year playing career. Robinson's statue in Heritage Park shows baseball's first black manager holding a lineup card with the Indians' batting order on April 8th, 1975 for a game against the Yankees. Robinson, who was hired as a player-manager following the 1974 season, made his managerial debut that day and hit second in the lineup as the designated hitter. He hit a home run in his first at-bat, one of 586 he hit as a player, and the Orioles went on to a 5-3 win.

Robinson is also depicted in a group of bronze sculptures at Great American Ball Park. The *Reds Legends of Crosley Field* was unveiled in 2003 to coincide with the opening of the new stadium. Joining Robinson in the exhibit are Ted Kluszewski, Ernie Lombardi and Joe Nuxhall. The four are displayed on a small field with the left-handed Nuxhall firing a pitch from the mound to Robinson with Lombardi crouching behind the plate. Kluszewski is waiting in the on-deck circle with both hands wrapped around a bat resting on his left shoulder.

· · · · ·

Robinson isn't the only Hall of Famer with three statues of his likeness at baseball stadiums. Red Sox great Ted Williams is also immortalized in bronze at a trio of parks — two of which are in Florida.

The first time we saw a statue of "The Splendid Splinter" was Fort Myers, as Williams is on display in front of the main gate at JetBlue Park. Williams is shown with a bat in his left hand, slung over his shoulder, while using his right hand to place his cap on the head of a small child. It is a duplicate of the Williams statue outside of Fenway Park. The team's spring home has several elements of Fenway, including a replica Green Monster and the "red seat" in right field to mark where Williams' famed 502-foot home run in 1946 landed.

A second statue of Williams' likeness is also at Fenway Park. "The Team-mates" statuary, located outside of Gate B at the intersection of Van Ness and Ipswich Streets, shows Williams standing with fellow Red Sox greats Bobby

Doerr, Dom DiMaggio and Johnny Pesky. The sculpture's name comes from the book, "The Teammates: Portrait of a Friendship," which tells the story of DiMaggio and Pesky driving to Florida to visit a dying Williams. The quartet became friends while playing together in the 1940s and remained close long after their playing careers were over.

Fenway Park is also home to a statue of one of the nation's founding fathers with the likeness of Samuel Adams located in the right field upper deck, which was renamed the "Sam Deck" in 2018. The Brookline Avenue Bridge that connects Commonwealth Avenue and Lansdowne Street near Fenway Park was renamed the David Ortiz Bridge in 2016, and a life-size LEGO statue of "Big Papi" was installed at JetBlue Park for the 2018 Spring Training. The LEGO statue shows Ortiz celebrating a home run with both hands raised and two fingers pointing toward the sky as he looks upward.

Williams was one of the best hitters ever and he is the centerpiece and namesake of the Ted Williams Museum and Hitters Hall of Fame at Tropicana Field. The statue of the left-handed swinging Williams is located just inside the museum's door in front of a painting that was the inspiration for the bronze sculpture.

· · · · ·

When we arrived at SunTrust Park in Atlanta and got to our seats, Patti said, "This just feels like baseball." The Braves christened SunTrust in 2017 after leaving Turner Field, which was the team's home for just 20 years. We liked Turner Field when we saw a game there in 2016, its final season. But the Braves did things right with SunTrust Park.

I am not wowed by many stadiums after spending two decades as a sports reporter, but SunTrust definitely has a wow factor. It starts before you even walk through the stadium gates. The Battery is analogous to Main Street, U.S.A. at Magic Kingdom in Disney World. The stadium itself then offers several amenities, including the Sandlot kids' zone. This place will make you want to be a kid again and it even has a zipline. Yes, you read that correctly. It's a baseball stadium with a zipline.

The Braves also do a wonderful job paying tribute to the franchise's history with over 300 pieces of Braves-themed memorabilia scattered throughout the stadium. Nowhere is the team's history from Boston to Milwaukee to Atlanta chronicled better than at the Camden Yards-esque Monument Garden. The focal point of Monument Garden is a nine-foot statue of Hank Aaron. The Hall of Fame outfielder is shown mid-swing, with a depressed baseball being struck by Aaron's extended bat. Aaron himself was on hand to see the unveiling of his likeness. The number "755" is on the wall behind the statue and a video of Aaron's 715th home run on April 8th, 1974 is shown above the number. Aaron passed Babe Ruth as baseball's home run king, a title he held until Barry Bonds surpassed him in 2007.

Flanking "755" are the 11 jersey numbers retired by the team, including Aaron's 44. A sculpture made up of 755 Hank Aaron Louisville Slugger baseball bats in the shape of the number 755 lives next to the Aaron statue. Pennants of the franchise's 17 National League championships and three World Series titles proudly line Monument Garden's walkway. The franchise's 55 Hall of Famers are represented by either a bat or glove while plaques honor the 31 former players or managers who are in the Braves Hall of Fame. A trophy case houses Greg Maddux's 1995 Cy Young award, Aaron's 1957 MVP award, Dale Murphy's 1982 Silver Slugger award, Andruw Jones' 2005 Gold Glove award and David Justice's 1990 Rookie of the Year award. Audio clips of some of the team's highlights since moving to Atlanta can be heard throughout Monument Garden, which is located behind Section 125 on the main level.

. . . . .

An Aaron statue also resides outside Miller Park in Milwaukee, where he began his career in 1954 as a member of the Braves and finished his career in 1976 as a member of the Brewers. Aaron was among the inaugural class of Miller Park's Walk of Fame in 2001. The others were fellow Hall of Famers Rollie Fingers, Paul Molitor and Robin Yount. Not every member of the Walk of Fame has his own statue, but Aaron's is one of the four statues guarding the entrances to the stadium.

The right-handed Aaron is shown in his batting stance, wearing the uniform of the 1957 Milwaukee Braves, who bested the Yankees in seven games to win the World Series. It was the Braves' last championship since the 1995 Atlanta team won it all.

The other three statues outside of Miller Park depict Yount, former Brewers owner and MLB commissioner Bud Selig, and Milwaukee native and longtime Brewers broadcaster Bob Uecker.

Yount, who spent his entire 20-year playing career with the Brewers, is shown swinging from the right side of the plate, arms outstretched and his straight left leg planted firmly in the pedestal as he follows through. Directly behind the Yount statue is the entrance to the Brewers' team store. Yount was the 1982 and 1989 American League MVP and was inducted into the Hall of Fame in 1999. He and Molitor were my two favorite players growing up as I fell in love with baseball watching the Brewers reach the 1982 World Series.

Selig, who moved the fledgling Seattle Pilots to Milwaukee following the 1969 season, stands wearing a suit while holding a baseball in his right hand. Selig was the Brewers owner from 1970 until 1992, when he transferred his ownership to his daughter after assuming the role of acting commissioner following the resignation of Fay Vincent. Selig had the "acting" designation removed in 1998 and he remained MLB commissioner until his retirement in 2015. He was inducted into the Baseball Hall of Fame in 2017 and his statue was unveiled in 2010. Aaron, who refers to Selig as a hero, attended the statue ceremony. Yount, Frank Robinson, Ernie Banks, Al Kaline, and more than a dozen team owners also witnessed the unveiling outside the stadium Selig pushed to get built.

Uecker has been calling Brewers games since 1971 and was the voice of my childhood as a kid growing up on a dairy farm outside of La Crosse, Wisconsin. I fondly remember listening to Uecker call Brewers games while helping my dad and grandparents in the barn. "Mr. Baseball" has also made a name for himself as a comedian and actor, known for his roles as broadcaster Harry Doyle in the "Major League" film franchise and as lovable family man George Owens in the 1980s sitcom, "Mr. Belvedere." Uecker often makes fun of his own baseball career, which was remarkable in that fact that he lasted six years in the majors, despite hitting only .200 with 146 career hits and 167 strikeouts in 731 at-bats. But he is a gifted storyteller and first became a national celebrity during the late 1970s, thanks to a series of class Miller Lite commercials. His self-deprecating humor is also immortalized inside Miller Park with the "Uecker Seat" in the last row of Section 422 high above home plate. During perhaps Uecker's most famous Miller Lite spot, he boasts of being a former big-league player who fans love and who gets free tickets from the team. When an usher tells him he is sitting in the wrong seat, Uecker says, "I must be in the front row." The camera then cuts to Uecker sitting by himself high in the upper deck.

Each seven-foot bronze statue stands atop a five-foot brick pedestal with a plaque detailing the men's respective accomplishments.

· · · · ·

Uecker, who received the Ford C. Frick Award for broadcasting from the National Baseball Hall of Fame in 2003, isn't the only broadcaster with his own statue. Phillies broadcaster Harry Kalas stands tall in the left-field concourse at Citizens Bank Park. Legendary Tigers play-by-play man Ernie Harwell greets fans at Comerica Park. A bust of iconic Cardinals voice Jack Buck adorns a section of Busch Stadium's exterior wall along Clark Street in St. Louis.

The statue of Kalas is not far from the entrance to the in-stadium restaurant at Citizens Bank Park that bears his name. The incomparable Kalas is shown in a suit with a sweater over his dress shirt, standing with his legs crossed while holding a microphone in his right hand and leaning on a baseball bat. His left hand is secured in his trousers pocket. A welcoming smile is on his face. Just a few yards behind him is the entrance to Harry the K's Broadcast Bar & Grille. Located just beneath the left-field scoreboard, Harry the K's offers superb outfield views of the field and is a first-come, first-served restaurant. It's even quite affordable, especially by ballpark standards, and does not require any special ticket to gain entry. Get the stuffed avocado, you won't regret it.

While Kalas greets visitors at the home-plate entrance, Phillies greats welcome fans at other gates. Hall of Fame third baseman Mike Schmidt stands watch at the third-base gate, seven-time All-Star pitcher Robin Roberts is at first base, and four-time Cy Young Award winner Steve Carlton is immortalized at the left-field gate. A statue of Hall of Fame outfielder and former Phillies broadcaster Richie Ashburn is in the outfield concourse, which is named Ashburn Alley and houses several concessions stands as well as the Philadelphia Baseball Wall of Fame. Granite markers along the walkway feature every Phillies player to be named to the All-Star Game since it was first played in 1933. Ashburn Alley is also home to Memory Lane, which chronicles the franchise's history as baseball's oldest continuous, single-name, single-city team.

Philadelphia is a city known for its statues, especially the one of Rocky Balboa in front of the Philadelphia Art Museum and of Pennsylvania founder William Penn atop Philadelphia's City Hall. The 37-foot bronze statue was once the highest points in Philadelphia and urban designer, Edmund Bacon, said no man should ever erect a building higher than the "brim of Billy Penn's hat." Bacon's 1894 mandate existed for almost 100 years until city developers allowed skyscrapers that towered over City Hall to be built. The result was a "curse" that resulted in zero Philadelphia sports teams winning championships. The Flyers won consecutive Stanley Cups in 1974-75 and the 76ers won an

NBA title in 1983, but the towering One Liberty Place was built in 1987. The "curse" existed until 2008, when a contractor placed a small William Penn figurine atop the new Comcast Center. The Phillies, who had won winning season between 1986 and 2001, won the World Series later that year. It was the team's first championship since 1980 and Kalas had the call as Phillies closer Brad Lidge, struck out Tampa Bay's Eric Hinske in Game 5.

"Swing and a miss. Struck him out! The Philadelphia Phillies are 2008 world champions of baseball," Kalas said as Queen's "We Are the Champions" began playing at Citizens Bank Park. "Brad Lidge does it again and stays perfect for the 2008 season, 48 for 48 in save opportunities, and let the city celebrate… And it has been 28 years since the Phillies have enjoyed a World Championship, 25 years in this city that a team that has enjoyed a World Championship, and the fans are ready to celebrate. What a night!"

Kalas, who began calling Phillies games in 1971 and received the Ford C. Frick Award in 2002, called his final game on April 12th, 2009. He collapsed in the press box at Citizens Bank Park the very next day and died of heart disease at the age of 73.

"We lost Harry," team president David Montgomery said in a statement. "We lost our voice."

· · · · ·

The Tigers lost their longtime play-by-play voice 13 months later when Ernie Harwell died at the age of 92. He stands inside the main entrance of Comerica Park, holding a microphone to his mouth with his left hand and his right hand in his pocket. He wears glasses and a smile that endeared him to Tigers fans for more than 40 years. The Georgia native was known for his Southern drawl that came across when he said Tigers (Ti-guhs) and his trademark home run call: "That one is LONG gone." He also began the first Spring Training broadcast of each year with the same excerpt from the *Song of Solomon*, "For lo, the winter is past, the rain is over and gone; the flowers appear on the earth; the time of the singing of birds is come, and the voice of the turtle is heard in our land." Harwell received the Ford C. Frick Award in 1981.

"Baseball is continuity," Harwell once said. "Pitch to pitch. Inning to inning. Game to game. Series to series. Season to season."

Walk past Harwell and you see one of ten towering stanchions in the concourse that pay tribute to each of the franchise's 20th century decades. The stanchion tower behind Harwell is a tribute to the 1980s, when the Tigers won the 1984 World Series over the San Diego Padres. Manager Sparky Anderson and Series MVP, Alan Trammell, both of whom are now in the Hall of Fame, are shown in celebration. Each of the franchise's four World Series titles and 11 American League pennants are honored as visitors walk back through time. Flags with the years of each World Series title, 1935, 1945, 1968, and 1984, wave over the Chevrolet Fountain above batter's eye in center field. To the left of the batter's eye are the most unique player statues in baseball. The six steel structures stand 13 feet high and honor Tigers greats Hal Newhouser, Ty Cobb, Al Kaline, Hank Greenberg, Charlie Gehringer, and Willie Horton. Each man is shown in motion. Kaline leaps to catch a potential home run ball, dirt flies in the air as Cobb slides into second base. Newhouser's right leg is raised as high as his head as he prepares to deliver a pitch. Gehringer is turning two as a mystery face in the steel dirt is shown beneath Gehringer's feet. Horton and Greenberg swing for the fences with motion trails following their bats. Greenberg is just making contact and three baseballs are shown flying off his bat in succession to depict the path of the ball. Horton's motion trail nearly surrounds his entire torso as he completes his swing.

Most statues at MLB ballparks capture players, managers, and broadcasters as a still image. Comerica Park's steel statues, which sit atop granite pedestals, depict larger-than-life players in motion as you might have seen them during their playing days.

There are also eight heroic-sized statues of Tigers that prowl the gates to the stadium. The most impressive of which is in front of the main gate. The 15-foot tiger roars while looking to its left and the left paw is raised and ready to strike its prey. Under that raised paw is where many fans choose to have their photo taken. Behind the guardian tiger is the Tigers Old English "D" logo above the home plate gate. Prowling tigers flank the entrance above as they do in right field. Two more tigers slink atop the left-field scoreboard; their eyes illuminate following each Tigers home run and victory.

We were fortunate enough to see the Tigers beat the Twins on June 13th, but more on that later.

. . . . .

Buck was the 1987 Frick Award recipient and began calling Cardinals games in 1954 alongside Harry Caray, who went on to greater fame calling Cubs games and received the Frick Award in 1989. His head-and-shoulders bust, which is protected by a green awning, shows Buck at what is presumed to be his press box seat with a microphone in front of him. He left hand is raised to his left ear as his right arm rests on the podium. Behind the bronze statue atop a dark granite podium is a photo collage of Buck throughout the years. His tagline, "That's a winner," is inscribed just beneath his name. Buck had one of the more memorable calls in 1985 during the National League Championship Series. The Cardinals were playing the Los Angeles Dodgers and game five was tied at 2-2, heading to the bottom of the ninth inning at Busch Stadium. Cardinals Hall of Fame short-stop, Ozzie Smith, hit a rare home run, going low to lift a Tom Niedenfuer fast-ball just over the left-field fence to give the Cardinals a 3-2 victory.

"Go crazy, folks. Go crazy," Buck shouted in a call that is now part of St. Louis baseball lore. Famed Dodgers broadcaster, Vin Scully, had television duties for that game. Scully retired following the 2016 season, but the 1982 Ford C. Frick Award recipient surprisingly did not yet have a statue outside of Dodger Stadium in 2018.

The Cardinals won the 1985 NLCS in six games but lost the World Series to the Kansas City Royals.

Buck was teamed with former Cardinals player, Mike Shannon, in 1972 and the two worked together for 28 years. Buck called more than 6,500 Cardinals games over nearly 50 years as the voice of the Cardinals. He was so synonymous with the Cardinals, he became known as "The Voice of Summer" in St. Louis. He died in 2002, but his legacy lives on, not only with his statue, but with his son, Joe, carrying the broadcasting mantle as one of the premier baseball and football broadcasters in the business.

Just around the corner from Buck's bust are the other Busch Stadium statues at the corner of Clark and 8th Street. Hall of Famers Stan Musial, Enos Slaughter, Dizzy Dean, Rogers Hornsby, Red Schoendienst, Lou Brock, Bob Gibson, and Smith are all depicted in front of the Cardinals team store. Former St. Louis Browns player and Hall of Fame inductee, George Sisler, is among the statues, as is former Negro league St. Louis Stars legend and Hall of Famer James "Cool Papa" Bell.

Hornsby is caught mid-swing with his bat pointed to the outfield. Schoendienst, who died June 6th, 2018, is turning a double play. Dean and Gibson are both delivering strikes to the plate, Dean with his arm cocked back before the pitch and Gibson falling off the mound on his follow through. Slaughter is shown sliding into a base and Smith, ever the wizard at shortstop, is shown mid-air diving for a line drive. Bell is watching his ball take flight after ditching his bat and springing out of the batter's box.

Musial was such an iconic player, he has two statues at Busch Stadium. He is included among the Hall of Fame cluster at the corner of 8th and Clark, his left-handed swing complete as he gazes toward right field to track the flight of his ball. The other, much larger, Musial statue is at the third-base gate and shows a barrel-chested "Stan the Man" in his corkscrew batting stance. An inscription on the statue's base reads, "Here stands baseball's perfect warrior; Here stands baseball's perfect knight."

Musial is the most revered of all Cardinals players, spending his entire 22-year career with the Redbirds. His career was interrupted in 1945 when he joined the U.S. Navy during World War II. When he returned to the big leagues in 1946, he won the second of his three NL MVP awards. Musial was a 24-time All-Star, MLB held two All-Star games a year from 1959-62, before retiring following the 1963 season. He had a .331 career batting average and recorded 3,630 hits with 475 home runs and 1,951 RBI. When Musial hung up his cleats, he held or shared 17 major league records, 29 NL records, and nine All-Star Game records.

When Jackie Robinson broke baseball's color barrier in 1947, one of his first road games was at St. Louis' Sportsman's Park. While some Cardinals players threatened to boycott the game if Robinson took the field, Musial would not protest and openly supported Robinson and other black players who followed.

· · · · ·

There are Jackie Robinson statues all over the country and even one on foreign soil. Robinson, who broke baseball's color barrier in 1947, was a star athlete at UCLA, lettering in baseball, track, basketball, and football. A pair of statues in the Los Angeles area honors his time with the Bruins. One of those statues sits outside of the Rose Bowl in Pasadena and depicts Robinson in his football uniform with a ball tucked under his left arm and his right arm outstretched to fend off a would-be tackler. At least nine statues of Robinson are scattered across North America. Those statues are believed to be the most for any U.S. athlete but deserving for a man Scully says is "the most courageous athlete" he ever met.

We saw our first Robinson statue outside of Olympic Stadium in Montreal. Even though we were on a 30-stadium MLB tour, we took advantage of a long Blue Jays homestand in May. We left our RV park in Mystic, Connecticut, where we stayed as a midway point between New York City and Boston, and left May 2nd, the day after we saw the Braves beat the Mets at Citi Field. We had never before visited New England, so we spent one night in Vermont, a night in New Hampshire, and three nights at Acadia National Park in Maine. We then entered Canada from Maine and crossed the border into Quebec. We spent two nights near Montreal and wanted to visit the former home of the Montreal Expos.

Olympic Stadium was home to the Expos from 1977 until 2004, when the franchise moved south to become the Washington Nationals. The final regular-season MLB game played at Olympic stadium was a 9-1 Marlins victory over the Expos on September 29th, 2004. It has hosted a few spring exhibition games since, including two games between the Cardinals and Blue Jays on March 26th and 27th, 2018. Vladimir Guerrero Jr., whose father was an Expos star and inducted into the Baseball Hall of Fame in 2018, lifted the Blue Jays to a dramatic 1-0 victory with a walk-off home run in the bottom of the ninth on March 27th.

There is a rich baseball tradition in Montreal, and Olympic Stadium hosted a handful of playoff series and the 1982 All-Star Game. What we learned during a tour of Olympic Stadium is that Montreal residents would love to see professional baseball return to Quebec. As we waited for our tour to begin, I saw a large chalkboard where visitors can leave messages. I grabbed a piece of chalk and wrote, "Bring back the Expos. #HomeRunOnWheels." Our tour was led by a man in his late 30s named Jeff, who carries around two tickets from a 1996 game he attended. The Padres shut out the Expos as Scott Sanders struck out ten over eight innings in a 6-0 win.

Baseball was part of Montreal long before Olympic Stadium opened in 1976 to host the Olympic Games that summer. Robinson played for the Montreal Royals at Delorimier Stadium a year before his MLB debut with the Dodgers. Delorimier Downs, which also hosted the Canadian Football League's Alouettes from 1946-53, was demolished in the 1970s and replaced with a school. A plaque honoring Robinson's accomplishments is posted on a stone memorial surrounded by a red batting cage in an adjacent park.

The statue of Robinson in Montreal is outside of the entrance to Café in Vivo at Olympic Stadium. A capless Robinson stands next to a pair of children on a stone slab holding the hand of one youngster. Both boys gaze up at Robinson, who looks down at them with a smile. A plaque on the statue's base pays tribute to the perseverance Robinson exhibited during his athletic career and life.

Robinson is also among the greats honored at Yankee Stadium's Monument Park, which does not house any statues but rather plaques to acknowledge the greatest players of baseball's most storied franchise. The Yankee Stadium Museum does have a statue exhibit of Yogi Berra catching Don Larsen's perfect game in the 1956 World Series. The two sculptures are appropriately 60 feet, six inches apart.

When we got to Toronto to see the Jays host the Red Sox on Mother's Day, we didn't see any player statues at Rogers Centre. There is a statue of former owner Ted Rogers, who ran the team for eight years from 2000 until his death in 2008. The Blue Jays were unremarkable during that team, failing to reach the postseason every year. The 2013 unveiling of the Rogers statue was controversial because many thought the team should honor Blue Jays greats, like Hall of Famer Roberto Alomar or 1993 World Series hero Joe Carter.

As Rogers stands in front of the stadium that bears his name, the façade of Toronto venue has an elaborate frieze depicting fans watching a game. There are 15 fans shown in the gargoyle-like fiberglass sculptures on the north side of the building along Blue Jays Way. Because Rogers Centre was built in 1989, as SkyDome using public funds, a city ordinance mandated that at least one percent of the construction costs be put toward a public art project. That project became known as the fans sculpture named, "The Audience."

There are different types of fans shown, heckling loudmouths shouting and pointing at the field, a dad with his son on his shoulder, a fan taking a picture, another using binoculars, a woman pointing up, presumably at the 1,800-foot CN Tower which rises above the stadium as its next-door neighbor, and a man guzzling a beverage. "The Audience" was one of the most unique statues we saw anywhere on our trip, at a baseball stadium or not.

· · · · ·

After flying to St. Louis for a wedding the following weekend and doing some sightseeing in Ontario (Niagara Falls), we were ready to return to the U.S. We stopped for a night in Buffalo to get some wings and watch a Bisons game, then made our way to Pittsburgh.

PNC Park is an amazing stadium and was our favorite MLB venue. The view of downtown Pittsburgh with the yellow Roberto Clemente bridge spanning the Allegheny River in the foreground is stunning. When you cross the Clemente bridge, you arrive at the stadium's left-field corner. There stands a colossal statue of "The Great One." Clemente was only 38 years old when he died in 1972 in a plane crash while on a humanitarian mission to Nicaragua. The 12-foot statue shows Clemente on his way to first base as he drops his bat and watches the path of the ball. His gave is fixed on the adjacent stadium, whose right-field wall is 21 feet high in honor of Clemente's retired jersey number. Clemente spent his entire 18-year career with the Pirates and he had collected his 3,000th hit three months before his death on New Year's Eve. The 12-time All-Star was fast-tracked for the Hall of Fame in 1973, bypassing the usual five-year wait.

The Clemente statue is one of four at PNC Park. The first former Pirates player to be honored with a statue was Honus Wagner, whose likeness guards the home-plate entrance of PNC Park. Wagner's time with the Pirates covered 51 years, 18 as a player from 1900-17. Wagner was an eight-time batting champ and led the Pirates to the 1909 World Series championship. He also managed the team in 1917 and was later a member of the coaching staff from 1933-51. His 1909 baseball card remains one of the rarest and most valuable cards ever printed.

We didn't see the Wagner statue ourselves because we entered by the Clemente statue. Nor did we see the Bill Mazeroski statue in the right-field grandstand. That statue depicts Mazeroski jubilantly sprinting around the bases after hitting a walk-off homer in Game 7 of the 1960 World Series. Mazeroski's ninth-inning blast against the Yankees remains the only Game 7 walk-off home run in World Series history.

We did walk past Willie Stargell's bronze sculpture near the left-field gate. Stargell, who helped the Pirates win the World Series in 1971 and 1979, is shown in his left-handed batting stance —— hands stretched back with his bat raised high above his head. The mustachioed Stargell endured racism early in his career but was selected to the All-Star Game seven times and was the 1979 National League MVP. He also claimed NLCS and World Series MVP honors that season. Known for his monster moonshots, Stargell hit 475 home runs over his career and was inducted into the Hall of Fame in 1988.

After Stargell died of kidney failure in 2001, Joe Morgan, who played for the rival Reds during the '70s, said, "When I played, there were 600 baseball players and 599 of them loved Willie Stargell. He's the only guy I could have said that about. He never made anybody look bad and he never said anything bad about anybody."

· · · · ·

We spent Opening Day in Miami; Easter Sunday at Tropicana Field; Mother's Day in Toronto; and Memorial Day weekend in the Pittsburgh area. When Father's Day arrived, we were at Guaranteed Rate Field in Chicago on a hot 92-degree day.

As we walked around during Detroit's 3-1 victory over the White Sox, we strolled past the numerous statues in the outfield plaza. The White Sox have 12 retired jersey numbers and there are eight players honored with statues at the "New Comiskey" Park. There is also a ninth statue of team founder, Charles Comiskey. "The Old Roman" stands behind the center-field batter's eye in a posh suit wearing a bowler hat and using a bat as a sort of cane.

Joining him in the outfield concourse are the effigies of White Sox greats Frank Thomas, Minny Minoso, Carlton Fisk, Billy Pierce, Luis Aparicio, Nellie Fox, Harold Baines and Paul Konerko. We didn't see each of the statues but were impressed by those of Aparicio, Fox and Baines.

With Aparacio at shortstop and Fox manning second base, the White Sox of the 1950s had one of the best middle infields in all of baseball. The two were selected to a combined 28 All-Star games and won 12 total Gold Gloves. Their sculptures are appropriately next to each other as Fox tosses a ball to Aparacio for one of the countless double plays turned by the Hall of Famers.

Baines had his 22-year career honored with a statue in 2008. It's unique because the bronze sculpture actually has some color to it. Shown in Chicago's bold-striped uniform of the 1980s, Baines' helmet is blue with a red brim. His long-sleeve undershirt protrudes from his jersey with a vibrant red that highlights his arms. His shoes, the right of which is raised as he begins his swing, are also red. Solid blue stripes on his jersey sleeve wrap his biceps. The wide blue stripe across his chest houses white letters that spell out "SOX." While Baines isn't in the National Baseball Hall of Fame, he was inducted into the Orioles Hall of Fame in 2009. He spent 14 years with the White Sox and seven with the Orioles while also spending time with the Athletics, Rangers, and Indians. Baines was a six-time All-Star who hit 384 home runs, 221 with the White Sox and 107 with the Orioles.

Statues with such color are not common, but there is another in Chicago.

Ernie Banks stands immortalized in front of Wrigley Field with a bright blue cap, blue sleeves, and blue stirrups as he awaits a pitch. Banks spent his entire 19-year career with the Cubs and was selected to the All-Star Game 14 times. "Mr. Cub" was also named NL MVP in both 1958 and 1959. The affable infielder was awarded the Presidential Medal of Freedom in 2013 but died two years later. His statue was temporarily moved from Clark Street to Daley Plaza in downtown Chicago, so fans could more easily pay tribute.

Two other Cubs Hall of Famers are honored outside Wrigley Field. While the Banks statue resides near the main entrance at the corner of Clark and Addison, statues of Ron Santo and Billy Williams are outside the right-field gate near the corner of Addison and Sheffield.

Santo was a fixture at third base for 14 seasons, making the All-Star Game nine times. When he was inducted into the Hall of Fame in 2012, his former teammates all did his patented heel click to celebrate in Cooperstown. Santo, who died in 2010 following a bout with bladder cancer, is shown with his arm cocked back as he prepares to throw across the diamond from third to first.

Williams holds a bat upright in his right hand as he gazes toward an unseen ball. His left arm crossed in front of his body, Williams begins his path down the first-base line. Williams spent 18 years in the majors, 16 with the Cubs. He led the National League in batting with a .333 average in 1972 and retired with a .290 lifetime average to go with 426 home runs and 1,475 RBI.

The Cubs celebrated Williams' 80th birthday when we saw them play the Dodgers on June 19th. Williams was in attendance and saw the Cubs win, thanks to Albert Almora's walk-off single in the bottom of the 10th to cap off an exciting night at the "Friendly Confines."

. . . . .

If you take the light-rail from the Mall of America to Target Field like we did, the first statue you'll see at the stadium is of a bull terrier. The depiction of Bullseye, the mascot of Target department stores, greets visitors as they exit the train at the Target Field Station near the left-field gate. We stopped to get a photo of Bullseye, his bronze body highlighted by a red target around his left eye. He is seated with his left paw resting atop a baseball mitt.

The canine sculpture was the first of many statues we saw at Target Field before entering to see the Twins take on the Orioles. After taking our pictures of Bullseye, we followed the crowd down through the left-field promenade. The walkway is lined with colorful sculptures of Peanuts characters.

Charlie Brown and Snoopy are joined by eight other Peanuts characters, all wearing Twins outfits. The six-foot statues were installed at Target Field ahead of the 2014 All-Star Game and have been greeting visitors ever since. The statues were created to honor Peanuts creator, Charles Schulz, who was a St. Paul native. I snapped a photo of Patti standing with Peppermint Patty and posted it to Facebook as we made our way around the stadium.

Gate 14 is the home-plate entrance at Target Field, and outside the entry point is a jubilant Kent Hrbek. The statue depicts the Twin Cities native with his arms raised as he celebrates the team's 1987 World Series championship. Hrbek spent his entire 14-year career with the Twins and was also a member of the 1991 World Series team. The banners of both championship seasons flutter on the stadium's façade above Hrbek.

Turning the corner around home plate, you enter Target Plaza, a park-like area outside of the team store on the first-base side. The plaza, which even has restrooms for those waiting to enter the stadium to use, stretches all the way down to the right-field entrance. A statue of the Twins mascot, T.C. Bear, is permanently seated on a bench in the plaza. At the plaza's center is a statue of former Twins owner Calvin Griffith, who moved the Washington Senators to Minneapolis in 1961. Griffith, wearing a suit, has a jacket slung over his left arm and is holding a baseball in his right hand.

Griffith sold the team to Carl and Elois Pohlad in 1984 and the Pohlads are also memorialized in Target Plaza. Both looking stoic while placed in front of the right-field gate, Carl has his arm around Elois, his right hand resting on her right shoulder, over which hangs a purse.

A bronze "Golden Glove" sculpture adds to the plaza décor.

Venture from the plaza and you see bronze statues of Twins Hall of Famers Harmon Killebrew and Kirby Puckett. Killebrew, who slugged 573 home runs, is captured in the middle of his swing, arms and bat fully extended with his legs wide. Puckett, a ten-time All-Star, is shown presumably rounding third and a gloved right fist is held high in a celebratory pump. Despite his portly stature, Puckett was swift of foot and a defensive dynamo who won six Gold Gloves in center field. He was also a superb hitter, finishing with a lifetime average of .318.

Standing watch nearby is former Twins manager Tom Kelly, who was at the helm for both of Minnesota's championship teams. A black slab in front of the statue holds a quote from the 1991 American League Manager of the Year:

> "There are no shortcuts to success. It takes a lot of hard work and effort. I tried to put players in a position where they will have a chance to succeed. I never felt that we should ask a player to do something that they cannot do. The name of the game is pitching. Pitch and catch; that is what it is all about and some have a difficult time understanding that."

The Kelly statue, which shows him in sunglasses and long sleeves with a bat resting on his left side and a baseball in his right hand, was unveiled in 2017. Six years earlier, it was Tony Oliva's turn to be honored. Oliva's statue is tucked into a vestibule just off the plaza. Like Killebrew, the left-handed Oliva is shown fully extended in mid-swing. The 1964 AL Rookie of the Year and eight-time All-Star is somehow not in the Baseball Hall of Fame despite a lifetime .304 average and 220 home runs. He led the league in hits five times and finished with 1,971 base hits, including an astounding 329 doubles and 48 triples.

But the greatest Twins player of all time was Rod Carew, and of course, he is also honored with a bronze sculpture. The problem with the Carew statue is that it's on the corner of 2nd Avenue and 7th Street, about 300 yards from the right-field gate. The stretch of 2nd Avenue between the Target Center, which is home to the NBA's Timberwolves and Target Field, is named Rod Carew Way. But if you take the light-rail train like we did and are new to the city, you have to sort of hunt to find the Carew statue. Fortunately, we located it following the July 7th game.

Carew, whose No. 29 is retired by both the Twins and Angels, is portrayed in his distinctive batting stance. Bending at the waist with his feet shoulder-width apart, Carew leans over the plate, his bat parallel to the ground as he holds it loosely in his hands. His dark, bronze eyes are staring at an unseen pitcher. Despite such a relaxed stance, Carew was one of the best hitters baseball had ever seen.

He led the league in hits three times, retiring after 19 seasons with 3,053, and was a seven-time batting champ. Carew had a career batting average of .328, highlighted by a .388 mark in 1977. Though he hit just 92 homers, Carew had 445 doubles and drove in 1,015 runs with only 1,028 strikeouts in 9,315 at-bats. He spent 12 years with the Twins before a falling out with Griffith led to his departure from Minnesota. Carew was traded to the Angels in 1979 and played his final seven seasons in Anaheim. He recorded his 3,000th hit in 1985, fittingly enough against the Twins. Carew retired following the '85 season as a player so beloved, the Angels paid tribute to his daughter three years after her death in 1996. Michelle Carew was only 18 years old when she succumbed to leukemia. The Angels dedicated a statue of Michelle smiling while holding a dog. A plaque beneath the statue says, "When she went to sleep, she woke up the world." Her death helped raise awareness of the National Marrow Donor Program. Rod Carew's eulogy for his daughter included a thank you to all those who support the non-profit organization.

Her statue is one of only two at Angel Stadium – the other being of former owner Gene Autry. The late actor, known as the "Singing Cowboy," is displayed on the first-level concourse with his trademark cowboy hat grasped in his left hand while his right reaches out to shake hands with visitors. Wearing a suit, bolo tie, and cowboy boots (of course), Autry's ever-present smile greets fans to Angel Stadium.

. . . . .

"The Player" statue in front of Coors Field pays tribute to former Dodgers owner Branch Rickey, who was the first to sign a black player when he inked Jackie Robinson to a big-league deal in 1945. Rickey also had a brief playing career with the St. Louis Browns and later managed the Browns and Cardinals between 1913 and 1925. But he's best known as the owner and general manager of the Brooklyn Dodgers. When Robinson made his MLB debut in 1947, he went on to be named the National League Rookie of the Year.

The 13-foot statue at the Coors Field entrance shows an anonymous player standing with a bat slung over his right shoulder. Standing under the clock tower, "The Player" gazes to his right with his left arm at his side and a baseball clutched in his left hand. On the reflective black plinth is a Rickey quote:

> "It is not the honor that you take with you but the heritage you leave behind."

Rickey was named the most influential person in sports in the 20th century by ESPN's sports century panel. The Branch Rickey Award was given annually to an individual in Major League Baseball in recognition of his exceptional community service from 1992 to 2014. The first recipient of the award was Hall of Famer Dave Winfield. Cubs first baseman Anthony Rizzo received the award in 2014.

Jamie Moyer, who pitched for eight MLB teams over 25 seasons, was the 2004 recipient while with the Mariners. Moyer was with the Mariners from 1996-2006 and one of his teammates during that time was Ken Griffey Jr. "The Kid" was a 13-time All-Star and the 1997 AL MVP. Junior called Seattle home for 13 of his 22 MLB seasons. He even got to play alongside his dad for 51 games over the 1990 and 1991 seasons. After eight-plus seasons with the Reds and a short stint with the White Sox, Griffey spent his final two years back with the Mariners. Blessed with one of the prettiest left-handed swings you'll see from anyone, Griffey blasted 630 home runs and had 524 doubles among his 2,781 career hits. He led the league with 56 homers, 125 runs scored, and 147 RBI in his MVP season of 1997. Griffey retired in 2010 and was inducted into the Baseball Hall of Fame in 2016. The Mariners revealed a statue of Griffey at Safeco Field a year later. The sweet-swinging "Kid" is outside of the home plate gate, his eyes staring at what we assume is a home run ball as his right hand drops his bat. That bat was stolen shortly after the statue was unveiled but discovered and re-attached three months later.

The larger-than-life bronze sculpture stands high atop a rectangular granite cube with his Mariners years beneath his name. The adjoining site of the base introduces Griffey as "One of the greatest players in baseball history."

We got our first chance to admire the Griffey statue before we ran a charity 5K at Safeco Field on July 21st. The annual Refuse to Abuse 5K benefits the Washington State Coalition Against Domestic Violence. When Patti told me she wanted to run the 5K, I told her I would do it with her, even though I loathe running. Many kids wind up in the foster system because of domestic violence or child abuse in the home.

We walked past Griffey again the next day when we returned to Safeco Field to see the Mariners host the White Sox in the final game of a three-game series.

Calling every one of Griffey's games with the Mariners was Dave Niehaus. The Hall-of-Fame broadcaster, who died in 2010 following a heart attack, was the Mariners play-by-play voice from 1977 until 2010. He is memorialized by an exhibit in the main concourse near Section 105 at Safeco. The display was unveiled September 16th, 2011 and depicts the 2008 Ford C. Frick Award winner in a suit and sitting behind a microphone, wearing headphones with his Mariners scorebook in front of him. Mariners fans could probably hear Niehaus say, "My, oh my, it will fly away," during both of Ryon Healy's home runs against the White Sox during our Safeco Field visit.

· · · · ·

We left the Seattle area the next day. San Francisco was next, but the Giants were heading north as we went south. We had a few days, so we took our time, spending a night near Portland, Oregon and then a couple of nights at the Redwood National and State Parks. Those stops are covered in detail later. This chapter is about statues and we saw several in the City by the Bay.

After looking at several options to get from our RV park in Vallejo to AT&T Park, we decided to suck it up and drive. There is a ferry that will take you near the stadium, but I wasn't sure of the return schedule and didn't want to take any chances of being stranded. I also wanted to drive across the Golden

Gate Bridge. Traffic is a nightmare in San Francisco and parking near the water is even worse. We made a rookie mistake by not going online ahead of time to reserve a parking spot, which would have saved us a few bucks. Parking at AT&T Park can run you up to $50, and parking at Fisherman's Wharf isn't much better. We wound up paying $30 at the Wharf.

AT&T Park is ridiculously expensive, so we decided to grab a bite to eat at the Wharf. We had a couple of hours to kill and went into the historic Boudin Bakery Café. Boudin is one of the oldest continuous businesses in San Francisco. Founded in 1849, Boudin is considered the originator of San Francisco's famous sourdough bread, which we of course had during our meal as the smell of baking bread wafted from the ovens.

The plan was to then take the F-Line tram from the Wharf to AT&T Park. The problem was the tram never arrived, and after waiting 15 minutes past the posted arrival time, we decided to walk. While annoyed at first, we were actually glad we made the three-mile walk. We saw a bit more of the waterfront and popped into Pier 23 Café that had a packed outdoor patio for a pregame drink. A trio of 20-somethings struck up a conversation with me. We told them about our trip and they gave us pointers about AT&T Park. I handed them a Home Run on Wheels card and we continued our walk toward the park.

We approached AT&T Park from King Street and got in the line to enter at the 2nd Street Gate, which is flanked by statues of Hall of Famers Gaylord Perry and Orlando Cepeda. Perry, who won 314 games over a 22-year career (ten with the Giants), is forever captured in his follow-through of a pitch that might have led to one of his 3,534 career strikeouts. Cepeda, who was an 11-time All-Star and the 1967 National League MVP, is depicted standing at first base with a ball in his right hand and a glove on his left. He spent his first nine MLB seasons with the Giants but helped the Cardinals win the 1967 World Series. Inducted into the Hall of Fame in 1999, Cepeda played for six teams over his 17-year career but will always be remembered as a Giants great. Cepeda's Number 30 is one of San Francisco's retired numbers, along with Perry's 36. A statue of Hall of Fame pitcher Juan Marichal whose Number 27 was retired in 1975, is located outside the opposite entrance in the left-field corner. We didn't see the Marichal statue on our visit but made a point to check out the Willie Mays statue in front of the main gate.

Following the Brewers' 3-1 victory on a chilly July night, we made our way to the exit behind home plate. Placed in the center of a crowded plaza lined by palm trees is the bronze sculpture of Mays atop a stone foundation. Mays won 12 Gold Gloves as the Giants center fielder but is shown dropping a bat after one of his swings that led to 660 career home runs. Matching his retired number, Mays was named to 24 All-Star games and was the NL MVP in 1954 and 1965. The "Say Hey Kid" is considered by many to be the best all-around player to ever grace a baseball diamond. His statue is one of the most popular attractions at a highly regarded venue with many cool features. A giant Mays bobblehead stands guard at the entrance to a bobblehead shop in the outfield concourse. Walk a few more feet and you're at the huge baseball mitt statue beyond the left-field wall. The giant Coca-Cola bottle, that houses a pair of slides for kids, leans over the top of the mitt. The oversized four-fingered glove, which resembles a mitt used in the 1930s, is believed to be the world's largest baseball mitt.

Just beyond the right-field concourse is the San Francisco Bay and Mc-Covey Cove, named for Giants Hall of Famer Willie McCovey, who hit 521 homers and was the 1969 NL MVP. We wish we could have enjoyed the view of the water, but San Francisco's ever-present summer fog, which is named Karl, prevented us from truly seeing AT&T Park in all its glory. We did watch an inning from the Ghirardelli Chocolate cable car that is permanently parked beyond the wall in right-center. It's a unique, first-come, first-serve spot to watch the game.

I had such high expectations for the Giants' home but felt disappointed because of the cold weather, fog, parking, and high costs of everything. The city of San Francisco even jacks up the price of the street meters for Giants games from $2 an hour to $7 an hour. Getting back to the car was another frustration because the tram back to the Wharf never arrived. We hoofed it again from the Embarcadero Station.

I really wanted to love San Francisco, and thought I would, but instead I was continually irritated by the traffic, cold July weather, cost of parking, unreliable public transportation, and the asinine prices at the AT&T Park concessions stands.

We did return to the San Francisco waterfront three days later to see more of Fisherman's Wharf. This time we reserved parking online and saved about ten bucks. We still paid $20 for the day but unexpectedly discovered some more statues. There were wax sculptures of legendary guitarist, Carlos Santana, San Francisco 49ers Hall of Fame quarterback, Joe Montana, and late comedian and actor,

Robin Williams, as "Mork" from the 1970s sitcom *Mork & Mindy*. After "meet-ing" the three Bay Area legends and grabbing some lunch, we did an hour tour on the Golden Gate Bay Cruise, which takes you right under the iconic bridge. The fog again hindered our view, though Karl does add a certain mystique to the bridge. It was also still quite cold, especially with the ocean breeze. You don't ex-pect to see people walking around wearing winter coats in July. The bay cruise took us past the infamous Alcatraz before returning to the pier, which was full of gulls and pigeons hoping to get some handouts from the many tourists.

It was just early afternoon when we got back to the pier, and we had plenty of time to get to Oakland for that night's A's game against the Blue Jays. Our walking tour of San Francisco continued as we trekked up Stockton Street about a mile to Coit Tower. The 210-foot tower built in the 1930s on Tele-graph Hill offer superb views of the city and bay, even through the fog. We're not sure why, but there is a statue of Christopher Columbus in front of the tower. We asked around, but nobody seemed to know why Columbus was given such a commanding view of San Francisco Bay. The statue stands amid a small flower garden in the center of a chronically clogged circular parking lot. We wanted to go to the top of the tower, but the line was extremely long and time was now running out on us. At just nine dollars per adult, it is rather inexpensive to climb to the top of the tower just be prepared to wait. The lobby of the tower is beautifully decorated with several murals of San Francisco's his-tory. After taking in some of the views, we took a different route back to our car. We walked down the steep steps through San Francisco's old hillside neighborhoods and back to the Embarcadero at the piers. From there, we headed to Oakland to see the A's play the Blue Jays. There aren't any statues at Oakland Coliseum, but several painted statues of the A's elephant mascot, Stomper, were placed around the city in 2018 to celebrate the team's 50th year in Oakland. The Coliseum does have several murals on the concourse ramps behind home plate that serve as a timeline of the franchise's history.

· · · · ·

The old Yankee Stadium was known as the "House that Ruth Built," but the Yankees also had iconic players, like Yogi Berra, Lou Gehrig, Joe DiMag-gio, Mickey Mantle, Roger Maris, and Derek Jeter. Stan Musial was "The Man" in St. Louis, but the tradition-rich Cardinals also employed the likes of

Rogers Hornsby, Bob Gibson, Albert Pujols, and currently Yadier Molina. Every generation of Yankees and Cardinals fans has enjoyed seeing a Hall of Fame player on their team.

There is perhaps no team in Major League Baseball more defined by one player than the San Diego Padres are with Tony Gwynn. He was Mr. Padre. The Los Angeles native played collegiately at San Diego State to begin his relationship with a city that would soon become synonymous with his name. Gwynn was one of the best hitters the game has ever seen.

He was a 15-time All-Star over 20 seasons, all with the Padres, and led the National League in batting average eight times. Gwynn was a contact hitter who never struck out more than 40 times in a season, and his career .338 average ranks 18th all-time. He was the last player to flirt with a .400 season, with a .394 average in 1994 before the final 45 games of the season were canceled because of a players strike. Gwynn was even a five-time Gold Glove winner in right field.

When Gwynn died of salivary gland cancer in 2014, over 23,000 fans attended a memorial service at Petco Park. His pallbearers included former Aztec baseball players, Quintin Berry and Tim Zier, former Padres manager Bud Black, who played with Gwynn at SDSU and became the Rockies manager in 2017, Aztecs director of baseball operations, Landon Burt, and former Padres teammates, Damian Jackson and Broderick Perkins.

"I could talk for hours about him. He was a huge mentor in my life," Zier said of Gwynn. "He was just a phone call away. I've grown very close with his family. I carried one of the best hitters of all time to his grave. I coach travel ball teams with his son. The main thing he implemented in me was to do things right."

Gwynn's number 19, retired by the Padres in 2004, is ubiquitous at Petco Park. A statue of Mr. Padre is atop a small hill behind the park overlooking center field. His perfect left-handed swing captured just before striking an invisible ball.

"You'd stand around Tony Gwynn in the dugout and he'd be telling stories about baseball and about hitting, guys he's met. It was mesmerizing," sports author and former Sports Illustrated MLB reporter, Jeff Pearlman, told me during a podcast interview. "Of all the people I covered and have come across, Tony Gwynn being dead still doesn't make any sense to me because his voice in my head is so vivid. He's from California, but he had, like, an Arkansas accent. He'd always have a big piece of chew in his mouth, which obviously ended up being very bad for him, but he was such a fascinating guy. He could get around on anybody, Randy Johnson, Curt Schilling – anybody. I could listen to Tony Gwynn talk all day."

· · · · ·

Johnson and Schilling helped the Diamondbacks win the 2001 World Series, but neither has a statue outside Chase Field in Phoenix. There is a statue of a Diamondbacks player, but it is an anonymous athlete who is interacting with a trio of fans.

The statuary entitled, "Baseball, A Family Tradition," depicts an unnamed D-backs player donning the number 98, ready to sign an autograph for a boy wearing a ballcap. The number signifies the Diamondbacks' inaugural season in 1998. The boy's left hand is covered with a tan ball glove that is tucked to his chest. The player has a ball in one hand and is taking a pen from the boy with the other. With the young fan is a woman, presumably his mother, and a girl assumed to be his sister. The word "Arizona" is stretched across the player's nameplate on the back of the jersey. The girl's dress and the player's number are both teal, and along with the boy's glove, represent the only colors in an otherwise bronze display. As the boy chats with the ballplayer, the mother stands between the children with a hand on each of their shoulders. She is looking at the girl, who is staring up at the uniformed player as the quartet stands in a circle surrounded by a lawn to the left of the main entrance. It's almost like the dirt circle is a flattened pitcher's mound. It's one of the most endearing statues you'll see at any ballpark.

· · · · ·

There are eight Hall of Fame players who have suited up for the Houston Astros at some point in their careers. Only two spent their entire careers with the Astros, Jeff Bagwell and Craig Biggio. They were forever immortalized with bronze statues outside Minute Maid Park in 2003, before their respective careers had even ended. Bagwell retired following the 2005 season, which ended with the White Sox beating the Astros in the World Series. Biggio didn't hang up his cleats until 2007, ending Houston's "Killer Bs" era. Bagwell and Biggio, as well as Lance Berkman, led the Astros to six playoff appearances from 1997 through 2005 and Houston's first World Series berth. Together, Bagwell and Biggio hold just about every Astros team record.

Biggio holds the franchise records for most career games (2,850), at-bats (10,876), hits (3,060), runs scored (1,844), doubles (668), total bases (4,711), and extra-base hits (1,014), and ranks second in runs batted in (1,175), walks (1,160), and stolen bases (414). He also holds the NL record for most times leading off a game with a home run (53) and is one of only five players with 250 home runs and 400 steals. He also holds the dubious distinction of being hit by a pitch 285 times, second all-time to Tigers Hall of Famer Hughie Jennings, who was plunked 287 times. Biggio, inducted into the Hall of Fame in 2015, never charged the mound and was never injured by a pitch.

Bagwell, a 2017 Hall of Fame inductee, retired as the Astros' all-time home run leader with 447, as well as intentional walks (155), RBI (1,529), and wins above replacement (79.9). He was the National League Rookie of the Year in 1991 and MVP three seasons later when he hit .368 with 39 homers and league highs of 104 runs scored, 116 RBI, .750 slugging percentage, and 300 total bases. He would have led the league in batting average had it not been for Tony Gwynn's remarkable year.

As good as Bagwell and Biggio were at the plate, they were also superb defensive players. Biggio won four Gold Gloves at second base while Bagwell was the 1994 Gold Glove winner at first. The duo solidified the right side of Houston's infield for over a decade. That is how they are shown outside of Minute Maid Park — a full 90 feet apart with Biggio at second base throwing to Bagwell at first. Bagwell's right foot is on the bag as he takes a wide step with his left. His left arm is outstretched as he awaits the throw with an open mitt to complete a double play.

"You don't see this happen anymore where two guys play their whole careers together," Bagwell told reporters in 2003 after the statues were unveiled in the plaza outside of Minute Maid Park. "They say it's all about money, but we've shown our loyalty to each other and to this organization. It's worked out. This is humbling. When we started out, we never thought anything like this would ever happen."

There is a third statue at Minute Maid Park, but it is not baseball-related. A bronze sculpture along the sidewalk on the edge of the left-field plaza depicts an aproned blacksmith, hammer in a raised right hand, ready to strike a piece of metal held atop an anvil. The statue, titled "Forging the

Future," was dedicated in 2002. It is a tribute to the Houston blacksmith shop that was founded on the ballpark site in 1902 and grew into the global manufacturing corporation known as Stewart and Stevenson.

· · · · ·

There aren't enough adjectives to describe how dominant Nolan Ryan was as a pitcher. Overpowering, ruthless, hard-nosed, tough, spectacular were all words used by scribes over Ryan's 27-year career. Blessed with a remarkably strong right arm, Ryan's noteworthy fastball that regularly exceeded 100 miles per hour paved the way for the power pitchers of today. Ryan recorded 5,714 career strikeouts – by far the most-ever, exceeding Randy Johnson's mark (4,875) by 839. Ryan, who also holds the career record for most walks (2,795), led the league in strikeouts 11 times. He is one of four Hall of Fame pitchers with more strikeouts than innings pitched — along with Johnson, Pedro Martinez and Sandy Koufax. Ryan's 383 strikeouts in 1973, while playing for the California Angels, are still a single-season record. Ryan tossed two no-hitters that season and his seven career no-nos are also an MLB record. He came close several other times and his 12 one-hitters are tied with Indians Hall of Famer Bob Feller for the most ever. Ryan won 324 games over his career, winning 21 in 1973 and 22 in 1974, but never led the league in wins. He also surprisingly never won a Cy Young Award, finishing second to Jim Palmer in 1973 and third-place finishes in 1974 and 1977.

Ryan began his career with the Mets in 1966 and joined the Angels in 1972. He was part of the 1969 "Miracle Mets" team that won the World Series. One of Ryan's teammates on that Mets team was fellow Hall of Famer Tom Seaver. Two-time All-Stars Jerry Koosman and Tug McGraw were also members of the pitching staff.

Ryan spent eight seasons in California before signing with the Astros in 1980. He posted a career-best 1.69 ERA in 1981 to lead the National League and again led the NL in ERA in 1987 with a 2.76 mark. Ryan spent nine seasons with the Astros, but the final five years of his lengthy career were with the Texas Rangers. By signing with the Rangers, Ryan became the first player to play for all four MLB original expansion teams. Ryan was 42 years old when he moved to Arlington but still led the American League with 201 strikeouts in 1989 and was selected to his eighth and final All-Star Game. His 232 strikeouts a season later again led the AL.

Ryan went 51-39 with a 3.43 ERA and 939 strikeouts in just 840 innings pitched. He finally retired following the 1993 season and fittingly recorded his final strikeout against the Angels on September 17th. His last two no-hitters were in those final seasons — on June 11th, 1990 against the Athletics and May 1st, 1991 against the Blue Jays. By keeping Toronto hitless in a 3-0 victory, Ryan tossed the Rangers' first no-hitter at home and became the oldest pitcher to ever record a no-hitter at the age of 44.

The Rangers paid homage to "The Ryan Express" in 1997 by unveiling a statue in the center-field concourse. Ryan's gloved left hand is at his side as he raises his cap to salute the crowd. An inscription on the mound-like base reads: "When Nolan Ryan came here, he was a superstar. When he left, he was a legend." His career numbers are also listed. A replica of the statue is located outside the main gate at Dell Diamond in Round Rock, Texas — home of the Rangers' Triple-A club.

You cannot see the field in Arlington from the Ryan statue, but a large high-definition screen is mounted to the back of the batter's eye wall to allow visitors to still follow the game. The bronze figure stands in the center of a courtyard surrounded by food and beverage stands. Unfortunately all of them were closed when we visited on September 4th, 2018. The Rangers were not very good in 2018 and attendance reflected that. The area is still prime for those who want to admire one of the baseball's greatest pitchers while watching the game on the big screen.

Despite an ugly breakup with the Rangers as a member of its front-office leadership in 2010, the Ryan statue is expected to be moved to the Rangers' new ballpark in 2020.

· · · · ·

George Brett led the American League in batting average three times, but none was more magical than his 1980 season. The former Royals third baseman was the last American League hitter to flirt with a .400 average that year, finishing with a .390 mark (Red Sox great Ted Williams was the last player to hit .400 with a .406 average in 1941). Brett also led the AL with a .454 on-base percentage and .664 slugging percentage thanks to 33 doubles, nine triples, and 24 home runs and was named the 1980 AL MVP. Brett had a career-high 118 RBI that year and is one of the Royals greats honored with statues in the outfield concourse at Kauffman Stadium.

Joining Brett, who was named to 13 All-Star games during his 21-year career (all with the Royals), are infielder Frank White, former manager Dick Howser, and former owners and stadium namesake, Ewing and Muriel Kauffman.

Brett is shown in his left-handed stance, reared back on his left foot and ready to swing. A lengthy inscription on the statue's foundation describes Brett as a baseball icon. He was at the center of one of baseball's most iconic controversies in 1983 — "The Pine Tar Incident."

The Royals were playing at Yankee Stadium on July 24th and trailed 4-3 entering the ninth inning. Brett's smashed a two-out, two-run homer in the top of the inning to give the Royals a 5-4 lead. Then-Yankees manager Billy Martin noticed a large amount of pine tar on Brett's bat and asked for umpires to inspect it. MLB rules state that a foreign substance on a bat could extend no further than 18 inches from the knob. The umpires measured the pine tar on Brett's bat and found that it extended about 24 inches from the knob. Brett was ruled out and the Yankees were declared winners – temporarily. Brett charged out of the dugout and had to be restrained by Howser and two field umpires as Brett unleashed a tirade of curses toward home-plate umpire, Tim McClelland.

"Obviously I disagreed with the call, so I calmly went out there to question them," Brett later said facetiously.

The Royals filed a protest, which was upheld by American League president, Lee MacPhail. He ruled that the bat should have been excluded from future use, but the home run should not have been nullified. The game was ordered to resume from the moment of Brett's home run on August 18th. The Yankees sued to prevent the game from being resumed but failed in court. Brett and Howser both had been retroactively ejected and the game resumed in front of 1,200 fans at Yankee Stadium. The Royals shut out the Yankees in the "bottom of the ninth" for a 5-4 win. Brett's pine tar bat has been in the National Baseball Hall of Fame and Museum since 1987.

Howser, who had a proclivity for watching a game from the top of the dugout, is shown in his trademark stance. One foot is on the dugout steps while the other is raised on the surface of an unseen field, think Captain Morgan's posture. Howser is leaning forward with crossed hands resting on his raised right thigh. Howser, who was a two-time All-Star as a shortstop, managed the Royals for six seasons and led the team to its first World Series championship in 1985.

White was also part of that 1985 team and spent his entire 18-year career with Kansas City. The five-time All-Star and eight-time Gold Glove winner was part of a superb defensive infield that included Brett at third, White at second, Onix Concepcion at shortstop, and Steve Balboni at first. That group committed a total of 65 errors in 3,511 chances for a fielding percentage over 98 percent.

White and Brett appeared in a franchise-record 1,914 games together. The former is depicted at Kauffman Stadium in the middle of a leaping throw to first while turning one of 1,382 double plays over his career. "Dirt" that has been kicked up connects second base with White's right foot with his left foot extended over an invisible player possibly sliding into the bag.

White, Brett, and Howser are the only three with their numbers retired by the Royals. They are also among the franchise greats in the Royals Hall of Fame, but only Brett is enshrined in Cooperstown. Ewing Kauffman was added to the Royals Hall of Fame on May 23rd, 1993, just 40 days before his death at the age of 76. His remains are interred at the Ewing and Muriel Kauffman Memorial Garden next to the body of his wife, who died in 1995, on the campus of the University of Missouri at Kansas City.

The Kauffmans statue captures the couple in jubilation — presumably in celebration of the team's 1985 World Series victory. Ewing's left arm is wrapped around his wife as his right hand is in the air. Muriel pose is reciprocal and both are smiling from ear to ear as they gaze to the heavens.

"Ewing and Muriel Kauffman stepped up to the plate to bring Major League Baseball back to Kansas City in 1968," the inscription on the statue's base reads. "A gracious and vibrant couple, they helped build a model organization, a spectacular stadium, and a championship team for their hometown."

While the Kauffmans left a standing legacy in Kansas City, what began at Camden Yards in 1992 has since permeated nearly every baseball stadium. Statues of the great ones are not only revered by those who appreciate the game's history but allow younger fans of any given franchise to connect with the prodigious figures of yesteryear.

CHAPTER 5:

'THINGS ARE GOING TO BREAK'

E very new adventure is always going to have some bumps in the road and we definitely had our share. We didn't exactly have the easiest transition from a three-bedroom house to an RV. The late start to our trip was only the beginning of the issues we faced.

What should be unacceptable in the RV world is that no matter what type of RV you get or how much it costs, you are told to take advantage of the warranty because "things are going to break." They tell you this at the dealer, whether you buy a camper that costs $40,000 or a 45-foot, high-end motorcoach that costs $400,000.

"Things are going to break."

We can't tell you how many times that phrase was repeated at dealerships or RV shows by salesmen who all recommended we get an extended warranty. There are lemon laws that exist for automobiles but no such regulations for recreational vehicles. Our Thor Windsport came with a one-year manufacturer warranty, which we took full advantage of at the conclusion of our trip in St. Louis. When we took it to the Camping World in Wentzville, Missouri on October 8th, we had 22 line items listed on the work order. One was simply an oil change, but the other 21 were mostly minor things that were covered under the warranty and needed to be repaired.

1. The slide topper on driver's side, main slide at sofa and dinette, has broken off the mounting brackets. The spring is weak, causing the fabric to become loose.
2. The flooring on front passenger seat area is coming up due to possible motor heat and adhesive failure.
3. The wall to the right top corner at fridge is pulling apart. The wall panel is cut too long and doesn't want to stay attached to the framing, causing the panel to bow out.
4. The furnace is coming on by itself and making a crazy clicking and humming sound.
5. The trim above the sofa is coming off.
6. The panel between the dinette slide and washer/dryer was not properly attached.
7. There is a silver box that looks like it should be behind and under the radio was not secured properly from the factory.
8. The LP (propane) comes on when the water pump is turned on even when the LP switch is not turned on.
9. The TV cable system, when plugged into cable hookup outside, shows a snowy picture.
10. The roof is bubbling at the ladder.
11. The driver's side mirror is missing the top portion of the mirror.
12. There is mold on the back wall in the back bathroom across the center up top. (Turns out this was mildew and not mold.)
13. The fan on passenger side; the blades hit the cage at front window.
14. The rear TV cabinet door latch is not staying closed, will not stay latched.
15. The pancake light on the right, if you are looking at the bed, has a short.
16. The window shade on the right side of the bed won't stay up.
17. Some sealant in the shower drain is coming out.
18. The half bath on the toilet seat is missing a mounting rod that holds the seat in place.

19. The backup camera works intermittently.
20. The sofa/dinette slideout seal at the bottom toward the sofa is showing light and letting in bugs.
21. There is a wire hanging at the passenger side rear wheel well that goes to the rear marker light.
22. Oil change.

Things add up when you're moving from city to city and don't have the time to pause to get minor issues fixed. Driving a New York City apartment 15,000 miles over the course of seven months is inevitably going to lead to some issues, but we weren't expecting such a lengthy list. We didn't get the RV back from Camping World until March 25th.

"My suggestion to anyone considering buying an RV, especially if you're going to go full-time, is to hire an independent inspector," Patti said, adding that we learned a lot throughout the entire purchasing process and subsequent journey. "There were some things that had gone wrong that an inspector probably would have found."

Traveling so far in a short time can be stressful, without the issue of broken equipment. There were a few times we thought our relationship was going to break. You get on each other's nerves when you spend so much time together in a small space.

Weather impacted our trip in more ways than one and was one of the reasons we were unable to leave Charlotte on March 10th. Though the Camping World in Concord was still waiting on parts for the slideout topper that broke February 20th, Charlotte Vehicle Wraps needed a week to complete what was supposed to be a two-day job. Our 36-foot-long motor coach, that is also 13 feet tall, was too big for their bay, so all the work had to be done outside. But of course, it rained for three days straight and the RV sat untouched during that time. When the wrap was finally completed, it looked fabulous and I drove the RV to Camping World to get that slideout topper fixed. If only we knew how much that slideout topper would be a pain in the ass on our journey.

The brackets that hold the slideout topper to the rig were replaced and the Camping World technician in Concord, who is also named Ron, worked on the tension of the slideout topper itself. This was the afternoon of March 12th, two days and several hours after we had originally intended on leaving Charlotte.

Though we were delayed in beginning our trip, none of the future issues created an interruption of our schedule.

"Come hell or high water, we're doing this trip," I told Patti. "We're just going to have to overcome the obstacles that have been put in front of us, most of which we have no control over."

As I assisted technician Ron with the tension of the slideout topper, he told me he couldn't guarantee it wouldn't unravel. This was a warning that concerned me, but there wasn't much I could do about it. We had to go.

The rest of March was spent in Florida for Spring Training and the start of the regular season. We still had a faulty water heater, the electric and propane heating elements were shorted together, meaning we were burning propane unnecessarily. That was something that had to be fixed on our way back through Charlotte when we traveled from Atlanta to Washington, D.C. We set an appointment for April 4th and told the service department they had two days to get it fixed. We had to be in Greensboro the night of April 5th.

Because it was an electrical issue and they had to check the wiring, everything we had in the basement storage compartments had to come out. We didn't want to clutter Maryalyce's home, like when did over those first 12 days of March, so we booked a room at a nearby Comfort Inn. We got a ground-level floor, and fortunately, the windows opened. Instead of making multiple trips with a luggage cart through the halls of the hotel, I parked the RV parallel to the building outside our room and handed our stuff to Patti through the window. I'm sure it was a sight to see. We got a late checkout the next day, and with some pestering, got the RV back in the afternoon. I drove it to the hotel to get our things, and this time it was Patti handing stuff to me through the window. Having to take everything out was sort of a blessing in disguise.

"That was actually quite convenient," I said in mid-April.

"It was," Patti laughed.

"We had a lot of stuff but not as much as we thought we had under there," I remarked.

"No, it didn't seem that bad," Patti replied. "Then when we started putting things back in, it was easier to organize."

. . . . .

With our visits to Nationals Park and Camden Yards over, we left Maryland and headed east to Delaware Seashore State Park. We had a few days as the Phillies wrapped up a road trip in Florida and Georgia. This was not the best decision we could have made.

Despite the fact that it was colder than normal, it was extremely windy. The rain, chilly temps and high winds kept most people away from the Delaware beaches. Only a handful of spots were occupied in the 88-site RV park between Rehoboth Beach and Bethany Beach. Remember that warning about the slideout topper tension? Yeah, it got caught in the high winds and began billowing. We spent most of the time inside the RV in a tight space because we retracted the main slideout in the living space that contains the stove, dinette, and sofa. We knew the roller had lost its tension and we didn't want the vinyl to tear. I started searching for a Camping World near Philadelphia. Fortunately for us, the Camping World in Swedesboro, New Jersey was able to fit us in. Camping World warranties its own service, which is why I wanted to take it there as opposed to another dealer. We also asked them to look at a couple other issues, like the water heater, which wasn't fixed in Concord. At least they had that extra set of keys and Blu-Ray remote for us.

Just as we did in North Carolina, we had to remove everything from the basement storage so the technicians could investigate the wiring issue. There was another issue that presented itself when I went to unlock one of the storage compartments during our stay in Maryland and the lock tumbler came right out with the key.

"You have got to be shitting me," I said as I turned to Patti to show her what happened.

Fortunately the compartment was for our middle grey and black water holding tanks. That was something that didn't need to be locked, though I did have to pull over to the side of the road once when the door missing a lock tumbler swung open as I made a turn.

The flooring in front of the passenger seat had also began to bubble up and that was another thing we wanted them to inspect.

We stayed at another Comfort Inn and requested a room on the first floor so we were able to hand things through the window in New Jersey like we did in North Carolina. My phone rang the next morning at 10. I recognized the number as Camping World.

"Oh, oh," I said. "This probably isn't good."

"Hello, Ron?" the voice at the other end said.

"Yes?" I replied.

"This is Jim Evans at Camping World. Your camper is ready to be picked up," he said.

"Seriously?" I exclaimed. "Wow, OK."

They took care of the water heater issue (sort of) and tightened the tension on the slideout topper. They also glued the vinyl flooring back down and took care of a couple of loose clasps on our indoor cabinets. The only issue they were not able to take care of was the lock tumbler because a part had to be ordered. Jim told us he would order it and have it sent to a Camping World of our choice. We just had to figure out where that would be. We were shocked the service department in Swedesboro needed a single day to address multiple issues that the Concord store wasn't able to fix given more than a month.

"Yeah, and now we have that experience under our belt," I said sarcastically. "I just hope, by the end of this week, all of the RV issues will be resolved and we can continue the rest of the season without any other issues."

If only. How stupidly naïve I was.

Jim never did order that part, and when I called to check on it a couple weeks later, he was no longer employed there. A man named Ed Urban replied to my email sent April 30th. He called me, and after I explained to him what was going on, he told me I needed to have the Camping World in Concord send that part. This was the runaround we often got. A few phone conversations later, Tom Johnson, Camping World in Concord, North Carolina, agreed to order the lock tumbler and send it to a Camping World outside of Pittsburgh. We arrived in Western Pennsylvania on May 24th and I drove straight to the Camping World in Apollo, about 35 miles northeast of downtown Pittsburgh. They didn't have the part. It was never ordered.

I cursed the store where we bought the RV, and this time I called the manufacturer. A Thor warranty representative named Ron Baker, with whom I would exchange several emails over the next few months, agreed to send the lock tumbler to our next stop by Cleveland. There was a Camping World in Akron and the lock tumbler was delivered a couple of days later.

Now it was a matter of getting the installation scheduled. I had hoped to get it done either on May 28th, when we were arriving in the Cleveland area, or on June 1st, when we headed toward Cincinnati. Neither date worked and Wednesday, May 30th was the only day they could squeeze us in. We had to unhook everything before leaving the RV park in Streetsboro, Ohio and then drove 40 minutes each way for what was a ten-minute job. But it was finally done.

Scheduling any sort of RV service is difficult, even for a simple oil change. We were coming due for an oil change as we arrived in Cincinnati. The Good Sam RV club offers discounts at Camping World, the club's dealership partner. Detroit was the next stop after Cincinnati, so I called the Camping World in Toledo about an oil change. They had no availability for a month. I tried Chicago, July 5th was the earliest opening. Milwaukee, same thing.

I wound up taking the RV to a small shop in Mason, Ohio for the oil change. The place opened at 10 a.m. and I called to see if they could get us in at that time. The owner, Willie, said no problem and he'd see us then. When I pulled into the dirt lot filled with RVs and landscaping vehicles, I had no idea where to park. We were early, so I drove around the RVs to pull it in front of the two bay doors marked as Coleman RV Sales, Parts and Service. The path was blocked by a wood chipper. I knew I was stuck.

The long rectangular building lined with large garage bay doors housed multiple businesses. The RV service center was flanked by a custom granite shop and a landscaping company. We were in the way. One of the landscaping trucks needed to get to the wood chipper and head to a job. I was asked to back up. Easier said than done. The tow dolly we had swivels to make turns less complicated. It makes going in reverse nearly impossible. The car and tow dolly had to come off.

I apologized and hopped out to unhook everything. I parked the car out of the way and rolled the tow dolly to a nearby vacant spot. The owner of the business then guided me around his equipment and vehicles as I backed up. The whole thing took about 20 minutes, but I was out of the way and parked near the row of RVs while we waited for Willie to arrive. He was late. Like, really late.

It was nearly 11 before he showed up, blaming his son and employee for not being ready to go. He told us his 30-year-old son had his license revoked after getting a DUI, maybe not the type of information you share with customers. But Willie didn't exactly care what we thought of his son. He assigned his son to change our oil while he returned phone messages, pausing every so often to vulgarly criticize his son. Willie was very nice to us, but every curse word directed toward his son made the hour spent there extremely uncomfortable. I also questioned how good of a job his son did with our RV while getting yelled at the entire time. Our RV engine requires an oil change every 7,500 miles. We were right at that number in Cincinnati. We had reached 11,000 miles a couple months later in Anaheim and I had the Camping World there do a full-service oil change. It was more of a peace of mind thing. I definitely didn't want our warranty voided because of a substandard oil change.

· · · · ·

Scheduling issues and broken parts aside, some of our RV issues were simply the result of ignorance and inexperience and a bit of bad luck. There were some definite growing pains, beginning with that initial test run. One of the last things we did before leaving Charlotte on February 22nd was buy a tow dolly. Based on the recommendation from the salesman at the Concord Camping World, we went to Big Tex Trailers in South Charlotte. It was essentially on our way, so I drove the RV and Patti followed in the car. After doing some research, we knew what type of dolly we wanted, a swivel Master Tow. Because it swivels instead of being a fixed tow dolly, navigating corners while towing a car behind a 36-foot long vehicle would be much simpler.

What we were unfamiliar with was strapping the car to the tow dolly. The two salesmen at Big Tex Trailers assisted us the first time we put the car on, but something wasn't right. The ratchet device kept hitting the apron of the car when I was tightening the straps. We asked if everything was set up correctly and the two "experts" helping us assured us that it all was good.

It was not all good.

We got to Jupiter less than an hour before the first Spring Training game of the year would begin. Needless to say, we were in a hurry. We had to check in, get the car off, and set the RV up in the lot. Checking in was easy. Getting the car off, not so much. Those ratchet devices were an issue. I could not get them to fully release the straps because of the car apron. The manager of the RV resort, an experienced road traveler, was also unable to get them off. The ratchet devices were on upside down. This is something the Big Tex sales guys should have realized when we asked if something was wrong. We were in a pinch, so instead of taking up any more time, I borrowed a scissors and cut the nylon straps. We would buy new ones. We had a game to get to and didn't want to miss the first game of the season. Tickets were already purchased. Once the straps were cut, I pulled the car off and we got everything set up in time to see the first pitch of the Spring Training season from Miami's Dillon Peters to Cardinals second baseman Kolten Wong. The Marlins scored five runs in the seventh inning to lift them to a 6-4 victory over the team with which they share Roger Dean Stadium.

When the game was over and we returned to the RV park, we searched online for nearby trailer companies. We still did not realize at the time that devices were not installed correctly, but our suspicions were confirmed three days later when we went to a trailer store in North Miami to get new straps. We wanted to ensure we wouldn't have any future issues, so grilled the salesman with questions about how to properly secure the car. He came outside with us — in the rain — to give a tutorial and immediately pointed out the issue with the ratchets. It was a simple fix — remove the bolt and flip it around, then put the bolt back in. That took less than five minutes to do both sides, something that should have been done a few days earlier in Charlotte. It was a $60 lesson — the cost of new tow dolly straps — but we did not have any future issues. Getting the car on and off the tow dolly became routine. It helped that we had a socket wrench with the perfect curvature to help push the latch down to release the straps.

· · · · ·

You live and learn through trial and error.

We saw another family struggle setting up their campsite a few months later near Milwaukee. As I stood at the sink one afternoon to do the dishes, I couldn't help but notice a man assign the set-up of a portable table to his two teenage daughters. They weren't getting it. Even Mom jumped in and couldn't figure it out. We had a similar folding table in our yard in Charlotte, but I didn't want to overstep. It was one of those small deck tables that had a divided top that would come together once the crossed legs were properly extended. I was softly chuckling, which Patti heard and asked what was so funny. When I told her, we both began staring out the kitchen window for what seemed like an eternity. In reality, it was only about five minutes when the dad exited the RV and was able to figure out how to get the table to stand. Once the table was set up, I did poke my head outside.

"I was wondering if you guys were going to figure that out," I said.

The man laughed before replying, "Yeah, that sucker wasn't easy."

We chatted for a bit and he asked about the logos on our RV, which I was happy to explain.

When I went inside, Patti said watching them struggle with that table made her think of how people were probably laughing at her back in February.

Before we bought the RV, we were a two-vehicle household. I had my Scion and Patti had her Infiniti. She was able to sell her car about a week before we finalized the purchase of the RV. The problem then was, after we moved out of our house and into the RV, we still had some things to arrange before our ultimate departure. I was still going into the office in Uptown Charlotte nearly every day, meaning some of the errands were left to Patti. She had no vehicle, except for the home on wheels. So to get a few necessary items for our trip, Patti made a couple of trips to Wal-Mart, the store choice because of their large, RV-friendly parking lots. Driving the RV to and from the East Charlotte Wal-Mart wasn't challenging. A late-night return to our campsite proved problematic.

The Camping World in Concord, North Carolina is next to the Charlotte Motor Speedway. Between the two is a campground owned by Camping World. They allowed us to stay there for two nights to get familiar with our new home. As Patti returned one night in the RV, she missed a turn inside the dark campground and wound up at a dead end. There was a fence on the right and a fence on the left and a fence at the end of the road. Patti was stuck.

"I ended up doing like a thousand-point turn to get out," Patti said. "I knew there were people in their trailers watching me and laughing. But I was actually proud of that thousand-point turn."

She eventually got out of the predicament and found our campsite. I couldn't help but laugh when she told me what happened after I got "home" following one of my final nights at the office in Uptown Charlotte.

The joke was on me a month later when I got stuck in a Pilot parking lot south of Atlanta. We had about a half a tank of fuel, but I saw a sign for the Pilot with gas prices about 20 cents lower than other stations we had passed. I decided to stop to top it off and maybe save a few bucks.

I exited the freeway and saw the station immediately on the right. There was just one way in and one way out. The pumps were all occupied, and I knew I had to get the RV at the right angle in order to exit the lot. I figured I could drive around the building to approach the pumps from the opposite angle, which would have made exiting much simpler.

So I headed to the rear of the lot, where I saw some space to the right of the dumpsters. I could not see from the pumps what was behind the dumpsters but assumed it was an opening for trucks to circle the building. You know what they say about the word assume? I was wrong. Behind the dumpsters was a fence. By the time I realized there was no access to the rear of the building, we were stuck in a tiny side lot. I turned the steering wheel as far as I could in a vain attempt to turn around. There were parked cars in the way. I tried to back up, but the swiveling tow dolly made that impossible. It immediately angled sharply and I was forced to stop. I was pissed. Here I am driving around an RV with a giant children's organization logo on either side and I am shouting every curse word that pops into my head.

A Pilot employee came out to offer assistance and tried to guide me forward and backward, but it was to no avail. The car had to come off in order for us to get out of this jam.

More curse words ensued.

I took the straps off the wheels of the car and backed it off the dolly. I then unhooked the dolly itself and rolled it out of the way. There was still one problem. Some guy decided to park his pickup right next to us — not in a parking spot, mind you — and watch us while he ate a sandwich. I shot a couple of glances his way. He wasn't taking the hint.

"Excuse me, sir, can you please move so I can get turned around?" I asked after motioning for him to roll down his window. I had calmed down by now.

He seemed surprised by my request but nodded and moved his truck. I still had to do some maneuvering but was able to get the RV in a spot to where it was facing the exit. We pulled the tow dolly back to the RV and hitched it up, then drove the car back on. I was so frustrated by the entire fiasco, which took about 30 minutes, that we left the station without getting any gas.

"I saw a pillow at a store that said, 'Sorry for what I said when parking the RV.' For us, it should be, 'Sorry for what I said when taking the car off the tow dolly,'" Patti joked.

· · · · ·

Then there was the border turnaround coming back into the U.S. from Canada.

As we approached the Peace Bridge between Fort Erie, Ontario and Buffalo, New York, we saw one sign directing truck traffic to the right and another sign pointing cars and RVs to the left. What we missed was the next sign that veered RVs to the right, between the automobile and semi lanes. I was approaching the automobile checkpoint and wondering how I'm going to make the tight turn once I'm through. I didn't have to wonder long because the female border patrol agent stepped out of her booth, waving both hands over her head, giving me a "high ten" telling me to stop. We were about 80 yards away from her. Two male agents then advanced toward the RV and asked if I could back up.

"How far?" I asked.

"Not far," was the response.

The tow dolly was again an issue, but I made an attempt. I threw it in reverse, trying to keep the steering wheel as straight as possible, but it was to no avail. The car started angling and was at about a 70-degree angle when the agents stopped me. I had only moved about ten feet. I had about another 30 to go. The two men started talking to each other and to someone on the radio, but I couldn't hear what they were saying. There was a lot of room to our left and two express lanes lined simply by blue traffic cones. I saw a solution, so I exited the RV — probably something I wasn't supposed to do — and told the border agents that if they briefly halted traffic and moved a few of the cones, I could turn around and get into the correct lane.

The only other option would have been taking the car off the dolly and unhitching the dolly before backing up the RV and putting the car and tow dolly back on. That would have been a much longer traffic interruption, so they agreed with my plan, and within five minutes, we were the second vehicle in the RV lane.

I'm certain there were some people waiting and watching in the halted vehicles who spent those five minutes cursing me out.

Once we got in the RV lane, we were in and out in about two minutes. The RV was being scanned electronically during our brief wait. The agent in the booth asked what we were doing in Canada. We told him we were going to all 30 MLB stadiums and had just seen the Blue Jays play. He asked if we were spending the night in Buffalo. We were.

"Do you like beer?" was the unexpected next question.

"Yes," I answered with confusion.

He then gave a brewery recommendation and told us to have a nice trip. That border encounter was far different than the one we had entering Canada from Maine at the Quebec border. There are just a couple of stop signs and no tollbooth-like structures on the two-lane road. We waited for about two minutes before a bearded Canadian man with a neck tattoo exited the adjacent building and walked toward the RV. He came on board and asked us about our trip as Holmes sniffed him up and down. He was friendly man and spoke with a slight French accent. He asked us if we had any firearms or other contraband aboard. We did not. He then took our passports and went back inside the building. He returned about ten minutes later and again asked if we had any firearms after explaining how Canada's gun laws are different than U.S. laws. We again told him we didn't have any weapons aboard. The whole process took about 15 minutes before he told us to have a safe trip.

We then proceeded down the bumpy provincial highway toward Montreal. I would not recommend driving an RV during rush hour in Montreal, especially when both bridges along Autoroute 10 are undergoing construction. I was so worried someone was going to clip us, but fortunately, we made it through unscathed.

· · · · ·

We did go through Hell to get from Detroit to Chicago. Literally.

Hell, Michigan is only about an hour west of Detroit. It wasn't exactly along Interstate 94, which we would take into Illinois, but it wasn't too far out of the way for us to decide to take a detour. The highway to Hell is scenic, yet bumpy. The two-lane between Ann Arbor takes you by Portage Lake before Patterson Lake Road leads you to Hell. There isn't much to the town, which isn't even an incorporated town. There are a couple of houses near the intersection of Patterson Lake Road and Silver Hill Road. There are two Hell-themed restaurants, each with a bar, and a souvenir shop called Screams. A sign on the outside of the store has a cartoon devil hovering over flames and reads, "Greetings from Hell, Michigan." Another sign outside of the Hell Hole Bar says, "Welcome to Hell. Admit it. You've been in worse places." A mini-golf course with another "Welcome to Hell" sign sits behind the store. A large parking lot separates the Hell Hole Bar from Screams.

We ordered a couple of Michigan pasties, a meat pie folded like a calzone, to go and then went into the adjacent store to look for a souvenir from Hell. I found a refrigerator magnet, something we collected from each state we visited, that had Hell and Paradise (a small town in the Upper Peninsula) marked. Though it wasn't the same style of the other magnets we had, we decided it was OK for this one to stand out. We also learned how the small community got its name. The site once held a popular trade post and had a sawmill and gristmill along the nearby creek. As traffic and business grew, a distillery, tavern, and a few houses were added. All four businesses were operated by landowner, George Reeves. Rumor has it as the small town grew, folks asked Reeves what they should name it.

His reply, "I don't care. You can name it Hell for all I care." The name stuck and became official in 1841.

From Hell, we made our way back to Interstate 94 and on our way to Illinois. Patti's parents were meeting us at the campground about an hour southwest of Chicago in Yorkville. We would be delayed.

The day before we left Detroit, the horn in my car began to beep intermittently as we drove down the highway. I messed with the steering wheel and got it to stop. There were no more issues as we did some sightseeing in downtown Detroit and even as the car was in tow along the bumpy road to and from Hell.

Once we got back on the Interstate, however, Patti began to hear the intermittent beeping again as she sat in the back at her workspace. Before too long it was one steady BEEEEEEEEEEEP.

I could even hear it all the way in the front of the RV. We were near the Indiana-Illinois border around 4 p.m. and stuck in bumper-to-bumper traffic. Truck drivers were staring into the windows of the RV as we slowly passed each other. One driver looked right at me and pointed backward. I looked back and just shrugged my shoulders. There was nothing I could do. The next exit was about two miles away. I eventually was able to move to the far right lane of the four-lane highway and took the first exit that had a truck stop. Though it seemed like an eternity, we made it to the exit in about ten minutes. The horn was still blaring.

Once stopped, I got out of the RV and hurried to the car. I messed with the steering wheel for a couple of minutes before I got the horn to stop. I then

94

pulled out the owner's manual to find out where the horn fuse is located in a 2011 Scion xD. It was under the hood on the driver's side, just beneath the windshield. I knew I couldn't get the horn fixed there because that would have taken time we didn't have. Patti's parents were already at the campground, and we still had another couple of hours to drive. I borrowed a fuse-removal tool from a shop mechanic and took out the fuse. The horn remained inoperable for the duration of the trip because there was a more serious issue going on inside the steering column. There was a short in the clock spring inside the steering wheel, something we learned at a shop in Denver. The shop would have had to order the part, something we didn't have time for, so we decided to go without a car horn until our trip was completed.

"I know you were frustrated," Patti said, "but I was sitting in the back giggling because it made me think of that scene in *Little Miss Sunshine* where the horn is going off in the VW van they have."

Life's all about the stories, right?

. . . . .

We were also slightly delayed leaving Wisconsin. After our two weeks in the Milwaukee area, we stopped in my hometown of La Crosse to visit my grandparents. I parked the RV on the street in front of my paternal grandparents' home.

My Grandpa Clements was 92 at the time and Grandma Clements was about to turn 88. They do not have Wi-Fi or even a computer in their home. They only get the local TV channels. Instead of bringing everything into their house, Patti kept her workstation set up in the RV. She worked out there for the Thursday and Friday we visited. If she needed some extra juice for the printer, microwave, or air conditioner, she ran the generator for a few minutes. But when she came in at night, she left the house power on. Neither she nor I thought anything about it. And had we known what awaited us the morning of Saturday, July 7th, we would have run an extension cord to one of the exterior outlets on my grandparents' home. Instead, when we woke up early Saturday morning to be in Minneapolis for a 1 p.m. game later that day, the RV batteries were dead.

I called the Good Sam roadside assistance number. It would be 90 minutes before they could get out there. We didn't have that much time. Minneapolis is about two-and-a-half hours north of La Crosse and we had to park the RV and then get to the Target Field by 1. Waiting until 9:30 would be cutting it too close. I had jumper cables in the car, and we hooked them up to the dual batteries on the side of the RV, just under the driver's window. Showing our ignorance, we charged the two house batteries instead of the engine battery. That would prove problematic.

After about 15 minutes of letting my little four-cylinder car engine run, we had enough juice to get the RV started. The house batteries and engine batteries are connected and charge each other if either the engine is running or the house is hooked up to an exterior power source. Even running the generator longer would have charged the batteries. Letting the batteries die was simply a rookie mistake.

In order to charge the RV batteries, we had to get the car off the dolly. After getting it back in tow, we were almost ready to go. I went back inside the house to grab a cup of coffee for the road and do one last sweep to make sure we didn't forget anything. As I was in the kitchen, my grandpa woke up and yelled from his bedroom door.

"Is somebody out there?"

"Yeah, Grandpa, it's me, Ron," I said, still in the kitchen and out of his sight.

He doesn't hear very well and shouted, "Who?"

I came around the corner into his view and said, "It's me, Ron."

He doesn't see very well either. He stared in my direction as he started to move down the hallway with the assistance of a walker. He stopped about ten feet from me.

"Oh. I thought you'd be gone by now," he said as we both began to laugh.

"Well, that was the plan," I said before explaining to him why we were delayed.

We had said our good-byes to my grandma the night before because she was still working part-time at a bakery and was out of the house by 5 a.m. We'd see them again in a couple of months, but for now, I bid my grandfather adieu and got back in the RV.

One more problem. The rearview camera display did not work. The screen for our dashboard stereo was also the display for both the rearview and sideview cameras. None of it worked. When we charged the house batteries instead of the engine battery, the car engine pumped too many volts into the system and we blew a fuse. We tried to troubleshoot it for a few minutes, but knew we had to hit the road. We went about three weeks without the stereo system and camera displays working. I tried to get the RV looked at in Denver but couldn't get scheduled. Fortunately, my cousin Camoren had all the tools needed to remove the display, then replace the fuse when we got to the Seattle area.

We stayed at Camoren's house during our visit to Seattle, but I had to back into his tree-lined driveway. Without the use of my backup cam, my cousin served as an exterior "backup Cam." Needless to say, once we had the radio display back, it made driving much less stressful.

At least the sideview cameras worked because I needed it a couple months later when the sideview mirror on the driver's side flew off as we approached the Oklahoma-Kansas border. The mirror was knocked loose while parked in front of my mom's house in Dallas. Someone in a moving truck or school bus clipped the mirror, cracking the glass but not damaging the housing unit. I saw my mom's neighbor across the street the day before we left Dallas on September 8th. After a couple days of heavy rain in Dallas, he was sweeping standing water off the sidewalk in front of his house.

I said hello and he responded in kind before asking, "What is this?" as he pointed to the RV. I explained to him what we were doing, and as I turned to look at the RV, I also saw the mirror and shouted an expletive. The neighbor, whose name is Ben, said the mirror had been like that for a couple of days, but he didn't know when the hit-and-run occurred. It's kind of unbelievable someone would knock the mirror off a parked vehicle on a residential street and not stop. Patti and I were able to snap the mirror back into place, but it flew onto the northbound lanes of Interstate 35 about 400 miles later.

"You know what happened, don't you?" Patti asked, unsuccessfully trying to stifle a laugh.

"What?" I curiously replied.

"The wind came sweepin' down the plain," she said, struggling to deliver the punchline through her chortling.

· · · · ·

There is a lot of road between the Twin Cities and the Puget Sound. We left Minnesota the morning of July 9th and didn't get to my cousin's place on the Kitsap Peninsula until July 19th. Neither of us had ever been to North

Dakota before, so we decided to spend the night of July 9th in Fargo. We had a free place to stay thanks to Harvest Hosts, a membership network that allows you to stay one or two nights for free at wineries, breweries, farms, orchards, or museums. The annual membership fee was just $46 in 2018, and we used several times during our trip. We stayed at a farm in New Hampshire, wineries near Montreal and Buffalo, an apple orchard by Columbus, Ohio, and the Fargo air museum. We later used it at a brewery in Nebraska, a winery outside of Portland, Oregon, and another winery near the New Mexico-Texas border.

The Fargo Air Museum is closed on Monday, and July 9th, 2018 was a Monday. But it's directly across the street from the FargoDome, home to the North Dakota State Bison football team. This is where Philadelphia Eagles quarterback, Carson Wentz, became a star, and because of my NFL background, the FargoDome was a place I really wanted to see. I walked across the street and was pleasantly surprised to find the building open. The lobby was filled with Bison football paraphernalia and signs. I walked up a flight of stairs to see a collage of former NDSU players who had made it to the NFL on the wall outside of the football offices. Beneath the lobby were meeting rooms where the NDSU women's soccer team had just met. A few hellos were exchanged, and I wandered back to the lobby to ask one of the ticket agents if I could go inside the seating area.

"Sure," the woman replied. "But I need to escort you."

I thanked her and we went inside, which was much more spacious than I thought it'd be. The artificial turf was being removed as the 19,000-seat venue was getting ready to host a bi-state youth wrestling tournament. Yellow banners honoring NDSU's 14 football national championships, including five straight FCS titles while Wentz attended the school, and the team's many conference crowns hung from the rafters. I took a couple of photos, thanked the woman again, and we headed out. As we were walking back to the lobby, I told her about our trip and she told me her son was a big baseball fan.

"Check it out," I told her as I handed her a card.

It was nearly 5 p.m. Central time, and I walked back to the RV to see if Patti was wrapping up for the day. We didn't have much of a lunch, so an early dinner was in our plans. We walked two blocks down the four-lane 19th Avenue, past a few chain restaurants, and settled on Labby's Grill & Bar. There weren't many people inside, but the service was wonderful as we sat at the bar. We struck up a conversation with a woman of about 50, who was nearing retirement from the Air Force. She was very interested in our baseball trip, as was a group of women putting together goodie bags for their sons' Little League team before they were traveling to a tournament the upcoming weekend. Cards were handed out and we were back in the RV a couple hours later, having no idea of the troubles that awaited us the next day.

The slideout topper would strike again.

· · · · ·

Summer winds can be rather blustery across the plains of the Eastern Dakotas. July 10th was especially breezy, with gusts over 30 miles per hour as we headed south down Interstate 29. We had more than an eight-hour drive from Fargo to Broken Bow, Nebraska, where we would use Harvest Hosts to spend the night at a microbrewery. We worked in a mid-day stop in Mitchell, South Dakota to see the famed Corn Palace and grab some lunch. We ate corn on the cob, of course.

There were two unplanned stops before we ever got to Mitchell.

We left Fargo around 7 a.m. A couple hours later, I was forced to stop on the side of the highway. The slideout topper had come unraveled and was billowing in the wind.

"What the farts! (I didn't say farts)," I yelled. "No frigging way (I didn't say frigging)."

"What?" Patti asked from the rear of the RV.

"The damn slideout topper came undone again," I answered as I moved the RV onto the shoulder of the Interstate.

A gas station was about 20 miles ahead of us and I wanted to at least get a temporary fix on the side of the road. I told Patti I'd go on top of the RV and handroll the vinyl topper out with the slideout as she extended it. Then I'd guide it back in with my hands once it was even and she retracted the slideout. This plan worked perfectly, and we were back on the road within ten minutes. I took it reasonably slow to the gas station, where two large flags were fully extended as they flapped in the wind. I climbed back on top of the RV and checked the slideout topper. Everything looked fine. I topped off the fuel tank and we continued our trek south. Once I took the on-ramp to merge back onto the freeway, we didn't make it 100 yards before the slideout topper was once again at full sail.

The same routine followed, only this time we used bus tape that we had inside to strap the vinyl to the RV, and I used the tape to cover the opening in the front of slideout to prevent air from whipping through. It seemed to work and we eventually made it to Kinkaider Brewing Company around 6 p.m. I had called ahead to see if they served food. They had a full menu. The car could stay hooked up for the night.

I parked the RV alongside a row of evergreen trees that separated the gravel lot from the adjacent road. I climbed onto the roof and began to remove the tape as Patti took Holmes out. Once all the tape was off, I was ready to do the same routine we did on the side of the road. We extended the slideout as used my hands to keep everything tight and even. And then we'd roll it back in. Once the slideout topper was smoothed out, Patti extended the slideout again. It moved about two inches and then, SNAP!

"Stop," I yelled. It was too late. Both brackets had broken in the same manner they did back in February. There was more cursing. Fortunately, there was nobody else in the parking lot, just a few empty cars.

We didn't know what to do. We couldn't drive like this, and I knew we had to remove the topper. It was a lot easier than I thought it would be. One single screw held the vinyl in place along a track that ran the length of the slideout. Remove the screw and then just slide the vinyl topper out toward the front of the RV. I moved it a few inches and then decided the rest could wait until morning. We fully extended both slideouts, fed Holmes, and then went inside for our own meal.

The dinner was fabulous and we had a couple of beers with our meal, joking that we hoped we could make it home after drinking. The RV was parked about 50 yards in front of the brewery doors. The beer was so good, we got a couple of crowlers — 32-ounce aluminum cans — to take with us. As things rattle around in the fridge while you're traveling, a crowler is much better than a glass growler for an RV.

We watched a movie after dinner and then went to bed. An early morning beckoned as we had to be in Denver by 3 p.m. Mountain time. The Rockies had donated 30 tickets to Lutheran Family Services Rocky Mountains and I was interviewing representatives of the foster care organization at their office prior to the game.

The slideout topper was easy enough to get off. I was up top guiding it out while Patti ensured it didn't crash to the ground. We put it inside, placing it on the floor of the RV, where it had spent some time in March before it was "fixed" in North Carolina. I called the Camping World near Denver to see if they could get us in. No dice. Tacoma, Washington? Nope. Anaheim? No can do. At least they got us in for an oil change there. Phoenix? Sure. OK, great. I made an appointment at the Camping World in Avondale, Arizona. We would be in the Phoenix area for ten days and had a place to stay thanks to Patti's childhood friend, Katie Harris. We'd stay with the Harris clan during that time and the slideout topper would get fixed. That would have been nice, but it didn't happen.

Even though I made an appointment and explained to them what was going on, even that the same issue had previously been worked on in Concord, North Carolina and Swedesboro, New Jersey, the Avondale service department still needed their tech to diagnose the problem and submit the work to the warranty department. When we arrived, no part had been ordered and it took over a week before the work was approved. That meant the new slideout topper would not arrive before we had to head toward Texas. We had removed most of the items from the refrigerator, including the dairy products, and thought our condiments would be OK for a couple of days. The RV would be getting power while being worked out. We wound up having to throw just about everything away because our home sat in the desert heat for more than a week, largely untouched.

It was a complete waste of time having the RV there. Katie's husband, Chris, is a Phoenix native and his aunt Peggy said we could park the RV at her place during our stay. We did for one night, learning our lesson from my grandparents' place, and plugged it in. Our Camping World appointment was the next day. Had we known nothing would get done, we'd have left it plugged in at Peggy's and the items in our fridge would have been fine. Instead, not only did we have to toss some food, having the RV at Camping World cost us some television coverage.

I was able to work in some NFL training camp coverage during our West-Coast swing. I stopped into 49ers camp, visited the Chargers, and then got the OK to cover a Cardinals practice. I was doing a feature on Cardinals linebacker Deone Bucannon. Media availability was before the afternoon practice with lunch sandwiched between. I sat at a table with two reporters I had just met, one of whom was from a Phoenix television station. I told them about our trip and the TV guy was very interested. He wanted us to drive the RV to their building and do a piece on us. I told him the situation and then it was, "Maybe you can drive the RV to the stadium and we'll do something there."

"That could work," I told him, still optimistic the work on the RV would be completed in the week before we were attending a game at Chase Field.

It didn't happen. Television stories are dependent on visuals, and we couldn't provide the primary visual that would have caught people's eyes. There would be no television coverage in Phoenix and the slideout topper sat in the middle of our RV for the duration of the trip.

"Despite the issues we had, everything was worth it when we got to see the impact of our partnership with Children's Hope Alliance and the kids and families enjoying the games," Patti reflected. "Seeing the kids like Heaven in Durham, saying she had never been to a baseball game before, or the boy in Denver and how engaged they were in the experience just made it feel worthwhile."

CHAPTER 6:

THE DETROIT UNICORN

If you are a Detroit Tigers fan and have attended a game at Comerica Park, you have probably seen Gordie Wykes. The Detroit native has regularly attended Tigers games since childhood, but it's his attire that makes him stand out. Gordie, who was born in 1984, goes to baseball games dressed as a unicorn. He first started dressing as a unicorn in 2016 as a way to meet people.

"I started dressing as a unicorn just a couple years ago, but I've been dressing like a weirdo for as long as I can remember," Gordie told me in June. "In eighth grade, I was voted most unique dresser, and at 33, I'm going to be the youngest person to receive the lifetime achievement award for unique dresser."

Despite his flamboyant attire, he is admittedly a shy person. When he goes out wearing a unicorn cap, he didn't have to initiate conversations, people approached him.

"I travel alone a lot, and the unicorn is sort of being symbolic of being the only one," Gordie said.

I first met Gordie in Port Charlotte, Florida during the Rays' wild walk-off Spring Training win over the Blue Jays. Before we spoke in the ninth inning of that game, I noticed him standing in one of the tunnels leading from the concourse to the main seating bowl. It was hard not to notice a bearded man with long and curly brown hair under a furry unicorn cap. The hat was solid white, with the exception of a rainbow-colored main and the gold spiraling horn. His shirt was an American flag with a huge eagle head across the chest. He wore a striped grey animal print scarf. His legs were covered by red-and-blue striped tights with the logo for legendary metal band, Slayer, running over both thighs. The American flag motif continued down to his red, white, and blue shoes. A tiger head fanny pack was around his waist.

As I walked past Gordie, not knowing who he was at the time, I couldn't help but to rudely stare. A couple of innings later, he was on the field as part of a between-inning dance contest. Gordie was matched against two young women. All three were asked to perform a ribbon-dance routine. None knew what they were doing, but Gordie owned it with leaps and spins while keeping his ribbon in constant rotation. He easily won the contest, decided by crowd applause.

"I don't think it was fair," Gordie said months later. "Unicorn against people is not an equal matchup."

I watched the game from the auxiliary press area just to the left of the press box. I took notes and prepared for my interview with Chris Archer. As the game drew nearer to its conclusion, I decided to pack up and head out to the outfield tiki bar and enjoy a beer during the final inning. I drank nothing but water prior to that and made a comment during the seventh-inning stretch that I missed my chance to get a beer. An usher informed me the tiki bar served beer through the end of the game. With beer in hand, I settled underneath the center-field scoreboard for a bit of shade and watched the Blue Jays erupt for five runs in the top of the ninth.

During the onslaught of runs, I happened to be standing next to that dancing unicorn.

"How long have you worked for the Rays?" I asked.

"Huh? I don't work for the Rays," the confused man replied.

"Oh, really? I just assumed you did. I thought you were a team employee who regularly did the dance competition," I explained.

"Nope. When I got here, someone asked me if I wanted to participate in one of the games," he said. "I was like, 'Sure.'"

Gordie told me he grew up in Michigan as a Tigers fan and was in Florida trying to hit as many Spring Training stadiums as he could. I briefly told him we were doing the same thing but didn't really go into detail. The game's wild ending didn't lend itself to much conversation.

"I remember seeing you speak something into a recorder and I was thinking, 'This guy is not just some fan. He's doing something else,'" Gordie later told me.

Following Tampa's walk-off win, I told Gordie it was nice to meet him and said good-bye before heading to my car. As I was driving away from the stadium down El Jobean Road, I saw Gordie walking on the sidewalk alongside the road. There isn't much on that stretch of Highway 771, and the temperature was hovering around 90 degrees, so I pulled into a paint store parking lot and asked where he was going.

"Hooters," he said.

"That's like two miles away. Want a lift?" I asked.

While a bit hesitant to accept a ride from a stranger, Gordie, still wearing his unicorn hat, accepted my offer.

I learned quite a bit from Gordie in our short ride to the restaurant. He explained his reasoning for dressing as a unicorn as a means to meet people. I also learned he worked for the Student Advocacy Center of Michigan, a non-profit that helps at-risk youth — many of whom are in the foster care system. This could not have been more of a serendipitous meeting. I told Gordie more about our 2018 plans and we exchanged contact information. The wheels were in motion.

When I got back to Jupiter, I was excited to tell Patti about my encounter. She was first taken aback.

"It's interesting when your husband comes back from somewhere and says, 'Oh, by the way, I gave a unicorn a ride,'" Patti recalled. "I wasn't sure whether I should call a doctor or what."

During my drive back to Jupiter from Port Charlotte, I received an email with the subject line, "Unicorn you met today."

"Thanks for the ride and the nice conversation. Let me know when you're in Detroit and I will try to set up an outing," Gordie wrote. "Thank you for the work you are doing! It is so important!"

Patti got to meet Gordie herself the very next day when we spotted the unicorn in Fort Myers at JetBlue Park.

Gordie's outfits vary day by day, from park to park, but the hat remains the same. He found the hat at a novelty store in Austin, Texas while on a trip that ended in New Orleans.

"I thought, 'This could make me some friends on Bourbon Street,'" he explained. "People thought I was a street performer and they were trying to tip me. My friends were asking, 'Why didn't you take the tips?' I'm just an amateur weirdo. I'm not a professional. After that New Orleans trip, I just kept rocking it."

When we saw him in Fort Myers, he was donning a powder blue Myrtle Beach Mermen jersey. The Mermen were a fictitious minor-league team featured in the HBO comedy, *Eastbound & Down*. He also wore silver leggings with white-capped grey and blue waves wrapped around the calves. Blood-red sneakers covered his feet.

I replied to Gordie's email the next morning and gave him the dates of our Detroit visit. He said he would submit a ticket request and did not foresee any problems because the Student Advocacy Center of Michigan had already received a donation of tickets for the April 15th game against the Yankees. That game had been postponed, however, because of inclement weather. The Tigers had six April games postponed in 2018, mostly because of lingering snow.

During one cold April day in Detroit, Gordie's outfit included a black sweater depicting Santa Claus riding a golden-maned unicorn. When we saw him in Detroit, Gordie was wearing a grey tank top with "#SquadGoals" in pink lettering emblazoned across the front. He wore his tiger fanny pack, which he named Carlos, and his leggings went from solid black near the waist, to a mixture of green and yellow stripes from the thighs down. Long purple socks decorated with pink donuts protruded from his bright purple shoes. Gordie picked up Carlos in Austin at the same store from which he got the unicorn hat.

A few days after Gordie's initial email, I shot a note to the Tigers community relations department to give them a heads up about a ticket request from the Student Advocacy Center for a game between June 12th and 14th. Gordie ultimately requested 20 tickets on behalf of the Student Advocacy Center for the June 13th game. I stayed in contact with Gordie, including an email on April 9th when I told him to celebrate National Unicorn Day accordingly.

By the time mid-May arrived, we had not heard anything from the Tigers. I was beginning to worry, and again, emailed the Tigers. That prompted a phone call from Courtney Kaplan, the Tigers community affairs manager. She left a voicemail asking for more details about the request. I called back and left a voicemail explaining what we were doing and told her she should contact Gordie for more details. The game of phone tag went on, but the ticket request was approved and we were set.

The Student Advocacy Center of Michigan (SAC) is located in Ypsilanti and its primary function to help kids who were either suspended or expelled re-enter school. It was established in 1975 by Ruth Zweifler, a woman Gordie described as "remarkable." Zweifler, who was inducted into the Michigan Women's Hall of Fame in 2003, noticed many minority, under-privileged, and at-risk youth were not receiving the same access to education. She introduced the idea of dual enrollment at local community colleges to help troubled high school students and thousands of overlooked children continue their education. SAC provides primarily non-legal support for Michigan children who aren't getting the special education rights required by law and mentors students through a "check-and-connect" program designed to prevent kids from dropping out of school. Gordie educated us by explaining that expulsions from private pre-schools are an issue.

He also cited one instance of an 18-year-old autistic student who was expelled for bringing a knife to school, though he brought the knife with him to cut an apple during lunch.

We arranged to meet Gordie at The Town Pump Tavern, a popular pregame spot for locals. Gordie was a regular there and the bartenders knew him by name and apparel. Gordie arrived with a guest, a young black woman named Erica who was raised in the foster system.

Erica was wearing mermaid leggings, as was Gordie, and had a unicorn horn strapped to the top of her head. Both Gordie and Erica were sparkling, thanks to the glitter they used to highlight their outfits. After exchanging pleasantries, Gordie presented us with a bag of gifts containing a pair of unicorn horns and a book by Tom Stanton called *The Final Season* – a memoir that chronicles the last season the Tigers spent at Tiger Stadium before moving to Comerica Park in 2000.

One of the gifted unicorn horns was blue, the other pink. Patti wore the pink one, but I kept the blue one in the bag. When a little girl at the stadium asked Patti where she got her unicorn horn, she said, "From a friend." She then handed it to the little girl, whose face lit up with joy. We also handed out some Children's Hope Alliance items, including a few of those orange cups, which went perfectly with the Tigers colors.

Gordie said the biggest benefit the kids from SAC get by going to a Tigers game is to see all the different career opportunities. Sure, there are the ball players, managers, coaches, and umpires on the field, but there are also food service workers, team employees in media relations, community relations, guest services, finance, marketing and ticket sales, not to mention the scouting department.

Gordie is no neophyte baseball traveler and had been to 19 of the 30 stadiums in use in 2018. He had also visited the old Tiger Stadium and Cleveland Municipal Stadium. He referred to Comerica Park as his "baby" and described AT&T Park in San Francisco as "a gorgeous place to watch a ball game."

"Different parks have different things to offer," he said. "The historic parks, you don't get the same feel as any modern park."

Patti replied with her adoration of Fenway Park, which does an admirable job of feeling nostalgic while including modern amenities.

Comerica Park was also one of our favorite stadiums. The stadium has several unique features and one we experienced was the baseball Ferris wheel near "Big Cat Court," a food court just inside the main entrance. Big Cat Court is home to Comerica Park's Tiger carousel, which is the centerpiece of a circular area surrounded by food stands and the Tigers team store.

We went inside the team store to add a Comerica Park lapel pin to our growing collection. Gordie and Erica patiently waited and then walked with us through the food court down a pathway toward the Fly Ball Ferris wheel. This isn't some rinky-dink gimmick. It is a legit carnival-size Ferris wheel. Each of the 12 cars, designed to look like baseballs, can seat up to five people. Because we're just a couple of big kids, Patti and I made the decision to pay the $2 to ride the Ferris wheel. Gordie and Erica declined to join us but offered to hold our bags.

From atop the Ferris wheel, you can see the city of Detroit behind you, but there isn't much of a view of the stadium. The Ferris wheel isn't exactly promoted as a spot for great views. It is, however, just one of the several aspects of Comerica Park that make it a very kid-friendly stadium. Comerica Park has the batting cages and kids zone of other stadiums but is the only one with both a carousel and a Ferris wheel. Heck, Kauffman Stadium in Kansas City is the only other ballpark with a carousel.

When we got to our seats in Section 139, we realized how generous the Tigers had been. Our group had a wonderful view from the left-field line. This was great foul-ball territory, though nobody from our group got a ball. We had a couple of close calls with a ball landing above us and another in an adjacent section. Line drives were out of the question because the Tigers added protective netting that extends beyond the dugouts down the left and right-field lines.

The kids were all in middle school, and though they were 12 and 13 years old, still got a kick out of sitting next to the shimmering unicorns. Gordie likes to use his unicorn persona as a way to bond with children who may need some levity.

"I take advantage of working with kids and having my wardrobe sort of look like a little kid's wardrobe," he said. "Sometimes I meet students on the worst day of their life. When you have a unicorn or Chewbacca, Zelda, or any number of various characters I choose, it seems more familiar. It can be kind of reassuring to see a unicorn on the worst day of your life."

Tigers pitcher Daniel Norris said in March he also relishes the opportunity to brighten a kid's day with what he called a "trickle-down effect."

"I remember I was that kid who was excited to meet a pro ball player," Norris told me during Spring Training. "I always try to keep that in perspective. Even if I'm having a bad day, you've got to focus on the other things, like the fans and the kids. Not only does it sometimes make their day, talking with them and seeing that you can inspire them, it can also bring your bad day up. That's something I value, for sure. I remember when I was a kid, me and my best friend went to see Rick Ankiel play in our hometown. He was with the Cardinals in Rookie Ball. We went to get his autograph and he looked at us dead in the eye and signed for us. That's one of the things I'll never forget."

· · · · ·

One thing to always remember is that people are generally good. I had a wonderful encounter in Detroit with a man named Anthony. One of the concession items suggested to me was Comerica Park's cinnamon-roasted almonds. As I went on a quest to find some local brews and food, I met Anthony while waiting in line to order some Chicken Shawarma Nachos, another recommended item at Comerica Park. The Shawarma Nachos, which are pita chips loaded with hummus and chicken, fed us both for the price of

$13. Anthony and I had already been talking as we waited for our food, but I had yet to tell him about our trip. During our conversation, I noticed the almond stand to my right and realized it was cash-only. I made the comment that I had to go back to my seat to get some cash from my wife. My name was then called and my nachos were ready for pickup. I retrieved my food and began to make my way back to Section 139 when Anthony stopped me and handed me a bag of cinnamon almonds. I was truly touched. His gesture meant a lot more than the six dollars he spent on a bag of almonds. I was someone he didn't know at all and he decided to pay it forward. I then told Anthony and his wife about our mission while on our stadium tour and told him we had some Michigan kids at the game with us. He asked a couple of questions and I gave him a card, thankful for this stranger's kind act.

When I got back to my seat, I told Patti about Anthony and we had our first cinnamon-roasted almonds. The middle innings of the game were uneventful, so Patti and I went on our usual stadium exploration. We stopped to investigate each historical tower in the concourse before venturing to the outfield area. Gordie and Erica had also decided to go for a walk and we crossed paths by the center-field fountain.

"Check out the face under Charlie Gehringer," Gordie suggested before we got to the statues in left field.

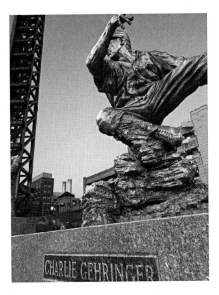

Sure enough, there is an unexplained face in the "dirt" under a leaping Gehringer. As we sauntered around the statues and took multiple photos, I struck up a conversation with a couple in their mid-50s. The Home Run On Wheels trip was explained and a card handed out.

It took a few innings, but we eventually made our way back to our seats to enjoy a thrilling finish. After the Twins jumped out to a 2-0 lead, the Tigers kept them scoreless the rest of the night en route to a 5-2 victory that was bolstered by a four-run eighth inning.

"Wherever there are ballparks, there are memories," Stanton wrote in his book. Hopefully we helped create some lifetime memories for those kids from the Student Advocacy Center of Michigan.

As we interviewed Gordie outside of Comerica Park following the game, we were interrupted several times by people who wanted to get their picture taken with Gordie. He is a bit of a local celebrity, though not many know his name.

"This is the most unique individual I've seen," one man said of Gordie. "This is inspirational. This is purely inspirational. Did you bring us the victory?"

"I bring the magic," Gordie replied.

"The glitter is the magic," the man said before moving on.

"That happens quite a bit," Gordie said as we resumed our conversation. "I was trying to estimate the number of pictures I've taken with people and it's gotta be in the thousands by now."

We left Detroit on Friday, June 15th, and I emailed Gordie to, again, thank him for helping to line up tickets. Unfortunately, he told me that he had been fired that same day, two days after we spent a night together in downtown Detroit. Gordie had been passed over for a promotion, leading to a confrontation with his boss. I felt terrible about situation because I knew how passionate he is about helping kids. Gordie has a huge heart and I offered words of encouragement for his pending job search. He genuinely cares about the kids with whom he worked and tried to improve their lives. As 2018 ended, Gordie was still out of work.

CHAPTER 7:
HALLS OF FAME AND MUSEUMS

I love history. In college, I took six history courses: Art history I and II, world history, U.S. history I and II and the Civil War. "To know your future, you must know your past," philosopher George Santayana once reminded us.

Textbooks can help historical events run through our minds like a film, but museums allow these people and events to come to life before our eyes. We made a point to see as many museums and halls of fame, which are at their core are museums, along the way. Those visits were part of our goal to experience as much of each city as possible.

But sometimes we didn't even have to leave the baseball stadium to take in a museum. Both Florida MLB parks have a museum and they could not be any different.

The Bobblehead Museum at Marlins Park is more of a giant display than actual museum, but it's still fun to see. Located in the main concourse, the double-sided display stands over ten feet high. The eight continuous rows hold the world's largest collection of bobbleheads. One side depicts players and coaches from the American League, the other side reserved for National League members. They are sorted by team and there are also sections for mascots, broadcasters, and other baseball personalities. The shelves are lighted to allow interested fans to inspect each of the more-than 600 figurines. The shelves even vibrate so the heads do indeed bobble. Mr. Met, the Phillie Phanatic, San Diego Chicken, Bernie Brewer and of course, Billy the Marlin are among the mascots included. The Marlins section contains, as its centerpiece, a portrayal of Craig Counsell pumping his fist in the air as he scores the winning run in Game 7 of the 1997 World Series.

Counsell finished his playing career in 2011 with the Brewers and was named Milwaukee's manager in 2015. He led the Brewers to the 2018 National League Championship Series. As a Wisconsin native and lifelong Brewers fan, I was particularly interested in the Milwaukee portion of the display. There are bobbleheads of Brewers greats like Robin Yount, Paul Molitor, Gorman Thomas and Pete Vuckovich.

The themed bobbleheads are especially neat with players dressed as superheroes and *Star Wars* characters, or sitting on the Iron Throne from the HBO television series *Game of Thrones*. Patti got a "House Banister" bobblehead of former Rangers manager, Jeff Banister, sitting on the sword-backed throne during our visit to Globe Life Park in Arlington. Bobbleheads have become a popular giveaway item at ballparks throughout the country. We each received a Mark McGwire bobblehead as part of a promotion at Busch Stadium on September 16th. That was one of 21 bobblehead games in 2018 at Busch Stadium alone.

Another treat was seeing giant bobbleheads at several other stadiums. The Oriole Bird at Ed Smith Stadium in Sarasota, giant caricatures of Tigers players Victor Martinez and Miguel Cabrera at Comerica Park, Giants Hall of Famer Willie Mays at AT&T Park, former Dodgers manager Tommy Lasorda in the outfield concourse at Dodger Stadium, and Cardinals catcher Yadier Molina at Busch Stadium were among the highlights. The Mays bobblehead is at the entrance to a small shop in the left-field concourse. Inside the store is an entire wall full of more bobbleheads.

For those bobblehead aficionados not satisfied with a giant display of baseball bobbleheads, there is an actual bobblehead museum located in Milwaukee. We didn't see it on our trip, but the National Bobblehead Hall of Fame and Museum in the heart of Brew City opened in 2018.

· · · · ·

The Ted Williams Museum & Hitters Hall of Fame feels a bit out of place at Tropicana Field, but it works. The museum first opened in 1994 and was located in Hernando, Florida, near where Williams lived following his retirement. An avid fisherman, Williams would spend winters in Florida during his playing career to go fishing in the state's rivers and lakes and would also go deep-sea fishing. An older Williams lived in Citrus Hills, Florida, and the museum in Hernando saw a surge of attendance in 2002, shortly after Williams died. The next few years saw dwindling attendance and it was forced to close in 2006. That's when the Rays stepped in and moved the museum, and its memorabilia, to a new wing of Tropicana Field.

The museum is located on the second floor above the main concourse and the 7,000-square-foot space displays mementos from Williams' playing career and his time in the Marine Corps during World War II and Korean War. One of his bats is enclosed in a glass case at the museum's entrance. A bronze statue of the left-handed Thumper is located just inside the museum doors. At the bottom of the stairs to the museum is a street-level lobby off the main concourse that pays tribute to some of the Rays greats over the franchise's brief history. Chris Archer, Tampa's 2018 Opening Day starter, is included alongside life-size murals of David Price and James Shields.

Ruth, Aaron, Mays, Thome and Robinson are among a list of other greats honored at the Hitters Hall of Fame: including Tony Gwynn, Alex Rodriguez, Barry Bonds, Joe Jackson, Ty Cobb, Pete Rose, Joe DiMaggio, Stan Musial, Lou Gehrig, Hank Greenberg, Al Simmons, Mickey Mantle, Johnny Mize, Mike Schmidt, Rogers Hornsby and Wade Boggs — who spent the final two seasons of an 18-year career with the Rays.

The Pitching Hall of Great Achievement was added in 2014 and later named for the late Roy Halladay. It has nine members, including Halladay and former Rays All-Star, James Shields.

The Ted Williams Museum and Hitters Hall of Fame is open before and during Rays games, through the seventh inning, and is free to all ticketed fans.

· · · · ·

Growing up on a dairy farm in Wisconsin, I went on one out-of-state family vacation. There were not any out-of-state school trips, either. Until 2017, I had never properly visited Washington, D.C. I did drive through D.C. on my way to Annapolis in 2006 to see the East Carolina football team play Navy. Annapolis is a neat, colonial city and that was a day trip Patti and I did take in 2018 while in Maryland.

When 2018 ended, I still had not been to any of the Smithsonian museums. The 2017 trip with Patti was to see the Cardinals play the Nationals at Nationals Park. We took advantage of the beautiful weather that April weekend to do some sightseeing. We hit the Lincoln and Jefferson Memorials, walked by the Washington Monument, which was closed at the time, and visited the U.S. capitol (though we did not take a tour). As addressed in Chapter 3, when we went in 2018, it was again a baseball trip. We did our walks around Georgetown and Arlington but did not have enough time to visit the Smithsonian Institution. The network of 11 museums in the National Mall basically requires a full day — or more — at each to do any visit justice. One of these times, we are just going to take a trip to D.C. for the Smithsonian alone. That said, the city of Washington itself is sort of one sprawling museum. Philadelphia and Boston are similar in that regard.

We also didn't have time to visit Cooperstown, New York for the National Baseball Hall of Fame and Museum. The route we took to Canada was up through New England and not across Upstate New York. A detour through Cooperstown, which is a tiny community of 2,000 people on Otsego Lake between Albany and Syracuse, would have been well out of the way. The Baseball Hall of Fame would have to wait for another trip. The same goes for the Naismith Memorial Basketball Hall of Fame, which was passed driving on Interstate 91 through Springfield, Massachusetts on our way to Vermont. There were a few stops between Washington, D.C. and Vermont. After we saw the Nationals play the Braves, our next MLB game would be at Philadelphia's Citizens Bank Park.

· · · · ·

We arrived in Philadelphia on a Wednesday and our first meal in the City of Brotherly Love had to be a cheesesteak. Though we were told neither Pat's nor Geno's are the best cheesesteaks Philadelphia has to offer, they are the two most well-known, so we felt obligated to try them. We didn't realize at the time that the two restaurants were right next to each other. That made the decision to eat from both places easier. Parking was limited on the narrow residential streets, but I found a spot in front of Pat's. We split one sandwich from Pat's before crossing the street to share another at Geno's. We agreed that Pat's is hands down the superior sandwich. You go to Pat's for the sandwich, Geno's for the tourist experience. Pat's is largely no frills, whereas Geno's is lit up like Las Vegas and has an adjoining gift shop.

After eating our sandwiches, we strolled into the bar that is in between the two for a beverage to wash them down. It's your typical neighborhood sports bar and the televisions were tuned into a hockey playoff game between the Flyers and in-state rival Penguins. After ordering a couple of Yuenglings — that's what you do in Pennsylvania — we got another cheesesteak recommendation from Joe the bartender. He said Ishkabibble's on South Street had the best Philly cheesesteak. Ishka-what? I think we asked him to repeat it four times and then spell it. We never did dine at Ishkabibble's, although we parked right in front of it when we visited Jim's the next night. We didn't realize it until we walked back to the car and noticed the tiny sandwich shop tucked between a pair of jewelry stores. Next time.

After seeing the Phillies beat the Pirates on Friday, our weekend was spent exploring Philadelphia's numerous historical sites.

Following a special lunch at Chickie's and Pete's (I'll explain later why this lunch was so special), we went to Old City and waited in line to check out the Liberty Bell. There was quite a line around 2 p.m., which should be expected on what was a mild April afternoon. We eventually made our way through the exhibit hall that tells the history of the Liberty Bell, how it came to be and the story behind its famous crack. When we finally got to the bell itself, it was rather underwhelming but is free to visit. Also free is the adjacent Independence Hall, but we couldn't get a time slot for Saturday, so we booked a tour for Sunday morning. We were able to enter Congress Hall, situated next door. Originally built to complement the Philadelphia County Courthouse, Congress Hall was home to the U.S. Congress from 1790-1800 and temporarily served as the U.S. capitol during that time.

There is so much to see and do in Philadelphia and we tried to cram as much as we could into two days. After leaving Independence National Historical Park, we walked toward the Delaware River to find the Tun Tavern marker. Tun Tavern was an 18-century drinkery where the Second Continental Congress met on November 10th, 1775 to form two battalions of Marines. Yes, the United States Marine Corps was founded in a bar. The actual building is long gone, but as a former Marine, it was one historical marker I needed to see. Across Front Street from the Tun Tavern marker are the Irish and Scottish immigrants' memorials. Tun Tavern is actually shown in a relief on the Scottish monument at Penn's Landing. The riverfront landing has several tall ships on display and is home to the Independence Seaport Museum. We did a quick 30-minute visit before the museum closed at 5.

On the way back to the car, we stopped in City Tavern for a drink. The tavern in Philadelphia's oldest bar, though these days it is more of a restaurant than a bar and the staff is dressed in colonial garb. We did sample a couple of ales, however, before continuing our self-guided walking tour of Philadelphia. Our next stop was One Liberty Place, which was about two miles away. We were in no rush, so we casually walked the streets of Philadelphia past the Independence Hall complex and City Hall. We paused for a few moments at City Hall to snap several photos of the impressive municipal building. Once we got to the One Liberty Place observation deck, we had a superb view of the 37-foot William Penn statue atop City Hall.

On the ground floor of One Liberty Place is a pair of large feet covered in colonial-era shoes. You realize who those feet belong to when you reach the 57th floor and a giant bust of Benjamin Franklin greets you as you exit the elevator. The Franklin bust is in the center of the 360-degree enclosed observation deck that is 883 feet above street level, which is the highest public access level in Philadelphia. Because of Patti's affinity for getting bird's-eye views of the cities she visits; One Liberty Place was on a list of observation decks that included the Empire State Building and Rockefeller Center in New York City, the Montreal Tower, Toronto's CN Tower, the Carew Tower in Cincinnati, and Seattle's Columbia Tower.

As you might expect, Ben Franklin's name and likeness are ubiquitous in Philadelphia. The Benjamin Franklin National Memorial, a giant statue of a seated Franklin, is at the entrance to the Franklin Institute — a massive science museum that would take an entire day (or two) to fully explore.

We didn't have that much time but took advantage of the 40 minutes we had inside before closing. After navigating the flow of blood through a giant heart that invites visitors to explore each atrium and ventricle, we raced professional athletes, tested our leaping abilities, and threw a few baseball's in the institute's sports zone. But the feature we enjoyed most was the Sky Bike. The bike sits on a high wire about 40 feet above the floor, though a safety net is between the rider and the people walking below. A 250-pound counterweight beneath the wire keeps the bike upright.

"You might rock a bit, but you won't tip over," we were told before getting on the bike.

For just three dollars, patrons can pedal across the atrium and back twice before giving way to the next person in line. Though we each only got about a minute on the suspended bike, it was the highlight of my weekend in Philadelphia outside of the game.

The best part of our Philadelphia sightseeing is that we didn't spend a lot thanks to the Philadelphia City Pass, which included admission to the One Liberty Place, Franklin Institute, and the two museums we visited Sunday. It also allows you to ride Philadelphia's Big Bus from site to site. The City Pass also includes discounts at places, like City Tavern, which we did not know until after we left. We did take advantage of the City Pass on Sunday, but we first returned to Independence Hall.

Though the building is two levels, it dwarfs the two-story Congress Hall thanks to its high ceilings. The building itself is still only 45 feet tall, but the clock tower steeple raises the total height of the structure to 176 feet. A statue of George Washington is in front of the building, though the visitor entrance is in the rear.

To see where our nation was born was spectacular. This is where our founding fathers met to draft the Constitution and adopt the Declaration of Independence on July 4th. The actual Declaration of Independence from English rule was made on July 2nd, but Thomas Jefferson's letter was adopted two days later. The document wasn't officially signed until August 2nd, giving us essentially three Independence Days.

The National Park ranger who led our tour said the staff at Independence Hall recognizes July 2nd as the true Independence Day. They hope it catches on but don't hold out much hope for convincing the rest of the country.

After going through Independence Hall, we had breakfast at Reading Terminal Market. The terminal has an overwhelming number of food options, though some are closed on Sunday. We browsed for several minutes before settling on our late-morning meal. We then hopped on the bus outside of the terminal and made our way over to Eastern State Penitentiary. The prison was in use from 1829 until 1971 and was influential in the construction of future prisons and in the treatment of inmates. The unique floor plan consisted of wings from a central point where guards could see down the passageway of each cell block. Castle-like walls form the exterior of the prison yard, which inmates were prohibited from entering. The prison was run by Quakers, who thought solitary confinement for each prisoner would help keep them safe and bring them closer to God. Each small cell had a skylight — or "Eye of God" — to let each resident know God was always watching. The Quaker rehabilitation strategy had the opposite effect. Many prisoners were driven mad without having other people to interact with and Eastern State had abandoned solitary confinement by 1913. Several areas of the prison are rumored to be haunted and the "Terror Behind the Walls" tour is a popular Halloween option. We didn't encounter anything out of the ordinary on an April Sunday afternoon.

One of the highlighted attractions at Eastern State is the cell block that once housed Al Capone. The infamous gangster was a "guest" at the prison in 1929. Capone received celebrity perks during his nine-month stay. His cell had a desk, nightstand, two lamps, and cushioned, high-back reading chair. Capone's old cell is made up to look now as it did when he occupied it.

Eastern State Penitentiary is within easy walking distance of the Philadelphia Museum of Art. We walked down Fairmount Avenue toward the Schuylkill River and were soon at the bottom of the museum's famous steps.

As we crossed Pennsylvania Avenue and rounded Kelly Drive, we first saw the statue of Rocky Balboa. The statue, which used to be positioned at the top of the steps made famous by the 1976 movie, is now situated to the right of the steps after a compromise with the museum director. The line for the statue was quite long, so we crossed the street to see a different statue.

The George Washington Monument is a massive bronze and granite sculpture in the center of Eakins Oval directly in front of the art museum. The sculpture, which was completed in 1897, depicts Washington riding a horse atop a fountain. Washington gazes toward Philadelphia City Hall, which is a straight shot down Benjamin Franklin Parkway. Beneath horse and rider are several other statues of animals and people indigenous to North America. The detail that went into creating the multiple statues that adorn the monument fountain and two flanking fountains is remarkable. There were again several pictures taken and uploaded to Facebook. But then we made our way back over to the Rocky statue and waited to get our photo taken. A couple behind us offered to snap a photo of us with our arms raised to mimic the statue of Sylvester Stallone's iconic character. He reciprocated the gesture and then ran up the flight of steps to the art museum (Yes, we actually ran up the steps). I had the Rocky theme song — *Gonna Fly Now*, not *Eye of the Tiger* — playing on my phone as we scaled the 72 steps. When I got to the top of the steps, I jumped up and down as Rocky did in the 1976 movie and my phone fell out of my jacket pocket. Fortunately, my East Carolina Otter Box did its job and the phone was OK. After reaching the top of the steps, Patti and I did something not a lot of people do. We actually went inside the art museum. We're glad we did.

The museum has an extensive collection, ranging from paintings to tapestries statues, to period furniture to religious artifacts. One interesting piece on the first level is an oil painting by John Singleton Copley. The 1763 portrait of Mrs. "Mercy Otis" Warren was on loan from the Museum of Fine Arts in Boston for three months as a reward for the Eagles beating the Patriots in Super Bowl LII. The second level rooms displaying several huge altars that date back to the 1400s and earlier. If you go to Philadelphia and run up the Rocky steps, do yourself a favor and go inside the museum. You won't regret it.

Down the hill on the opposite side of the steps is Fairmount Park on the Schuylkill River. Lining the riverbanks is "Boathouse Row," which is exactly what it says, a row of boathouses used by the rowing teams of Philadelphia's many colleges. Also along Boathouse Row is the Cosmic Café, where we got a couple of sandwiches for a late lunch around 3:30. We watched several rowing teams practicing on the river as we ate.

We hopped back on the Big Bus in front of the art museum a little after 4 and made our way back toward Old City where our car was parked. But we hopped off to make that brief visit to the Franklin Institute. Once that closed, our tourist travels for the day were done and we were back in the RV by 7. We cooked a late dinner and then had to record the next day's podcast entitled, "Phillies baseball, U.S. history and Philly cheesesteaks."

· · · · ·

The world was forever changed on September 11th, 2001. Most people remember exactly where they were and what they were doing when two hijacked airliners slammed into the sides of the World Trade Center towers in New York City. Thousands had been killed in the attack, and the United States has been in a perpetual war since.

As first responders rushed toward the rubble to save whomever they could find, I was sleeping in Pamlico County, North Carolina.

It was after 3 p.m. before I even learned what happened seven hours earlier. I had my first post-Marine Corps job as a sports reporter at the New Bern

Sun Journal. I worked the night before and didn't get home until 1 a.m. I got up the next morning around 7 to get the kids off to school, then went back to bed. I woke up around noon, made coffee, and ate some cereal at the kitchen table while reading that day's Sun Journal. Nobody had called or texted. I didn't have a smart phone, and social media platforms like Facebook and Twitter did not yet exist. I did not turn on the TV or the radio. I was enjoying a quiet afternoon before I had to go to work.

After going through the paper and making sure the sports section didn't have any typos, I read a book for about an hour and then got ready for work. I don't remember if there were any typos or what book I read. Those details were soon lost once I learned of the day's news. When I got in my car and turned the ignition key, the radio came on immediately. A Nirvana song was playing on the local alternative rock station, which one, I don't recall. The song ended and another one began.

Then the DJ cracked his mic, "In light of today's events," he began.

"Today's events? What happened?" I said aloud to myself.

My question wasn't answered before a new song filled my car's speakers. I began flipping to other stations.

"What the hell happened?" I said again. FM, nothing but commercials or songs. I switched to AM and landed on a news station. That's when I heard. I nearly drove off the road. I was stunned, angered, and saddened. I was just seven months removed from the Marine Corps and had thoughts of re-enlisting, even though I knew I had fulfilled my eight years of obligatory military service, all active duty. My feelings were not unique and there were many recently separated Marines, soldiers, sailors, and airmen who returned to the military. Some who had never before served soon found themselves at their local recruiting station.

When I walked into the newsroom, every eye ball was fixed on the handful of televisions in the office. The sports department had its own TV, which was mounted on a back wall. There were four desks in the Sun Journal sports department, and in order to get to mine, I had to wiggle my way through the group of people gathered in front of the TV. Once I set my bag down, I joined them. I had yet to actually see what happened. The sports TV was tuned into CNN. Footage of the attack from WABC in New York was re-aired. My mouth dropped. Tears began to form. I sat down in my chair and cried. Images of the damage at the Pentagon and the downed plane in Pennsylvania were shown. It was 4 p.m. by now and I was seeing everything for the first time.

My mind leapt to Gunnery Sergeant Ricky Heyward, who was my boss at Camp Lejeune before he was sent to work at the Pentagon. I called around and learned he was OK. Gunny Heyward had been very good to me, and I was relieved to learn he was unharmed. I stayed on the phone, either making or receiving calls about that day's scheduled sporting events, all of which were now canceled. Most would be rescheduled, though nobody was concerned with the dates.

Patti was also driving to work when she heard the news. Only she was hearing it in real time. She spent much of that day with her co-workers at Anheuser-Busch in St. Louis, clustered around the breakroom television.

Every emotion we felt that day came flooding back when we entered the 9/11 Memorial and Museum in Manhattan on May 1st, 2018. A week earlier, Patti and I had visited the two reflecting pools located where the Twin Towers had once stood. The North and South pools are recessed and water cascades over the coated granite walls into the basin before spilling into a deep hole at the center. The two waterfalls are the largest man-made falls in the United States.

The names of every victim are listed on bronze parapets surrounding each pool. Flowers had been placed near some of the names, presumably by loved ones. A forest of more than 400 swamp white oaks fill the plaza. The one exception is a callery pear tree, planted in the 1970s. It was badly burned and had just one living branch following the 2001 attacks but was replanted and now stands tall as a symbol of hope and rebirth. "The Survivor Tree" had grown from eight feet in 2001 to over 30 feet in 2018.

Patti and I visited the pools at night, taking the subway in from Jersey City. It was only two stops away. The museum was closed, but the plaza is always open to those who want to pay their respects to those lost. The buzz of the city seems to disappear in this solemn place. The new One World Trade Center towers over Memorial Plaza. Also called Freedom Tower, it is the tallest building in the United States at 1,792 feet. We didn't make it to the observation deck on the 102nd floor (of 104). Gazing up, the tower's illuminated spire set against a starry backdrop seems to touch the clouds.

This was our first night in Manhattan, and we wanted to explore the area. A permanent barricade next to a security booth limits traffic to One World Trade Center. The other World Trade Center buildings create a boundary for the plaza and museum. The white Oculus PATH station spreads its wings in the northeast corner of the plaza. Centered in the station's roof is a giant sky-light that runs the length of the building. A steady stream of passengers enters and exit through the street-level doors day and night.

A few hundred yards to the south, past 3 and 4 World Trade Center, is the FDNY Memorial Wall along Greenwich Street. The wall, which was dedicated in 2006, honors the 343 firefighters who lost their lives trying to save people from wreckage of the fallen towers. We slowly walked by, examining the bronze frieze, which is cleaned regularly. Across the street was a bar we were told is a popular hangout for police and firefighters. We spent over an hour walking around Memorial Plaza and the World Trade Center complex. It was approaching 8 p.m., and our stomachs were reminding us that we had not yet eaten dinner. Steve's Pizza was a couple blocks away and did the trick. We grabbed a couple of first New York Style slices, one of which, of course, was just cheese and pepperoni, and stood at one of the high-top tables to eat. Steve's is a small counter shop that shares the space with a sandwich shop. Eating gave us time to sort of process our initial visit to the World Trade Center. Our hunger satisfied, we then took the subway to see the Empire State Building; we did go to the observation deck there. One World Trade stands out among the Manhattan skyscrapers.

It was daylight when we returned to Memorial Plaza on May 1st. We walked from Battery Park after taking the ferry from Liberty Island. Our day began back at Liberty Harbor, where we had stayed for three nights beginning April 23rd.

May Day would be spent as New York City tourists, beginning with Ellis Island and the Statue of Liberty. We had originally planned on taking the Liberty Harbor cruise during our stay in Jersey City but didn't have enough time. The cruise terminal in Liberty State Park was walking distance from the RV park. We did walk over there with Holmes early one evening.

There isn't enough time and/or money to see everything New York has to offer in just a few days or even a month. It's the city that never sleeps, and whether it's shopping at Times Square, going to a baseball game, visiting Central Park and the multitude of museums there, the Central Park and Bronx zoos, going to see a Broadway show, or simply wandering through a neighborhood to sample some local cuisine, New York is fantastic. The City Pass is a great way to see many sights for a discounted fee and bypass some lines.

Just don't drive. Use the subway and you'll be much happier. That is, unless you're trying to get back from a night game and they're doing some work on the track line you need.

Patti took this Tuesday off from work and we still nearly ran out of time to do everything we had planned before heading to Queens to see the Braves beat the Mets at Citi Field. Liberty Harbor would be followed by the 9/11 Memorial and Museum and the Museum and the Metropolitan Museum of Art. The Met before the Mets.

The Statue of Liberty and Ellis Island form the Statue of Liberty National Monument. The Ellis Island National Museum of Immigration is in the main building of what was once the hub for migration to the United States. Here those hoping to live the American dream were screened for illnesses and other eugenics principles. The screening process was sometimes cruel, but an estimated 12 million people passed through Ellis Island and eventually found roots in the U.S. Ferries from Liberty State Park and Battery Park in Manhattan drop you off right in front of the main building. Glass panes atop a steel frame cover the ramps leading to the center doors.

Inside the lobby are various interactive exhibits and informative displays. But the second floor is the location most visitors seek. This is home to the Registry Room, or Great Hall. A third of the current U.S. population can trace their roots back to this rectangular room, where hundreds of people stood in line every day, waiting to speak with immigration officials and doctors. Encircling the room, which is 200 feet long and 102 feet wide, is a balcony that is popular today for tourists to better appreciate the magnitude of the space. Each level has various side rooms, many of which are open to the public. Old photos of how the hall appeared when full of families awaiting entry to the U.S. are at either end of the balcony. Even today as tourists wander about, noise carries well under the high, vaulted ceiling. It was even worse when in use as an immigration center was often a loud, confusing, and frightening place.

Back on the first floor is a room where you can search for ancestors who were processed at Ellis Island. Outside is the Immigrant Wall of Honor, a permanent exhibit that contains over 700,000 names. Visitors scan the wall looking for either names of their ancestors or simply their surname. We found several Wright and Clements, but only one Cavadini, my maternal grandmother's maiden name.

An entire day could be spent at Ellis Island, but we didn't have an entire day. We were back on the ferry in less than an hour for a short ride to Liberty Island. The ferry takes you to the opposite side of the Statue of Liberty, giving riders an all-sides view of Lady Liberty as she strikes her impressive pose over the Upper New York Bay. We really wanted to get tickets for the crown, but those have to be purchased months in advance. The same is true for tickets to enter the statue's pedestal. Our visit to Liberty Island would be restricted to the island itself.

When we got off the ferry, a line had quickly formed at the Crown Café. We weren't interested in dining on the island. We walked at a brisk pace past the café toward and made our way to the front of the statue. We stopped a few times along the railed sidewalk to get a few photos. One of the many birds gathered on the island's rocky seawall had a fresh catch in its bill.

As you face Lady Liberty, the Manhattan skyline is in the background. It really is quite stunning to see the 150-foot statue up close. We had viewed it from Liberty State Park on our walk with Holmes a week earlier, but now we were right there. Her right arm extended above her head with the torch lighting the way to the American Dream. There were so many people from around the world joining us in our admiration. I took photos of people from Vietnam and France. They, in turn, snapped a couple photos of us. Some selfies were also taken because we finished our lap around the statue. An image of "The New Colossus" sonnet inside the pedestal is displayed in the causeway behind the statue.

> "'Keep, ancient lands, your storied pomp!'" cries she
> With silent lips. 'Give me your tired, your poor,
> Your huddled masses yearning to breathe free,
> The wretched refuse of your teeming shore.
> Send these, the homeless, tempest-tost to me,
> I lift my lamp beside the golden door!'"

Instead of taking the ferry back to Jersey, we hopped on the Battery Park ferry to Manhattan. The World Trade Center site was our next stop and was a short walk away.

As soon as we entered the 9/11 Memorial and Museum and passed the last remaining trident support columns of the old World Trade Center, we were humbled. Just as it was on September 11th, 2001, the sky was a clear blue. Sunshine gleamed off the windows of the new One World Trade Center as we took an escalator down to the museum's main floor.

The recessed lobby is below ground level. A pair of reception desks are at the bottom of the escalators. A coat room and the restrooms are around the corner. Continue walking straight from the escalators and you find yourself in a hallway filled with voices. The words you hear are not of tourists but the real-life voices of the victims' families. Some tears were shed as we walked through the wood-floor corridor. Photos of the Twin Towers before and after the attacks are displayed side by side. Graffiti painted as tributes to first responders is prevalent on much of the debris inside the museum. One column in particular honors the 37 officers from the Port Authority Police Department and the 343 New York City firefighters who lost their lives that day. More could have died had the slurry wall collapsed. That wall, which reinforced the soft earth near the Hudson River, prevented a mass flooding in Manhattan. It is still intact and lures most museum visitors, including us.

We spent two hours inside the museum that occupies what was once the foundation for the World Trade Center towers. As the path takes you deeper, you walk past an American flag created from pictures of each victim's face. Across from the flag is a mangled iron beam from the South Tower. A portion of the antenna atop the North Tower is on display nearby. You can see the Vesey Street stairs, where hundreds of people escaped death by fleeing the building. The steps are now known as the "Survivors' Stairs."

But the one exhibit that stopped each of us in our tracks was a mangled FDNY truck. Patti immediately thought of her nephew, Kristopher, who is a fire chief in Illinois.

"It took my breath away. It was overwhelming," she later said. "That was so emotional, especially when I thought of Kris."

The truck from FDNY's Ladder Company 3 is in the bottom level of the museum and is one of the last things you'll see before the exit. Eleven of the company's firefighters were lost that day after leaving JFK Airport to respond to the North Tower. Most of the firemen killed were last known to be on the 35th floor when the building came down. The truck was parked on West Street and the rear of the vehicle took the brunt of the damage. The ladder was folded over a disintegrated back end. The rear wheels were gone. The front tires were shredded. Open storage compartment doors were charred. The cab was crushed. But the yellow block letters and white numeral that spell out "LADDER 3" on the side of the telescopic ladder are still clear, as is the image of the soaring bald eagle to the left of the "L" in "LADDER." The truck was lowered into the museum in 2011 and represents all of the FDNY casualties.

There really aren't any words or photos that can do the 9/11 Memorial and Museum justice. We would like to return and spend more than just a couple of hours there, but our schedule this day was tight. We were in a rush to get to the Met before it closed at 5:30. We should have had an hour at the Met. We had 15 minutes.

I did a search for which subway line to ride and which exit to take for the Met. We needed to get off at Lexington Avenue. Except, in my haste, I didn't realize there are three Lexington Avenue exits. The cross streets are important. Instead of getting off at Lexington and 77th with about a three-block walk to the art museum, I led us off the subway at 59th and Lexington. By the time I realized our mistake, it was too late. We were already in Central Park at the opposite end.

We didn't run, but it was a pretty fast walk through the park, with 5th Avenue running parallel to the park's pathway. We passed by the Central Park Zoo and The Lake before finally getting to the museum at 5. We had the New York City Pass but didn't need it.

"The museum closes in 15 minutes," a docent told us.

"We have 30 minutes. It's only 5. I thought the museum closed at 5:30," I replied.

"5:15," came a flat, matter-of-fact response.

Here's where you have to read carefully. Google lists the Met's hours as 10 a.m. to 5:30 p.m. But there is some fine print there that tells you security begins to clear the museum 15 minutes before closing. The Met's website, which I should have checked, lists the hours as 10 to 5:15. We had 15 minutes to see as much as we could inside one of the world's largest art museums.

Armless marble statue of Athena in the Great Hall. Cool. Up the stairs. Hey, look, a huge painting of a biblical scene. Nice. Let me get a photo of that. There are more Medieval and Renaissance paintings in the next room. There was no time to see who or what was depicted. Snap, a couple more photos for Facebook. Let's go down this hallway to the American Wing. Nope. Closed.

How about the other way toward the European sculptures? Nope. Time to go.

It was 5:13.

"We still have two minutes," I softly said in protest, knowing it would do no good. We joined the line of people being ushered out of the building. We were disappointed and irritated, more so by my subway mistake than anything.

Patti was upset. I was annoyed. We were both hungry. Our phones were about to die. We grabbed a quick bite from a street vendor and walked to the nearest subway station. We made it to Citi Field in plenty of time to see the first pitch.

· · · · ·

New Jersey is probably a fine state in which to live if you never want to leave New Jersey. There are beaches, large cities, and lovely parks. You don't even have to pump your own gas at the fuel pump. But if you do decide to leave New Jersey, there are exit fees.

Every highway out of the Garden State has a toll at the border. When you're driving an RV with a car in tow, those tolls can get expensive. When we left the RV park in Jersey City to head to Mystic, Connecticut, we had to pay $42 to cross the George Washington Bridge. The toll to cross the Delaware River into Philadelphia was $38. To make matters worse, even in 2018, all New Jersey toll booths were cash-only.

You don't pay to enter New Jersey, but they make you pay to leave. E-ZPass can save you money, but there really is no way to avoid the tolls.

When we did finally arrive in Mystic three hours later, we were delighted to be in an RV park that had grass and trees. We had our "urban camping" experiences in Philadelphia and Jersey City and now it was time to get back to nature. Holmes loved it. He wasn't too fond of the parking lots where we had spent the last week.

Mystic is pretty much the midway point between Boston and New York, about two hours each way (depending on traffic). Fenway Park was our next stadium, but we had to return to New York to see the Mets at Citi Field, so Mystic became our home for a week. It's also where we "broke up" with a family who had been our accidental travel companions. We met Toby and his Texas family in College Park, Maryland. They were living in their fifth-wheel fulltime while traveling and home-schooling their two children. Their son was 12 years old and their daughter might have been the most well-spoken 9-year-old I've ever met. They were then at the Campus Park and Ride in Philadelphia and joined us at the Liberty Harbor RV Park in Jersey City, Jersey. This was all coincidental. Our respective travel plans just happened to overlap, and it was nice to see a few familiar faces as we ventured into new places.

131

We spent a couple of days exploring Mystic, eating dinner one night at the famed Mystic Pizza, and ambling through the Seaport Museum. There is a fee to tour the large collection of 19th-century sailing ships and boats docked there. We passed on that but did visit the gift shop and art gallery. Mystic is a neat little port town with a history that dates back to the 1640s.

We didn't get to experience much of Mystic's history or visit its renowned aquarium. We did try to cram as much history as we could during a one-day trip to Boston on April 28th.

The Red Sox were playing host to the Rays at 4 p.m. That gave us most of the day to explore before heading to Fenway Park. We would even have some time after the game to do some more sightseeing. We thought about taking Holmes with us and getting a hotel for the night, but that would have been cost-prohibitive. Holmes has an iron bladder and can go 12 hours without feeling distressed. Still, we didn't want to be out too late. We left the RV park around 9 and were at the Brookline Village train station by 11.

Boston's T-line is the old subway system in the country, with sections dating back to 1897. The T has nine routes, — and another eight commuter rails, — that transport riders to different parts of the city. We used one of the four Green Line routes and soon found ourselves in downtown Boston. The day's itinerary was The Old North Church, Paul Revere's house, Boston Harbor, Red Sox game, Cheers bar. Easy, right?

Boston's Old Town looks how you'd expect it to look. Narrow, cobblestone streets are lined by tall, thin brick buildings. Brick sidewalks are usually crammed with tourists ducking in and out of the many shops that now occupy many of the 300-year-old homes.

The Old North Church is located at the north end of Old Town — just blocks from where the Charles and Mystic rivers meet Boston Harbor. To the west, across the Washington Street Bridge, is Paul Revere Park. A few blocks south of the church on Salem Street is Paul Revere's former home.

Though the oldest church in Boston, it is best-known for the role it played in the American Revolution. Revere ordered a pair of lanterns to be hung in the steeple to inform rebels of when and how British soldiers were arriving. "One if by land, two if by sea" is the line included in Henry Wadsworth Longfellow's poem, *Paul Revere's Ride*.

Patti and I walked up the stone streets and were able to walk right into the church. We could have paid $8 for a tour, but the only available times were later in the afternoon when we needed to be at Fenway. The church is open to the public and self-guided tours are allowed at no charge. Guided tours give customers access to the bell tower and crypt.

White boxes that resemble modern-day cubicles are on their side of the aisle, which leads to a modest altar. Each box has an L-shaped bench, hymnals, and missals. A gold cross sits on the altar. A paining of Jesus is directly behind the altar and is flanked by four tablets containing prayers. Colonial flags hang from columns that run from the second level to the vaulted ceiling, from which chandeliers hang. A large pipe organ adorns the balcony wall above the entrance. A bust of George Washington, regarded as a remarkably accurate likeness, rests in a concave section of the wall to the left of the altar. Plaques commemorating other presidential visits are scattered throughout the church. Episcopal services are still held every Sunday. Our visit was on a Saturday.

We could not have asked for better weather for our first visit to Boston. There wasn't a cloud in the sky and April 28th was the first day of the year with a high temperature of 70 degrees or above. The streets and sidewalks were both jammed with cars and people. Schools had groups of kids on Saturday field trips. Families from out of town joined the other tourists (like us) to see the varied historical sites Old Town had to offer. Patti and I explored the city wearing matching Dropkick Murphy's T-shirts we got at the band's concert in Charlotte on March 9th. Because neither of us are Red Sox fans, we figured that was one way to represent Boston at Fenway Park.

After leaving the church, we began our stroll through the Paul Revere Mall on our way to Revere's home. As Ben Franklin is in Philadelphia, Paul Revere is omnipresent in Boston. A statue of Revere atop a horse is at the opposite entrance of the park. But the most interesting thing we saw in the Revere Mall had nothing to do with history. A large turkey was perched on a wall behind the church gift shop, preening itself in the sun. The turkey had not a care in the world and ignored me and every other person who stopped to watch and take a few photos. I did manage to get a picture of the bird looking in my general direction. As random as this was to us, seeing wild turkeys in Boston is rather common for those who live there.

When we got to the Paul Revere House, we learned only cash was accepted to pay the modest admission fee. We didn't have any cash on us, but fortunately there was a CVS nearby. We got a couple bottles of water and some cash back with our debit card purchase. Back to the Revere House we went.

The two-story grey wooden home isn't anything spectacular. Revere lived simply with his wife and growing family. The house, built in 1680, was already 90 years old when Revere bought it. The silversmith (and amateur dentist) lived there for 30 years and wound up fathering 16 children – eight with his first wife, Sarah, and eight with Rachel Walker, whom he married after Sarah died giving birth to a daughter who also died less than a year later. Five of Revere's children never survived to adulthood.

The house is surrounded by a brick wall, broken only by the entrance to a brick-paved plaza. The wooden ticket hut matches the architectural style of the house.

The first floor of the home has the kitchen, dining room, and a living room. Two large bedrooms are upstairs. Each room is furnished to reflect the era. A walkway from the second floor was added to lead modern guests to a small museum that houses some of Revere's dental equipment. Stairs then take you to the gift shop before guiding you back into the plaza. The exit is at the same point of the entry.

Our Paul Revere tour of Boston was now over and we were now in search of a place to have lunch. While I'm not a huge fan of clam chowder, I did want to try some authentic New England "chowdah." A couple of women at the Old North Church suggested The Boston Sail Loft Café and Bar, which is right on the water. The chowder, served in a large coffee mug, was excellent. I was shocked at how much I liked it. We each ordered seafood entrees and after lunch, continued our walk along the harbor. Several yachts were docked in the marinas that line the harbor.

The Boston Tea Party Ships & Museum is located near the Congress Street bridge that spans the Bass River just before it dumps into the harbor. The bright red building has a small gift shop and houses Abigail's Tea Room, named after former First Lady Abigail Adams. A pair of ramps on the back end of the building lead to a wooden sailing ship, where patrons can re-enact the 1773 rebellious act of tossing bricks of tea into Boston Harbor. Five copper chafer urns are lined up in front of the windows that face the harbor. We had just eaten lunch, so we didn't order any of the available pastries, but Patti did get a cup of tea. Take that, England.

From there, it was back on the T and onto Fenway, which in itself is sort of a baseball museum as MLB's oldest ballpark. The atmosphere around Fenway Park is amazing. Rising above Lansdowne Street is the left-field wall affectionately known to baseball fans as the Green Monster. On the opposite side of the street is a row of bars and restaurants that are always packed before, during, and after Red Sox home games. The street is lined with vendors on either side as fans and tourists alike walk between. We got a pregame beverage at Loretta's Last Call at the end of the street, based on a recommendation we received. We maneuvered our way through the tight crowd to order a couple of drinks and found a spot to stand near the small stage, where live music was provided by two men and a woman plucking away at their guitars. Televisions above the bar aired the Red Sox pregame show. A few people complimented us on our Dropkick Murphy's shirts, which are white with green sleeves and a shamrock above the band's name.

We entered Fenway Park through Gate E off Lansdowne. Though our seats were down the left-field line, near the Monster, we stopped to catch a glimpse of the field from the right-field bleachers. One red seat in Section 42 marks the spot where a 502-foot home run hit by Ted Williams in 1946 landed. As we walked through the concourse, we passed a wall decorated with the various logos the Red Sox have used since the franchise was founded in 1901. Old newspaper clippings from championship seasons and images of the teams Hall of Fame players are also displayed throughout the stadium. There's a great sense of history at Fenway Park, which unquestionably lived up to our expectations.

Following Tampa Bay's surprising 12-6 spanking of the eventual World Series champions, our walking tour of Beantown continued. We wanted to see the *Cheers* bar, also known as the Bull & Finch Pub on Beacon Hill. We probably should have taken an Uber, but the two-mile walk allowed us to really see the houses, apartment buildings, and businesses along the Charles River.

Boston was a city in which we could see ourselves living. The *Cheers* bar itself is small and rather underwhelming. Memorabilia from the 1980s sitcom decorates the place and a gift shop separates the bar from the Hampshire House, a Boston mansion now a popular wedding venue. We crossed paths with a few wedding guests when entering the bar, where we had a couple of beers and shared an appetizer plate. A studio light track hangs above the bar. It was fun to imagine George Wendt as Norm sitting there next to John Ratzenberger's Cliff Clavin with Sam (Ted Danson), Coach (the late Nicholas Colasanto) and Woody (Woody Harrelson) serving drinks. Directly across from the bar is Boston Public Garden, which we walked through to get back on the

T-line so we could head back to Brookline. A 16-foot tall statue of George Washington is one of the many sculptures located within the 24-acre park.

The night was later than we had anticipated, but fortunately when we got back to Mystic around midnight, Holmes had not peed in the RV. But, boy, did he have a stream when we let him out. We made sure we would not leave him alone that long again.

. . . . .

Where in the hell is the entrance to the Hockey Hall of Fame? That was the question we kept asking each other after we got to the ornate building in downtown Toronto. A beautiful example of rococo architecture, the building was once home to the Bank of Montreal. Columns that run vertically up the façade are topped with fastidiously decorative capitals and separated by windows. When we visited on May 13th, each window was covered by banners of the 2017 Hall of Fame class that included Mark Recchi, Dave Andreychuk, Paul Kariya and Teemu Selanne.

The entrance to the Hockey Hall of Fame is not on the street level, despite a large door that faces the intersection of Yonge and Front streets. There are a few signs that direct you to the Hall's entrance, which is actually underground on the shopping concourse level of Brookfield Place. A statue of Gordie Howe, Mr. Hockey, stands just outside the entrance to greet visitors. Glass classes in the atrium contain the jerseys of that year's Hall of Fame class. Once through the turnstile, a video plays on a large television on the opposite wall. The NHL Legends video plays on a loop and highlights each Hall of Fame player and coach. As we walked in, a tribute to St. Louis Blues great Chris Pronger had just begun. As two people who became Blues fans while living in St. Louis, we thought that was quite special.

The Hockey Hall is a blast, and we wished we could have spent the entire day there. It opens at 10 a.m. and we got there shortly after. We were seeing the Blue Jays and Red Sox play at Rogers Centre with a 1 p.m. start. It would be our third and final time seeing the Red Sox play in 2018. This would be our second of three Blue Jays games. We had already seen them in Baltimore and would watch them again in Oakland.

We had less than three hours to explore the Hockey Hall, which is divided into different zones. The NHL zone is the largest, containing artifacts and memorabilia from some of the game's greats like Howe, Maurice Richard, Wayne Gretzky, Mario Lemieux and Bobby Orr. One of the high-lighted exhibits is a complete to-scale replica of the dressing room used by the Montreal Canadiens at the Montreal Forum. Sweaters of Habs legends Guy Lafleur, Jacques Plante, Jean Beliveau, Ken Dryden and Howie Morenz, hang in the stalls. The Canadiens played at the Forum from 1924 through 1996, and it's where the Habs won 22 of their 24 Stanley Cup championships. The walls of the replica locker room are adorned with por-traits of Montreal Hall of Famers and plaques that list the roster from each season the team called the Forum home.

We made a point to check out the displays honoring former Blues players like Gretzky, Pronger, Al MacInnis, Brett Hull, Bernie Federko and Brendan Shanahan. There is also a really neat case spotlighting Gretzky, who began his NHL career in Edmonton, and Oilers wunderkind Connor McDavid — the MVP of the 2016-17 season at the age of 20.

One of the coolest exhibits at the Hockey Hall of Fame is the Evolution of the Goalie Mask. It's subtitled "From Protection to Expression" and con-tains over 150 masks used between 1929, when Montreal Maroons goalkeeper Clint Benedict donned the first mask — and present day. Benedict wore a pro-tective mask after suffering a broken cheekbone. Once healed, he ditched the mask and it would be another 30 years before another goalie wore another. That goalie was Plante, who had also been hit in the face by a puck. More goalies began to wear the face-hugging fiberglass masks, and by the end of the 1960s, every netminder was behind a mask. The style of mask, popularized by horror icon Jason Voorhees of the *Friday the 13th* film series, was eventually dumped in favor of a helmet/cage combination. The helmet protects the entire head while the facemask-like cage gives the goalie more than just a couple of eyeholes through which to see the rink. A hard, plastic extension to protect the neck was added following a life-threatening injury to former Calgary Flames keeper Clint Malarchuk in 1989. The evolution of the masks did not stop there as goalies began to personalize their masks with elaborate decora-tions. Former New York Rangers goalie Henrik Lundqvist had the Statue of Liberty painted on his helmet. Marc-André Fleury wore a mask covered with the Pittsburgh Penguins logo and a small Stanley Cup image on the back to commemorate Pittsburgh's 2009 championship. Brent Johnson, who played for four NHL teams, would place Led Zeppelin graphics on his mask. Curtis

Joseph, whose nickname was "Cujo," had a snarling dog on his mask, alluding to the Stephen King novel and movie of the same name.

Some of the featured masks at the Hall of Fame exhibit are the bone mask worn by Vancouver Canucks goalie Dunc Wilson, the skull mask used in the 1986 movie, *Youngblood* (former Canucks keeper Gary Bromley wore a similar mask from 1978-81), and the crossed sabres helmet donned by former Buffalo goalie Gerry Desjardins.

A fun interactive area gives visitors the option to either play goalie or try to score. The two games are called "Shoot Out" and "Shut Out." The line for each was rather long, so I could only do one. I waited in line surrounded by members of a youth hockey team in town for a tournament. The shorter of the two lines was for the goalie simulator. You can choose the degree of difficulty; I selected the "rookie" level. NHL players skate toward the net on a screen displayed in front of you. Soft pucks are then fired through slits in the screen from the point where the shot is taken. I stopped five of the eight shots that came my way.

The one exhibit every visitor comes to see is the Great Hall, which is the room on the other side of that grand door that faces Yonge Street. The Great Hall is where you have the opportunity to see and touch the Stanley Cup, which I have always regarded as the best trophy in all of sports. Each of hockey's most prestigious trophies are kept under the 45-foot domed ceiling. The stained glass that adorns the ceiling adds reverence to the rotunda. The names of every player and coach to win the Stanley Cup are added to the trophy's rings. The trophy on display and awarded annually remains the same size as rings that have no more space to add rosters are removed. Those rings are then kept in a room adjacent to the Great Hall. The original Stanley Cup from 1892 is inside a glass case in this side room that is known as Lord Stanley's Vault. Patti and I stood in line to get our photo taken with the modern Cup. A trio of Canadian women were taking a lot of time to get multiple photos. Each woman by herself. One of all three taken by the Cup's on-duty caretaker. Then several shots with varied combinations of two of the women.

"Oh, come on," I mumbled to Patti as I rolled my eyes.

I think they sensed our annoyance and finally moved on. We were quick with our photos. I took a couple of the trophy itself and then we had one taken of us with the Cup — Patti wearing a long-sleeved blue T-shirt with Canada emblazoned across the chest and I in a teal Children's Hope Alliance T-shirt.

"That was cool," I said to Patti as we left the Hall, which had several signs to remind everyone 2018 was the 125th anniversary of the Stanley Cup. We were getting close to the first pitch, but Rogers Centre is just a 15-minute walk from the Hockey Hall of Fame. After exiting Brookfield Place, we walked past the Spirit of Hockey gift shop and "Our Game" statuary, which shows youthful hockey players smiling as they lean over the boards of an invisible rink. One player is straddling the wall as he prepares to take the ice.

We could not have asked for better weather on Mother's Day in Toronto. As we walked to the stadium, we spoke with a man named Chris, who was going to the game by himself so his kids could spend time with his wife on Mother's Day. We told Chris of our trip and gave him a card. We also had some Children's Hope Alliance items to give away and there were some folks in Toronto who went home that day with a new cup or a pair of sunglasses.

We knew we were lucky to see a May game at Rogers Centre with the roof open under a clear blue sky. Downtown Toronto is easily walkable no matter what you want to do, attend a Blue Jays game and the Hockey Hall of Fame like us, watch either the Raptors or Maple Leafs (or both) at Scotiabank Arena, stroll through Roundhouse Park outside of Rogers Centre, visit Ripley's Aquarium, or go up in the CN Tower, which rises beyond the right field wall of Rogers Centre.

The Mother's Day game was a sellout and we sat next to a pair of kind season-ticket holders in Section 214 to watch the Red Sox take the series with a 5-3 victory. The home teams were now 2-8.

. . . . .

Cleveland rocks. The city may get a bad rap, but it is indeed progressive with hip neighborhoods, a thriving restaurant scene, and quaint waterfront.

Prior to our June visit, neither of us had really thought of Cleveland as a destination spot. But it is. There are halls of fames, professional sports, a sprawling waterfront, and even a national park all within an hour of the city.

Definitely on the menu for a trip to Cleveland should be the Hall Pass, which gets you into the Pro Football Hall of Fame in Canton and the Rock & Roll Hall of Fame in Cleveland for one discounted price. The *A Game for Life* exhibit in Canton, which hologram Joe Namath narrates, contains great inspirational messages for children and adults. I may have had tears in my eyes (as did Patti).

Also inspiring is a visit to The Rock & Roll Hall of Fame, which will leave you feeling nostalgic and wanting to go listen to all the greats. There are so many things to see at the Rock Hall, it's almost overwhelming. Make sure you have multiple hours to spend and get through all six floors. It may sound daunting, but it is certainly doable.

We began June 2nd in Canton, where I had been two years earlier. As an NFL reporter, I traveled from Charlotte up Interstate 77 to Canton to cover the 2016 Pro Football Hall of Fame induction. Brett Favre's induction to the Hall made this a must for me. I was there for four days, most of which spent in Canton. I did head out to the Browns facility in Berea to do something on the upcoming season. I repeated that trip in 2018 when I checked out Browns minicamp and spoke with linebacker Christian Kirksey for my website.

Patti had never before been to the Pro Football Hall of Fame and that was something I wanted to remedy. She wasn't really excited about going to Canton but that changed when we walked past a banner with Brian Urlacher on it. The former Chicago Bears linebacker was part of the 2018 Hall of Fame class, along with former Washington Redskins and San Diego Chargers general manager Bobby Beathard, Houston Oilers linebacker Robert Brazile, former Philadelphia Eagles safety Brian Dawkins, legendary Packers guard Jerry Kramer, former Ravens linebacker Ray Lewis, and flamboyant wide receivers Randy Moss and Terrell Owens. We were a couple months early for the induction ceremony.

Urlacher became the 28th Hall of Famer to spend most or all of his career with the Bears. Kramer was Green Bay's 25th Hall of Famer. Patti, who is a lifelong Bears fan, made sure to point out the Bears had more Hall of Famers than any other NFL team.

As much as I was looking forward to Patti seeing the Hall of Fame for the first time, I was probably even more excited for my second-ever trip to Canton. When I went in August of 2016, it was induction weekend and there were people everywhere. The place was abuzz with activity. But when on June 2nd, 2018, it was relatively quiet. We parked the car in the adjacent McKinley High School parking lot and I hurried us to the Hall of Fame entrance.

"You were like a little kid going to Disneyland," Patti said of my excitement. "It was really cute.

"I enjoyed it, but I was not nearly excited as you were."

One of Patti's highlights, outside of the Urlacher locker displayed with the rest of the 2018 class, was seeing all of the Walter Payton memorabilia in the Hall. Payton, who starred for the Bears from 1975-87, was one of Patti's very players. She was 13 when the 1985 Bears won Super Bowl XX. He ran for over 1,500 yards that season and retired as the NFL's all-time leader in rushing yards. Before we left, Patti had a brand new Walter Payton, Number 34, Bears shirt.

The first exhibit you see after entering the Pro Football Hall of Fame is a massive card collection. Patti was among the majority of people who associated sports trading cards with baseball and was stunned to see an entire room dedicated to football cards.

A ramp lined with a mural of Hall of Famers then leads to a room that tells the origins of the National Football League. A statue of 1912 Olympic gold medalist and league founding father, Jim Thorpe, dominates the center of the rotunda.

The Pro Football Hall of Fame has more artifacts and league memorabilia than any other North American sports hall of fame. You could spend an entire day there and not see everything. We only explored for about three hours because we had to drive an hour north to see the Rock & Roll Hall of Fame later in the afternoon. I wanted to make sure we hit the highlights — the gallery of Super Bowl champions, the Lombardi Trophy, the display of Super Bowl rings and *A Game for Life* exhibit. It's amazing to see how the championship jewelry has evolved from trinkets of simple design to the gaudy diamond-studded rings of today.

A Game for Life is a must-see. You're led into a room lined with lockers filled with the jerseys of Thorpe, John Randle, Jim Brown, Merlin Olsen and Derrick Brooks among others. Rows of benches are in the center of the room. Screens are in the front of the room above a glass wall. Behind that wall is a "magic" chalkboard that comes to life when a hologram of former New York Jets quarterback, Joe Namath, walks out. Namath talks about the life lessons football can teach and introduces inspirational videos of Hall of Famers like Curtis Martin, Warren Moon, Jim Kelly, Steve Largent and Alan Page. Each man explains how they were able to overcome adversity and shape who they are, not just as players, but as men before eventually reaching the pinnacle of their profession. I had to wipe tears from my eyes more than once. Actors portraying famed coaches George Halas and Vince Lombardi are cast in holographic form to deliver motivational speeches. It's a 20-minute presentation that is included with the price of admission and well worth a wait in line. As wonderful as *A Game for Life* is, the hall's main attraction is the gallery that contains a bronze bust of every person inducted into the Pro Football Hall of Fame. I tried to get a photo of each Packers bust but missed a few. I only got 19 of them but did get the big guns like Lombardi, Brett Favre, Bart Starr, Reggie White and Curly Lambeau.

There are several interactive exhibits where you can put on football equipment or measure yourself against a former player. For the record, Hall of Fame running back, Marshall Faulk, is a normal-sized human being. Former Packers defensive lineman, Gilbert Brown, who weighed 350 pounds when he helped Green Bay win Super Bowl XXXI, is not. Small children could fit into the mold of his leg.

No matter which room you're in at the Pro Football Hall of Fame, you can count on seeing at least one quote from a player or coach. Two stood out to us as lessons anyone can apply to their own lives:

> "Football has taught me accountability — to be accountable to your teammates, your family, the fans and to yourself." — Seattle Seahawks Hall of Fame offensive tackle, Walter Jones

> "Success isn't owned, it's leased, and rent is due every day." — Houston Texans defensive end, J.J. Watt

The Pro Football Hall of Fame is a bucket-list item we were happy to add to our bucket-list trip to every MLB stadium. We were back in the car around 1 and hopped on I-77, which the Pro Football Hall overlooks. Because the Rock Hall didn't close until 9 p.m., we stopped to get lunch and were in downtown Cleveland around 3.

· · · · ·

Vincent Furnier was born in Detroit on February 4th, 1948. He was born into a family of Tigers fans. He attended games at old Tiger Stadium as a child and was 5 years old when future Hall of Famer Al Kaline, make his MLB debut. Kaline, an 18-year-old from Baltimore, had skipped the minors and entered the big leagues with much fanfare. Two years later, Kaline was selected to his first All-Star Game. There would be 17 more. Kaline quickly became a fan favorite and his legend grew every season. He was, and still is, beloved in Detroit. He was a hero for kids like Furnier, who attended his first game when he was 7 — his mouth agape upon seeing the green grass of Tiger Stadium for the first time.

Baseball was a passion for Furnier, but becoming a big-league player and perennial All-Star like Kaline was not in his future. He was a sickly child and his parents decided the dry, desert air would be best for their son. It worked. Furnier's health improved and he became active at his new Phoenix-area high school. He still followed the Tigers, who won the 1968 World Series with Kaline in right field.

Furnier ran cross-country and participated in track at Cortez High School, where he and three of his new teammates decided in 1964 to start a band. The group's first performance was the school's talent show. They were a hit and decided to become a "real" band. Only one of the quartets even knew how to play an instrument, but Furnier could sing. The Spiders recorded their first single a year later. A second song was recorded the next year and the band began to get local radio play. The Spiders started booking gigs as far as Los Angeles. They had achieved status as a real band. Furnier was their energetic front man and relished this new taste of fame. He wrote in his high school yearbook that he wanted to sell a million records. But as much as music was his darling, baseball was still his first love. He had once dreamed of being teammates with his childhood hero.

"If somebody had told me you have a choice of being a rock star or playing left field for the Tigers, there would not have been a choice at all," Cooper once told reporters. "I would have said, 'Where's my locker?'"

Baseball may not have been in the cards for Furnier but music was.

Vincent Furnier legally changed his name to Alice Cooper in 1975.

Cooper was inducted into the Rock & Roll Hall of Fame in 2011, along with his original band mates. Cooper has remained involved with the Hall, appearing to open a pinball exhibit in 2018 and recording some of his music memories in 2017 for a booth called "Say It Loud!" Patti and I each stepped into the booth during our visit to the Rock & Roll Hall of Fame. A video with

Cooper immediately begins as he welcomes visitors to the booth and explains its purpose. Fans can record memories of their favorite concerts or albums. You only get once chance to record, and it goes quickly. I talked about the first albums I ever owned — Terence Trent D'Arby, Tone Loc, Billy Idol, Michael Jackson, Public Enemy, N.W.A. and Guns N' Roses — and how they created my eclectic musical taste.

The Rock & Roll Hall of Fame is a monstrous building on the Lake Erie waterfront in downtown Cleveland. It sits in front of a short pier that leads to a lakefront restaurant and the quaint Voinovich Bicentennial Park. FirstEnergy Stadium, the home of the NFL's Browns, is separated from the Rock Hall by the Great Lakes Science Center. A U.S. Army Corps of Engineers building and the Coast Guard's Cleveland Harbor station are directly across 9th Street from the Hall's plaza. Six-foot red letters spell out, "Long Live Rock" in front of the Hall's glass pyramid entrance.

The Rock Hall is loaded with memorabilia from legendary musicians. Outfits worn by Michael Jackson, David Bowie, and Joan Jett, guitars used by Guns N' Roses, The Who, Soundgarden, and B.B. King, and hand-written lyrics and set lists from Prince, Jimi Hendrix, and Frank Zappa are among the Hall's massive collection of rock and roll treasures.

Hendrix's notes were on hotel stationary, which sort of puts visitors back to the place and time when he wrote them. Hendrix, The Beatles, The Rolling Stones, Michael Jackson and Elvis Presley are some of the artists who have their own sections in the Hall. One very large room is split in half between The Beatles and the Stones. The adjacent room is devoted to Hendrix. A couch from the living room in Hendrix's house is one of the items on display.

"It sort of humanizes this rock legend," Patti remarked.

Prince, who died April 21st, 2016, and Tom Petty, who died October 2nd, 2017, also had special displays. We were again in tears while watching the Power of Rock Experience, which ends with a video of Prince and Petty performing *While My Guitar Gently Weeps* with other artists. Petty sings the song, which ends with an epic guitar solo by Prince. A month later, Patti and I would be at Prince's former home outside of Minneapolis (keep reading).

Kurt Cobain's death certificate is displayed in the exhibit dedicated to 1990's grunge rock. There are retrospectives for cities that greatly influenced music — Seattle, Memphis, Detroit, London, San Francisco, Los Angeles, New York and of course, Cleveland.

The Legends of Rock exhibit includes items from James Brown, Diana Ross, the Allman Brothers, Blondie, Bruce Springsteen, and The Doors. The Rapper's Delight retrospective pays tribute to the rise of hip-hop and Hall of Fame members, like N.W.A., Public Enemy, Run DMC, Grandmaster Flash, Tupac Shakur, and the Beastie Boys. The Right Here, Right Now exhibit is not only named for the 1990 Jesus Jones song but is an homage to modern artists, like Bruno Mars, Katy Perry, Taylor Swift, the Arctic Monkeys and Cee Lo Green.

Each year's Hall of Fame class also gets its own exhibit on the third floor. For us, that meant we saw items belonging to Bon Jovi, The Cars, Dire Straits, The Moody Blues, Nina Simone and Sister Rosetta Tharpe. The 2019 class will have mementos from The Cure, Def Leppard, Radiohead, Janet Jackson, Stevie Nicks, Roxy Music and The Zombies.

Each floor of the Rock Hall is smaller as the pyramid nears its apex. The sixth floor consists of just one room that houses rotating exhibits. In 2018, it contained a tribute to music videos. A storyboard from A-Ha's *Take On Me* was one of the many items hanging on the wall. Televisions scattered throughout the room play videos, like Michael Jackson's *Billie Jean* and Paula Abdul's *Opposites Attract*. The "Mad Hatter" top hat worn by Tom Petty in the video for *Don't Come Around Here No More* was behind a glass case in the center of the room. Also displayed was the outfit Andre 3000 wore while shooting Outkast's video for *Hey Ya!*

Days could be spent at the Rock Hall without seeing everything. We saw as much as we could over five hours. By 8 p.m., we were hungry and headed to the Tremont neighborhood for a late dinner.

There aren't many things that can bring people together more than sports and music. They are two of my passions, and it was truly special to combine them into a single-day experience.

Long live rock... and the city of Cleveland.

· · · · ·

Berry Gordy was one of the first members of the Rock & Roll Hall of Fame when he was inducted as a non-performer in 1988 – seven years before the Hall even had a building. Gordy is the founder of Motown Records and helped spawn the careers of fellow Rock & Roll Hall of Famers like Marvin Gaye, Diana Ross and the Supremes, Michael Jackson, Stevie Wonder, The Temptations and Smokey Robinson and the Miracles.

Gordy also has his own museum in Detroit — The Motown Museum. Hitsville, U.S.A., as it's known, consists of two adjacent buildings. One was the Gordy family home, which contained a small studio on the ground floor. The other, which Gordy purchased after his fledgling record label outgrew the home studio, became the new administrative building and contained a larger state-of-the-art recording studio.

The entrance to the museum is through the original Gordy home, a two-story red brick building trimmed in white. The adjacent house is an architectural match but is solid white with blue trim to go with its solid blue door. The words, "Hitsville, U.S.A," and "I Am Motown" adorn the façade. A white gable embellishes the roofs of each building. There is only about a six-foot gap between the buildings, which are connected with a second-story walkway. A sign that designates the museum as a Michigan Historic Site in on the front lawn.

> "The 'Motown Sound' was created on this site from 1959 to 1972. The company was started with an $800 loan from the savings club of Bertha and Berry Gordy, Sr., family. Originally called Tamla Records, the company's first national release was *Money (That's What I Want)*, in August 1959. The founder, choosing a name that reflected the Motor City, coined the word 'Motown' for the company that was incorporated as the Motown Record Corporation on April 14th, 1960. That same year it produced its first gold record, *Shop Around*. In 1968 the company, which had grown from a family-oriented business to an international enterprise, moved its business operations to 2457 Woodward. Motown provided an opportunity for Detroit's inner-city youth to reach their full potential and become super stars."

There wasn't much of a crowd when we visited the museum on June 14th. We paid the $15 to enter and waited in the lobby before our tour guide began her spiel about Motown's origins. An hour-long tour followed as we were walked through 60 years of Detroit's musical history. The tour guide's words were augmented with the sounds of Michael Jackson, Smokey Robinson, Diana Ross, Lionel Richie and the Four Tops, among others. You can't help but to sing along. Dancing was encouraged by our vibrant tour guide.

The group that really helped launch Motown records was the Miracles. Smokey Robinson and Berry Gordy met in 1957 and instantly clicked. They collaborated on songs and *Shop Around* became Motown's first million-sales record. Robinson and Gordy were soon business partners as the singer became one of the growing label's executives.

The Motown Museum has among its collection the white, crystal-beaded glove worn by Michael Jackson during his *Thriller* tour. The glove was actually stolen in 1991 but recovered and returned to the museum in 2016. The glove is located in the center of a second-story room in the original home. The room is shaped like an "L" and one of the walls is a glass case filled with album covers. One that stood out was *Sugar 'n' Spice* by Martha Reeves and the Vandellas. It caught our eye because, days earlier, we had eaten breakfast at a Cincinnati restaurant of the same name and spelling.

There are no photos allowed inside the Motown Museum until you get to the end. The primary studio, in which hundreds of hit songs were recorded, is the last stop on the tour. Microphone stands are lined up against the back wall, behind a grand piano and drum set. Coiled cords dangle from hooks on two sides of the room. The wall near the door has a window to the control room. A larger window forms the fourth wall and allowed guests to watch the recording process. An hour earlier, we were on the other side of that tinted soundproof glass to watch a short video. We saw some folks dancing in the studio. It was our turn and we sang along and danced to *My Girl* by the Temptations. We were given one minute to take as many selfies and other photos as we could. We ended up getting two decent selfies.

The Motown Museum isn't polished or flashy; the video shown at the beginning of the tour was from the 1980s. The museum is, however, a wonderful look into a grass roots movement that changed the world of music.

Our tour had begun at 4:30 p.m., and by 5:45 — after perusing the gift shop — we were back in the car and headed to our next museum. The Detroit Institute of Arts had a particular exhibit I wanted to see.

· · · · ·

"Star Wars and the Power of Costume" was developed by the Smithsonian Institution Traveling Exhibition Service. It had previously been on display in Seattle, New York City, Denver, Cincinnati, and St. Petersburg. Its final stop was Detroit. When I realized we'd have the chance to see various items on loan from the Archives of Lucas Museum of Narrative Art, I started to geek out.

There aren't many more recognizable movie scores than the brilliant work John Williams composed for *Star Wars*. The main title theme can be identified by most with the first note. It's probably playing in your head right now. The score was played throughout the Power of Costume exhibit, with the main title theme coming through the speakers at the entrance.

The sprawling exhibit, which was displayed throughout several rooms on the second floor of the Detroit Institute of Arts (DIA), presented more than 60 original costumes from the first seven films of the Star Wars saga.

Each room has its own theme and isn't a chronological retelling of the Light Side versus the Dark Side. The exhibit instead focused on the creative process behind each costume and prop.

The first room was a circular space dedicated to the iconic lightsabers. Sith and Jedi knights are displayed side by side. Darth Maul, with his spiked read head and double-bladed lightsaber, stands on a podium in the center of the room. He is frozen in combat against four Jedi knights, one of whom is identified as Samuel L. Jackson's Mace Windu. Placards for each of the five characters describe the inspiration for their respective outfits. One display along the wall had a mannequin with outstretched arms covered with the dark robe belonging to the evil Emperor Palpatine. Even Palpatine's disgusting fingernails were on display. Standing across the room were effigies of Obi-Wan Kenobi and Anakin Skywalker dressed in the brown robes worn by Ewan McGregor and Jake Lloyd in *The Phantom Menace*. Because *Star Wars* creator, George Lucas, envisioned Obi-Wan Kenobi and the other Jedi as sort of warrior monks, he wanted their robes to reflect that.

In the next room were various outfits worn by the women of *Star Wars* — most notably Carrie Fisher as Princess Leia Organa and Natalie Portman as Padmé Amidala.

Portman's character goes through a significant transformation in the prequel trilogy. She was the Queen of Naboo and then a Senator before falling in love with Anakin and getting married in secret. As Anakin was lured to the Dark Side, Padmé became one of the leaders of the Rebel Alliance. Each step along her story arc is shown through the multiple gowns, headdresses, and disguises she wore. Padmé's headdresses were especially elaborate and their costume designers found their inspiration in Chinese, Mongolian and Russian culture.

After walking past four of Padmé's ornate gowns, we stepped into the droid room. A video of Anthony Daniels explaining how difficult it was to move in his C-3PO costume played on a loop. Daniels is the only actor to have appeared in each of the films in the series. The various pieces of the C-3PO outfit rested on a table covered by a glass bubble. A podium centered on the back wall has intact replicas of C-3PO, his sidekick, R2-D2, and rolling Resistance droid, BB-8.

Other rooms were dedicated to the uniforms worn by the stormtroopers and other Empire guards, whose garb was inspired by uniforms worn by Nazi soldiers in the 1940s, and the Rebel Alliance, who were dressed in uniforms resembling World War II-era British attire. We see Ewoks, Tusken raiders (Sand people), bounty hunters, and Imperial guards. Then there are the costumes of the main characters in the Star Wars saga, Luke, Leia, Han Solo, Chewbacca, Yoda and of course, Darth Vader.

Luke and Leia's costumes varied from film to film, although the budget was so tight for the first movie that Leia mostly wore the same white outfit. One Leia costume that stood out in the exhibit was the bikini she wore as Jabba The Hutt's slave in *Return of the Jedi.* The skimpy outfit was life-changing for a 9-year-old boy like me in 1983. Carrie Fisher was less fond of the outfit, calling it "the bikini from Hell."

Han Solo's vest and gun belt were inspired by Old West cowboys. Han's sidekick is, of course, Chewbacca, and it's hard to imagine the Wookiee as anything other than a creature resembling a Sasquatch. But early concept art had Chewie looking like some sort of werewolf with giant bat ears. The two are, of course, shown side by side against a backdrop of the Millennium Falcon jumping to lightspeed. Good thing the hyperdrive was functional.

The last thing you see before exiting the multi-room exhibit is Yoda. The Jedi master is posed with hands crossed at his waist under his robe. The pedestal on which he stands is surrounded by some of his most memorable quotes. "Do. Or do not. There is no try," is one of my favorites.

The exhibit's main attraction, however, was Vader. There is no more iconic movie villain, in my opinion, than Darth Vader. The imposing black costume famously worn by David Prowse and Hayden Christiansen was at the room's center. It was complete with the flowing cape and shimmering helmet. Another helmet was disassembled and on display behind a glass case against the wall. Vader's own theme music, the *Imperial March*, bellowed from the room's speakers. We also heard Vader's signature mechanical breathing and the baritone voice of James Earl Jones delivering some of the character's best lines: "No. I am your father. Search your feelings, you know it to be true." "The circle is now complete." "Be careful not to choke on your convictions." "I find your lack of faith disturbing."

The bad guys always get the best lines, don't they?

As much as I love Star Wars, the exhibit in Detroit was the only Star Wars experience on our trip. Almost every MLB team has a *Star Wars* night – May 4th is a popular one with the Braves, Reds, Royals, Brewers, Yankees, Mariners and Nationals all running a promotion that day in 2018. We did not attend a game on May 4th as we traveled through New England on our way to Canada. The schedule worked out for us to attend three "Bark in the Park" games but did not line up with any *Star Wars* promotions. Poor timing on my part, I guess, but at least the RV wasn't cluttered with *Star Wars* souvenirs at the end of the trip.

. . . . .

When a home run is hit by the home team at Target Field, the Prince song, *Let's Go Crazy* is played and Twins fans oblige. Prince was and still is beloved in the Twin Cities — a place where he was born and remained, even after achieving superstar status. He loved his hometown sports teams — especially the NBA's Timberwolves. Though it's simply a coincidence, it is rather fitting the NFL's Vikings have purple as their primary color.

After Prince's death on April 21st, 2016, the Twins paid tribute to the singer by turning the stadium into a purple palace. It rained in Minneapolis the day Prince died, fitting given his most famous song was "Purple Rain," and the Twins didn't even have a home game scheduled that day. The team held a free viewing of the *Purple Rain* movie at Target Field a day later. When the Twins returned home on April 25th, 2016 to play the Indians, every Minnesota player used a Prince song as his walk-up music. Outfielder Oswaldo Arcia went with, *I Would Die 4 U*. The Twins released seven white doves before the game and players wore purple wristbands during Minnesota's 4-3 win. The team played *Little Red Corvette* during the seventh-inning stretch for the remainder of the 2016 season.

Prince was one of several notable celebrity deaths in 2016 but was the only one that made me cry. I watched his memorable Super Bowl XLI halftime performance through watery eyes before heading into the office. Patti also gets emotional when thinking about Prince and his untimely death of an accidental overdose at the age of 57.

Even before Prince died, he had always envisioned Paisley Park becoming a museum. We paid a visit to Paisley Park on July 8th, 2018 before heading to Target Field to see the Twins beat the Orioles.

Paisley Park is an unassuming white building in the Minneapolis suburb of Chanhassen. Driving by the building, you might never guess it was home to multiple music studios, entertainment venues, and an impressive film studio. Did you know that some interior scenes from the 1993 comedy, *Grumpy Old Men*, were filmed there? We did not.

The tour is not cheap, setting us back $38 a pop, but is worth it — especially for Prince fans. Purchasing tickets ahead of time can save you some money. There are also VIP tours and options that include a live DJ dance party. We went with the basic 70-minute guided tour and were led through the complex where the multi-talented Prince once lived and worked.

Our visit to Paisley Park was a surreal experience that began even before we got out of the car.

My iPod is always on shuffle. I love music and have quite the eclectic taste. There are over 4,400 songs on my iPod from every music genre imaginable. I never know what's going to come next. It could go from Mozart to Snoop Dogg to Garth Brooks to Metallica to Nina Simone.

As we pulled into the parking lot off of Audubon Road in Chanhassen, Minnesota, the previous song ended. The next song was *Adore* – not exactly a Prince staple.

"You have got to be kidding me," I shouted, shocked that a Prince song would begin playing just as we were about to visit the late singer's home.

"Oh my God! How cool," Patti added before joking, "It's destiny, man."

Having a relatively obscure Prince song playing in my car as we parked in front of the place where Prince lived and worked could not have been more appropriate. Had I told people that *Purple Rain* or *Let's Go Crazy* was playing in my car, they probably would have looked at me like, "Yeah, sure," or, "Whatever. You probably played it on purpose." But this was a complete coincidence and we were amazed.

Paisley Park has very tight security and they go to great measures to ensure no photographs are taken inside the estate. A young woman greeted us at the door.

"Do you have a cell phone?" she asked.

"Yes," we both said.

"Take them out please and turn them off," came the command.

Disappointed, I hit the power button and started to put my phone back in my pocket.

"Sir, your phone's not off," the woman said.

I pulled my phone out, and sure enough, she was right. The screen was displaying the options, "Power off," "Restart," and "Emergency Mode."

"Oh, sorry. My bad," I said as I hit the power off button.

I had not even checked in on social media yet, something I really wanted to do, and tag our friend, Craig, back in Charlotte. He is a huge Prince fan and once even tried to sneak a peak at Paisley Park while Prince was still living there. But no go. Craig would have to wait until our tour was over to see us bragging about our visit to Paisley Park.

With our phones off, we stepped to the reception counter and were asked again to pull out our phones. We were each handed something called a Yondr pouch and instructed to place our phones inside of it.

"Seriously? Our phones are already off," I said softly to Patti.

Once secured inside the Yondr pouch, something I had never before heard of, the pouches were handed back to us and we were told they would be unlocked at the conclusion of the tour. The no-photos policy was in accordance with Prince's wishes. We got our phones back in the gift shop and took a couple of photos there; one was of us in front of the purple banner with his "Love Symbol" ⚲ draped on the wall near the exit. I was wearing a purple V-neck. I snapped another of a yellow guitar placed in front of a four-foot portrait of Prince with pearl beads hanging in front of his face and grasped in his hands.

Despite the nearly windowless façade of Paisley Park, the interior is elaborately decorated and there is Prince memorabilia hanging everywhere. The tour guide informed us that almost all of the decorations and memorabilia were placed in their current locations while Prince still lived and worked there. Prince did love him some Prince.

Prince didn't just live at Paisley Park, he worked there. The sprawling two-level building has multiple wings with administration offices and a pair of state-of-the-art recording studios. The large film studio wasn't just used for *Grumpy Old Men*. Several commercials and music videos were also filmed at Paisley Park Studios. Perhaps the most ambitious thing Prince ever did at his motion picture studio was shoot nearly the entirety of his 1987 self-directed concert movie, *Sign o' the Times*.

One of the last things you see on the tour is the cavernous film studio. As the doors open, you hear the opening chords to *Let's Go Crazy* with the words, "Dearly beloved, we are gathered here today to get through this thing called life…" The studio is filled with outfits worn by Prince and guitars he played. A few cars used in movies and videos are included in the collection. We were given about 15 minutes to explore the studio before exiting into a lobby outside of the gift shop.

More Prince memorabilia adorns the walls that contain enclosed shelves. A flat screen TV hangs on a wall between a pair of double doors on opposite ends. One leads to the gift shop, the other a quaint banquet hall that was set up to host a brunch later that day. Playing on the television is Prince's epic performance during halftime of Super Bowl XLI in Miami. Prince would not let a steady rain alter his plans. When told of the forecast beforehand, Prince shrugged it off and asked if they could make it rain harder. He, of course, played his iconic *Purple Rain* during the show, which is still regarded as perhaps the best Super Bowl halftime show ever.

Prince was a Minneapolis native who could have lived anywhere in the world but stayed home. One of the reasons he did was because he "wanted his creativity to remain pure." He didn't want to be pushed in certain directions or thrown off course in places like New York and Los Angeles. That was just one of the things we learned about Prince during our visit to his home. There were hand-written letters Prince wrote to himself for a press conference explaining why he changed his name back to Prince after using an unpronounceable symbol for years. He became "The Artist Formerly Known as Prince" in 1993, when he started using what he called a "Love Symbol" ⚧. The symbol's origin was out of a contract dispute with Warner Brothers because of creative differences. He wanted out of his contract with Warner Brothers and churned out five albums from 1994-96 to fulfill his contractual obligation. He signed with Arista Records in 1998 and dropped the symbol by taking back the Prince name in 2000.

When we left Paisley Park around 11:30 a.m., we hustled to the Mall of America to meet Patti's cousins, Shelley and Santiago. The four of us took the light rail to Target Field, where the Twins hit three home runs in a 10-1 victory over the Orioles and we heard *Let's Go Crazy* after each blast.

. . . . .

We may have spent the night in the Fargo Air Museum parking lot, but we couldn't go inside. It was closed that Monday and we left before it opened the next day. That doesn't mean we didn't see a museum in Fargo.

Yankees slugger, Roger Maris, was a Fargo native and there is a museum dedicated to him at the West Acres Shopping Center. The museum was born out of a breakfast meeting Maris and former Yankees teammate, Bill "Moose" Skowron, had with organizers of the 1983 American Legion World Series in Fargo. Bob Smith and Jim McLaughlin suggested creating a Maris Museum in Fargo, where the 1961 home run champion spent his formative years and attended Fargo Central High School. Maris agreed to a museum with a caveat: it had to be free.

"Put it in a place where people from all walks of life will see it and where they won't have to pay for it," he instructed.

The West Acres Shopping Center was chosen as the site for the museum, which opened June 23rd, 1984. The museum is essentially a long display case lining one of the mall's walkways. Standing in the middle of the walkway is a plaque erected by the Yankees on July 21st, 1984.

"Roger Eugene Maris
Against All Odds
In 1961, he became the only player to hit more than 60 home runs in a single season. In belated recognition of one of baseball's greatest achievements ever, his 61 in '61, the Yankees salute him as a great player and as author of one of the most remarkable chapters in the history of Major League Baseball."

The plaque was placed in the center of the large display that is a couple hundred feet long. Small banners numbered 1 through 61 line the top of the glass case. A timeline of Maris's career stretches the entire display, which is filled with a multitude of items from his career. The centerpiece is a portrait of Maris in his Yankees uniform. He's leaning on a bat with his right hand on the knob of the bat and his left hand on his hip. Two crowns identifying him as the "Home Run King" flank 16 bats displayed on a circular rack topped with eight of the home run balls he hit in 1961. There are spots for ten base-balls, but two of them were missing at the time of our visit. To either side of the crowns are glass shelves filled with various awards like his 1961 American League MVP trophy and 1960 Gold Glove.

Various newspaper clippings, magazine covers and baseball cards comple-ment the other memorabilia. One placard is composed of a baseball-card-like portrait with his bat resting over his left shoulder and his career stats listed to the left. That placard is among a huge collage of photos taken throughout his legendary career.

Maris's single-season home run record stood for 47 years until Cubs out-fielder Sammy Sosa and Cardinals first baseman Mark McGwire both eclipsed the mark in 1998. Sosa finished with 66 homers that year while McGwire blasted 70. Sosa hit 63 in 1999 with McGwire besting him again with 65 homers. Sosa smashed 64 homers in 2001 but was again second in baseball with Giants slugger Barry Bonds setting the all-time single-season mark of 73 home runs.

Because Sosa, McGwire and Bonds all played with the stigma of alleged steroid use, many fans still regard the 61 home runs Maris hit in 1961 as the pure single-season record. It remains one of baseball's most-hallowed numbers.

· · · · ·

Late in the 1800s, a crop palace race began in the Midwest. Several cities throughout the Great Plains constructed grain palaces, beginning in 1887. A Corn Palace propped up in Sioux City, Iowa; another in Gregory, South Dakota; a Grain Palace in Plankinton, South Dakota; and a Bluegrass Palace in Creston, Iowa. Mitchell, South Dakota was a town founded in 1879 and incorporated in 1883. It opened its Corn Palace in 1892 when the fledgling city had just 3,000 residents. Each grain palace built was erected with the purpose of promoting the town and its product while hopefully luring tourists to inject some revenue into other businesses. The one in Mitchell is the only one that remains.

The World's Only Corn Palace has become Mitchell's premier tourist at-traction, drawing about 500,000 annual visitors. We were among those in 2018 who wanted to see the uniquely designed corn murals on the building's exterior. The murals change from year to year using naturally colored corn and other grains and native grasses to make it "the agricultural show-place of the world."

The 2018 design was not yet complete when we were in town on July 10th. Two sides were complete, one depicting a church in a lightning storm and the other showing a farmer standing above some crops just sprouting from the soil.

With a pair of towers that flank the entrance and three elaborate Russian-style onion domes, the Corn Palace sort of resembles a mosque. The two Moorish minarets are more like totems that rise 70 feet above North Main Street. The middle dome, the largest of the three, is topped with a flag pole from which "Old Glory" waves. The two smaller domes are adorned with the flags of South Dakota and the city of Mitchell.

The words, "World's Only Corn Palace," stretch across the façade under the crowned dome. Three large arched bay windows are on the second level and face the street. Beneath those windows are two sets of double doors that lead to the lobby.

The Corn Palace abuts Mitchell City Hall and is an active multipurpose facility. Initially used as a fall festival gathering place, the Corn Palace is now home to the Dakota Wesleyan University Tigers and the Mitchell High School Kernels basketball teams. It was once regarded as the finest basketball arena in the upper Midwest area. It has also hosted various concerts, rodeos, and festivals over the years. The annual harvest festival is still held in late August every year. Former U.S. President Barack Obama held a rally at the Corn Palace during his inaugural campaign in 2008. When Patti and I visited in 2018, the basketball court was dotted with myriad stands as part of a community market. The walls above the court are also decorated with colored ears of corn. Western images of cowboys, bison, Native Americans, and Mt. Rushmore frame a large stage that was covered by a black curtain during our visit.

Free RV parking was available in a nearby lot and we spent about an hour inside the Corn Palace. We watched a short video explaining the history of the building before grabbing some lunch — corn on the cob, of course, and resuming the day's long drive from Fargo to Broken Bow, Nebraska. From there it would be onto Denver to see the Rockies take on the Diamondbacks for our final game before the All-Star break.

. . . . .

Like many MLB teams, the Seattle Mariners have a section of their stadium dedicated to the franchise's history. But the Mariners Hall of Fame is much more than Ken Griffey, Jr., Randy Johnson, Jay Buhner, Lou Piniella, Ichiro Suzuki or Edgar Martinez. It doubles as the Baseball Museum of the Pacific Northwest and tells the long history of professional baseball in the region. The "Celebration of a Rich Tradition" dates back to 1877 with a few roving teams. The Pacific Northwest League was founded in 1890 and featured teams from Seattle, Portland, Spokane, Tacoma, Butte, Helena and Victoria, British Columbia. The league was short-lived but laid the groundwork for the Pacific Coast League, which began in 1903 and is currently one of the three leagues that play at the Triple-A level. The Western International League was a Class B circuit that fed the PCL with franchises in Oregon, Washington, Idaho, and B.C. The WIL operated from 1923 until 1955, when the name was changed to the Northwest League — which still operates today as a Single-A league.

The Tacoma Rainiers are the only PCL team remaining and have been affiliated with the Mariners since 1995. Tacoma's first team was the Tigers, who began play in 1904 but ceased operations in 1951. The Rainiers were founded as the Tacoma Giants — affiliated with the San Francisco Giants — in 1960. The name has changed over the years, from the Cubs to Twins to Yankees to Tigers and even one season as the Tugs.

While the history of baseball in the Pacific Northwest is certainly interesting, the main attraction is the Mariners Hall of Fame. There are nine members of the Mariners Hall — Alvin Davis, Dave Niehaus, Jay Buhner, Edgar Martinez, Randy Johnson, Dan Wilson, former manager Lou Piniella, Ken Griffey, Jr., and Jamie Moyer. A surprising omission is Alex Rodriguez, who spent his first seven MLB seasons in Seattle and was the MLB batting champion in 1996. He hit .358 that season and was selected to the first of 14 All-Star games.

While Johnson and Martinez figure prominently in the Mariners Hall of Fame, the two most honored players are Griffey and Ichiro Suzuki, who will join the others in the team's Hall. There are multiple displays dedicated to the two, who spent the bulk of their Hall of Fame careers with the M's. Griffey has a pair of lockers that house three of his Number 24 jerseys, a Wheaties box with his image, a few bobbleheads, and several photographs to go with other items. Ichiro has his own glass display with a blown-up black-and-white photo serving as the backdrop. The display includes his jersey, more bobbleheads, a couple of magazine covers, and shoes, gloves, and wristbands he wore.

Ichiro also shares a display with Martinez. Griffey's number, as well as the Number 11 worn by Martinez, are the only two numbers retired by the Mariners, as well as the Number 42 retired by every MLB team to honor Jackie Robinson. Ichiro's playing days ended in 2018 and his Number 51 is sure to be retired someday soon by the Mariners.

During a time when home runs were being hit at a record pace, Ichiro slapped single after single over 18 MLB seasons. He was already a Japanese star when he made his MLB debut with the Mariners in 2001. He led the American League with 242 hits, 56 stolen bases, and a .350 batting average to be named AL Rookie of the Year and MVP. He went to his first of ten straight All-Star games and led the league in hits six more times. His best season was 2004, when he knocked 262 hits and batted .372, 32 points higher than the next qualified hitter. But the Mariners went 63-99 that season and Ichiro was not in contention for MVP. Ichiro spent three seasons with the Yankees and Marlins respectively before rejoining the Mariners in 2018. He retired at the age of 45 following the 2018 season and joined the Mariners front office. He played in just 15 games in 2018, but we were not in attendance for any of them.

Ichiro's MLB career ended with a .311 batting average and 3,089 hits, including 362 doubles, 96 triples, 117 home runs (15 was his season-high), and 509 stolen bases. He had 1,278 hits over nine seasons in Japan and his 4,367 career hits are the most by any professional baseball player. The Mariners require a two-year wait following the end of a player's career before inducting someone into their Hall of Fame. The National Baseball Hall of Fame has a five-year wait. Ichiro is a shoo-in for both in his first year of eligibility.

There are more than just the displays of each franchise great in the Mariners Hall of Fame. The area includes an interactive exhibit to call famous Mariners plays, test your Mariners knowledge with team trivia, or pretend your Griffey robbing someone of a home run by scaling the outfield wall. Patti did that in high heels and looked much better doing it than I. Pegs protrude from the wall and fans can step onto them to "climb" the wall to snare a ball attached with a cable in front of a panoramic photo of fans reaching for a souvenir.

Another great thing about the Mariners Hall of Fame is that it has its own bar with a huge selection of local beers. We grabbed a couple before rejoining our group in Section 109 but returned a couple innings later for a free beer. When we told the bartender at the Power Alley Bar of our trip and mission, he gave us a voucher to return for a complimentary brew. I thanked him and gave him a Home Run On Wheels card.

. . . . .

I thought it would be cool to see a couple of movie premieres while in Los Angeles. I knew it wouldn't be some huge blockbuster but maybe some independent film that strikes it big. We could say, "Yeah, we saw that movie premiere in L.A."

I found a pair of free tickets to a couple of premieres for films I had never heard of. I asked Patti if she wanted to go.

"Sure, what are the movies?" she asked.

I told her the titles, which prompted the question, "Who's in them?"

"I don't know any of the names, except one. Steve-O is in one," I said.

"I guess so," Patti acquiesced.

The first movie was at the Los Angeles Film School on Sunset Boulevard. It was a dark comedy and this was the one with Steve-O. I should have known something was amiss when there were no concessions available. The movie was not ready for public viewing. Everything was bad, the lighting, the sound, the dialogue, most of the acting. Then we found out there was no script and it was one long improv. It showed. There was no direction. It was the worst movie we had ever seen. Before it began, we had told the people sitting next to us about our trip. A couple of them were actresses in the film. I wish I had kept my mouth shut. We wanted to leave 20 minutes in but stuck around the entire 90 minutes and then felt captive during the awkward post-film Q & A session. A few people asked questions and most were complimentary in their preamble. They must have been relatives. I won't give the movie's title, to spare the filmmakers and actors any more embarrassment, but we learned our lesson. We would not attend the other premiere for which we had tickets.

We did see a movie that night, however. Patti and I had been clamoring to see a film at Grauman's Chinese Theatre in Hollywood. *Mission Impossible: Fallout* was playing. Say what you will about Tom Cruise, he may be a weirdo, but his films are almost always good. *Fallout* was no exception. It was action-packed, fun, intense, and had plenty of twists to keep us guessing. But the real treat was the theatre itself.

Fastidiously decorated inside and out, the Chinese Theatre is gorgeous. The iconic pagoda entrance on Sunset Boulevard is flanked by two stone Ming Dynasty guardian lions. Above the trio of decorative golden double doors is a 30-foot stone frieze of a Chinese dragon writhing toward the copper roof that towers 90 feet above Hollywood Boulevard. The entrance is edged with two coral red columns adorned with wrought iron masks.

The lobby serves as a mini-museum with outfits worn by Judy Garland in *The Wizard of Oz*, Grace Kelly in *To Catch A Thief*, and Vivian Leigh's green dress from *Gone with the Wind*. There was also the jacket worn by Arnold Schwarzenegger in *The Terminator* and the tablets from *The Ten Commandments* movie released in 1956. The main theatre, which underwent an IMAX conversion in 2013, is where we watched our movie.

Before the lights dimmed, Patti and I gawked at the brilliantly ornate ceiling. At the center of the 40-foot ceiling is a blue chandelier surrounded by crystal pendants in the middle of a massive wood starburst medallion. The beautiful walls and ceiling have been unaltered since the theatre opened in 1927. We were seeing the same carvings and paintings as those who attended the three Oscars ceremonies the theatre hosted in the 1940s. Following the movie, we took a few moments to once again marvel at the 932-seat theatre.

We had seen an early Saturday afternoon matinee, and when we exited the theatre through those gorgeous golden doors, we joined a horde of people in the forecourt. The throng was there to see the famous handprints and footprints of Hollywood stars. It's tough to get your own photo when everyone else is trying to do the same thing. I did learn that Gene Kelly had very small hands and feet. Patti and I sought out our own concrete prints. I took pictures of the *Harry Potter* block with the hand and footprints of Emma Watson and Daniel Radcliffe. Wands were included. I got Michael Jackson, Paul Newman and Joanne Woodward, Humphrey Bogart, Roy Rogers and his horse, Trigger, and Shirley Temple. Patti was much more productive with the prints of Norma Talmadge, George Clooney, Matt Damon, Clint Eastwood, Sylvester Stallone, Bing Crosby, Jack Benny, George Burns, Cecil B. DeMille, Cher, Sandra Bullock, Dwayne Johnson and of course, Tom Cruise, among others.

The mass of people sprawled onto the adjacent sidewalk, which was also crowded. The Hollywood Walk of Fame runs along 15 blocks of Hollywood Boulevard and three blocks of Vine Street. There are more than

2,600 five-pointed stars included, and I managed to get a photo of 28 of them as we walked back to the car. One star is actually not on the sidewalk but on a wall in front of an entrance to the mall that adjoins the Chinese Theatre. That star is of boxing great Muhammad Ali, who did not want his name stepped on. So while the names of Jackie Chan, Michael J. Fox, Cuba Gooding Jr., Nicole Kidman, Mike Myers, Susan Sarandon and Michael York were added to the sidewalk, Ali's star went on a wall near the Dolby Theatre.

It was about 5 p.m. when we returned to the car. I had the brilliant idea of going to the Griffith Observatory to watch the sunset. It was only five miles away. It took over an hour to get there.

Hollywood Boulevard was a cluster, so I took Franklin Avenue, which was also congested. Once we got across the Hollywood Freeway, traffic began to thin. Then I turned onto Fern Dell Drive, which becomes Western Canyon Road. Not only does Western Canyon twist and turn its way through the Hollywood Hills, but it is a very narrow road that results in traffic stopping to allow someone going the other way to navigate one of the many hairpin turns. Congestion is also the result of tourists driving slowly to gawk at the mansions that dot the hillside. We were not immune to that affliction. If we were able to see a street number, Patti Googled the address to see not only the value of the home, but if someone famous lived there. We didn't learn the names of any residents.

But the main reason for the traffic jam was a three-way stop at Observatory Road. Seemingly nobody could grasp the concept of one car goes, then another from the intersecting road and repeat. There was some foot traffic, causing even more confusion for drivers. When we finally turned onto Observatory Road, I stopped about 100 yards up the hill to park. We decided to walk up the rest of the way up Mount Hollywood. There is a nice wide hiking trail that leads to the observatory. The problem was Patti was wearing heels. They were short heels, but still heels, and not conducive to trekking up the side of a mountain. We got about halfway up and begrudgingly headed back to the car. When we finally made it to the pay lot in front of the observatory, the sun had already set. The L.A. lights now dominated the sky. We could see Dodger Stadium lit up in the distance. The Dodgers took a beating that night, losing 14-0 to the Astros. We were there three nights earlier when Yasmani Grandal's two-run homer in the bottom of the 10th inning lifted Los Angeles to a 6-4 win over my Brewers. Milwaukee got smacked the next night with a

21-5 shellacking. I was glad we picked the Wednesday game. I viewed Houston's rout of the Dodgers as karmic payback for the beating they gave the Brewers two nights earlier.

During the daylight, the Griffith Observatory offers a wonderful view of the Hollywood sign. But it was barely visible through the night sky, even with the city lights. We were surprised the sign itself wasn't illuminated. We could hear the faint sound of music from the Jackson Browne concert taking place down the hill at the nearby Greek Theatre.

The domed Griffith Observatory is one of the most recognizable buildings in Los Angeles. It has been a popular film location over the years with notable appearances in movies, like James Dean's *Rebel Without A Cause*, *The Terminator*, Jim Carrey's *Yes Man*, and of course, 2016's Oscar-nominated *La La Land* with Emma Stone and Ryan Gosling.

The observatory's lawn was packed with people standing in line to get a glimpse of Venus, Saturn, and Jupiter using one of the three outdoor telescopes. We bypassed those lines and made our way to the rooftop, where even more visitors were in line for the primary telescope. There was no way we were going to see the stars through the powerful lens. We took a few photos of the L.A. skyline, got a couple of selfies, and then went inside.

The observatory is much more than a few telescopes to see celestial bodies or a place to get a wonderful view of the San Fernando Valley. It's an expansive space and science museum.

I was enraptured by the Cosmic Connection timeline, which tracks the history of the universe from the Big Bang to present day. Significant events are marked by placards along the timeline, which is tracked using a variety of "celestial" jewelry. The "ribbon of time" is comprised of over 2,200 trinkets of stars, moons, and planets. The timeline winds down a long hall, taking visitors through the curtain of light, formation of the Milky Way galaxy, our solar system, and the first signs of life of Earth. The exhibit ends with a photograph of the footprint Neil Armstrong left on the moon in 1969 with the words, "He leaves behind a footprint. It's one small step across time and space." How infatuated was I with the timeline display? I stopped to read every placard and took 18 pictures that were posted to Facebook.

The hallway leads to the Leonard Nimoy Event Horizon Theater, which was empty and did not have a scheduled show during our visit. Just past the theater is a huge room displaying our solar system. The moon sits in one corner and is described as "Our closest neighbor in space." Each planet is mounted side-by-side on a wall. Infographics and videos are displayed beneath each to-scale planet. On the floor beneath each planet is a scale which tells you how much you would weigh on each planet. You'd be light as a feather on Pluto, Mars, or Mercury but heavier than an elephant on Jupiter.

The room's marble floor is even colored to resemble a night sky. Sitting on a bench at one end of the room, with his right leg crossed over his left, is a bronze sculpture of Albert Einstein. He is looking up at his right index finger, which he is holding about a foot in front of his face. Einstein's finger represents how much of the night sky you'd see with the naked eye compared to the "Big Picture" view you'd view with the observatory's powerful telescope. The wall to Einstein's right is filled with stars and galaxies from the known universe.

It would have been nice to see "The Big Picture" for ourselves, but that will have to be for a future visit. We also did not have enough time to enter the planetarium. I really wanted to see if we could dance on the ceiling like Sebastian and Mia — or Lionel Richie. We did have time to use one of the outdoor telescopes, waiting a brief while to gaze upon Saturn. The rings around the planet were easy to see thanks to the cloudless sky back here on Earth. The image was so clear, it didn't even seem real.

The exit from the Griffith Observatory was much easier than the trek up the hill. The Jackson Browne concert was still going strong when we passed the Greek Theatre. It was 10 p.m., and we had yet to eat dinner. We tried to avoid chain restaurants during our trip, so when I saw a place called "Rick's Drive In & Out," I stopped. The Astros' romp over the Dodgers was winding up. We ordered a couple of burgers as the postgame show aired. A couple walked in just as our food arrived at the table. The man and woman were each wearing Dodgers gear.

"Go to the game?" I asked.

"Yeah," the man said.

"That was rough, eh?" I said.

"Oh yeah, but we stayed to the end," he replied.

I then told him I'm a Brewers fan and we were at the game with Grandal's walkoff and that I was happy we didn't go to the Thursday night game. We both laughed, not realizing then that our two teams would meet in October with the World Series on the line.

. . . . .

The San Diego Padres were not expected to contend for a postseason berth in 2018 and they lived down to expectations. The Padres were the basement dwellers in the National League West with a record of 66-96. They were 46-71 on August 10th when we made our first visit to Petco Park. This was one of our favorite stadiums.

It was rather controversial when the Padres decided to leave the suburban Jack Murphy Stadium for a downtown ballpark. There were concerns of congestion, land, and a clear path for plans to the nearby airport. The Padres did it right, however, and have themselves one of the gems of Major League Baseball. It's easy to get to thanks to an efficient public transportation system and the stadium itself is gorgeous. Developers made the wise decision of incorporating the Western Metal Supply Company building into the left-field wall. The building was an original structure of downtown San Diego and now houses several bars and restaurants, including those with balcony and rooftop views, as well as the main team store. But also in the Western Metal Supply building are the Breitbard San Diego Sports Hall of Fame and the Padres Hall of Fame.

Patti and I entered Petco Park through the right-field gate, past a large number 19 sculpture that honors Padres great Tony Gwynn. We were on our way to the Park at the Park in center field for a pregame wine-tasting event. I chose games on August 10th and 11th because of the team's promotions those days. The Friday wine tasting included a stemless Padres wine glass and the next day was Patti's birthday and the Padres were giving out beach towels. Happy birthday, Patti.

Our route through the concourse took us into the Breitbard Hall of Fame, a walkway on the main level of the Western Metal Supply Co. building. We made a point to return but continued on past the Padres Hall of Fame and to the grassy knoll beyond the center-field wall. We went back to each area during our walkabout but also studied the halls of fame when we came back to the ballpark the next day. We again entered via the right-field gate, collected our beach towels, and headed toward the left-field corner.

Just outside the entrance to the Padres Hall of Fame is a large display that says "PADRES IN COOPERSTOWN." The exhibit features National Baseball Hall of Fame players who have spent time in the Padres organization.

There were 17 plaques on the wall in 2018, including that of St. Louis Cardinals great Ozzie Smith. The "Wizard of Oz" spent the first four seasons of his career with the Padres before he was traded to St. Louis in 1982. He then helped the Cardinals win the '82 World Series against the Brewers and was a defensive stalwart on Cardinals teams that captured National League pennants in 1985 and '87. Another Hall of Famer and former Padre who played in the 1982 World Series was Rollie Fingers, who was Milwaukee's closer from 1981-85. Fingers was the first relief pitcher to win both the Cy Young Award and MVP in the same season when he was awarded both in the strike-shortened 1981 season.

Also on that Cooperstown wall is Dave Winfield, who spent the first eight of his 22 MLB seasons with the Padres and was the first to wear a Padres cap in the National Baseball Hall of Fame when he was enshrined in 2001. The only other player wearing a Padres cap in the Baseball Hall of Fame is Tony Gwynn. He has his own spot in Petco Park's Cooperstown shrine. Gwynn's plaque is atop a blue pedestal that stands about ten feet in front of the wall. Gwynn, the only Hall of Fame player who spent his entire career with the Padres. After 20 seasons, he tops the Padres' career charts in nearly every offensive category. He's fifth in home runs, however, behind Nate Colbert, Adrian Gonzalez, Phil Nevin and Winfield.

To the right of the Cooperstown wall are the doors to the team hall of fame. The entrance is marked by grey bricks to offset the red-brick surrounding. Standing like monoliths in the center of the room are glass-encased tributes to Gwynn, Winfield, and Nate Colbert, pitchers Randy Jones and Trevor Hoffman, former manager Jack McKeon and others. We noticed one name we didn't expect. Ray Kroc. Yes, that Ray Kroc. The self-proclaimed McDonald's founder.

Patti and I had recently watched the movie, *The Founder*, in which Michael Keaton plays Kroc. After seeing how Kroc swindled the original McDonald's brothers out of millions, I swore off McDonald's forever. My McDonald's boycott was broken in April when we were in New York City. We needed to use a restroom late one night and McDonald's was the closest spot. The restrooms were for customers only, so we shared an order of fries and relieved our bladders before taking the subway from Manhattan back to the RV in Jersey City.

A couple from Minnesota joined us by the Kroc display. I asked them if they had seen the movie. He had not. She had. We agreed Kroc was awful. That said, he did found the Ronald McDonald House, a non-profit organization that provides free housing for parents close to medical facilities where their children are receiving treatment, and started the Kroc Foundation to support medical research. His wife, Joan, increased her charitable contributions following Kroc's death in 1984. Why is Ray Kroc in the Padres Hall of Fame? Without him, the team probably would have moved to Washington, D.C. in the 1970s. Kroc bought the club in 1974 and the franchise drew one million fans the next season for the first time ever. After he died, the Padres wore a special patch with Kroc's initials, RAK, on their jerseys as they played in their first World Series.

The most recent member of the Padres Hall of Fame was former general manager Kevin Towers, who was the architect of the 1998 team that won the NL pennant. Towers was only 56 when he died of thyroid cancer on January 30th, 2018. One of his best moves was acquiring slugger Greg Vaughn from the Brewers in 1996. I saw Vaughn play in person at Jack Murphy stadium in 1997, just before I was transferred from Camp Pendleton to Camp Lejeune, North Carolina. I was able to get his attention and shouted that I wished he was still in Milwaukee. He smiled, nodded, and gave me a thumbs up. Vaughn hit 50 home runs in 1998 to bolster a lineup that still had Gwynn batting in the leadoff spot. All-Star pitcher Kevin Brown was also a Towers acquisition and won 18 games with a career-best 257 strikeouts. Hoffman was the team's closer and saved 53 games, a career-best for a Hall of Fame reliever who retired in 2001 as the all-time saves leader with 601. That number was eventually passed by Yankees closer, Mariano Rivera, who retired in 2013 with 652 saves.

Hoffman is among several Padres also included in the Breitbard San Diego Sports Hall of Fame, which honors more than 140 people who either excelled athletically in San Diego or who are native San Diegans and achieved athletic fame elsewhere. It's named for Robert Breitbard, a native San Diegan who played football at San Diego State before coaching the Aztecs in 1945. "Mr. B" brought the NBA to San Diego in 1967 with the expansion Rockets and owned the team until the franchise moved to Houston in 1971. He also owned the San Diego Gulls of the defunct Western Hockey League. Breitbard laid the foundation of the San Diego Sports Hall of Fame when he founded the Breitbard Athletic Association in 1946 to honor local high school, amateur, and professional athletes. The San Diego Hall of Champions opened in historic Balboa Park in 1961. The San Diego Sports Hall's charter member was Harold "Brick" Muller, who starred for the University of California football team from 1920-22.

The Hall was moved to Petco Park in 2017. Hall of Fame broadcaster Dick Enberg was the master of ceremonies for the unveiling, which took place just months before he suffered a fatal heart attack at the age of 82.

Bronze plaques of San Diego sports stars line the walls that cut through the concourse level of the Western Metal Supply building. We noticed Muller in the top corner of one section. As a football fan and reporter, I was drawn to the plaques of Pro Football Hall of Famers Charlie Joiner, Dan Fouts, Lance Alworth, Ron Mix, Kellen Winslow, Junior Seau and LaDainian Tomlinson, who all starred for the Chargers. Seau was a San Diego native, as are fellow Hall of Famers Marshall Faulk, Marcus Allen and Terrell Davis, who went onto football stardom with other NFL teams.

Padres greats, like those in the team's Hall of Fame, are also included. Gwynn's glove and jersey are displayed beneath a mural of Ted Williams, Jones, Winfield, Gwynn and Hoffman. Bordering the mural are the plaques of White Sox great Floyd Robinson, journeyman pitcher David Wells (who threw a no-hitter for the Yankees in 1998), Hoffman and former MLB first baseman Tony Clark.

Breitbard's prize possession is the bat Williams used in 1941, when he hit .406. Williams was a San Diego native who went straight from Herbert Hoover High School to becoming a member of the original Padres team in 1936. Williams was just 17, the youngest player in the Pacific Coast League by four years, and hit .271 over 42 games in his first minor-league season. He led the Padres to a PCL title as an 18-year-old, hitting .291 with 23 home runs. Williams was a 19-time All-Star during an MLB career interrupted for three years because of his Marine Corps service during World War II.

Williams was added to the Padres Hall of Fame in 2016, along with the late Ken Caminiti. Williams may have played only two seasons for the Padres while they were a minor-league team, but his role in making San Diego a viable baseball market cannot be understated. The Padres joined MLB in 1969 and made World Series appearances in 1984 and 1998.

· · · · ·

San Diego is a city rich in history. We tried to see as much as we could before and after each game. It helped that the Old Town San Diego State Historic Park was only four miles from the RV park where we stayed. With a trolley stop just outside the park's entrance, Old Town became our hub to get to and from downtown San Diego.

Settled by pensioned soldiers in the early 1800s, Old Town had about 40 adobe houses and several garden plots by 1835. The population continued to grow as California gained its independence from Mexico in 1847 and was ushered into American statehood in 1850. Still standing in Old Town are San Diego county's first school, the Mason Street School that opened in 1865, and San Diego's first courthouse and city hall. Behind the small building that held both the courthouse and city hall was a single-person jail cell. The cell was locked, but Patti pretended to be locked up as I took a picture of her through the crisscrossed iron bars. Abutting the single-story courthouse museum is the three-story Colorado House, a hotel founded in 1851 that today houses the Wells Fargo Museum. The centerpiece of the museum, as is the case at the Wells Fargo Museum in Uptown Charlotte, is an old stagecoach.

Though posted signs clearly state, "Please Do Not Touch," several visitors, mostly grey-haired white men, couldn't resist poking at the tattered cushioned seats or running their hands down the wooden exterior painted red with gold trim and lettering. A mural of an old west landscape adorned the back wall of the museum, which is restricted to a small, ground-level room.

Old Town is a tourist trap chock full of souvenir stands, coffee shops, bars, and restaurants but does contain multiple adobe structures built in the 1830s. The most notable is La Casa de Estudillo, one of the oldest extant adobe mansions in California. The mansion served as a backdrop in Helen Hunt Jackson's story *Ramona*. We spent a couple hours exploring the area by foot, but chose the right time to leave as various buses arrived. Each was packed with visitors scheduled for a Saturday-afternoon guided tour. There is no admission to the park and self-guided tours are free. There is an Old Town Trolley that takes you around the district's historic sites, but we were taking the modern trolley south. As we waited on the platform, a middle-aged man began yelling at a group of teenagers standing on the other side of the tracks. The youngsters ignored him, but his chirping continued on the train. Lucky for us, he got in the same car we did. He ranted incoherently to nobody in particular. When the train made its first stop, he poked his head outside to yell at people walking by. He had to be told to either get off or put his head back inside so the doors could shut. He retreated back inside the car and his shouting continued.

"Will you shut the fuck up?!" an older man shouted. While purchasing our train tickets, I heard this man tell the clerk he was having a bad day. "Shut the fuck up already," he added.

The ranting man responded with his own cursing.

"I have medication I have to get home and don't need to hear your shouting on my way there," the older man said before repeating his order of silence.

The ranting man got off on the next exit. The man with the medication exited at the next stop. With both men gone, Patti and I shared glances with the other remaining passengers. Each look had the same meaning, "What the hell was that?" All we could do was laugh at the incident.

When we took the train from Old Town on Friday, we went right to Petco Park. But our first Saturday stop was Seaport Village. Here is a collection of shops and restaurants right on the water. We had a pregame dinner reservation at The Fish Market, a seafood restaurant recommended by my sister, Faith. It could not have been better in terms of food and location.

The restaurant is in the shadows of the U.S.S. Midway aircraft carrier. Now a floating museum complete with its own restaurant, the Fantail Café, the Midway towers over everything else in the harbor. Tours are available and you could spend all day exploring the ship. We didn't have all day and decided not to purchase tickets to rush through in less than an hour. Just outside The Fish Market are two other popular attractions, the 25-foot "Unconditional Surrender/Embrace Peace" statue and the Bob Hope Memorial.

"Unconditional Surrender" depicts the famous scene caught by a photographer of a sailor kissing a nurse on his return from World War II. Patti and I were among the many visitors to have our picture taken in front of the statue. We tried out a couple of poses to replicate the statue's embracing muses. A few steps away is the Bob Hope Memorial, a circular, open-air court with 15 life-sized bronze statues of soldiers gathered to watch one of Hope's USO shows. At the center of the plaza is a bronze likeness of the famous comedian standing behind a microphone while some of Hope's best one-liners play on speakers that surround the piazza. Also in the park with a view of the Midway are memorials dedicated to members of the armed forces who lost their lives during World War II.

Up the shore from the Midway is the Maritime Museum of San Diego, which has a world-class collection of historic vessels including sailing ships, steam-powered boats, and submarines. The featured ship is the Star of India, which first set sail in 1863, is the world's oldest active sailing ship. We took a few photos from the adjacent sidewalk, but again, did not have the time to explore the ships themselves.

While I lived in San Diego County for five years, Patti had never before been there and wanted to see more than some statues and the exterior of old ships. After searching through several pamphlets at an information kiosk, we opted for the San Diego City Lights Tour after the game. With the Padres game starting at 5:40 and the tour beginning around 8, we knew we'd have to leave the stadium early. Because it was our second game at Petco Park, we figured that was acceptable.

The Padres offer a free ice cream sundae to anyone celebrating their birthday, and Patti had to take advantage of that freebie before we left. As she waited in line, I spoke to others at the concessions stand. They learned of the Home Run On Wheels trip and mission and a few cards were handed out. One conversation was interrupted by a roar from the crowd. Phillies second baseman César Hernández smacked a solo homer to the right-field corner. This is where we were just sitting. I sprinted to our section only to find out that Hernandez's homer landed one section over. Relieved I didn't miss out on getting my first home run ball, I went back to the ice cream line.

"The next section over," I said to Patti when she noticed me.

"Ah," she said with a bob of her head.

The Phillies added another run in the inning to take a 5-0 lead. Patti had her sundae, served in a miniature Padres helmet that we would later give to Celeste, and it was time to go. The Padres added a run in the seventh, but the Phillies avenged Friday's 2-0 loss with a 5-1 victory. The Padres took the series with a 9-3 win on Sunday. The home teams were now 16-14 on our trip.

The City Lights tour left from Seaport Village and took us through the historic Gaslamp Quarter, with bars and restaurants that were congested on a Saturday night, and then to Coronado Island. Coronado has a large Naval base but is really an affluent resort city. Coronado Beach is considered one of the best along the Pacific Coast. There would be no nighttime beach visit for us, however. When the trolley arrived at the ferry landing, we were given 30 minutes to search the multitude of shops or just admire the view of downtown San Diego across the bay. Our 30-minute break was extended once an unexpected fireworks display began. Our tour guide decided to wait until the show was over before leaving.

"Did you arrange that for my birthday?" Patti jokingly asked me.

"Sure," I said. "Yeah, exactly. Let's go with that."

As we watched the fireworks display, the tour guide did a head count. We had somehow added a person.

"Excuse me," our guide said. "This is the City Lights trolley and will return to Seaport Village. If you did not pay to be on this tour and don't want to wind up at Seaport Village, you need to exit."

Nobody moved.

He repeated this twice more before leaving. Once the trolley jerked into motion, an inebriated blonde woman, about 30 years old, stood up.

"Stop," she yelled.

The driver obliged and our stowaway exited.

. . . . .

Before Patti enrolled at Bradley University as a music major and transferred to Illinois State with her major changed to information technology, she had dreamed of working for NASA. Space exploration has always fascinated my wife, which is why a trip to the Johnson Space Center in Houston was a must. She was disappointed we didn't have the chance to visit the Kennedy Space Center at Cape Canaveral while we were in Florida. She let me hear it, too, and I definitely didn't want to argue about it in Texas.

The Johnson Space Center is NASA's primary hub and has worked its way into popular culture because of the phrase, "Houston, we have a problem," uttered during the problem-filled Apollo 13 mission in 1970. Sitting in the Mission Control room where those words were first heard through a radio box still sitting on the control panel is rather surreal.

None of the scenes for the 1995 movie, *Apollo 13*, were filmed in Houston, even though director Ron Howard wanted it to be as authentic as possible. But many people inside that room in 1970 were smokers, but the Mission Control building in Houston no longer allows smoking. So those scenes were created in a Hollywood studio, but some Mission Control scenes for the 2000 movie, *Space Cowboys*, were actually filmed at the Johnson Space Center in Houston.

Mission Control is one of the last things you see on the tram tour that takes you around the sprawling campus. The space center was a good 45-minute drive from our Houston RV park, which was closer to Sugar Land than down-town Houston. We really wanted to see a Sugar Land Skeeters game but didn't have time to visit the minor-league park.

As we traveled east on Highway 288 before taking Interstate 45 South, Patti remarked upon the Houston landscape.

"There isn't much to see," she said. "Just a bunch of shopping centers."

She's not wrong. Traveling on the freeways in the Houston suburbs isn't exactly a scenic drive, and even after we crossed over Clear Creek and entered Nassau Bay, the highway was still lined with businesses ranging from bars and restaurants to miniature golf courses and hotels.

Greeting us as we turned onto Saturn Lane were a pair of small jets, off-white with blue stripes running up either side, and the NASA logo on the rudder and angled at 45 degrees. Behind them, a small white space capsule. Outside of the entrance to the museum is the Space Shuttle Independence piggy-backed on the back of a modified Boeing airliner.

It's amazing to think of the engineering that went into making that aircraft into a piggy-back jet for a space shuttle. All the guts were removed to lighten it and the fuselage was reinforced so it could support the weight of the shuttle. We were able to tour both the jet and shuttle. Patti was like a kid in a candy store.

"I love space stuff," Patti said, being purposefully non-specific. "I considered going into aeronautical engineering, but I ended up not doing that, obviously. I just really enjoy the science aspect of it. I can't imagine getting into some of those space capsules."

The capsules are ubiquitous inside the museum. There are the original single-man capsules used by Alan Shepard and John Glenn, two-man capsules that had hatches capable of opening to allow "space walking," and the three-man Apollo capsules. Each provided little room for the astronauts to move. They are shown in chronological order, some mounted on walls, other hanging from the ceiling. A faux starry night surrounds you on the walls and ceiling and you walk through the darkened halls.

A diorama of the first moon landing is beyond the Apollo 17 command module.

"So this is where they filmed the moon landing," I joked to anyone within ear shot. Patti groaned, her usual response to my frequent bad jokes.

Apollo 17 was the last of the Apollo missions, lasting from December 7-19, 1972. It is the last manned spacecraft to have traveled to the moon. Commander Eugene Cernan was the last man to walk on the moon and said, "We leave as we came, and God willing, as we shall return: with peace and hope for all mankind."

We have not been back to the moon, though space exploration did continue. The Johnson Space Center houses a replica space station, allowing visitors to see the areas where the astronauts work, eat, sleep, bathe, and relieve themselves. "Floating" mannequins are mounted to the bulkheads. After taking a gander inside the piggy-backed shuttle, we got a couple of drinks in our NASA souvenir cups and stood in line for the tram.

Nobody likes to wait in line, but it does allow you to meet people. We spoke with foreign visitors from Japan, a pair of University of Florida students, France, Germany. A couple from Texas was in front of us and there was another family from North Carolina, the patriarch wearing a University of North Carolina T-shirt. It was September 1ˢᵗ, the first full Saturday of the 2018 college football season. Maryland upset Texas, which did not please the Texas folks. I told the UNC fan that East Carolina would beat the Tar Heels the following week.

"We'll see," he said with an optimistic, almost sarcastic, grin. My Pirates won just three games in 2018 but did hand the Tar Heels a 41-19 spanking on September 8ᵗʰ. North Carolina won only two games in 2018, and both teams fired their head coaches following the season.

The tram is equipped with a speaker system and our guide gave a brief overview of NASA history before pointing out various things on the Houston campus. There is a working longhorn farm at the Johnson Space Center and the cattle graze the undeveloped acres adjacent to the campus.

Outside of Mission Control, the coolest thing about the tram tour is the stop it makes at Rocket Park. Outside a huge rectangular warehouse are a pair of vertical rockets and unattached thrusters. The Little Joe II rocket launched in 1966 as an unmanned craft with a dummy payload to test the viability of the rockets used for the Apollo missions. The larger Mercury Redstone 2 launched in 1961 with a chimpanzee named Ham aboard. Ham was the first primate launched into space by the United States. The Redstone rocket is towering at 83 feet, red letters spelling out "United States" running vertically down the white exterior. But the Mercury rocket is miniscule compared to the rocket inside the building.

Just one rocket is inside the huge structure, the 363-foot long Saturn V. Displayed horizontally, Saturn V is broken into sections to allow visitors a glance inside one of the most impressive rockets NASA ever built. Saturn V was a powerful, heavy-lift vehicle that was used for several Apollo missions during the 1960s and '70s. It also launched the Skylab space station into orbit in 1973. The Saturn V remains the most powerful rocket ever built and was launched 13 times from 1967 to 1973. It launched eight missions to the moon, with six of landing on the surface. The rocket is so large that trying to get the entire thing into a single photo was difficult. It has five huge thrusters at the rear. Another set of thrusters, five J-2 Rocketdyne engines, are at the end of a middle section and helps the rocket escape the planet's orbit as the other sections detach and fall back to Earth. The sections of Saturn V were not re-used but rebuilt for each mission. The names and photos of each astronaut carried into space by Saturn V are posted on the wall opposite the entrance. It's an impressive engineering feat, especially when you consider there was a single loss of life or payload in 13 launches.

Rocket Park was the last stop on the tram tour. After returning to the main museum building, Patti and I refilled our drinks and checked out the gift shop. While Patti selected a T-shirt, I began chatting with a rather tall gentleman wearing Houston Texans sweatpants.

"You a Texans fan?" I asked.

"No. Player," he said, confirming my suspicion.

"Oh, really? What's your name?" I asked.

He was Jevoni Robinson, who played basketball at North Carolina State before spending a brief time playing professionally in Europe. The 6-foot-7 Charlotte native was attempting to make it as a pro football player but got injured during training camp and had just been released with an injury settlement. I told him I was an NFL reporter, used to live in Charlotte, and went to college at East Carolina. We shared a couple of friendly jabs at each other's university. N.C. State whipped ECU in the 2018 finale, 58-3. He asked what I was doing in Houston and I told him of our trip and mission and handed him a card.

I never expected to run into a professional athlete at the Johnson Space Center. It's amazing who you meet along the way.

After leaving the NASA center, we headed toward downtown Houston for dinner. This was really the only time we walked around downtown Houston. We strolled past the Harris County Courthouse, which is a six-story building that opened in 1910, and was added to the National Register of Historic Places in 1981. Bold letters spelling out Harris County line granite blocks that border the sidewalk. Its neo-classical architecture is topped with a clerestory drum and dome. The 1910 courthouse occupies an entire city block with a more modern courthouse and other Harris County offices across the street. Because it was Saturday, we were unable to go inside the courthouse. We decided to satisfy our hunger by grabbing dinner at Jackson Street Barbecue, which is a next-door neighbor of Minute Maid Park. We were hoping my brother in San Antonio would join us, but he didn't get to town until the next day.

We knew we'd eat well in Houston and we did with some of the most tender beef we've ever had in a fajita and excellent barbecue at Jackson Street. But if there is one city most identified by barbecue, it's Kansas City. The slow-cooked meat we had at Joe's KC on the Kansas side of the border did not disappoint.

· · · · ·

We checked into our RV park in Merriam, Kansas during the early-afternoon hours of September 9th. It was a Sunday and relatively quiet, despite construction equipment along the narrow road. The RV park was less than a mile off the Interstate 35, and I was a seasoned driver by now, so the orange-lined street wasn't difficult to navigate. Knowing we'd be arriving early enough to see some of Kansas City, we planned on taking a tour of Boulevard Brewing Company. The brewery is just blocks from the Kansas-Missouri border and the tour is excellent. For five dollars each, we got an intimate experience with just three other people on the tour with us. The tour began with a small glass of a beer of our choosing and ended with a trio of samples in the tasting room. In between was an entertaining and informative history lesson on the brewery's origins in 1989 and growth into one of the nation's largest craft breweries.

One of the people on the tour with us plays violin for the Kansas City Symphony and offered us tickets to their next performance after learning of our trip. Unfortunately for us, it was a Tuesday show and we were going to the Royals game that night. We had to pass.

After the brewery tour, we headed to Joe's, which is housed inside a gas station. The convenience store and restaurant are separated by a few booths. Joe's has its own entrance and a walk-up counter to order. The restaurant was full on a Sunday evening, but we didn't have to wait too long. We watched the Chiefs complete a 38-28 win over the Chargers in their NFL season opener. Had that game been in Kansas City instead of Los Angeles, we would have made plans to attend. Arrowhead Stadium is a venue neither of us had visited and remains on our bucket list. When the Packers later completed an improbable comeback to beat the Bears, a game we watched back at the RV, Patti was not pleased. It's tough living in a split sports household.

Kansas City is a pretty cool town, and we wished we could have spent more time there. One of the highlights of our short stay was the Negro Leagues Baseball Museum. No baseball trip would have been complete without a visit there. The Negro Leagues museum shares a building with the American Jazz Museum in Kansas City's 18th and Vine district. One combo ticket for both museums was a modest $15.

Founded in 1990, the museum features multimedia displays, hundreds of photographs, and various statues of the great players who paved the way for Jackie Robinson to break baseball's color barrier in 1947. Some of the greats who have their own exhibits are Satchel Paige, Buck O'Neil, and Rube Foster. All three are among those inducted into the Baseball Hall of Fame and the Negro Leagues museum includes lockers for each former Negro Leagues player who is enshrined in Cooperstown. Each player's jersey hangs in the locker, which is stuffed with memorabilia and other items they wore during their respective careers, both in the Negro Leagues and at the MLB level.

Photographs, infographics, newspaper clippings, and placards with quotes dot the walls, alongside the names of bygone franchises. Many Negro leagues teams used the monikers of MLB teams in their respective cities and simply added the word, "Black," before it. There were the Black Yankees, Black Giants, Black Sox, and Black Senators. There were other variations of Giants, Cubs, Sox and Tigers. Another popular team designation was Stars, with at least 19 teams scattered across the country using the nickname. Kansas City's team was the Monarchs, for whom Hall of Famers Ernie Banks, James "Cool Papa" Bell, Hilton Smith and Norman "Turkey" Stearnes played.

Once inside the museum, one of the first things you see is a statue of O'Neil standing near a bench made of baseball bats with three bases serving as cushions. The back of the bench is comprised of eight bats with the names of Buck Leonard, Paige, Bell, Oscar Charleston, John Henry "Pop" Lloyd, Martin Dihigo, Josh Gibson and O'Neil from left to right. O'Neil's name is the one closest to his bronze effigy. His left leg is raised as his foot rests on the ledge of a short wall. He's peering through a chicken-wire fence at a replica field. Life-sized statues of Negro Leagues legends fill the diamond. Dihigo is up to bat with Gibson behind the plate. Gibson is said to have hit 80 home runs in a single season. Here he's crouched behind the plate, awaiting a strike from Paige on the mound. Leonard is at first with Lloyd, Judy Johnson and Ran Dandridge going around the horn to complete the infield. The outfield, from left to right, is Bell, Charleston and Leon Day. On the other side of the right-field wall is another statue. This one shows Foster, who founded the first Negro National League, in a suit and cap with a cane in his right hand. Behind Foster is a timeline showing when the first league began play in 1920 to when the final Negro game was played in 1966.

The timeline isn't just about baseball but also the civil rights struggle African-American citizens faced. A theater just past the O'Neil statue shows a short video detailing the plight of early black players and the racism they faced. The 15-minute video titled, *They Were All Stars*, is narrated by legendary actor James Earl Jones. Because I'm a softy, I was tearing up by the time I left the theater's bleacher seating.

White baseball players long resisted black players joining their ranks until media pressure finally led to Robinson and Larry Doby joining MLB teams in 1947. Hall of Famer Cap Anson was done playing in 1897 and died in 1922 but was one of the most vocal opponents of black players. He's shown in his Chicago White Stocking uniform, posed with a bat and a curled, black handlebar moustache above his lip. Next to the image are placards detailing his refusal to play exhibition games against teams with "dark-skinned" players.

When you think about the diversity of professional sports today, it's hard to imagine that type of intolerance existed through 1959 when the Boston Red Sox were the last MLB team to integrate.

Paige has his own wall, and rightfully so. He was already a five-time Negro League All-Star before making his debut with the Indians in 1948 at the age of 42. He went 6-1 in seven starts that season and recorded two shutouts to help the Indians win the World Series. Paige had a 28-31 record over five MLB seasons but was an All-Star in his final two years after he had turned 45. Twelve years after his initial retirement in 1953, Paige returned to MLB and pitched three innings for the Kansas City Athletics. He was 59 years old, but surrendered just one hit and zero runs in a 5-2 loss.

O'Neil, whose adjacent exhibit includes the Presidential Medal of Freedom he received from George W. Bush in 2006, was a longtime friend of Paige. He said in Ken Burns' 1994 *Baseball* documentary that Paige once faced Yankees great Babe Ruth, who hammered a 500-foot home run. Paige was so shocked by the towering blast, he met Ruth at home plate to shake his hand. O'Neil's account is refuted by Paige's own words, saying in a 1948 book that the biggest disappointment of his career was that he never faced Ruth.

"I wish I had a time machine to go back and watch Satchel Paige pitch," I told Patti. "He was an unbelievable talent, arguably the greatest pitcher of all time. If I had a time machine, that's what I'd do. Number one, kill Hitler, and two, go watch Satchel Paige."

Patti and I spent so much time in the Negro Leagues Museum that we had to speed through the Jazz Museum before it closed. We hit the highlights of the Charlie Parker, Duke Ellington, Louis Armstrong, and Ella Fitzgerald exhibits before poking our heads into the Blue Room, a still-operational jazz club that hosts live music acts multiple times each week.

Each room is illuminated by neon lights mounted on the walls. We buzzed through the small museum in about 30 minutes and then ate dinner at a downtown restaurant recommended by a museum usher.

· · · · ·

Newspaper headlines adorn the walls of the vestibule at the Royals Hall of Fame. The ceiling reads, "KANSAS CITY" in bold, neon blue light. "KANSAS CITY BASEBALL" is spelled in black lettering above a headline from 1985, "Royals head for first World Series." Contrasting the light Ashwood walls is a display of stained wood lockers that house the franchise's three retired jersey numbers — infielders George Brett and Frank White and former manager Dick Howser. All three have statues in the outfield concourse, as do the Kauffman Stadium namesakes.

Howser was the manager of that 1985 club that beat the Cardinals to win the I-70 World Series. Brett and White were mainstays, appearing in a then-MLB record 1,914 games together between 1973 and 1990. Each player spent their entire careers with the Royals.

Turn to the right and a white wall directs you to the exhibit entry. Small windows in the Royals Hall of Fame face the field, allowing you to check in on the game. The Royals Hall of Fame is a neat feature loaded with memorabilia from the franchise's two World Series victories as well as other MLB items that are not Royals-related. It's more of a baseball museum than a Royals-centric attraction. The giant George Brett baseball shrine, however, is a nice touch.

Baseballs stacked six wide form Brett's number 5 as a three-dimensional tribute to the Hall of Famer. The monument was created by using 3,154 base-balls, one for each of Brett's career hits. In the center of the 5 is the bat used for his 3,000th hit in 1992 and the ball he struck.

Just before you get to the Brett shrine, which is in the middle of the walk-way, is a tribute to the National Baseball Hall of Fame in Cooperstown, New York. The two-walled area includes a "History of the World Series" and the "Kansas City Connection" to Hall of Fame players and managers. Photos of former Monarchs, Athletics and Royals members are displayed along with oth-ers who have achieved baseball immortality in Cooperstown.

A quote from longtime Detroit Tigers broadcaster Ernie Harwell is above the World Series display case, "Baseball is just a game, as simple as a ball and bat, yet as complex as the American spirit is symbolizes."

Howser's jersey is displayed a second time inside the Royals Hall, in an exhibit called, "Lasting Memories." The glass case honors postseason berths, George Brett's first batting title in 1976, the five Gold Gloves won by former center fielder Amos Otis, World Series MVPs Brett Saberhagen in 1985 and Salvador Perez in 2015. The jersey worn by Perez, who has been Kansas City's catcher since 2011, is displayed. Saberhagen won a pair of Cy Young Awards — in 1985 and 1989 — and was added to the Royals Hall of Fame in 2005.

There are 26 members of the Royals Hall of Fame, including former groundskeeper, George Toma. Each member's portrait is displayed on an off-white wall above a beautiful hardwood floor. That room is at the end of the exhibit, just past the team's two World Series trophies.

Kauffman Stadium hosted the All-Star Game in 1973 and 2012. The Roy-als Hall has memorabilia from those two games but also artifacts on loan from the National Baseball Hall of Fame & Museum from other All-Star Games dating back to the first played in 1933.

Ewing Kauffman has his own exhibit with photographs telling the story of how the Kansas City native was able to bring baseball back to his hometown. Kansas City was without Major League Baseball for two seasons after the Ath-letics moved to Oakland. The city was granted an expansion franchise in 1969.

The Royals joined the big leagues that year, along with the Padres, Seattle Pilots (Milwaukee Brewers), and Montreal Expos (Washington Nationals). Led by Brett and White, the Royals were the first of that group to reach the playoffs in 1976. Kansas City reached the World Series in 1980 but lost to the Phillies in six games.

Buck O'Neil is also featured in the Royals Hall, serving as the narrator for a 15-minute video that guides you through the history of Kansas City baseball — including the Negro Leagues Monarchs. The video is shown in the Dugout Theatre, which sounds like exactly what it is. Visitors sit on a pair of long benches inside a replica dugout to watch the film that puts them right onto the field with sights and sounds of the game. O'Neil died in 2006, so footage of Kansas City's World Series championship in 2015 is not included.

Kansas City has a long baseball history, dating back to the 1880s with minor-league teams, like the Blues and Cowboys. Just as MLB players start in the minors, some MLB franchises do as well. The Kansas City Blues became the Washington Senators, who are now the Minnesota Twins. The Kansas City Cowboys became the Pittsburgh Alleghenys, who changed their name to the Pirates in 1891.

CHAPTER 8:

BACK TO THE MINORS

There may not be any Major League Baseball teams in North Carolina, but there are several minor-league clubs, including a trio along the Interstate 85 corridor. We had to cut diagonally across the Tar Heel State on our way from Atlanta to Washington D.C. Because Children's Hope Alliance operates solely in North Carolina, we wanted to do something for the kids served by CHA.

We reached out to the Charlotte Knights, Greensboro Grasshoppers, and Durham Bulls about doing events with Children's Hope Alliance. Charlotte, the Triple-A affiliate of the Chicago White Sox, opened the 2018 season in Durham.

The Grasshoppers, then a Marlins Single-A affiliate, provided 20 tickets for their opener on April 5th. Greensboro played host to the Hickory Crawdads (aren't minor-league names great?) to begin the 2018 campaign. The Bulls, who are perhaps the best-known minor-league team there is, came through in a huge way. The Bulls hooked us up with 60 tickets for their April 6th game against the Knights.

We weren't sure any of this was going to happen a week earlier. Nothing had been set up as of March 30th, despite my belief getting kids to games in North Carolina would be an emphasis. It was something Patti and I had discussed with Celeste and Children's Hope Alliance chief development officer, Abigail Lord-Ramsey, prior to leaving Charlotte. Abby had admittedly dropped the ball. Now we were in scramble mode to make this happen. I shot off a few emails to each of the teams while Abby spent the weekend trying to coordinate with families in the Greensboro and Durham areas.

Patti and I were still in Florida on March 31st when I received an update from Abby: "We will have tickets. Will get swag out to the areas as well. Really appreciate you and Patti."

My Saturday morning was off to a great start.

"OK. Great. Thank you. Let us know when and where we need to be," I replied.

Though we had missed the deadline to request Grasshoppers tickets through Greensboro's Guilford's Kids program, Abby was able to acquire 20 tickets. I'm still not sure how, but we're glad it happened. But I still didn't know who I was supposed to meet or where. This wasn't exactly well-organized, but we thought we could figure it out when we got to Greensboro.

We had spent a couple of days in Charlotte before making the short drive to Greensboro on April 5th. The Home Run On Wheels RV rolled up Bellemeade Street to First National Bank Field around 4 – about three hours before the scheduled start. I didn't realize it before we got there, but Children's Hope Alliance has an office a block away from the stadium. Patti stayed inside the RV, which was in the bus parking lane, and I walked over to the office to figure out who I was supposed to meet and where I should park the RV. I called Abby. Voicemail. I immediately began to text her when she called back and told me my contact's name is Tammy Bradley. Now I had a name. I just had to find her.

Children's Hope Alliance's Greensboro office is a former residence in a neighborhood bordering downtown. A short sidewalk and three concrete steps lead to covered porch of the two-story grey building. I knocked on the door and a confused middle-aged man opened the door.

"Can I help you?" he asked.

"Yeah. Hey, I'm Ron Clements, the guy traveling to all of the baseball stadiums this year," I said.

His expression was unchanged.

"We're supposed to be meeting Tammy from Children's Hope Alliance for tonight's Grasshoppers game," I continued. "Is she here?"

"No," was the matter-of-fact response.

He let me come in and I again called Abby. She shot me Tammy's contact information. A couple minutes later, I thanked the man and called Tammy as I walked back to the RV. I still didn't know where I was supposed to park and was fairly certain I couldn't leave it in the bus lane.

Tammy answered and said she was making home visits all day and would be at the stadium around 6. Parking had been arranged in one of the nearby lots, but we had to pay the $5. That's a bit of a bargain considering how many spaces a 36-foot RV towing a car actually fills. The problem was nobody told the parking lot attendant.

I circled the stadium — which is quite large for a Single-A park — and entered the lot before I was stopped by a grey-haired white man of about 50 years. I stepped out of the RV and explained to him the situation. He radioed someone and then told me to park in the back.

I began to pull forward but quickly realized where the man had stopped me put us in a slight predicament. Traffic cones were in front of us, but the right turn I was forced to make was at less of an angle than I would have liked. I couldn't back up because there was a line of cars behind us. I went out as wide as I could, but the car still leaped up on the curb and slammed back to the concrete. The jerk startled me a bit, but I continued toward the back of the open lot and parked the RV as close to the concrete wall as I could. We were too close to extend the awning but close enough to open the door on the passenger side.

Then we waited. I told Tammy where we were located and she arrived with her husband, Chris, about 20 minutes later. She had the tickets and some of the Children's Hope Alliance swag we would eventually hand out, not just in Greensboro and Durham, but across the country.

The families joining us at the game were instructed to meet Tammy by the home-plate entrance. Once the boxes of giveaways were loaded into the RV, we grabbed some items, and followed Tammy and Chris to the stadium.

We had excellent seats about 20 rows up and to the right of home plate. First National Bank Field was packed on opening night to see the Grasshoppers begin their season with a 6-1 victory. Opening night was just one reason a crowd of 6,604 people filled the stadium. The team had Thirsty Thursday drink specials that drew in a horde of college students from nearby UNC-Greensboro, North Carolina A&T and Guilford College. The Grasshoppers set an attendance record in 2017 and got off to a great start in 2018. That atmosphere made what was the first professional baseball games for most of the kids with us even more special.

One of the main attractions at Grasshoppers games is Miss LouLou Gehrig, the team's bat dog. She made national news on August 28th, 2018 when she tried to grab a Grasshoppers player's bat during an at-bat. Jhonny Santos thought he had walked and was about to place hit bat on the ground but lifted it back up when the pitch was called a strike. LouLou, a black Labrador, was already in retrieve mode and ran toward Santos. She twice attempted to snag the bat before she returned to the dugout.

LouLou continues a tradition of bat dogs in Greensboro. Miss Babe Ruth and Master Yogi Berra began retrieving bats and carry buckets of baseballs to the home-plate umpire in 2006. Yogi, who died in 2017 at the age of 9, was used sparingly. Babe was the star of the show. She worked 649 consecutive home games beginning August 2nd, 2006, when she fetched catcher, Trent D'Antonio's bat and retiring September 2nd, 2015, after retrieving the bat of left fielder Austen Smith. Babe's 6-year-old niece, LouLou, took over the following season. Babe did work the final eight home games of the 2016 season. She was diagnosed with cancer in January of 2018 and died May 18th. The bucket she used to carry baseballs to home plate is now in the National Baseball Hall of Fame.

· · · · ·

"Hit Bull Win Steak. Hit Grass Win Salad."

Those words are on the now-iconic sign of a giant, snorting bull above the left-field wall at Durham Bulls Athletic Park. The bull sign was just supposed to be a movie prop for the 1988 classic baseball film, *Bull Durham*. Installed at the old Durham Athletic Park, which was used to shoot many of the movie's scenes, the sign was an instant hit with fans. When the Bulls moved into their new downtown stadium in 1995, a new bull sign was displayed in the first-base concourse but was put out to pasture 13 years later. A larger, double-sided replica was placed in left field in 2008. That bull, made of wood and sheet metal, is the one we saw April 6th, 2018. It is 20 feet wide and 30 feet tall and stands 10 feet above a 32-foot wall that is 305 feet from home plate. It would take a mighty shot to hit the bull or the grass at its feet.

But that's what Durham Bulls first baseman Jake Bauers, did in 2017 — an amazing accomplishment considering Bauers bats left-handed and needed some real opposite-field power to reach the sign.

"I felt pretty good, got a good steak out of it," he told me prior to the game we attended on opening weekend of the 2018 season.

MLB games are fun to attend, but the fun is taken to another level by minor-league teams. Every club has various things they inject to the game to add to the experience. The Bulls are no different and the success of the movie ensured that 30 years later, the Durham Bulls consistently play in front of sellout crowds.

"The community support for the team is second to none," Bauers said of playing in Durham. "If you have to play in the minor leagues, this is where you want to do it."

Bauers has seen the movie "about ten times" and quotes it often. He even hit the bull in 2017. That was a pretty amazing accomplishment for the left-handed hitting Bauers, considering the bull is above the left-field wall.

He knew from the moment he picked up a bat as a 4-year-old that he wanted to be professional baseball player. Bauers began the 2018 season confident he was ready to make his MLB debut. The Rays agreed June 7th when they promoted the 22-year-old California native to the big club.

"Anytime you walk into a major league stadium, it feels special and it's something not everybody gets to do. It's something less people get to do as a player," Bauers said. "To get there, that feeling is indescribable. I hope I can give back to kids who are like me and maybe are less fortunate than I was… It's a big responsibility. It's a lot of weight on your shoulders sometimes, but I think the guys who manage that well wind up being the best role models."

Bauers had a pair of hits, including an RBI double off the left-field wall in the bottom of the fifth inning of Durham's 11-1 victory. The bull's red eyes light up, his tail wags, and he snorts smoke from glaring nostrils every time the home team hits a home run. Though the Bulls scored 11 runs, they did not hit one out of the park. But the bull's animatronics are activated following a win, so we were able to see the iconic bovine in action.

My interview with Bauers was right after batting practice, so I had to be there about three hours prior to first pitch. I just had to figure out where to park the RV. Abby had emailed me parking instructions from the Bulls earlier in the day. I was supposed to use the bus parking at the intersection of Jackie Robinson Drive and Blackwell Street in front of the stadium's right-field corner. The streets are blocked off around 6 for a 7 p.m. start, but we were there at 3. I circled the stadium a couple of times before I noticed there was ample street parking near a greenway a block from the stadium. But it wasn't free and I didn't know how obliging those checking the meters would be with an RV occupying several spots.

I was standing on the sidewalk trying to figure it out, probably looking bewildered, when a woman stopped to ask me about Children's Hope Alliance. I was happy to tell her. She then told me she owned a business a couple of blocks away and I could use her lot. I appreciated the gesture, but it was a small lot and did not have the space I needed to turn around with the car in tow. There was, however, a grocery store with a large lot across the street. I found a few spaces away from the building and parked. Patti stayed inside to finish up her work for the day while I hiked back toward the stadium.

Meeting me in front of the stadium when Neil Yentsch, who is married to my cousin, Mandy. Neil works in downtown Durham and knocked off a couple hours early to show me around. He led me to the American Tobacco district that abuts the stadium's third-base side. The campus is full of shops, bars, and eateries. Neil and I went into one establishment and chatted while sharing a basket of garlic fries. Once content, Neil asked if I wanted to see his office. "Sure," I said.

I wasn't ready for what he showed me.

Neil works for the corporate tax company, Alvara, which is headquartered in Seattle. The company's Durham office overlooks the Bulls stadium. That's actually simplifying things. The stadium's right-field backdrop is Alvara's building.

We entered the building on the opposite side and walked through the lobby to a break room that was open to the rest of the office. The first and second floors were both dotted with cubicles.

"You want a beer?" Neil asked.

"Excuse me?" I said.

"We have a few beers on tap here in the breakroom," he said with a gesture toward three taps installed on the back wall.

"Holy cow," I exclaimed. "That's pretty cool. Sure, I'll take one."

Neil poured me a Kölsch and said the taps are opened at 4 for the end of the work day. When the Bulls are home, many employees stick around to watch the game from the huge windows that border the right-field concourse. Glass double doors even open to a small, field-level patio to allow an "outside" view. We eventually made our way to the second floor, where Neil's desk is a few feet away from another door that leads to balcony overlooking the stadium. From there we watched the Bulls take batting practice. A few balls came close to hitting the building, but none quite made it. Neil said he and his co-workers have been startled more than once by batting practice balls striking the shatter-proof glass. Several office buildings line the stadium's outfield boundary and nearly everyone has some sort of field-viewing area.

As batting practice was wrapping up, I told Neil I had to get down to the field to speak with Bauers. I was very thankful for the tour and a bit envious he worked at an office with that view. After speaking with Bauers, I walked back to the RV to park it in our designated spot at the corner of Jackie Robinson and Blackwell.

Our contact this night was Miya Atchison. She met us with a couple other Children's Hope Alliance representatives. We put the awning out and placed several Children's Hope Alliance items on a table we set up on the sidewalk. As Miya met the foster families to give them their tickets, Patti and I were handing out cups, T-shirts, and lanyards to those families and others who walked by.

Among those who received tickets were a 9-year-old girl named Heaven and her foster mother, Barb. They ended up sitting right behind me and Patti in the right-field bleachers. Heaven, who was accompanied by a classmate, did not know baseball very well and began to ask several questions in the first inning. Barb didn't know many of the answers, so I turned around to offer the requested information. During the third inning, I overheard Heaven say something that confirmed what I had suspected.

"I've never been to a baseball game before," she said to her foster mom.

"Did you hear that?" I leaned over to ask Patti as my eyes began to well with tears.

"Yeah," Patti replied. "That's awesome."

It wasn't just that Heaven had never been to a game before or that she was asking questions, it was that she was genuinely interested. She barely left her seat and followed every pitch. She was into it and we may have helped birth a life-long love of America's pastime.

As the game stretched into the later innings, Wooly Bull threw some foam baseballs into the stands. I caught one and handed it to the girl sitting next to me. It was Heaven's friend. I didn't realize who the girl was and Heaven's disappointment was clear as day. She began to softly cry and I felt awful for inadvertently creating some friction. But just for a minute. Her friend handed her the ball, and when Heaven realized it wasn't an actual baseball, her sadness quickly evaporated. We all wound up exchanging high-fives before leaving.

A scheduled fireworks display followed the game and most of the foster families, including Barb and Heaven, stuck around to the end.

We were ecstatic when we got back in the RV and hopped back on Interstate 85 around 11 p.m. We slept at a rest area just past the North Carolina-Virginia border before spending Saturday on the road to College Park, Maryland — our home while we visited Washington D.C. and Baltimore.

. . . . .

Sahlen Field is located right in downtown Buffalo right off Interstate 190 and the Highway 5 Buffalo Skyway. It's also served by the Seneca station on the Buffalo Metro Rail and is just a ten-minute walk from KeyBank Center, home to the NHL's Sabres. Sahlen's hot dogs acquired the ballpark naming rights on October 9th, 2018. When we visited on May 23rd, it was known as Coca-Cola Field.

Built in 1988 as a failed attempt to lure a Major League Baseball team to Buffalo, the 17,000-seat stadium is still the largest minor-league park in the country. Its state-of-the-art video board installed in 2011 is the largest high-definition LED video display in all of Minor League Baseball at 80 feet wide and 34 feet tall. A million-dollar lighting system was also put in the same year. The stadium once held over 21,000 fans, but renovations in 2014 and 2015 included the installation of new, wider seats that cut the capacity. All of the improvements made at Sahlen Field made our visit that much more pleasant. Though a bit on the chilly side with a temperature of 57 degrees at first pitch, we enjoyed seeing the Bisons play host to the Syracuse Chiefs. Syracuse, the Triple-A affiliate of the Nationals, used a four-run eighth inning — courtesy of a Hunter Jones grand slam — to secure a 7-2 victory over Toronto's top farm club. We joked that we were seeing "two Canadian teams" play with teams affiliated with the Blue Jays and the former Expos club. The Chiefs ended their ten-year affiliation with the Nationals following the 2018 season and are now the Syracuse Mets.

For just $14 apiece, we got two tickets in Section 109 down the third-base line and sat in front of a group of employees from a local healthcare company. The four men and two women hailed from Chicago, Detroit, and Pittsburgh. We gave each of them a Children's Hope Alliance cup after telling them about our trip and mission. As we did at every other ballpark on our trip, we took a self-guided tour of Sahlen Field. We got up after the third inning and did not return to our seats as we explored the ballpark.

The four-tiered Bully Hill Party Deck in right field is popular for groups of 25 to 200 people and has some of the best food in the ballpark, including wings, of course. The Consumers Craft Brew Corner, located just inside the main entrance, features several local beers. We stopped to get a couple and met a pair of newlyweds in the concourse. Once we told them about our trip, they were very inquisitive and began sharing stories of their handful of MLB ballpark visits. They had seen both New York and Chicago stadiums, Toronto, Pittsburgh, Cleveland, Detroit, Boston, and Philadelphia. We agreed that PNC Park was the best of that group. It is also, in our opinion, the best stadium in all of Major League Baseball.

The couple suggested we hit up the Pub in the Park, located behind the Labatt Blue Zone on the first-base side. The pub is open to anyone with a game ticket and serves food through the end of the sixth inning. By the time Jones hit his grand slam, we were already inside the pub to escape the chill. We were still able to watch the game thanks to the large windows forming the pub's interior wall to provide fantastic sight lines to the on-field action. When the weather is warmer, the windows do open.

With the game well in hand for the Chiefs, we left the park after the eighth inning to get to the Anchor Bar before it closed. While we were told that Duff's or Gabriel's Gate had the best wings in Buffalo, the Anchor Bar is known as the home of Buffalo wings. Given Patti's affinity for wings, it was a must-see and got our stamp of approval.

"I don't care what anybody else says, they were delicious," Patti stated.

We likened the Anchor Bar to Pat's in Philadelphia. While Pat's may not have the best cheesesteak in Philadelphia, it is widely accepted as the first to serve the iconic sandwich. It was a place we had to see, just like the Anchor Bar. We'll check out Duff's and Gabe's on our next trip to Buffalo.

· · · · ·

Scheduled doubleheaders rarely occur in professional baseball these days.

It's nearly unheard of to have two teams play a pair of games in the same day at two different stadiums. The last time it happened in Major League Baseball was July 8th, 2000, when the Mets and Yankees faced off twice in a day-night, home-and-home doubleheader. The Yankees won both those games — the first at Shea Stadium and then the nightcap at Yankee Stadium — by identical 4-2 scores. It was the first time since 1903 that two MLB teams played two games in different stadiums on the same day.

A pair of Frontier League teams played a scheduled, day-night, home-and-home doubleheader on June 20th, 2018.

The Joliet Slammers and Windy City Thunderbolts first played at Joliet Route 66 Stadium with a scheduled 10 a.m. start. Following Joliet's 6-5 win, the two independent-league teams packed up and moved 26 miles to the east for a 6 p.m. tilt at Standard Bank Stadium in Crestwood, Illinois.

"It feels like travel ball," Slammers infielder Justin Garcia, who was a draft pick of the Houston Astros in 2015, told me following the first game in Joliet. "You play a game; you got a big break, then you go somewhere else to play. It's crazy. It's funny. I don't think I'll ever do this again… It's definitely an experience."

Garcia drove in a pair of runs in the nightcap to help Joliet sweep the doubleheader and win its eighth in a row. Watching Joliet's 5-1 victory in Crestwood with me was my high school classmate, Jason Stevens, who lives in the Chicago area. We talked some about baseball but mostly Jason wanted to hear about our trip and what it's like to live in an RV. There is an adjustment period, for sure, but we knew what we were doing was special and not something everyone has the opportunity to do. When Patti and I saw the Cardinals and Brewers play the next night at Miller Park, it was my fourth game at four different stadiums in four different cities in three days. We watched the Dodgers and Cubs play at Wrigley Field the night before the minor-league doubleheader.

The home-and-home double-dip wasn't new to the Slammers. They did the same with the Schaumburg Boomers, who are also in the Chicago area, several years earlier. While it may not have been new to the Slammers club, it was new to the players on the independent Frontier League rosters in 2018.

"Throughout my career, I've played in many doubleheaders but never one where you have three to four hours in between," Thunderbolts second baseman Tim Zier told me in Joliet. "It's something different."

Zier, a 2014 draft pick of the Phillies, was in his fifth professional season and third with the Thunderbolts. Zier, who played for Padres great Tony Gwynn at San Diego State, said he had never played a game that started at 10 a.m. prior to his first season in the Frontier League.

"We have a few (early) starts and they're called kids days and a bunch of kids come out an it's a lot of fun, which, in the end, it's all about the kids and the fans enjoying the game," said Zier, who left San Diego State as the school's all-time hits leader. "It's a grind in the morning, but sometimes waking up early in the morning is fun because you see all these kids out here."

The early start coincided with "Camp Day" at Route 66 Stadium. Several kids attending area summer camps were at the game, each group wearing different-colored T-shirts to turn the main bowl seating sections into something resembling a rainbow.

"I love hanging out with them," Windy City pitcher Connor Bach said of the kids. "It's a time for them to relax and just have some fun."

Bach was a 2014 draft pick of the Washington Nationals but was released by three separate teams before winding up in the Frontier League.

"It's tough, especially because I felt my skills were able to compete at the professional level," Bach told me. "When three teams say they don't want you, it hurts. It gives me more motivation to try to get back up."

I love the Frontier League. It's a ten-team independent league in the Midwest and is loaded with players who were drafted by MLB teams and are trying to get back to affiliated baseball. There are some players who were not drafted and are trying to get noticed by MLB teams.

"You go your whole life wanting to play in the big leagues, but you never know if it will ever happen," Garcia said. "When I was drafted and saw the Astros logo next to my name, it was crazy. That's a moment I could not believe and I'll remember it for the rest of my life. But when I got released, I kind of knew it was coming. There was more work to be done. Getting released sucked, but I got cut twice in college. It's not the end of the world and there's still an opportunity to make it. I'm lucky to be here," Garcia added. "Every day I turn around and look at the stadium. Just to be here is an honor. You appreciate the game, every single moment. There are people who wish they were me, being able to play professional baseball."

I spent the entire 2014 season covering the Frontier League — primarily the Gateway Grizzlies in Sauget, Illinois, outside of St. Louis. It's always special when you are told a player was leaving the team because he had been signed by a big-league club. Those are the moments that made me fall in love with the Frontier League. The 2014 Frontier League All-Star Game was played at GCS Ballpark in Sauget. The game was halted after the first pitch to recognize River City Rascals third baseman Taylor Ard who had been signed by the Arizona Diamondbacks earlier that day. Ard left the game to a standing ovation and caught a flight to Oregon, where he joined Arizona's single-A short season team in Hillsboro. Joliet pitcher Blair Walters was signed by the Atlanta Braves a day earlier. Walters was in Double A two years later but didn't play beyond 2016. Ard played Double-A ball with the Jacksonville Jumbo Shrimp in 2017 but was back in independent ball in 2018 with the Long Island Ducks of the Atlantic League.

"This is your second chance," Garcia said of independent baseball. "You're kind of on your own and you have to remember why you're here… I don't want to be the guy later in life when I'm watching major-league baseball with my sons thinking, 'That could have been me.' I don't want to have any regrets. If it doesn't work out for me, God has another plan for me."

Garcia, Bach and Zier all finished the 2018 season still in the Frontier League.

· · · · ·

Jeren Kendall was stuck in no-man's land.

The Rancho Cucamonga Quakes center fielder slapped a single to right field in the third inning of a 19-6 win over the Lake Elsinore Storm at Loan-Mart Field.

Kendall's teammate, Connor Wong, went from first to third on the hit and Kendall thought the throw from the outfield was going home. He was wrong as the throw went to second, catching Kendall in a pickle. But Kendall used some nifty footwork and a little body contortion to avoid the tag and wound up on second.

"I was going for two the right away, so when he cut it off, I was a little surprised," the Wisconsin native told me after the July 31st game. "I just kind of stepped backwards. I told the outfielder, who ran in for the pickle, I should have played football instead. That was a good little move and I got around it. It was nice the umpire saw it as it is and called me safe."

Kendall later scored on Jared Walker's three-run homer, one of five homers hit in the game. Kendall, Wong, and Walker the Quakes win the California League for the second time in four years.

"We're having a lot of fun," Kendall said of his first season with the High-A affiliate of the Los Angeles Dodgers. "The first half was a little different. We kind of struggled and had to win our way to secure a playoff spot, and then the second half, we've just been taking off. It feels pretty good."

Kendall hit just .215 in 2018, a far cry from his explosive debut in rookie ball. He hit .455 with the Ogden Raptors but slipped to .221 when promoted to the short Single-A season with the Great Lakes Loons.

"I'm starting to get used to the playing style here," Kendall said. "I'm not saying the playing style on the field, just coming here every day at the same time, doing the same thing. Everybody knows it, everybody's gone through it. Once you start getting into a little bit of a slump, the days kind of catch up on you. We don't have any time to relax and regain your focus like you do at school when you're playing three games on the weekend and you've got a couple days off. But (in 2017) I just jumped right into it, didn't really think much of it and then coming here out of Spring Training feeling really good. The days kind of catch up on you, but things are going a little bit better. As a good baseball player, you're always trying to make adjustments," he added. "I'm just trying to find that right adjustment."

We had the Home Run On Wheels RV parked out front of the minor-league stadium about 50 miles east of Los Angeles. We attended the game so I could speak with Kendall, who was the Dodgers' first-round draft pick in 2017. The La Crosse Tribune, which profiled our trip on Easter, reached out to me to ask if I could write a feature on Kendall. The 22-year-old went to Holmen High School outside of La Crosse and was the Wisconsin state player of the year in both 2013 and 2014. The Red Sox selected him in the 30th round of the 2014 MLB Draft, but he remained committed to play collegiately at Vanderbilt. Kendall's freshman year ended with the Commodores reaching the College World Series for the second straight season. They were unable to defend the national championship they won in 2014, but Kendall was selected as a freshman All-American. He then was a third-team All-American as a sophomore and first-team All-SEC player as a junior before the Dodgers selected him 17th overall in the 2017 MLB Draft.

"It worked out perfectly," Kendall said. "I love it."

As he works his way through the minors, Kendall leans on the baseball advice he's always received from his father, Jeremey, who reached Double A with the Phillies.

"He's always told me just to go out and have fun," Kendall said. "At the end of the day, whether you're playing well or not, when this stuff is over, you're going to miss it. You don't want to look back on this experience and miss what it really is. It's a game. You've got to be really patient with his game. Finding the right adjustment, the results aren't going to be immediate. For me, it's just enjoy the time you have out here. I have a lot of friends who are just working right now, and as much as coming out here and going 0 for 4 or 0 for 5, I think it's a lot better than working behind a desk. I don't take anything for granted."

Kendall's Holmen team actually faced off against my high school alma mater of La Crosse Aquinas. He didn't quite remember how he did personally but was able to get in a dig.

"Holmen was always the better team," Kendall said, "but it was a fun rivalry."

. . . . .

The San Gabriel mountains provide a gorgeous backdrop for Loan-Mart Field and I enjoyed my visit to the quaint stadium that seats about 6,600 people. When the game was over, we headed toward our RV park in Orange. We should have arrived around 11:30 p.m. It was nearly 4 a.m. before we got there.

It is a long drive from Vallejo to Rancho Cucamonga, and somewhere along the way, one of our tires had picked up a nail. It was the rear inside tire on the passenger side. As that tire deflated, the outside tire absorbed the weight of our 20,000-pound rolling home and blew. We first smelled burning rubber, then we heard the pop, and I asked, "What was that?"

"I don't know," Patti replied.

A few seconds later, we heard the rumbling of the blown tire on the Highway 57 freeway. That is one of the worst sounds you can hear while rolling down a highway in an RV. We were thankful we purchased Tyron bands to go on the tires for this very reason. The bands allow the driver to maintain control of the motorhome and avoid an accident in case of a flat tire. I don't even want to imagine what might have happened without those steel bands.

I was in the second-from-right lane and put the signal on to move over but nearly clipped a car that was trying to pass on the right after I flipped the turn signal. The vehicle backed off and I pulled onto the shoulder. Fortunately it was wide enough to fit the RV. We had roadside assistance, so I called the number after going outside to see that we did indeed need a new tire. I couldn't tell if we needed two. One new tire and roadside installation would set us back $800. I was praying we didn't need two. We were only ten miles away from the RV park.

We waited about an hour and I called again for an estimated time of arrival. I was told about 40 minutes. Another hour went by. I called again. There was an issue finding a tire, but the driver was now on his way. Patti and I tried to rest a bit, her on the bed and me on the couch. Patti even worked on some of our stadium reviews, sitting at the dinette as the sound of vehicles cruising past us shook the RV. A vehicle pulled up behind us.

"Finally," I exclaimed and opened the door, only to be greeted by a pair of California Highway Patrolmen.

"Everything OK?" one of the officers asked.

"We got a flat tire and are waiting for someone to come out to change it," I said as I exited the vehicle.

I pulled out my phone and used the flashlight app to show them what had happened.

"Someone's on their way?" the same officer asked.

"Yes," I replied.

"OK. Be careful," he said and the two returned to their vehicle.

About 20 minutes after the cops pulled away, our tire technician arrived. I showed him what had happened and he went to work. I used the RV's leveling jacks to raise the vehicle and he removed both rear passenger tires. The outside tire was shredded. After removing the inside tire, he discovered the culprit, the aforementioned nail. He was able to remove the nail and repair the hole (thank God). It took about an hour from the time of his arrival until we got back on the road. Ten minutes later, we pulled into the Orangeland RV Park. I hooked up the water and electric, but that was it. We had to go to bed.

Our trip to see the Rancho Cucamonga Quakes had been costly, literally. Fortunately, we had tire insurance and eventually got reimbursed, though it took a couple of months. Life's all about the stories. We now had another memorable one.

We saw the Quakes parent team a couple nights later. Yasmani Grandal delivered a walk-off home run in the bottom of the 10th to give the Dodgers a 6-4 win over the Brewers. While Dodger Stadium is expensive, it was Dollar Dog night, so we were at least able to load up on Dodger Dogs for only a buck.

CHAPTER 9:

MILWAUKEE

It was only about a two-hour drive from our RV park south of Chicago to the Jellystone campground outside of Milwaukee.

Matt Roesler would be meeting us there around 3 p.m. on June 21st to give us our two tickets for that night's game and be interviewed for the Home Run On Wheels podcast. I met Matt at the reception building and he rode with me into the campground. Matt brought his dad with him, but the older Roesler napped in the car while Matt joined us in the RV.

Back in March when Patti and I spent our wedding anniversary at Disney World, we went on the "It's a Small World" attraction. That song began playing in my head early in my conversation with Matt.

And it started with that run-in I had with Cheryl Larson during the Pirates Spring Training game in Bradenton.

"She was all excited when she got home and told me a little bit of the story," Matt recalled. "She said, 'You've got to call this guy.' I love baseball and love making those connections. It was clear I needed to give you a call back. She just kept saying, 'What a small world.'"

Cheryl had no idea how right she was.

When Matt first called me and told me his last name is Roesler, I began to wonder if he knew my aunt's former husband, Mark. When Matt told me he grew up in Westby, Wisconsin, less than an hour from my hometown of La Crosse, I had to ask him.

"You're not related to Mark Roesler, are you?" I asked.

"Oh, yeah, Mark's my cousin," he answered. "We're third cousins."

"No way. He used to be married to my Aunt Gail," I said.

"I remember Gail. I didn't know her well, but I remember meeting her," Matt said. "Wow. What are the chances?"

That was a phone conversation we had in April. Matt truly blew my mind in June when he arrived at the Jellystone Campground in Caledonia, Wisconsin to record the podcast interview before we headed to Miller Park.

"Hey, what's your dad's name?" he asked almost immediately after entering the RV.

"Bernie. Why?" I replied.

"I thought so. My mom knows your dad somehow," he said. "After talking with you in April, I was telling my mom and said, 'You've got to hear this story,' and she's like, 'What's his dad's name? Is it Bernie?'"

"I wasn't really sure at the time."

"But somehow through the Catholic church in Middle Ridge (an unincorporated community with St. Peter's church, a few houses, a ball field, cemetery, and of course, a tavern), she knew him. So, yeah, here we are."

It's crazy how a chance meeting in Bradenton, Florida at a Pirates Spring Training game led to meeting a Wisconsin man whose family has ties to my family. It also helped us get some foster kids to a Brewers game.

After some nudging on my part, the Brewers wound up donating 50 tickets to Anu Family Services for the June 21st game against the Cardinals.

Matt had submitted the ticket request soon after our initial phone call, but weeks went by without a word from the Brewers. Matt sent a couple follow-up emails and when I called him the first week of June to ask about the status of his request, he said he still hadn't heard one way or another. My next call was to the Brewers' community relations manager, Erica Bowring. I got her voicemail but left a detailed message explaining the situation and mission.

Matt emailed me two days later to let me know the Brewers were donating tickets. The tickets arrived at the Anu office in Eau Claire the next week.

Matt said he hopes Anu now has "a foot in the door" with the Brewers and can give other kids the "tremendous opportunity" by making a Brewers trip an annual event for the families Anu serves.

"A lot of these kids come into foster care never having a sense of belonging to a family, a home, or community," Matt said. "Chances are, they may have never been able to go to a game because nobody's ever taken the time to take them to any sporting event."

Like Children's Hope Alliance and most foster care organizations, Anu's definitive mission to find children their permanent "forever" home.

"I grew up with an almost picture-perfect childhood, two loving parents in the same house, so when I go home, there's this sense of belonging," Matt said. "It's just a calming. I could have the most stressful week, but I go back to Mom and Dad's for dinner on a Friday evening and all the stress just goes away. It's that sense that I have a place to belong. It's safe. Kids in our programs don't have that. They've been in and out of institutions; they've been in and out of homes. They just need somebody to love them. That's one of the big misconceptions about foster care," Matt continued. "A lot of people thinking about foster care are sometimes resistant because they think, 'I'll get too connected to the kids.' That's actually the opposite. We WANT you to be connected. We want you to love that child as if they're your own. We have foster parents whose foster kids are their own, being involved in every family event. I've seen obituaries that list foster kids right along with biological kids and making absolutely no differentia between the two. That's what we want. The ultimate therapy for kids is love."

Matt's words struck a chord with me and a proverbial light bulb went on for me. Though I knew kids need a loving home, the message I wanted to spread didn't quite hit me until I heard what Matt was saying. Any child can survive in a home but a loving home helps that child thrive.

"When your brain is just surviving, you don't dream. Kids need to dream," Matt added. "They need to be in a safe place to dream and not let any of their past hold them back."

Children's Hope Alliance gave us 15 and 30-second commercials to run during our podcast. Adam Hicks voiced the shorter spots, and in one, says, "There are enough kids in foster care to fill the rosters of almost 1,500 MLB teams and their entire farm systems." One of our goals was to inspire people across the country to become foster parents, or at the very least, get involved by donating time, money, or items to a foster care organization.

"The world needs more foster parents, wherever they are," Matt said in June. "There are thousands of kids who are sleeping on the street or in unsafe situations because there aren't enough foster homes."

When Celeste laid out her mission for us, it wasn't to get as many kids to MLB games as possible. The real meat and potatoes of the trip was to spread the word to raise awareness of the needs of children in the foster system. Getting kids to games was just the gravy, but it was really good gravy.

After recording our interview, I took Matt to his car and told him we'd see him at the park. A high school classmate of mine, Kevin Kadrmas, and his wife and parents were going to the same game and we wanted to see them beforehand. Kevin was one of my closest friends in high school and was the only classmate of mine to attend our wedding. I wanted to see him, so we made arrangements to meet at a local restaurant for a pregame meal. Two other high school classmates of mine, Eric Petzold and Nick Hotchkiss, were also attending that night's game but had tickets in a different section. We said our hellos to Eric and Nick at the TGI Friday's inside Miller Park and then headed to our seats.

We sat next to Mark and his dad in Section 422 at Miller Park on June 21st to see the Brewers roll to a 11-3 win over the Cardinals. The Kadrmas clan was in a section just beneath us. It was fun and exciting for me, not so much for Patti as a Cardinals fan. We found out Mark, though a Wisconsin native, grew up a Cubs fan. Matt also revealed that another distant cousin of his is Seattle Mariners manager Scott Servais, who starred at Westby High School before going on to play in the 1988 Summer Olympics. Servais then had an 11-year playing career with the Astros, Cubs, Rockies, and Giants. The four years Servais spent with the Cubs are a big reason why Matt Roesler became a Cubs fan.

Patti and I got up after the third inning, with the Brewers already up 4-0, to go on our usual stadium walkabout. We didn't make it far, however. We were stopped by a group of women who were impressed by Patti's shoes.

This is a common occurrence whenever Patti attends a baseball game. She has two pair of high-heeled baseball-themed shoes. One pair is shoes made to look like a baseball with white leather stitched by red seams. The heels look like a miniature wooden baseball bats. The other pair is solid red with the Cardinals "STL" logo and a cardinal on one side with the St. Louis skyline, complete with the Gateway Arch on the other. Patti was wearing her Cardinals shoes to see her team play in Milwaukee.

Miller Park hosted "Pride Night" on June 21st and the group of women who inquired about Patti's shoes were lesbians and all wearing black T-shirts with Brewers' classic "m-b" baseball mitt logo centered in rainbow colors. Patti told the women she got her shoes from Etsy and she had another pair that she got from a website called HerSport. Four of the five women then began to talk among themselves while one continued her chat with us. She was from Madison, but now lived in Milwaukee, and was very curious about our venture. We answered her questions before one of her friends, who identified herself as Duckie, returned with a gift.

"Hey, man," she said, looking at me. "You guys are so cool. You're just talking to my friend here and you don't even care that we're gay."

"I don't," I said. "You're people just like us."

"That's awesome, and hey, I wanted to give you this because you've been so nice to my friend," Duckie said, handing me one of the black Brewers Pride shirts. "We have an extra shirt, and I want you to have it."

"Thank you," I said. "This is great. We're actually seeing the Brewers play in San Francisco on my birthday this year, and I am totally going to wear this shirt. It'll be quite appropriate."

And that I did. When the Brewers beat the Giants on July 27th, I was wearing that rainbow-logoed Brewers shirt at AT&T Park.

We eventually parted ways with our new friends, and with new beverages in hand, returned to our seats.

A married couple in their early 30s was sitting in front of us at Miller Park, holding their 4-year-old foster son. We were in the front rows of our section, but Section 422 is high above the field. It didn't matter to this little boy at his first MLB game. He was cheering and shouting at the players like he was sitting in the front row directly behind home plate. Every time I heard him yell or wave his brand new foam "No. 1" hand, I couldn't help but smile and chuckle a bit. This kid was having the time of his life and it nearly brought me tears of joy.

"That was a blast," Patti said of seeing the boy. "That's the whole point."

· · · · ·

We spent 16 days in Wisconsin, which was longer than anywhere else we stayed during the regular season. After arriving on June 21st and going to the Cardinals-Brewers game that night, we didn't leave the Milwaukee area until July 5th. We drove across the state and spent two nights near La Crosse to visit my grandparents before traveling to the Twin Cities on the morning of Saturday, July 7th.

Our second Cardinals-Brewers game was on June 23rd and we were again sitting with a group of people. My dad drove down from his home in the Upper Peninsula of Michigan. He arrived with my sister, Faith, her husband, Bob, and son, Brock, who all live outside of Appleton in a tiny town called Fremont. Our friends, Pete and Maria Shuleski, drove up from St. Louis with their daughter, Elle. The Shuleskis also invited a few of Maria's cousins, two of whom live in the Milwaukee area, to join us. Our group in Section 210 consisted of 16 people.

Saturday was a bright, sunny day — unlike Thursday, when the roof was closed while a steady rain fell all day. Not only would we see a game with the roof open, but the clear skies allowed us to tailgate before the game.

So we could all be parked next to one another, we decided to meet at the Hampton where the Shuleskis were staying. We agreed to meet at noon and make the short drive to Miller Park for the 3 p.m. game. We weren't exactly grilling by 12:15. Maria had a cousin driving up from Chicago with his two children and they were running late. We had grown increasingly upset by the time he pulled up about 12:45 and we finally drove as a mini-convoy to the Molitor lot at Miller Park. But all was forgiven by the time we were biting into burgers and hot dogs fresh off the grill at 1:30. We still got over an hour of tailgating in. The late cousin even took a few of the kids to an open spot in the lot to play catch. One great thing about the Miller Park lot is there are several recycling bins right next to the trash dumpsters.

Aside from the many tailgaters in the lots surrounding Miller Park, there is also a Little League park called Helfaer Field. Beyond the outfield fence of the tiny Brewers-owned stadium, Miller Park serves as a giant backdrop. There were a few kids with their parents playing a game on the field, where home plate is in the same location of Milwaukee's old County Stadium. Helfaer Field hosts various Little League tournaments throughout the summer.

We started to pack up about 2:15 and most of us were inside the stadium by 2:40. Patti and I wanted to make a Home Run On Wheels sign after seeing fans with signs at Thursday's game. Kohl's had set up free sign-making stations on each level, so we took advantage of that by making our first sign of the season:

"Miller Park is #17 of 30 in 2018
#HomeRunOnWheels"

We took the sign with us when we returned July 4th to see the Brewers take on the Twins.

Miller Park is easy to navigate and the many escalators make it simple to reach the upper levels. It's also a kid-friendly stadium with multiple interactive exhibits for kids. There is a fun display of five six-foot statues on the main level near the right-field corner. The statues were near one of the Kohl's sign-making stations, and after Patti and I made our sign, she snapped a photo of me and Brock "racing" the five sausages, Brat, Polish Sausage, Hot Dog, Italian Sausage, and Chorizo. A short while later, we watched the actual sausage competitors race at the end of the sixth inning.

· · · · ·

My dad and sister's family arrived Friday night. Dad and Brock slept in the RV, Brock in the drop-down bed above the cab and Dad on the pullout sofa. Faith and Bob chose to sleep outside in a tent they brought with them. Saturday's game was a 3 p.m. start and we weren't meeting the Shuleskis until noon, so we had time for a good breakfast. I made pancakes using some batter we got in Canada. We topped those pancakes with authentic Canadian maple syrup, also obtained in Ontario.

After we finally got to Miller Park, Bob transformed into the tailgating master. He pulled the portable grill from the back of their SUV and got to work. Patti and I brought folding chairs and a table from under the RV and set those up while my dad lifted the cooler from the back of his vehicle. Pete and Maria and her cousins had their own grill, chairs and drinks and the whole thing turned into a makeshift potluck. We even shared with the folks parked next to us; they had some condiments we forgot to bring, so it was a mutually beneficial barter. I brought some Children's Hope Alliance cups, T-shirts, and lanyards with me and those got handed out, along with some cards.

Faith and Bob left following the game, but Brock stayed with us through the weekend. My dad would drive his grandson home on his way back to the U.P. Brock was only 15 years old but over 6 feet tall. His once bright red hair had darkened a bit. Unlike me or his mom, he's soft-spoken. He stopped playing sports when he reached high school but is still a big fan of the Packers, Badgers, and Brewers. I was happy he was there with us.

While disappointed Bob and Faith couldn't stay the entire weekend, Patti and I enjoyed our time with my dad and nephew. We spent the entire next day touring the Milwaukee area. My dad volunteered to drive everyone in his Jeep Cherokee. It's a *tad* bigger than my Scion xD.

Our first stop was the 34th annual Strawberry Festival in Cedarburg, a municipality of 11,000 people north of Milwaukee. We found free street parking a couple of blocks away from festival's downtown entrance. The quaint downtown was packed with people and vendors lined each side of the closed streets. The handful of bars and restaurants were open and overflowing with customers spilling onto the sidewalk. One bar had live music that I initially thought was a recording. They were that good. The grey-haired female singer may have been in her 50s, but her Lady Gaga impression was perfect.

One tent was selling locally grown strawberries, and there were a couple other places with strawberry wine and beer. I would not recommend the latter. Other vendor's things had clothing, paintings, woodwork and metal works, Christmas ornaments and ice cream. It took about an hour to walk down and then back up the few downtown blocks that were the festival grounds.

The only other thing we really had planned for our lazy Sunday was a visit to Lakefront Brewery. But instead of taking Interstate 43 south, we decided to enjoy a scenic route along Lake Michigan. This turned out to be an excellent idea.

I began covering the NFL in 2009 as a St. Louis Rams beat reporter. Every year I covered the Rams, they held training camp at their team facility in Earth City, Missouri. The team held training camp at Concordia University in Mequon, Wisconsin in 2008. I just missed it. So when we drove past the campus on our drive from Cedarburg to Milwaukee, I told my dad to stop.

The campus is picturesque, situated on a bluff overlooking Lake Michigan. A small beach of white sand and driftwood is at the bottom of the bluff. Paved paths wind down the side of the hill to lead visitors there. We didn't venture down to the beach because we didn't really have that much time to descend and ascend the hill. Swimming in the cold Lake Michigan water is not exactly encouraged.

"I can't imagine going to college at a place like this," I said. "This is gorgeous. I'd never be able to concentrate."

"I'm sure that's not a problem in the winter," my dad said.

"Good point," I replied.

Statues dot the campus, the most impressive of which is the "Fishers of Men" sculpture on the edge of the bluff. Concordia is a private network of Lutheran universities, so there is a Christian theme on the campus. "Fishers of Men" depicts the apostles Peter and Andrew in their boat, pulling a net in from a "sea" composed of blue flowers that surround the statue.

Lake Shore Road becomes North Lake Shore Drive near the Concordia campus. We turned onto Lake Shore Drive and headed south. Downtown Milwaukee was 18 miles away, via the lakefront, 15 if we took the freeway. We were stopped again in three miles.

Virmond Park is a 63-acre park overlooking Lake Michigan from the bluff. It's a habitat for chimney swifts, small dark gray-brown birds that resemble swallows but beat their wings rapidly like hummingbirds. A bench under the cover of trees sits along the bluffside to offer wonderful views of the lake and beach below. A flowery meadow abuts an open field where a family was playing a game of touch football. Next to a tennis court is a playground, where kids were enjoying the slides, swings, and merry-go-round.

Our stop was brief but not before we took a few photos of each other standing at the bluff's edge with the lake in the background. We could not have asked for a nicer June day, 72 degrees and clear skies. Our leisurely drive took us through Whitefish Bay before hitting the village of Shorewood and crossing the Milwaukee River. Despite its name, Lakefront Brewery is actually on the river and a good 12 blocks from the lakeshore.

The brewery serves food, which was a good thing because we were rather hungry when we arrived. We got some chicken strips and fries, along with a few beers, Brock drank soda. The beer is good; I was especially fond of the Lager and Pilsner. But the real draw for us was the giant mug in the corner of the tasting room. Above the seven-foot mug is a tap handle and the words, "Go Brewers." This was Bernie's mug. The mascot of Milwaukee's MLB team is Bernie Brewer, a yellow-haired figure with a giant moustache. Bernie used to glide down a slide into the mug following a Brewers home run at the old

Milwaukee County Stadium. He still goes down a slide after Brewers homers at Miller Park, but there is no mug. We got the obligatory shot of my dad in front of the mug.

"Bernie slid into town," Patti joked.

The giant mug is where the Lakefront Brewery tour begins. We didn't have time to take the tour, which includes four drink tokens, but I poked my head through the open door into the next room. It was Bernie's Chalet, which housed the mug at County Stadium.

We went to three games at Miller Park and the Brewers hit a total of four home runs in those games. I didn't see Bernie go down the slide following Manny Piña's home run on June 21st because I was in the concourse getting a brat. When the Brewers hit three solo homers on July 4th in a 3-2 victory over the Twins, I only witnessed Bernie sliding once. I was chatting someone up when Travis Shaw smacked a solo shot to center field in the second inning. A restroom visit during the seventh inning resulted in missing Brad Miller's homer to center field. I was paying attention from our party-deck seats in right field when Nate Orf lifted a Jose Berrios curveball to left. I lifted my eyes and there, for the first time in my life, I actually witnessed Bernie Brewer sliding down his yellow slide.

· · · · ·

July 4th was a hot day in Milwaukee. The Brewers and Twins were set to start at 3 p.m. at Miller Park and the temperature at first pitch was 87 degrees. The humidity was high as a storm front approached, making it seem even hotter. As that front got closer, the Brewers decided to close the roof at Miller Park but left the outfield bay windows open. That didn't do much good. The airflow was minimal and fans were roasting inside the stadium. It was probably worse on the field. Miller Park does not have air conditioning, as the original idea behind a retractable roof was keeping fans and players warm during early and late-season games when the Wisconsin temperatures can dip into the 40s or lower. The roof had the opposite effect on July 4th as Miller Park was essentially turned into an oven for about 20 minutes until the Brewers wised up and re-opened the roof. The first crack of sunlight to beam through the widening gap drew a round of sarcastic applause those in attendance, us included.

Despite the heat, we did enjoy ourselves and used one of Milwaukee's many shuttles to get to and from the stadium. We opted for the Milwaukee Brat House shuttle, mainly because when in Wisconsin, you seek every opportunity you can to get a good bratwurst. The shuttle doesn't cost any extra and you can take a "to-go" beverage on the bus. Several St. Louis establishments offer the same service to Busch Stadium.

Following the July 4th victory, we hopped back in the shuttle and got a ride to the Summerfest grounds. Def Leppard and Journey were the headliners and we had lawn tickets at the American Family Insurance Amphitheater. We wish we would have had covered seats.

That storm front that threatened to soak Miller Park earlier in the day was now upon us. We got drenched, along with thousands of others, as Def Leppard was in the middle of their set. We tried to use our blanket as some cover, but that didn't last long. It was a downpour and we joined the horde huddled in the stairwells or bathrooms in a vain attempt to stay dry. Women who couldn't find space in their restroom gathered in the men's room. Some even posed for photos, making goofy faces while men stood at urinals behind them.

The rain and lightning lasted for about 30 minutes as Def Leppard, who opened with *Rocket*, kept playing. We saw that opening song — as well the next one (*Animal*) — before seeking cover. We returned to the lawn in time to see their final four songs — *Hysteria*, *Pour Some Sugar On Me*, *Rock of Ages* and *Photograph*.

Journey was up next, though as Patti says, it's not the "real" Journey without longtime leader singer, Steve Perry. Perry had left the band in 1998 and Journey found Filipino singer Arnel Pineda in 2007. Pineda was discovered on YouTube singing covers of Journey songs. He does sound a lot like Perry. The band opened with *Separate Ways* before performing *Only the Young* and *Be Good to Yourself*. There was then a rendition of the *Star-Spangled Banner* performed by guitarist Neal Schon as members of the military joined the group on stage. There was a huge applause for both Schon and the service members, and during the ovation, Patti and I decided to leave. We wanted to change out of our waterlogged clothes. We could hear the faint sound of *Lovin'*, *Touchin'*, *Squeezin'* as we exited the amphitheater.

Neither of us had ever been to Summerfest before. It bills itself as the world's largest music festival for good reason. Over 800 bands performed across the park's 12 stages. I made sure to bring plenty of Home Run On Wheels cards with me.

We saw Imagine Dragons with Grace VanderWaal on the amphitheater stage on June 27th, the first night of the festival and fireworks were shot off in the middle of the set. Imagine Dragons put on one of the best performances we'd ever seen. We also saw the Dave Matthew Band on July 1st. Patti ducked out two hours into the three-hour set to see Pat Benatar on an adjacent stage. Rick Springfield was playing at the other end of the park at the same time. I stuck around for the entirety of Dave Matthews, seeing him for the second time in my life. I saw the band on July 26th, 1994 but was a bit disappointed in 2018 because he didn't play many of his 1990s hits.

We also took in the The All-American Rejects, A Flock of Seagulls, also in the rain, Great White, the Pixies, and The Fray. We walked past a stage where Kesha was playing and it wasn't good. We also discovered a couple of artists we had never heard of but enjoyed watching Caroline Rose, Ida Jo, Digbii, Madison Ryan, and Danielle Juhre. Ryan played to the largest crowd she ever had on July 1st thanks to a covered bandstand as an afternoon downpour interrupted the set of A Flock of Seagulls on the next stage over. A Flock of Seagulls had to stop after just two songs because of the heavy rain and open stage. We didn't even get to hear *I Ran* as we hustled over to the covered area.

One of my Summerfest highlights was stumbling upon a miniature Lambeau Field setup, where former Packers safety LeRoy Butler was holding a question-and-answer session. We stopped to listen and I explained to Patti hold dominant of a player Butler was in the 1990s and he helped the Packers win Super Bowl XXXI. His sack of Drew Bledsoe is one of the all-time greats because he took down Patriots running back Dave Meggett in the process. Butler is still waiting for his call to the Pro Football Hall of Fame, despite being named to the 1990s All-Decade team. He also invented the Lambeau Leap in 1993 when he returned a fumble for a touchdown in a 28-0 win over the Oakland Raiders. Butler was, and still is, one of my favorite players and it was an unexpected treat to be able to meet him at Summerfest.

Butler may be a Florida native, but he still lives in Wisconsin and hosts a radio show in Milwaukee. He has become of a fan of Milwaukee sports and even offered some Brewers opinions during the Q&A. The Brewers' 3-2 win over the Twins completed a three-game sweep. When we left Milwaukee, we had seen 20 games in 17 stadiums and the home teams were 8-12. They would improve thanks to the Twins winning twice at Target Field.

CHAPTER 10:

THE TWIN CITIES

The news arrived within minutes of each other. Antigone Vigil was the first to contact me with a phone call. As I'm on the phone with her, an email came in from Onoma Ejiya.

It was June 26th and both women delivered excellent news.

Antigone is the manager of community affairs with the Colorado Rockies and she wanted to know how many tickets Lutheran Family Services Rocky Mountains needed for the July 11th game. I had to get back to her and emailed my contact at LFSRM, but more on that in the next chapter.

Onoma was an intern with Family Alternatives in Minneapolis. Patti and I had nearly given up on getting kids out to a Twins game the weekend after July 4th. Matt Roesler had put me in touch with Family Alternatives director, Mary Lennick, on May 22nd. Mary, a lifelong Twins fan, was more than happy to join our cause. The problem is there was some confusion over how to submit the ticket request to the Twins. When I emailed her June 6th for an update on the request, she had not yet done it and wasn't sure of the proper channels. I walked her through it and she finally had Onoma submit the request on June 10th. I did my part to help by leaving a voicemail for Stephanie Johnson, the team's senior manager of community relations. Then we waited and had heard nothing. Patti and I assumed the worst and ended up buying tickets for the game on Sunday, July 8th. We were leaving my grandparents' house Saturday morning and didn't want to be rushed to get from Bangor, Wisconsin to Minneapolis. I purchased four tickets for Sunday's game; we would be joined by Patti's cousin, Shelley, and her husband, Santiago, at 10 a.m.

"Tickets are purchased," I told Patti. "Now watch, we'll find out the Twins are donating tickets for the Saturday game."

Onoma emailed me at 4:26 p.m. that very same day.

"I guess we're going to two games at Target Field," I said.

This wasn't exactly a bad thing.

Patti and I arranged to meet Mary at the right-field gate and interview her for our podcast inside the stadium before the game. She didn't realize being interviewed would be "part of the deal" but was more than happy to talk about the services Family Alternatives provides.

· · · · ·

As people wait in Target Plaza outside the right-field gate at Target Field, a recorded message comes through the speakers affixed to the light poles.

"Everyone is welcome at Target Field."

A nearby sign reads, "It's a beautiful day for baseball."

We were thankful to the Twins for opening their doors to a group of foster families from Family Alternatives in Minneapolis for the July 7th game against the Orioles.

Family Alternatives had previously received tickets to Twins games but never before did those tickets come directly from the team. They were acquired by a third party and then donated to the non-profit organization that was founded in 1978. They did have an existing relationship with the NBA's Minnesota Timberwolves and the Minnesota Lynx of the WNBA, and Mary was excited and hopeful to build a relationship with her beloved Twins.

"We, as an agency, really prioritize kids in care having normal childhood experiences, and when I say normal, I mean things like going to baseball games and other sporting events, concerts, sleepovers," Mary said. "This was an opportunity to let our kids do things that otherwise wouldn't be able to do in the home settings they're coming from. We like kids to have fun. You heal through having fun and you heal through experiences such as this."

Mary said her favorite baseball memory was the Twins' 1991 World Series championship. While a 7-year-old Mary didn't attend any of the World Series games that year, her dad did and brought home several "Homer Hankies" that were made famous when the Twins won the 1987 championship.

"I wasn't able to go to the games because my dad wanted to go instead of me. Thanks, Dad," Mary quipped. "But we took those now-infamous 'Homer Hankies' and made them into pillows. Those bring back some nostalgic memories for me."

She joked that she's gotten over the "bitterness" of not being able to go to any of those postseason games.

"I'm working through it," she cracked. "I'm aware of that bitterness now more than I was when I was 7 because I didn't understand the magnitude of the victory."

"That's funny," I said while trying to contain my laughter as we chatted at the top of an escalator at Target Field.

Matt wasn't the only common link Mary and I had. One of my favorite players growing up was Paul Molitor, who finished his Hall-of-Fame playing career with the Twins. The St. Paul native later served as the Twins manager from 2015-18. Mary grew up with Molitor's daughter and she said she got to know her friend's dad over the years.

After our podcast interview got sidetracked by talk of the Vikings collapsing in the 2017 NFC championship game against the Philadelphia Eagles, we brought it back to foster care. As Celeste, Michael, Gordie, and Matt had done previously, Mary explained to our listeners how people can get involved and directed them to the Family Alternatives website as a first resource.

"The most important need is foster parents," Mary said. "Baby boomers are retiring and that's an age group that is maybe looking to give back now that their biological kids have moved out. It's hard work, but it's the most rewarding and remarkable journey on which I've had the privilege of walking with people."

Mary is a huge sports fan and her family has had Twins season tickets for years. They would improve their seats on a regular basis, and in 2018, had a pair of tickets right behind home plate. Mary sat in her parents' seats while the donated tickets were in Section 319, but sitting next to her behind home plate was a 16-year-old girl who Family Alternatives had helped place in a home. The girl, who was nice enough to take a picture of Mary with me and Patti, was thrilled to not just be at an MLB game but to have such a wonderful view.

From our seats in 319, we had an excellent view of the Minneapolis skyline behind the giant Minnie and Paul sign in right field set against Target Field's yellow limestone walls.

· · · · ·

We had moved down to Section 121 for Sunday's game and were joined by Patti's cousin, Shelley Garcia, and her husband, Santiago. The Garcias had driven over from their home in Marshfield, Wisconsin, about three hours due east of Minneapolis. We met Shelley and Santi at the Mall of America and took the light-rail train right to Target Field.

We did the same thing a day earlier, except this time we had parked my car at the mall. Both the July 7th and July 8th games had 1 p.m. Central Time starts. We could not check into the Dakota County RV park in Apple Valley, just south of St. Paul, before 1. We did a little research and found that the Mall of America had a lot for RVs and we could park there until the mall closed. We didn't need that long, just a few hours from about noon to 5 on a Saturday.

After Sunday's game, we took the train back to the Mall of America, rode one of the many rollercoasters inside the mall, and then said our goodbyes to Shelley and Santi. Patti and I weren't quite ready to leave the mall. I wanted to see the recently released *Ant-Man and the Wasp*, which we watched at the Mall of America's only movie theater.

The movie, which we thoroughly enjoyed, capped off a full day of activity in the Twin Cities. Prior to meeting up with Shelley and Santi at the Mall of America, Patti and I had taken our tour through Paisley Park.

The Twins completed a four-game sweep of the Orioles over the weekend and the home teams were now 10-12 through 18 stadiums.

CHAPTER 11:

ROCKY MOUNTAIN HIGH

Denver was our final stop before the All-Star break, and we hit the unofficial halfway point of the season on a high note.

The Rockies had donated 30 tickets to Lutheran Family Services Rocky Mountains for the July 11th game against the Arizona Diamond-backs. Despite the frustration of now having the slideout topper in the middle of the RV floor, I was happy that the efforts I began in late January had paid off.

The first thing I did was research foster care organizations in the Denver area. I emailed a couple and got a return email from Lauren Knudsen of Lutheran Family Services Rocky Mountains. A conference call with Lauren, LFSRM vice president of development, Jane Pope Meehan, and Abby Lord-Ramsey of Children's Hope Alliance was scheduled for January 30th. We agreed to a partnership by the end of the call.

I then emailed Dallas Davis, a former Colorado State football player who now served as the assistant director of community affairs for the Rockies. My email prompted a phone call from Dallas, who wanted to know more about our trip. I spoke with him on February 3rd while sitting in my car in the Perform Media office parking lot and explained our objective. He was on board and walked me through the ticket request process.

I relayed that information on to Lauren and the request was made but then we went months without hearing anything. She and I both pestered the Rockies with emails until I finally got that call from Antigone Vigil on June 26th. It was finally happening.

"Wonderful!" was the response from Lauren when I told her.

Lauren told me I would be interviewing Dona Dalton, the group's director of marketing, at their Denver office at 3 p.m. on gameday. I was looking forward to meeting Lauren to thank her for helping to make this happen. Unfortunately she was out of the office when I arrived. Jane wasn't there either. But Dona was and she led me into a conference room where I would interview her, program director, Cindi Noah, and office administrator, Nicole Vail, about the donation of tickets from the Rockies. Cindi is a New Jersey native and proud lifelong Yankees fan who attended Mickey Mantle's final game in 1968.

"I grew up watching him play, and then you say good bye, only to welcome other players," she said.

As LFSRM celebrated its 70th anniversary in 2018, the Rockies were in their 25th anniversary season. Dona attended the team's first-ever home game in 1993.

"It was great. Everybody was excited to go to the games, and the fun thing was the Rockies had to play in Mile High Stadium because Coors Field wasn't built yet. It was a lot of fun being in the football stadium and watching this new Rockies team play there," Dalton said of the inaugural Rockies season.

Lutheran Family Services Rocky Mountains, which serves families in Colorado and New Mexico, had never before received tickets from the Rockies. The Denver office had about 80 children in the foster system in 2018. Dona and Cindi were hopeful the Rockies' donation would lead to a continuing relationship with the club.

"Baseball is America's game, but there are a lot of Americans who don't get to watch it in person," Cindi said. "To see our kids' faces light up with the opportunity to go, that's meaningful. The whole focus is to make sure they feel safe and secure and that they're provided with opportunities they might not otherwise have and that eventually they are reunified with their families or they are adopted by somebody else," Cindi added. "Finding their forever home or returning to people they know best, who they had to leave, temporarily, and making sure we give them as many opportunities as possible."

LFSRM doesn't just help with foster care and adoption but also provides services for refugee resettlement, senior citizen assistance, and natural disaster recovery.

"Any one of the programs could be meaningful to someone on a personal level, whether it's helping an older adult adjust to lifestyle changes or it's someone who's interested in adopting a child locally or from another country, or it's being a foster parent, adopting a child from foster care, helping refugees settle here in this country," Cindi explained. "There are a variety of ways to help. It just depends on what taps into the passions you might have or you didn't know that you had. In foster care, we need tutors, we need mentors, we need people who can be a big brother or big sister in order to help these kids feel more comfortable."

When the interview was over, all three women thanked me for helping to obtain tickets. Dona and Cindi would not be attending the game, but Nicole would serve as the organization's liaison to ensure each family received their tickets. The seats were in prime home-run location, Section 156 in the left-center field bleachers. We had no idea just how good they would be.

The Diamondbacks jumped out to an early lead with Paul Goldschmidt's solo home run in the top of the first. The ball landed in the third row, two sections to our left.

The Rockies pounced in the bottom half of the inning with five runs, punctuated by Ian Desmond's monster 472-foot blast that sailed over the left-field seats. The ball caromed off the sign above Todd Helton's Burger Shack behind Section 153. Two homers to left field in the first inning. This was promising. I was thinking that I just might get my first home run ball.

The Diamondbacks pulled starting pitcher Shelby Miller after one inning, but the Rockies added four more runs in the second off reliever, Jorge De La Rosa. Charlie Blackmon and Carlos Gonzalez both homered to center field in the third. Gonzalez sent another blast to center — off infielder Daniel Descalso — to cap a six-run fourth and the rout was on. It was 18-1, and Patti and I had already begun our exploration of the stadium.

It began with food, as it usually did. I ordered a burger from the Helton Shack while Patti got adventurous with some Rocky Mountain Oysters. If you're not familiar, those are bull testicles and Patti said they were chewy. As we ate our respective sandwiches in the left-field corner, I recognized a Rockies employee walking by. It was Dallas Davis. I stopped him to thank him again for the team's donation of tickets.

"No problem. Hope you're having a good time," he said before telling us he was actually on his way out to attend one of his children's functions.

Gonzalez's second home run landed in the center-field batter's eye, which is certainly unique. Coors Field has perhaps the most incredible outfield scenes in all of baseball. The batter's eye is a microcosm of Colorado's landscape, as a wall of ivy serves as the backdrop for a miniature forest of conifers. The trees, which stretch into the visiting team's bullpen, are accompanied by rocks and small waterfalls that help form a tiny stream.

"That is absolutely the best center field and bullpens in baseball," an impressed Patti remarked.

Nicole advised us to check out the views from the "Purple Row" in the upper deck. The 20th row of the upper deck stretches from foul pole to foul pole and is known as the "Mile High Row" because it is exactly 5,280 feet above sea level. Nicole said we'd be able to see the Rocky Mountains in the distance. How right she was and we picked a perfect time to be up there.

The first pitch of the game was thrown by Colorado right-hander German Marquez at 6:40 p.m. Sunset in Denver that evening was at 8:29, which is right around the time Patti and I sat down in the Purple Row along the first-base side. We didn't purposefully plan to be in the Purple Row at sunset, but our timing could not have been better.

"Yeah, we're not that smart," Patti quipped when I mentioned our excellent, yet accidental timing.

We watched as the sun, with rays beaming through a few sparse clouds, slowly disappeared behind the Rocky Mountains. It was stunning.

"This is the best view in baseball," Patti said. "I love the view of the Arch in St. Louis, but this is a completely different kind of view.

"The moral of the story is nature trumps architecture," I replied.

We continued to admire the view, ignoring the game until the sun was completely behind the mountains. The top of the fifth ended with the score still 18-1. We used the mid-inning break to make our way to The Rooftop in right field. The Rooftop stretches from the right-field corner to center field and has several bars and food options. Despite being a Wednesday night, it was teeming with casual fans socializing while enjoying views of the mountains and the downtown Denver skyline. Patti and I maneuvered through the crowd with several excuse mes and were eventually looking down at the batter's eye foliage. The fountains and waterfall cascading over the multiple rocks were even more impressive.

Then the incredible happened. Marquez, who had pitched brilliantly, stepped to the plate with two outs. With the infielder Descalso still on the mound for Arizona, Marquez lifted a 72 mile-per-hour "slider" over the wall in left-center.

"Um, babe," I said as I watched the ball land in the bleachers.

"Yeah?" she said with an inflection.

"I think that's our section," I said before we hurried back to our seats.

The ball landed on the stairs between sections 156 and 157, about eight rows up. Just missing the outstretched glove of one young man, the ball bounced left and found the waiting hands of a boy in Section 156. He was from Lutheran Family Services Rocky Mountains. He was about 10 years old and this was his first-ever MLB game.

The boy was sitting in the row behind the one we had vacated an inning earlier. If we remained in our seats, that could have been my ball.

I jokingly told the kid, "You know, if I was here and got that ball, I would not have given it to you."

One of these days, I'll get my own home run ball.

Nicole took a picture of the boy with his new baseball and two other kids holding a sign thanking the Rockies for the donation of tickets.

Seeing that kid hold a home run ball he got at his first-ever MLB game is precisely why we chose to do what we did. When we first got the idea for a baseball road trip, it was just something to cross off our bucket list. But we wound up being grateful for our partnership with Children's Hope Alliance and proud of our mission to raise awareness of the needs of children in the foster system. The experiences these kids got are something they'll have for a lifetime. We said that a lot on our trip, and it's true. That boy has a memory for life, and even the kids who didn't catch it are going to remember that their friend caught that ball.

It was the first career home run for Marquez, who was pulled after the Diamondbacks scored a run in the sixth inning. He had allowed two runs off five hits and struck out eight to improve his record to 8-8 on the season. Marquez finished the season 14-11 and had lowered his ERA from 4.88 in July to 3.77 by October.

As we watched the final three innings, we spoke with some of the families there with us. One foster dad was there with his two biological sons while his wife was at home with their sick 3-year-old foster daughter.

Even though she was not yet 100-percent legally theirs, they considered her their daughter. She had been with them for over a year at that point, but they were still trying to get the adoption finalized. The couple went through the foster system and found the girl, with whom they immediately fell in love.

I asked the man why he and his wife wanted to be foster parents. He said that even before he and his wife were blessed with their own bio-kids, adoption was something they had always considered. Following the birth of their two sons, they still decided to adopt and went through the foster system to do so. You could hear the passion in the man's voice when he spoke about his daughter, whom he said is "very much" their daughter. But the adoption process is a long one.

"The system is complicated," Cindi said emphatically. "The system is not easy to navigate and it's not easy to understand. What I'm most proud of here with Lutheran Family Services is the focus we place on children and how we can best take care of children."

On the same night, we saw the Rockies cruise to their 19-2 victory, the Indians trounced the Reds by a 19-4 count. I don't know what was going on that night, but between Ohio and Colorado, the baseballs were flying out of the yard. And one went home with a foster kid.

CHAPTER 12:

NATIONAL PARKS

When KHOU television reporter, Jason Bristol, came out to do a story on us in Houston, he began the segment that aired in September by saying, "Like most baseball stories, this one begins in a park. But not a baseball park – an RV park."

But those weren't the only parks we visited. On our 15,000-mile trek across 38 U.S. states and two Canadian provinces, we entered six national parks.

Our first was Acadia National Park in Maine.

When I put our schedule together in September of 2017, I noticed the Toronto Blue Jays had a long homestand in May. The Jays had 13 home games between May 8th and May 24th. Rogers Centre would be our tenth stadium and would follow our visit to Citi Field in Queens. We had a three-week window to get from our RV park in Connecticut to Toronto, and I wanted to capitalize on it. I had never been to New England, so I asked Patti what she thought of doing single nights in Vermont and New Hampshire and then spending a few days in Maine. Without any hesitation, she was on board.

We spent May 4th in Brattleboro, Vermont, which is barely in Vermont but still counts. Brattleboro is in the southeast corner of the state, right on the New Hampshire border and just a few miles north of Massachusetts. We had dinner at a restaurant with a balcony overlooking the Connecticut River and New Hampshire bluffs. We sat outside and struck up a conversation with a couple of women seated next to us. Gail and Danielle were from Boston and their sons had a college baseball game earlier in the day. They informed us their sons' team won to qualify for the NCAA Division II tournament. After telling them about our baseball trip, they told us they were each host families for the Cape Cod League, a college summer wood bat league. When their husbands arrived, I gave them cards before they were seated inside. When it was time to pay our bill, we were told it was already taken care of. Those two couples bought our dinner, which was something we never expected but were extremely grateful. We thanked them on our way out, hoping they were the kind of people who would get involved with a foster-care organization.

The next night, we stayed at a farm in New Hampshire with our Harvest Hosts membership. We arrived at Acadia National Park around 5 p.m. on May 6th. We were the last to check in that day and the staff was waiting on us before they closed the office.

The Bar Harbor/Oceanside KOA had just opened for the 2018 season and it was sparsely populated. Some amenities, like Wi-Fi, weren't yet ready. That was frustrating as we tried to work from the road. We were led to our lot, which was maybe 100 yards from the water. Because the RV park was on the interior of Mt. Desert Island, the water was calm with just ripples splashing the rocks on the pebble beach. Though there weren't many people at the campground, within five minutes of pulling into our campsite, we were asked three times about Children's Hope Alliance and Home Run On Wheels. We were happy to tell them and cards were issued. One of the inquiring parties was a couple from Vancouver, who were living in their RV full-time and had traveled across Southern Canada. They had a dog named Meatball, who spent about an hour running around with Holmes while the humans talked over some drinks.

Acadia National Park preserves more than half of Mt. Desert Island. Acadia's natural beauty is stunning with its mountains and granite cliffs that form a craggy coastline. Because of its location on Maine's central coast, Acadia has one of the earliest sunrises in the United States.

We attempted to see one, but even a 5 a.m. wakeup wasn't early enough. We got dressed and I fixed myself come coffee before hopping in the car. We arrived at the Schooner Head Overlook just before 6, but the sun was already in full view. Its reflection off the ocean water was extraordinary. There was one car parked there when we arrived. They were from California and had slept in their car overnight to see the sunrise. I had to admire the dedication. We had a couple hours before Patti's first conference call of the day, so we decided to explore a bit. I had read about a cave full of anemones in the area. It's a large sea cave aptly named Anemone Cave. We walked up and down the rocky shore with no luck.

We were ready to give up when we sat down on one of the large boulders when Patti glanced to her left and shouted, "Found it."

That she had. I wanted to see if I could get inside.

"Be careful," Patti yelled from the boulder as she watched me descend to the rocks below. Waves slapped my feet as I moved toward to the cave opening. The closer I got, the more I realized I would not be going inside. The cave is accessible only at low tide, which wouldn't be until about 11 a.m. that day. They were far too high at 7:30 and attempting to enter the cave would have been a very bad idea. Others have been trapped inside the cave, some even dying, and I wasn't going to be added to the list. Because of that danger, the cave has been removed from official Acadia National Park maps and guides. I got a couple photos and climbed back up to rejoin Patti on the boulder. We returned to the car and made a couple more stops along Park Loop Road.

Sand Beach is exactly what it says, a sandy inlet that stretches 290 yards between two mountainsides. Up the road is Boulder Beach, which is also exactly what is says. There you find Thunder Hole, a spot where waves crashing between the boulders at high tide create a thunderous sound. The water wasn't quite that violent during our morning visit, though I could feel droplets atop the boulders as I hopped from one to another to each the edge.

Acadia's rocky terrain was created by glaciers that swept across the land some 17,000 years ago. Those glaciers created the mountain valleys filled with lakes and the only fjord on the East Coast. Also left behind were the sloping mountains, their smooths summits void of any foliage. The highest and most popular peak is Cadillac Mountain at 1,530 feet. While the majestic centerpiece of Acadia National Park is a favored spot to view sunrise, we took the winding road to the top on the evening of May 7th. Holmes went with us and happily trotted across the granite blocks as we enjoyed a 360-degree view of the Atlantic Ocean. The Porcupine Islands, named for how the evergreen-topped islands rise from the water, lie to the east in Frenchman Bay. Four of the five islands are in a line while a fifth sits to one side to form an upside-down L. The archipelago is just off the shore from the town of Bar Harbor, the island's only real municipality.

The islands are popular with kayakers who leave from the town's waterfront, which is where visitors can also catch touring boats to cruise around the island or go whale watching.

We didn't take any cruises but did venture into town a couple of times to find some Wi-Fi and pick up a few grocery items. Downtown Bar Harbor offers free Wi-Fi, though it wasn't strong enough for me to upload a podcast episode or photos to our website. A coffee house on Main Street did not have public Wi-Fi, but a bar next to it did, so that's where I did my work. I got a lot done on the trip with a beer next to my computer.

Patti and I had dinner that night at Fish House Grill, which is on the water next to one of the whale watch cruise terminals. The restaurant has its own boats, so everything was fresh. I ordered some halibut, while Patti got some lobster. When in Maine…

We left the next morning to begin our seven-hour drive to Montreal.

· · · · ·

It was rather surprising to learn that Niagara Falls is not a national park in Canada or the United States.

Arguably the world's most famous cataract, Niagara Falls, is a New York state park on the U.S. side and a provincial park on the Canadian side. Queen Victoria Park is maintained by the Ontario government and houses the Table Rock Welcome Centre. That's where we purchased our tickets that included a 4-D film, the Journey Behind the Falls, the Hornblower Cruise, and White Water Walk.

The Hornblower Cruise lives up to its name. We weren't on the boat for five minutes when our conversation with a couple of German tourists was interrupted by a bellowing honk. We were standing directly under the horn and it scared the bejeezus out of us. The 16-year-old German girl, who was traveling with her father as a birthday present, nearly leapt out of her skin — as did I. The horn did not catch us off-guard again.

There is a reason they give you ponchos on the cruise because you definitely get wet as the boat nears the mist. The boat takes its passengers past the American Falls and Goat Island, on the New York side, and directly into the basin. Luna Island and Bridal Veil Falls are on the boat's port side with the massive Horseshoe Falls directly in front of the spectators. We tried to take some photos, but it was very tough to see through the profuse mist. Again, we tried. After a couple futile attempts to snap a few pictures, I put my phone away and just took in the view. Talking was impossible because of the turbulent sound created by the gushing water. The boat began to turn after a few minutes with the Horseshoe Falls now on the starboard side. We were soon back at the dock to disembark — soaked but stupefied. An outdoor restaurant adjoins the landing and we stopped to have a local brew while enjoying live music provided by a young man and his guitar.

We were also given ponchos for the Journey Behind the Falls, which takes you into the tunnels near the bottom of the Horseshoe Falls on the Canadian shore of the Niagara River. A two-level observation deck provides a vantage point looking up at the falls to the right. The platforms are continually sprayed from the cascading water as it drops 187 feet to the half-mile basin below. Seeing Niagara Falls for the first time, we were in awe. With tons of water falling per second, the sheer power of Niagara Falls can be felt behind the falls or on the cruise boats. Even hundreds of yards downstream from the whirlpool basin, that power still manifests itself in the form of violent whitewater rapids gushing over huge boulders in the riverbed. The water moves so quickly that plumes over ten feet high shoot up in the air. Lining the riverbed is a walkway that takes you within a few feet of the rapids. Just stay on the path. Swimming is not advised.

. . . . .

Excluding Niagara Falls, Ball's Falls were the most impressive waterfalls we saw in Ontario.

A small mill town once existed between the two waterfalls on Twenty Mile Creek, but the establishment of the Great Western Railway resulted in industry moving away from the Glen Elgin area and the town was abandoned. The buildings still exist in what is now a nature conservation park, and those structures were in use during our visit.

The park was very close to the RV park where we stayed and we wanted to take Holmes for a hike. Upon arrival we were told that the Lower Falls were closed because a film crew was there shooting scenes for *Star Trek*. I said I didn't even realize a new *Star Trek* movie was coming out. I asked all sorts of questions about who might be on site; the clerk didn't know. She had never seen a Star Wars movie or episode. She did recognize one actress of African-American descent. I assumed she had spotted Zoe Saldana, who plays Uhura is the most recent *Star Trek* films.

We made our way up to the shorter Upper Falls, which are still an impressive 35 feet high. You can view the falls from above and below as the shallow creek careens over the rocky cliff. We first went to the top of the Upper Falls and let Holmes get a drink as I spoke with another trio of visitors. Our conversation was interrupted by a snake that swam out of the water and slithered onto the bank. It was a harmless Northern Watersnake, but we left it alone and moved down the hill. I stood on the banks below while Patti led Holmes out into the water on a path of stepping stones that had naturally formed.

A few photos were taken and we then headed downstream. I was still curious about the film set and wanted to see the Lower Falls and its 90-foot drop. The village was located at the Lower Falls and several of the original buildings still stood and had been restored. Usually open to the public, the original Ball family home, an operating gristmill, a lime kiln, a restored church, a blacksmith shop, and a carriage shed were being used to shoot the *Star Trek* scenes. We noticed some activity outside of the church with multiple camera dollies moving about. We walked along a path across the creek from the town to catch a glimpse of the falls from above. It was an obstructed view because of the many trees between us and the limestone precipice. Across the way was a viewing platform. The same trio of people we saw at the Upper Falls were now on that observation deck. You had to walk through the town to get there and we just assumed they were part of the crew. As we headed back to our car, we saw them cross the narrow bridge that led to the hamlet. I asked if they were part of the crew. When they said no, we turned right around.

One woman approached us as we walked across the bridge. She introduced herself as a producer but not for a *Star Trek* movie. They were filming scenes for Season 2 of the CBS show, *Star Trek: Discovery*. Turns out that African-American actress wasn't Zoe Saldana but Sonequa Martin-Green, best known for playing Sasha Williams on *The Walking Dead*.

The producer told us they were on a break from shooting and we were free to walk through to the falls viewing area. We thanked her and walked down the path, which was lined with power cords leading to various lights, trailers, and tents. Holmes trotted along behind us. One male member of the crew stopped us to give Holmes an extended rub on the head.

A covered wooden bench is at the entrance to a large, concrete deck overlooking the creek below. A railing is embedded into a stone foundation on the cliff's edge. The impressive Lower Falls are to the left. Because of the film set, we did not have access to the creek bed, but seeing the water drop 90 feet was still quite something. We admired the view for a few minutes and snapped some photos of the falls before turning to head back to the car. Three people, two women, and a man were now sitting on the bench and a small dog was sitting at the feet of the man. The dog and Holmes locked eyes, though neither made a sound nor moved toward the other, just staring and waging their tails. The man and I exchanged some small talk about our dogs, but it was clear to us now he and the two women were actors on the show. We later realized who they were. The man was Anson Mount, who plays Captain Christopher Pike and the two women were Oyin Oladejo, who portrays Joann Owosekun, and the aforementioned Sonequa Martin-Green. This was our brush with celebrity in Canada, though we barely realized it at the time.

We told ourselves we were going to watch *Star Trek: Discovery*, but the year ended without us viewing a single episode.

· · · · ·

TLC told people in 1995 not go to chasing waterfalls, but we happily ignored that advise. We couldn't pass up the opportunity to see the many falls within the Niagara Escarpment. The bucolic region is dotted with waterfalls and wineries from Hamilton all the way down to the majestic Niagara Falls. One of the more difficult to find is Rockway Falls minutes east of Ball's Falls. Our GPS took us to a trailhead, but we realized we after a few minutes walking along the creek we had a long walk to get to the waterfall. After doing a search, we learned the falls were next to the Rockway Community Centre. That was an easy find and there below was the 45-foot waterfall. A narrow path took you to the top of the waterfall, but there was no real water access like we had at Ball's Falls. Now the question was how to get to the bottom of the falls. Well, there is an answer to that question, just not a simple one. This is where we had to truly hike. We walked down the narrow path and crawled over a few boulders before carefully stepping down the gorge's steep slope. Once at the rocky creek bed, we still had a bit of a hike over the large stones to get to the waterfall basin. About 15 minutes later, we were there. Rockway Falls isn't the most impressive waterfall in Ontario, but for us, it was the most satisfying. We had truly earned our view because the path can be treacherous without any railings to grasp in case of a slip. We took a few minutes to relax and enjoy watching the fast-moving water cascade down the step-like shale. The trek there was efficacious, but leaving the gorge wasn't any easier and we had to help Holmes get over some of the bigger rocks. He may transform into a mountain goat when on trails like these, but some of boulders were a little too large for him to climb. He hates to be picked up, but in this situation, he had no choice.

"It was a little challenging and not for the faint of heart," Patti said of the path to Rockway Falls.

Much easier to find was the Devil's Punchbowl, which sounds much cooler than it actually is. The ribbon waterfall is alongside Ridge Road near Hamilton with a farmer's market across the road. Water from a tiny stream drops from a small hole and into a large, bowl-like basin 110 feet below. The basin walls are multi-colored with layers of Queenston Formation red shale, Cabot Head grey shale, limestone and shale dolomite. There is an excellent view of Hamilton Harbour, but the waterfall itself was rather underwhelming.

· · · · ·

Ohio's Brandywine Falls, on the other hand, is very cool. Located just south of Cleveland in Cuyahoga Valley National Park, Brandywine is surrounded by an abundance of hiking trails. Water cascades 65 feet over a series of sandstone ledges. Viewing platforms at different levels provide vistas of the falls and gorge below. Spring wildflowers lined the riverbanks.

The Cuyahoga River winds away from Cleveland and into the Cuyahoga Valley, where the national park is located less than an hour from Cleveland. We just got a taste of Cuyahoga Valley National Park but loved every minute we spent hiking with Holmes. We did get in a bit of trouble when we took him off leash. We had gone about ten minutes without seeing another person, so we let Holmes run free. He is the type of dog who will sprint off and evens turns around to make sure we're still there if he thinks we've fallen too far behind.

Creeks that serve as tributaries to the river line the hiking trails. Patti stopped to take some pictures and I continued on with Holmes. A blonde jogger approached and slowed as she saw Holmes, who was wagging his tail. She stopped to pet him and we introduced ourselves. Our conversation was interrupted by a man's voice, "Is this your dog?"

"No," the woman quickly said.

"It's mine," I replied to the man, who was about 40 years old and wearing a park ranger uniform.

"Do you have a leash for him?" the ranger asked.

"Yeah. My wife has it," I answered.

"Where is she and why is he not on his leash?" came another question from the man, who stood about 6 feet, 2 inches. He was authoritative, yet polite.

I explained there was nobody around, so we took the leash off and that Patti had stopped to take pictures. I yelled to her, and a couple minutes later, she appeared with the leash, which was reattached to Holmes' harness. The ranger told us National Parks require all pets to be leashed to protect the wildlife in the park and the pets from any predators. We weren't ticketed but were issued an official warning. We learned our lesson and Holmes was never taken off the leash at a National Park again. I did use the opportunity to explain to the man what we were doing on our trip and left him with a Home Run On Wheels card.

We eventually made our way back to the waterfall, this time standing on a bridge directly over the falls. There again was the jogger, who was now accompanied by her husband. She asked about our encounter with the ranger and I told her we got off with just a warning. Official introductions were then made, followed by the question of where each other was from. That question when proposed to us always led to an explanation of our trip and mission. I had some cards on me and handed one to the couple, who made a dinner reservation for a spot in the valley. We took their recommendation and found a restaurant with outdoor seating, where we ate as Holmes lay quietly at our feet.

. . . . .

The drive from Denver to Yellowstone is a lot longer than I thought it would be. It took over 11 hours for us to make the 700-mile journey, but there were a couple of stops as we admired Western Wyoming. I had no idea how beautiful the western part of the state is, especially along U.S. Highway 287. We took Interstate 25 North from Denver until we exited onto Highway 287 in Fort Collins. There, the highway skirts the Arapaho and Roosevelt National Forest before reaching the Wyoming border. The road goes through Laramie, where it briefly merges with Interstate 80. It separates from the freeway in Rawlins, where 287 transforms into the Washakie Trail. The scenic track spans 140 miles through colorful valleys as green mountainsides eventually give way to rocky, snow-capped peaks. Ghost towns that were once booming mining communities dot the route.

The trail is named for Chief Washakie, who was a prominent leader of the Shoshone people during the mid-1800s. He was renowned for his expertise in battle but also his willingness to peacefully coexist and trade with white settlers. He befriended soldiers and an Army outpost was renamed Fort Washakie in 1878, 22 years before the chief's death. It was the only fort the U.S. military ever named for a Native American. Chief Washakie was also the only known Native American to be given a full military funeral.

The fort is long gone, but the town of Fort Washakie exists in its place inside the Wind River Reservation. Indian reservations often have gas prices lower than the towns around them, so we topped off in Fort Washakie. Patti had done some research during the drive and learned that Sacajawea's burial place was in Fort Washakie. She told me we had to see it.

Patti has an obsession with cemeteries. She tries to find the headstone with the oldest date on it and wonders out loud what type of life the person occupying the grave might have had. There were no questions about Sacajawea's life, which has been recounted in detail by every U.S. history book. The young

Shoshone woman was the guide and interpreter for explorers Merriweather Lewis and William Clark on their 1805 journey along the Missouri and Columbia rivers from St. Charles, Missouri to Oregon's Pacific Coast. While some historical documents suggest Sacajawea died in North Dakota in 1812, her Wyoming tombstone lists the date of her death as April 9th, 1884. The inscription adds she was identified by "Rev. J Roberts who officiated at her burial." Flowers and other trinkets left by visitors rest on the headstone, which is flanked by the markers for her two sons, Bazil and Baptiste. The gravesite is in the center of the Native American cemetery, which is about two miles off the highway. The green grass is offset by flowers of various colors next to small crosses and gravestones. Across the street from the cemetery is a statue of Chief Washakie. More charms and flowers rest at the bare feet of Sacajawea's bronze statue, which is located at the rear of the burial ground. Some beads and bracelets were placed over her right hand, which is held across her torso. She's looking down at a sand dollar clutched between her thumb and index finger.

We didn't spend too much time at the cemetery, maybe 15 minutes, before we got back on the road. We still had five hours to go before we got to Yellowstone.

· · · · ·

When we drove the RV off the lot in Concord, North Carolina, the odometer read 818. It rolled over to 10,000 miles inside Grand Teton National Park.

Highway 287 merged with U.S. Highway 26 just east of the Wyoming town of Crowheart, named for a nearby butte inside the Wind River Reservation. We stayed on Highway 26 through the Bridger-Teton National Forest before it intersected with U.S. Highway 191. We were now inside Grand Teton National Park. The America, The Beautiful pass paid off because it would have cost us $70 just to drive through the park. It was the same fee for an RV towing a vehicle to enter Yellowstone. The annual pass cost $89. It had paid for itself.

The park ranger at the gate, a man of about 30 years whose name tag read Shaw, asked about the Children's Hope Alliance logo. Just as we were every other time someone inquired about our trip, we were happy to tell him and gave him a card. Shaw then told us that he's from Milwaukee and that his mother works for a foster care organization there. He was pretty pleased to learn the Brewers donated 50 tickets to Anu Family Services for that June 21st win over the Cardinals.

The Tetons look out of place rising from the forested terrain without any foothills. They are what you picture in your mind when you think of mountains, towering snow-capped peaks, barren rock, sharp crags, and steep slopes. I was in awe when the domineering Grand Teton, for which the park is named, came into view. It's the highest peak in the Tetons at 13,775 feet and rises above the equally impressive mountains with summits between 11,000 and 13,000 feet. At the base of the granite massif is the pristine Jackson Lake. From the Colter Bay Village convenience store, Highway 191 borders the northeastern shore of the lake. It was along this stretch of highway the odometer went from 9,999 to 10,000. Though it's just a two-lane road, there wasn't much traffic, so I stopped just long enough to snap a picture of the odometer. It was the only stop we made inside Grand Teton National Park. We had hit 10,000 miles, though not all of those were ours. We'd officially put 10,000 miles on the RV while leaving Snoqualmie Falls in Washington a few weeks later.

· · · · ·

Just seven miles separates the northern edge of Grand Teton National Park from the South entrance to Yellowstone on Highway 191, which is named John D. Rockefeller Jr. Memorial Parkway between the parks.

We weren't inside Yellowstone for five minutes when we saw our first waterfall. I noticed a sign for Moose Falls with a pullout a few yards ahead. I steered the RV into the pullout on the side of the road and parked. We got Holmes out and took him with us toward the nearby trailhead. Another couple was coming the other way. We held Holmes close but soon extended the leash when the young man and woman came over to pet him. They inquired about the RV, and after briefly explaining to them what we were doing, a card was handed out and we went our separate ways. The waterfall was only about 100 feet off the road. The short trail leads to a rocky 30-foot cliff over which Crawfish Creek gushes. Our stop lasted only about 15 minutes before we hopped back in the RV and headed to the campground, passing a female elk chewing on some grass alongside the road.

We spent the first of three nights at Yellowstone inside the park, staying at the Grant Village campground at the West Thumb of the sprawling Yellowstone

Lake. We could only spend one night at Grant Village and moved to an RV park in the town of West Yellowstone, Montana for the remaining two nights. We had our first Yellowstone meal at the Grant Village restaurant, which has a wonderful view of the lake. Our server was from Minneapolis and we shared with her our experience at Target Field. She was a college student working a seasonal job, as many National Park Service employees do.

There is a lot to see in the 3,500 square miles atop a volcanic hot spot. Around every turn is something new, canyons, geysers, hot springs, rivers with falls and rapids, smaller lakes, mountains, and cliffs. We tried to see as much of it as we could. While the diverse terrain is mystifying, the one constant is bison. They, along with herds of elk, are everywhere in the park.

We woke at 6:15 a.m. to begin our first full day at Yellowstone, returning to the RV around 10 a.m. to move it to West Yellowstone. Once checked into our new RV park, we didn't return home until 11 p.m. That first morning provided our first bison encounters.

We took Holmes with us as we headed toward the Mud Volcano area. Because the park sits in a massive and active caldera, steam from hot springs and geysers are ubiquitous. There are approximately 4,000 fumaroles in Yellowstone. The steam was even more prominent in the early-morning hours. Before we arrived at the Mud Volcano, I pulled off the road alongside a large meadow. A few hundred yards off the road, a lone bison was grazing. I got out of the car and whipped my phone out. I took a couple of pictures and then began shooting video while providing narration. Patti had taken Holmes out of the car on his leash and walked him to the top of a small hill just off the shoulder. Though we were nowhere close to the bison, he spotted Holmes and began moving in our direction. His meandering walk turned into a slow trot.

"Time to go," I said before we got back in the car. The bison was still a football field away, but I didn't want to take any chances. We sat in the car and watched as his trot slowed again to a walk and he altered his course, crossing the road to graze on the opposite side.

The Mud Volcano is more than the bubbling hole that flings muck into nearby treetops. There is a hotbed of thermal activity along a looping mile-long path. Dragon's Mouth Spring is a steaming hot spring that boils out of a deep cave just above the Mud Volcano. When the water shoots out of the cave and into the adjacent pool, the gurgling sound echoes off the cave walls. The sound coupled with the plume of steam is what gives the spring its name. Other hydrothermal features in the area also have fun names like Grizzly Fumarole, Sour Lake, Black Dragon's Caldron, Churning Caldron, Sizzling Basin, and Cooking Hillside. Black Dragon's Cauldron is a boiling mud pit, like the Mud Volcano, though it doesn't spew any mud into the air. The Mud Volcano area overlooks the putrid Sulphur Cauldron, which is filled with bubbling muddy acid. Holmes had to stay in the car as we made our way along the loop — dogs aren't allowed on the trail. As we reached the end, we had our second bison encounter. Lying on a hill just about 30 feet off the trail was a bison simply chewing its cud. Patti and I each snapped a picture of the relaxing animal and then turned to take a "bison selfie." We couldn't believe how close it was. We would have closer encounters, one of which was just minutes away.

As we headed back to Grant Village, the three cars in front of us slowed. Seeing their brake lights, I followed suit. They had slowed to 10 mph in a 25-mph zone because a pair of bison were walking down the double-yellow center line. They were shaded to the north-bound side of the road and we were heading south. We slowly crept by as the bison walked in the opposite direction. Holmes was lying down in the backseat and we were thankful he didn't notice the wild beasts as they moseyed by my car. I could have reached my hand out of the window and touched them. A line of north-bound vehicles was stalled behind the sauntering bovines. When the bison were out of sight, I rolled my window down to inform the bewildered drivers headed the other way why they were stopped. We were warned of bison roadblocks before our visit and now we knew they were very much a real thing. The next day in a gift shop, I noticed some cans of Yellowstone Road Block Pale Ale. The logo was a bison walking down the center line. I felt obligated to grab a couple to commemorate the experience.

When we got back to the RV, we loaded the car onto the tow dolly and rolled out. On the way out, we rode right past one of Yellowstone's trademark features — Old Faithful. The Upper Geyser Basin is dotted with various geysers that either bubble or burst out of the ground. Old Faithful is one of the most reliable, erupting about every 90 minutes. After parking the RV in the spacious Old Faithful lot, we followed the crowd to the visitor center. Approximate eruption times are posted there and Old Faithful's next burst was soon. A crowd had already gathered on the benches that surround the geyser. The benches are well out of harm's way from the boiling water that is blown over 100 feet into the air. We only had to wait about 20 minutes before we saw our first eruption.

The Upper Geyser Basin is a dish-shaped valley about two miles long with the Firehole River cutting between the hot springs and geysers. Like the Mud Volcano area, the geyser basin also has great names — Anemone Geyser — which has a bubbling eruption every few minutes — Lion Geyser, Heart Spring, Beehive Geyser, Castle Geyser — which looks like a castle turret — and Spasmordic Geyser. Castle Geyser has one of the most impressive eruptions, mainly because there is 11 to 13 hours between eruptions when water shoots 80 feet into the air from its 30-foot cone. We walked to the far end of the flat basin before taking one of the hiking trails up the hill.

A family from Switzerland was walking alongside of us. They had two young children, a boy and girl. The father was about my age, a tall blond gentleman who spoke perfect English. When we told him what we were doing and that we had come from Denver, he asked what we thought of the Tetons. I told him we were amazed. He, however, was unimpressed because he sees the Swiss Alps every day back home. That added some perspective.

The trail from the basin leads to a bubbling pool and a secluded fountain aptly named Solitary Geyser. It has frequent eruptions, so we waited a few minutes before it gurgled and shot a burst of water about five feet high. Small waves ripple from the minor eruption and slap the edge of the clear blue basin. As we left, a family of four arrived. They asked about the geyser and we told them it should erupt again in a few minutes.

The trail led up Geyser Hill to the Old Faithful Observation Point. Before getting to the end of the trail, we stopped with a group of college students from Wisconsin at a spot with several large rocks on which to sit and an unobstructed view of Old Faithful. The five students, four male and one female, had rented a van and were on a summer trip through the Western U.S. They attended the University of Wisconsin at Oshkosh, where my cousin Andrew was also a student. I asked if they knew him: they didn't. Patti and I then told them of our trip and issued a few Home Run On Wheels cards. Soon after we stopped, our group was joined by a solo hiker named Lance Williams. He was a teacher from El Paso and ventured up the hill with his camera to get a panoramic shot of the basin once Old Faithful erupted. As we patiently waited, a fearless chipmunk looking for a handout darted between our feet. We watched a couple of the other geysers go off during the hour spent basking in the sun on an 80-degree day. Then the one we waited for – Old Faithful blasted a towering plume of water in the air. We could faintly hear the oohs and ahs from the crowd below as we all took photos. As the eruption ended, we made our way back down the hill. We made a stop in the gift shop, where I spotted some bottles of Old Faithful Golden Ale. Again, we had to commemorate the moment.

Back to the RV we went. The beer bottles were secured inside the fridge and we pulled away. It was time to check in at the Grizzly RV Park in West Yellowstone. Once settled, we took Holmes for a brief walk and went back to the park. After flashing our America The Beautiful pass at the West Entrance, the ranger posted there asked if we got caught in the bison roadblock that morning. We told him we were inside the park all morning. Good thing, too. Traffic at the West Entrance was blocked for more than two hours because of bison roaming on the road. We felt fortunate that our morning bison encounter only cost us about five minutes of drive time.

While we had already seen multiple bison, we had only seen one elk and zero moose, bears, or wolves. We were told that Lamar Valley in the northeast quadrant of the park provided the best opportunities to see wildlife. Between slow traffic, summer road construction, and multiple stops, it took us awhile to get there. We stopped at the terraced 150-foot Kepler Cascades, the 84-foot Gibbon Falls, the impressive Upper and Lower Falls of the Yellowstone River, and Tower Falls, where water plunges 132 feet between a pair of natural stone spires. The next day we'd see Lewis Falls (30 feet), Undine Falls (60 feet), and Wraith Falls (100 feet). Yes, there are a lot of waterfalls inside Yellowstone Park.

A territorial squirrel chirped at me as we walked past it on the way to the Lower Falls. He looked me right in the eye and told me where to go in Squirrelish. I tried to get video of the squirrel cursing me out in his native tongue but instead all I did was take a picture of a log. I was truly disappointed with my photo fail.

The steep trail zig-zags down the hill until you get to the brink of the majestic falls. The Upper Falls can also be seen from the trail along the Yellowstone River. Standing above the 308-foot drop of the Lower Falls is astonishing, but just as breath-taking is looking out at Yellowstone's own Grand Canyon. The Lower Falls is the second-most photographed site in Yellowstone, behind only Old Faithful. Patti and I each stared in amazement, surrounded by others also captured by the scenic beauty.

The golden-colored walls of the canyon are anywhere from 800 to 1,200 feet high and the canyon is approximately 24 miles long. The same type of rapids we saw downstream from Niagara Falls, we saw more than a mile down from Yellowstone's Lower Falls.

Back in the parking lot atop the hill from the Lower Falls, another bison had attracted attention as it slowed traffic near the lot's entrance. Being careful not to spook the bison, I walked toward it to get a photo. A family with several small children followed. The kids got excited and started to shout.

"Shhhh!" I hushed them as I turned around. "You don't want to scare it."

Maybe that was a job for their parents, but they were not saying anything and I didn't want the bison to charge at anyone. The bison could not have cared less. It didn't even look in our direction as it stood behind a No Parking sign in the small patch of grass between the lot and Grand Loop Road.

Our trek to Lamar Valley did not turn up any moose, bear, or wolf sighting, though I thought I might have seen a bear roaming a ridge. But it was doubtful. What did see were hundreds of elk and a couple herds of bison. One group blocked our way out of the valley once we turned around. We were stopped for about 30 minutes as the group meandered across the road. Evening had fallen by the time we got by the herd. Taking a different route back, we went through the Mammoth Hot Springs area and then south by the numerous cliffs before following the Madison River to the West Entrance. More elk and bison awaited us the next day, but moose, bears, and wolves eluded us. A grey fox did scamper in front of my car while driving back to West Yellowstone.

We didn't wake up quite as early the next day, which was a Monday and the first official day of the All-Star break. We took our time to eat breakfast inside the RV and Patti got on a few calls while I updated our website with photos. We were inside the park around 2 p.m. and drove toward Mammoth Hot Springs. There would again be stops along the way, the first of which was the Norris Geyser Basin. Located there is Steamboat Geyser, which is in a constant state of steam but rarely erupts. When it does, however, it is the tallest geyser in the world with a blast between 300 and 400 feet. We weren't fortunate enough to see it erupt. Steam is omnipresent at the Norris Basin, with surface temperatures approaching 200 degrees in some places. Those hot spots are off limits for the public.

I wish we had more time to hike at Yellowstone. Every mountain I saw, I viewed as a challenge, especially Tuff Cliff along the Madison River. I wanted to find out just how "tuff" it was. The road north to Mammoth Hot Springs took us by a couple more named cliffs, Obsidian and Sheepeater. One name is self-explanatory; the other, not so much.

Though we drove through the Mammoth Hot Springs village the night before, seeing it during the day revealed unexpected features. It's a small city complete with a luxury hotel, restaurants, grocery store, gift shops, a museum, a couple neighborhoods with houses for employees with families, and apartments for single employees. Thought just a stone's throw from the Montana border and the North Entrance, Mammoth Hot Springs village is the heart of the park and home to the park headquarters. It's also where you find the namesake springs that cascade over the travertine terraces. The limestone is outlined in white by crystalized calcium carbonate. Rising 8,000 feet above the village is Terrace Mountain, which is home to the largest known carbonate-depositing spring in the world. The terraces overlook the village from either side. We parked near the Liberty Cap, a dormant hot spring cone that is 37 feet tall and named for the peaked caps worn during the French Revolution. We walked along Palette Springs, pausing every so often to not get in the way of a family photo. I pretended to join an Indian family, dressed in saris and dhotis. Thankfully the family laughed and my antics drew the desired effect.

From there we headed to the Minerva Terrace, which is the primary feature of Mammoth. A boardwalk takes visitors through the various levels of the multi-colored terrace, which is resplendent. As we strolled down one of the walkways, I heard quick footsteps behind me. An 11-year-old boy was running to a lower level, so I also bolted. Even with a brief head start, he beat me to the finish line, an observation deck overlooking one of the steaming pools. There we met the boy's parents, Brett and Dina, and his older sister. The family was from San Francisco, and of course, Giants fans. We told them about our trip and they gave us a few pointers on where to go for a good meal. I handed Brett a Home Run On Wheels card and we parted ways.

In the time we spent wandering the terrace, a herd of elk had invaded the village. They were casually strolling through the streets and parking lots, grazing front lawns and the nearby parade ground, which were used for military ceremonies when the village was the site of Fort Yellowstone.

The visitor center is across the street from the parade ground and we walked over there to see if it was open. It was 5:05 p.m., and it had just closed. But sitting outside of it was our hiking buddy, Lance, who we met at Old Faithful. This time we talked some more, and after we told him we would be driving through El Paso in a few weeks, we exchanged numbers and agreed to get together for dinner. I almost didn't recognize him. He was wearing jeans and a leather vest with a cowboy hat the previous day. His tanned skin and dark hair made him look Hispanic. But now he was without a hat and his short beard was freshly trimmed. He was wearing a dress shirt and slacks. He was waiting on a friend who works at the park and they were having dinner that night. Lance's friend arrived and he left. We were about to get going, too, before Patti spotted a woman in a Chicago Bears shirt and began asking the couple where they were from. Patti striking up a conversation with strangers? All the time spent together in the RV must have made me rub off on her. Her new friends were in their 60s — the woman was from Galesburg, Illinois — not that far from Peoria — and the man from Southern Wisconsin. Much to my chagrin, he was also a Bears fan. Patti asked if I had any cards, which I did, and they were given one.

The elk were still hanging around. A female was chewing on some grass about 15 feet from my car. It was unbelievable to be that close to these wild animals, but I wasn't about to get any closer. I slowly pulled out my phone to get a picture and then got in the car. We were headed back out to Lamar Valley to see if we'd spot any moose or bears. You already know we didn't.

There is no cell service inside Yellowstone, but the National Parks book my mom sent us the previous Christmas was helpful to figure out what to see. We used the book some for Acadia and Cuyahoga Valley, but it was especially useful at Yellowstone. That said, words and pictures do not do Yellowstone any justice. We had read quite a bit about Yellowstone and viewed a bunch of photographs, but nothing could have prepared us for the astonishing allure of the park. It's one of those places you have to see with your own eyes.

· · · · ·

It wasn't with the RV, but we did drive through a tree during our brief stop at the Redwood National and State Parks. We were unable to see the core of the parks at the Avenue of the Giants. We were on the northern edge of the collection of parks along the Northern California coast. The artery of giant redwoods in Humboldt Redwoods State Park was 90 miles to the south of our stop near Klamath.

As we wound down U.S. Highway 101, I felt a little melancholy when I saw the exit for the Avenue of the Giants and knew we couldn't stop. Time was the least of our worries, it wasn't not knowing if there was a place for the RV. The last thing I wanted to do was get stuck in a tree.

Fortunately for us, we were able to take my car through a tree near Klamath. The exit for that tree, which is aptly named the Klamath Tour-Thru Tree, was just one up for our Highway 101 exit for the Kamp Klamath campground, where we spent two nights.

Getting to Kamp Klamath was nerve-wracking. When I drove the RV through Montreal during rush-hour traffic, I was concerned someone would hit us as they often cut me off while weaving their vehicles between lanes. When we came down the Pacific Coast on Highway 101, I feared for our lives. The road is narrow in some places as it snakes along the rocky cliffs. Redwood roots and trunks venture onto the shoulders, which lack any railings. You veer off the road, you're tumbling down the cliff. It also didn't help that there was heavy construction along the route, causing the already heavy traffic to back up for miles.

When we finally made it to the campground, Patti apologized profusely for suggesting we take the RV on Highway 101. She spent most of the drive in the back of the rig at her desk but heard some of my complaints.

She was sitting in the cab when we got to Klamath and passed the 49-foot Paul Bunyan statue outside the Trees of Mystery museum. Next to Paul Bunyan is a 35-foot statue of his trusted ox, Babe. Some kids were sitting on Paul Bunyan's left foot while others were attempting to climb Babe's legs.

We continued to the campgroun but returned to the statue so Patti could recreate a childhood memory of when her family visited the same Paul Bunyan statue over 40 years earlier.

Patti was so young at the time, she asked of her sisters, "How big is his ass?" because she couldn't pronounce the word "axe." Photos were taken the next day and posted to Facebook with the same childlike question. We had Holmes with us and discovered a hiking trail on the other side of the highway that led to a "hidden" beach. The trail's end is met with a pile of driftwood that had gathered on the sandy beach, which is tucked between a pair of cliffs. Rock islands are just off the shore. It was cool and foggy, so there was no getting into the water, even though I was tempted to traipse out toward one of the larger rock formations. North California's ever-present summer fog takes on a certain mystique as it filters the sun's beams through the giant trees.

Kamp Klamath is also secluded, located along a narrow road two miles from Highway 101. Trees surround the park, which is divided between an RV area and traditional camping sites. The campground is at the northern tip of the Redwood National and State Parks. It's a dead zone for cell service and the campground did not offer Wi-Fi. Needing to update our website, I drove up to Crescent City to have lunch at SeaQuake Brewing and utilize the brewery's Wi-Fi.

I sat down at the bar and a man next to me told the bartender he would have a beer while he waited on his wife and their 8-year-old foster son to arrive. When I heard him mention his foster child, I introduced myself and told him what we were doing on our travels. His family soon arrived and I handed him a card before he was seated at a table. The bartender, Hailey, heard our conversation and inquired about our journey and mission. After explaining everything to Hailey, she said the director for the local CASA office was having lunch with two members of her staff. CASA stands for Court Appointed Special Advocates and is a national non-profit organization that provides a courtroom voice for foster children. People who volunteer go through 36 hours of intensive training over the course of a few weeks before having a child assigned to them. The volunteers then serve as advocates for the children through legal and familial issues.

We first heard of CASA from a St. Louis friend of ours named Tim Snow. He asked in March if we knew of CASA and briefly described what it does. I didn't get around to doing much research on CASA, as I was still in the mindset of focusing on having MLB players join our podcast. But while in Cincinnati in June, we met a woman who is a CASA volunteer. I gave her a card and she said she would put me in touch with someone from CASA to interview for our podcast. I never heard from that woman, so I took matters into my own hands.

I went to the CASA website and searched for its leadership team. The organization has its national headquarters in Seattle and the CEO was Tara Perry, who used to work for the Atlanta Braves. This was perfect. Here was someone who led a group that helps foster children and she has ties to baseball. I shot off an email and followed it up with a phone call the next day. I spoke with her assistant and told her we would be in Seattle from July 19th through the 23rd. Unfortunately, however, Tara had a vacation scheduled that weekend and would be out of town. I inquired about a phone interview but that never came to fruition. So I was ecstatic when this bartender at a brewery in Northern California said she would introduce me to the CASA director for the Del Norte County office.

A few minutes later, a blonde woman in a white blouse and grey skirt walked up and asked, "Are you Ron?"

"I am."

"I'm Christine Slette. I understand you wanted to speak with me."

I told Christine what we were up to and asked if she could drive out to our RV to be interviewed for the Home Run On Wheels podcast. She agreed and we finally had someone on to speak about the work CASA does.

"Our nation has an epidemic with the foster care system; it's an overburdened system," Christine began. "Our volunteers do so much. The goal and mission of the CASA program is recruit, train, and supervise volunteers in the community to advocate for children in foster care. What they're really doing is being the extra eyes and the ears of the court, but the volunteers don't work for the court. They work for CASA and have a non-biased opinion. They're advocating for the best interests of the child."

Christine, who had spent over ten years with CASA, spoke passionately about the organization that was founded by Seattle judge David Soukup in 1977.

"He knew he was making decisions for the sake of foster children and didn't feel like he had enough information," Christine explained. "He was just basing his decisions off of social workers' reports. He asked some friends if they would be willing to be trained and sworn in under the jurisdiction of the court to become officers of the court. The program has just grown since. California now asks for CASA to be assigned to every single child's case. The end result is that advocate writes a thorough report and submits it to the court, so the judge has more information to make better decisions for the sake of the child."

Meeting Christine was serendipitous and all thanks to a young bartender who overheard a conversation.

"Yeah, we're sitting there eating chicken wings and had sauce all over our fingers and face and Hailey comes over and says, 'There's a guy who is interested in talking to you about children in foster care.' I said as soon as I get finished eating my wings, I'll walk over there," Christine explained.

The California native then told us she is a San Francisco Giants fan but did not attend a game until she was an adult — and it was a Padres game in San Diego.

"Baseball is like the American dream and it's a family thing, and if you look at it from a foster child's perspective, they don't get to participate in things like that," Christine added. "Typically, even in their hometowns, extracurricular activities are oftentimes something foster kids don't get to do."

One aspect of the foster system is something called respite care, which is when children spend a few days at a different home to give their foster parents a break. Christine told us a heartbreaking story of a couple of children who went to a respite home for a week while their foster parents took their bio-kids on a vacation to Disneyland.

"Foster parents don't get paid very much and so often the foster kids don't get to go on family trips," she said. "A lot of the kids in Del Norte County come from poverty-stricken homes, so they would never get the opportunity to go to a baseball game or anything like that."

Fortunately for the CASA office in Del Norte County, Disneyland did donate tickets so kids could take that trip south to Anaheim and enjoy some fun at the theme park. Christine said one of the kids came back and reported he was "so excited he got to go to Disneyland and be included on that family vacation."

"The mission of the CASA program is for a safe and secure, permanent home for these children," Christine said. "We want to make sure they're not falling through the cracks. The ultimate goal is to reunify the kids with their families. Foster care is really intended to be a temporary placement. There should be efforts to connect those children with their families… because it helps with the long-term stability of the child."

· · · · ·

Kamp Klamath was where we saw the only bear on our trip. After speaking with Christine, Patti and I went into the town of Klamath for dinner. We ate at a restaurant inside the Redwood Holiday Inn, which also houses a small casino. We were actually in our car to head to the restaurant when Christine showed up because she was running late. She had no way to contact us, however, because of the service dead zone. But it worked out.

We returned to the campground around 10 p.m., and as I approached our RV, a small black bear darted in front of the car and disappeared into the woods below. We had finally seen a bear, even if it was only for half a second.

We left the next morning and headed to Vallejo, where the RV was parked while we saw the Brewers beat the Giants in San Francisco on my birthday and the A's crush the Blue Jays a few days later. From there it was onto Los Angeles to see the Dodgers and Angels play at home and then San Diego for a pair of games at Petco Park over Patti's birthday weekend.

Our trip was on its final leg as we left San Diego and headed east for the first time in weeks. We were excited to get to Phoenix, where we would stay with the Harris family. We were also stoked to see the Grand Canyon for the first time ever.

· · · · ·

A late night was met by another early morning. August 16th was Katie Harris' birthday and there was a party. We were staying at the Harris home, so we were obviously invited and had a wonderful time eating street tacos and drinking beer and margaritas. By the time the last person left and we crawled into bed in the Harris' guest room, it was 1 a.m. We were getting up at 6 for our day trip to the Grand Canyon. We got out of bed at 7.

Knowing we were behind schedule, the one we set a couple days earlier, we hustled to get ready. We knew Holmes would be OK hanging out with the Harris beagles, Porkchop and Meatball. By 7:30, we were in the car and began our three-and-a-half hour drive north. We were tired and hungover and needed to eat, so there was a brief breakfast stop and another for gas. The route from Phoenix to the Grand Canyon is rather simple. Take Interstate 17 North until you head west on I-40 in Flagstaff. Around Williams, State Highway 64 takes you the rest of the way. It's a beautiful drive through the Coconino National Forest, past exits for Prescott and Sedona. We wished we had the time to visit those cities. As lovely as the drive through Northern Arizona is, it pales in comparison to the Grand Canyon. A mile deep, 277 miles long, and up to 18 miles wide in some spots but as narrow as four miles in others, it is a natural wonder.

When we arrived around 11 a.m., there was still a foggy haze hovering over the canyon. It didn't even seem real. It was more like staring at a giant postcard. Never before I had seen something so vast. It was breathtaking.

We were on the South Rim of the canyon, which is not quite as long as the North Rim but is said to have the best views of the canyon. By noon, the haze had dissipated and sun shined brightly on the layers of red, white, black and grey stone that form the canyon walls. The Grand Canyon is a geologists' playground with granite, limestone, Bright Angel shale, and lava stone.

Most of the services are on the South Rim, and we parked at the visitor center before walking two miles along the canyon to the Grand Canyon Village. There is a hotel and restaurant, where we grabbed a late lunch, and some gift shops.

It took us awhile to walk those two miles because we kept stopping to take photos. I would stravage to the edge of the cliffs, then sit with my feet dangling over the edge. The 100-foot tall cottonwood trees on the canyon floor looked like tiny bushes. Patti wasn't quite as adventurous. We later learned of an Indian couple who fell 800 feet to their deaths in Yosemite when trying to get a photo at the edge of a cliff for their popular Instagram account. Though some rocks were smooth as erosion was accelerated by people constantly walking on them, I was careful not to do anything too dangerous. One young woman from Scotland put the fear of death in everyone around her when she decided to step onto the edge of the canyon and raise one leg over her head while standing on just one foot. She nearly lost her balance the first time and attempted it again while her friends took photos. Everyone standing near her yelled, "Don't do that again." She heeded our advice.

A geology museum along the South Rim helps to explain how the canyon was created from a continental shift that picked up some volcanic islands — resulting in the current canyon plateau to rise. The river and erosion then cut the canyon even deeper. A diorama points out various features of the canyon, like the Dome, Holy Grail Temple, Shiva Temple and Isis Temple — each named for their respective shapes and colors.

From the Village, we walked some but used the shuttle about 80 percent of the way to complete the remaining seven miles to Hermit's Rest. Described by National Geographic as a "medieval jumble of stone with a cairn-like chimney," Hermit's Rest was a shelter for early 20th-century hikers. They'd get supplies, use the alcove fireplace to cook or just warm up in the winter, and rest before moving on. The fireplace is still there, in front of which tourists pose for photos, but the building now houses a small gift shop and a popular ice cream shop.

Before we got back on the shuttle, I spoke with a ranger who grew up in the park, but his name tag identified his home state as Wisconsin. His father was actually from Wisconsin and worked as a ranger at Grand Canyon. Because of that, his children grew up there and this man had followed his father's footsteps. I didn't how to process that the stunning vistas we were seeing for the first time were old to him. He still appreciated the canyon's natural features, and I'm certain he was just as in awe we were the first time he saw the prodigious ravines.

Former President Theodore Roosevelt was integral in the creation of the National Park Service and was also mystified by the Grand Canyon. He said it's Arizona's "natural wonder which is in kind absolutely unparalleled throughout the rest of the world." He never wanted anything to "mar the wonderful grandeur, the sublimity, the great loneliness, and beauty of the canyon."

The South Rim shuttle makes nine stops between the Grand Canyon Village and Hermit's Rest, each with an overlook. At Maricopa Point, you can look down at the ruins of the Orphan uranium mine that closed in 1969. Hopi Point juts into the canyon to offer spectacular views of the muddy Colorado River below. It's also one of the more popular spots to watch the sunset. We were already back at the Village at sunset, which was still a glorious site as the canyon shadows grew longer as the sun got lower on the horizon.

If only we had more time to actually go hiking along the canyon floor or visit the North Rim. We would have loved to have gone whitewater rafting on the

Colorado River. Rafting usually requires a reservation made a year in advance. If and when we do return to the Grand Canyon, we will spend more time and do an excursion or two. I'd love to experience a donkey ride down the Bright Angel trail, which you can also walk if you desire a ten-mile hike from South Rim to North Rim.

The wind had shifted in the evening and we now knew the cause of that morning haze. Wildfires were in the area and an evening haze that was actually smoked had crept in. As we drove back to Phoenix, we saw a sign that said, "Wild fires in the area. Do not report," and "Wildfire risk high. Use you ashtray."

As long as the drive from Phoenix seemed because of how tired we were, the drive back went by quickly and Patti and rehashed our day. "What did you like best?" "Can you believe how massive that is?" "What'd you like better, Yellowstone or the Grand Canyon?" That last one sparked a debate that last for a while. There is no right or wrong answer.

We had a few more days to spend with the Harris family before we all went to Chase Field on August 21st to see the Diamondbacks take on the Angels. We appreciated their hospitality for ten days while the RV sat untouched at Camping World in Avondale, but it was time to move on. We would be in Texas on August 24th.

· · · · ·

It took use two full days of driving to span the 1,000-mile trek from Phoenix to Austin. Our Texas itinerary included one night in Austin, two nights in San Antonio, a week in Houston, and five nights in the Dallas area. On the way from Phoenix to Austin, we spent a night in Anthony— a city that straddles the New Mexico-Texas line just west of El Paso. We used Harvest Hosts to stay at a winery, which was closed by the time we arrived and met up with our new buddy, Lance, there for dinner. We were back on the road early the next morning. I wanted to ensure we got to Austin in time to see the bats leave the Congress Avenue Bridge for their nightly forage. It was close, but we got there in time and that is a sight to see.

About 1.5 million Mexican free-tailed bats have been using the crevices under the bridge as their home for more than 30 years. Just after sunset each night, they begin to creep out from under the bridge to feed. Thanks to such a large population of bats, Austin has one of the lowest mosquito populations in the country. Even after Patti and I got dinner at a downtown barbecue restaurant, the bats were still going strong a few hours later.

The detour to Austin was solely to see the bats. Our stop in San Antonio was supposed to be a visit with my brother, but because one of his co-workers had a death in the family, Ben had to work through the weekend and we were unable to connect. We were grateful he was able to join us in Houston for an Astros game. Patti and I were left to our own devices for a weekend in San Antonio. There are worse places to be.

We strolled up and down the famed River Walk, eating lunch at Casa Rio, a Mexican establishment that claims to be the city's oldest restaurant. We also had a lunch at the revolving restaurant atop the Tower of the Americas. Patti loves to get those bird's-eye views.

We had both previously visited The Alamo, so that wasn't on our list of things to do. But San Antonio is home to several early Spanish missions, one of which was less than a mile from our RV park. Mission San José is part of the San Antonio Missions National Historical Park. There is no charge to enter the mission for a self-guided tour.

Mission San José was founded in 1720 and remained active until 1824. Restoration of the stone buildings began in 1933. The original Catholic church remains intact, as do the arched exterior passageways. It is an active parish today with regular mass every Sunday. A small statue of mission founder, Fray Antonio Margil de Jesus, is behind the church.

The walls surrounding the church form a rectangular courtyard. Inside the thick walls were guest rooms, offices, kitchens, and pantries. About 350 Native Americans lived inside those walls, as did soldiers tasked with defending the presidio. Smaller buildings closer to the church housed clergy and visitors. Some of the wall's rooms are used now to house artifacts and other exhibits.

The primary entrance to the church is a set of heavy, wooden double doors. The exterior wall above the doors is adorned with white stone reliefs that depict a cross, Jesus Christ, St. Joseph holding the infant Jesus, St. Dominic and St. Francis, and the Virgin Mary as Our Lady of Guadalupe. The church interior is rather simple with white walls that support a high-arching ceiling. The powder-blue altarpiece is something spectacular, crowned by a gold ornament with a white dove in its center. Beneath that is a crucified Jesus on a blue cross. Four figurines, stack by two on either side, flank the cross.

A dome topped with a bronze cross covers the altar. At the corner of the church, to the right of the double doors is a bell tower that would call residents to service or warn them of danger. One of the more interesting features of the church building is La Ventana de Rosa, or the Rose Window. Framed with baroque sculptures, the window was where the communion host was shown during the Feast of Pentecost. But the window's name is what makes it interesting. No one knows for sure why stone roses were added to the exterior frame. A vase of fresh roses sits inside the window on the south wall of the church sacristy. Those flowers are replaced regularly. The window frame is believed to have been sculpted by a man named Juan Huizar and it's believed he included the roses as a tribute to his betrothed, a young woman named Rosa. At least that's how the legend goes.

Once known as the "Queen of the Missions," Mission San José has a massive, open courtyard where livestock used to graze. Around the perimeter are several wells and outdoor ovens used by the mission's residents. As we walked around, we pretty much kept to ourselves except for one couple from France. They were of retirement age and seemed fascinated by our baseball trip, even though they knew very little about America's Pastime.

One of the really neat things about visiting the national parks, especially Yellowstone and the Grand Canyon, is how many people from different parts of the world you meet. We met people from France, Germany, Sweden, Scotland, England, Wales, Australia, Holland, Italy, India, Pakistan, Belgium, Mexico, Spain, Colombia, Brazil, Canada, and all over the United States. Just on the day trip to the Grand Canyon, we met folks from Wisconsin, North Carolina, Idaho, Illinois, Missouri, Washington, Montana, Minnesota, Virginia, Florida, New Jersey, and Connecticut. When the question, "Where are you from?" came back to us, we told them what we were doing and I handed out a lot of Home Run On Wheels cards. We were able to spread our message across the U.S. and the world.

CHAPTER 13:

FRIENDS AND FAMILY

Just shy of Exit 17 on Interstate 85 in South Carolina is where we spent the night of April 2nd. Our stop was a rest area on the banks of Lake Hartwell, a snaking reservoir that forms South Carolina's western border with Georgia, between Denver and Anderson. Clemson University is not far away. I pulled the RV to an open spot at the end of the designated row for truck parking. I always like to find spots at the end of a row because it gives us a little more room to extend a slideout. It was late. We left Atlanta around 11 p.m. after seeing the Nationals hand the Braves an 8-1 shellacking. By the time we crawled into bed at the I-85 North rest stop, it was nearly 2 a.m. We didn't get much sleep as an early morning beckoned with an appointment in Charlotte to get a portion of the vehicle wrap touched up. We were up before 8. After a bowl of cereal and some coffee, I was in the driver's seat by 8:30. We'd shower when we got to Charlotte.

Just as I put the key in the ignition, there was a tap on the driver's side window. A grey-haired man in a Waste Management jacket was standing there. His truck was parked next to our rig.

"Are you Ron?" he asked after I opened the window.

"I am," I replied.

"I thought so," he said. "I just looked you guys up. It's pretty cool what you're doing. I just wanted to say hello."

"Oh, well, thank you," I said, a bit stunned by this interaction.

We weren't quite used to people coming up to the RV yet. But it happened often as we moved from city to city and campground to campground. We met a lot of strangers who walked up to the RV asking, "What is Children's Hope Alliance? What is Home Run On Wheels?"

We were happy to tell them. While it was a joy to connect with hundreds of strangers across the United States and Canada, it was also nice to see some familiar faces along the way. Patti and I both have family and friends scattered across the U.S. One of the great things about traveling was being able to see most of them.

We saw our first familiar faces during Spring Training when our St. Louis friends, Mike and Ginny Kempf, joined us for dinner in Jupiter. They were in Florida staying at her aunt's house in Port St. Lucie while their school-aged kids were on spring break. Based on the recommendation of two folks staying at the same RV park we were, we met Mike and Ginny at a waterfront tiki bar for drinks and then walked to an island-themed spot called Guanabanas Restaurant. Carlos and Tracy Rodriguez, our new RV park friends, also joined us. The food was great, the company better. A visit to an ice cream shop followed dinner to cap a wonderful evening.

Mike and Ginny didn't go to any Spring Training games with us, but we knew we'd see them in St. Louis for our September finale.

Carlos and Tracy were just two of the new friends we made in Jupiter. Bruce and Mary Knight from Evansville, Indiana were a lot of fun. We first started talking with them because Bruce was wearing a Yadier Molina jersey. Chris and Kelly Ochs, the Jupiter-Palm Beach Motorcoach Resort reservationist, were so hospitable, they invited us over to their house one evening. Bruce and Mary and Carlos and Tracy were also there. Not only was that RV park one of the best-maintained places we stayed, the people there could not have been nicer. There was a true sense of community that made it feel like home. We didn't have a lot of that once we got into the regular season.

· · · · ·

There is actually a word for your brother-in-law's brother. It's "co-brother-in-law" and mine is Neil Agarwal. Neil lives in Arlington, Virginia, and I had not seen him since his brother married my little sister on May 4th, 2013. Neil then lived in Dallas, where he and his older brother, Shivum, were raised. Their parents, Sanjiv and Neetu, had emigrated to the U.S. from Northern India and began a family in Texas. Shivum stayed in Texas after finishing medical school and began a family of his own with my sister, Danielle.

Neil moved to the D.C. area after graduating from college and worked at an engineering firm. I had almost forgotten he lived near Washington until Danielle reminded me when she called as Patti and I were walking through Georgetown with Holmes. I called Neil as we walked past the Key Bridge Boathouse near the Georgetown Waterfront Park. We made plans to meet for dinner the next night.

Neil recommended a downtown Greek tapas restaurant called Zaytinya. As you do at a tapas place, we shared several dishes while talking about the latest things in our lives. He is a big sports fan and grilled us about our trip so far and where we were going. We learned he had a serious girlfriend, who couldn't join us for dinner because of a previous engagement. Neil is what most would consider a handsome man, tall and thin with short dark hair and trim beard that doesn't hide his strong jaw line and high cheek bones.

We didn't know much about Neil. The only time we had ever spent with him was the week of our siblings' wedding five years earlier. Somehow we got on the topic of middle names. Shivum simply has the letter K as his middle name, and when Neil told us his middle name in the loud restaurant, I heard Kenneth. "Neil Kenneth?" I asked?

"Yeah," he said.

"Shiv gets Shivum Agarwal and you're Neil Kenneth?" I replied.

"I guess my parents wanted an Indian son and an American son," he joked.

What Neil actually said was "Kenth" — a much more traditional Indian name. I had misheard him and he just played along without correcting me. For the record, I am Ronald Bernard and Patti is Patricia Lee.

The restaurant wasn't far from Chinatown, and Neil wanted to take us to a permanent pop-up bar called Drink Company that has ever-changing themes. It's taken on décor for Christmas and Halloween and had *Game of Thrones* and *Stranger Things* themes. We were there in early April, there was a Cherry Blossom Festival theme with faux trees on the wall and bar and

Japanese designs. The tavern had two main rooms, each with a bar. The larger room had a long bar that ran the length of the narrow room. The smaller room had a bar similar to something you'd see in someone's basement. One woman was serving up drinks there while a trio of bartenders took orders behind the elongated counter. The restrooms were off the smaller room, but to get there, you had to walk past Godzilla and Mothra.

A four-foot replica of Mothra hung from the ceiling above a ten-foot Godzilla that moved, roared, and breathed fire. Well, actually his mouth opened and lit up while steam was emitted. Godzilla came to life about every ten minutes, stunning unsuspecting patrons who were simply on their way to the restroom. It was all a pretty neat experience and one we wouldn't have had without Neil's knowledge.

We all had the same stomach grumbling when we left Drink Company, and Neil suggested a late-night snack at Ben's Chili Bowl. We were told about Ben's a year earlier but didn't get a chance to visit it. Nationals Park has a Ben's Chili Bowl concession stand, but we passed on it because we wanted to eat at the original location first.

While the chili is good, the atmosphere is even better. It's simple with a counter to place your order. The food is then brought out to your table. The walls are filled with photographs of celebrities who have visited the Washington landmark over the last 60 years. Washington Nationals players and other D.C. athletes, Muhammad Ali, presidents Barack Obama, George Bush, and Bill Clinton, singer, George Clinton, and other performers like Bruno Mars, Questlove, Jimmy Fallon, Gabriel Iglesias, Kevin Hart, and Dave Chappelle.

Nobody took our photo during our initial visit with Neil, so I guess we'll have to return to see if Home Run On Wheels makes it on the wall.

· · · · ·

I found myself in Philadelphia. Well, sort of.

If you're a fan of Walt Disney animated movies, you have likely seen the name Ron Clements in the credits alongside John Musker. The two are Disney animation's dream team. They received Oscar nominations for *Treasure Planet*, *The Princess and the Frog* and *Moana*. They also wrote, produced and directed *Aladdin* – which was the first film in which I noticed my name in the credits – *Hercules*, *The Little Mermaid* and *The Great Mouse Detective*.

After the release of *The Princess and the Frog* in 2009, I got curious about other people named Ron Clements. I searched Facebook and found several people with my name. I sent a few of them messages, asking to connect. I had one positive response from a guy who lived just outside of Philadelphia.

After almost nine years of online correspondence and nine years of birthday messages along the lines of, "Happy birthday to me," we were excited to finally meet in person. We picked an iconic Philadelphia to meet, at the original Chickie's & Pete's location in North Philadelphia.

"I can't wait to meet myself," I told the other Ron Clements in a Facebook message.

"That sounds creepy," he facetiously replied.

After a few more weird jokes, and agreeing that Pat's cheesesteaks are better than Geno's, we settled on a Saturday lunch.

"Is it weird that I feel like I'm going on a first date?" Ron asked me.

"Haha. No," I answered. "There probably won't be a handshake on the first meeting."

Patti and I arrived well ahead of the agreed-upon time. We walked around the neighborhood near Robbins Avenue for a bit before entering Chickie's & Pete's. The place was fairly empty, and we were led to a four-top table past the bar. Patti and I ordered a couple of a drinks and some of the crab fries that helped make Chickie's & Pete's famous. Ron and his wife, Lisa, walked in a few minutes later, around 12:30. There was indeed no handshake. Just a big hug.

Within minutes of sitting down for lunch, it felt like the four of had known each other for years. Ron and I had chatted on Facebook for years, but finally meeting him in person was more like seeing an old friend you hadn't seen in a while and not like meeting a stranger.

As for our meal, Patti stuck with the crab fries theme by ordering the delicious crab nachos with aioli sauce. I got the Ultimate Tailgate burger, which is a beef patty topped with a crab cake.

We spent about two hours chatting with the "other" Clements couple, learned about their family background, and saw pictures of their kids. Ron, who is a junior, has a son also named Ron. That's three Ron Clements in one family. And here, I was almost Bernie the third.

Ron and Lisa, who are both Philadelphia-area natives, asked us what we thought of Citizens Bank Park. We shared our favorable opinions of the ballpark and mentioned that the only cheesesteak sandwich we got at the stadium was "The Heater" from Campo's. The buffalo sauce and jalapeños helped keep us warm on a chilly Friday night.

The Phillies were the first home team to win in six games, thanks to Odubel Herrera's go-ahead RBI triple in the eighth inning of what was a 2-1 win over the Pirates. Though our tickets were on the first-base side, Patti and I had strolled over to the third-base side and had a perfect view of Herrera sliding head-first into third.

We enjoyed Citizens Bank Park, which is very easy to get to. We ordered an Uber from the Campus Park and Ride RV spot that is just four miles from the stadium. There is ample parking around the stadium, which is part of the South Philadelphia Sports Complex. Lincoln Financial Field, home to the NFL's Eagles, and Wells Fargo Center — where the NHL's Flyers and NBA's 76ers play — are all in the same location. In between the stadiums is the Xfinity Live! entertainment venue, which Patti and I visited after the Phillies victory.

"Other" Ron was very familiar with that area and offered some pointers for future visits Patti and I might take. He and Lisa are huge Philadelphia sports fans and were still riding high from the Eagles' first Super Bowl championship a few months earlier. They even like soccer and Ron wore a Philadelphia Union hoodie to our meetup. I am not a big soccer fan. It's not that I don't like soccer; it's more apathy than anything. Ron and Lisa's kids play in youth soccer leagues.

Following the Ron Clements-squared lunch, we posed for a couple of photos outside of Chickie's & Pete's, in front of the ground-level marquee. We did share a handshake for the pictures, but before Patti and I headed toward Old City Philadelphia to take in some history and Ron and Lisa left for a family function, there was one last hug. You can't love anyone unless you love yourself, right?

· · · · ·

The La Crosse Aquinas class of 1992 had a small 25-year reunion meetup during the summer of 2017. Patti didn't go with me to my 20-year reunion because we had met just months earlier. Five years later, she was my wife of just a few months. Our group met at a bar in downtown La Crosse. We talked about our respective lives and families and reminisced a bit about high school. Your typical reunion conversations.

One classmate of mine unable to attend was Kevin Kadrmas. He and his wife, Melissa, had other plans that night. Patti and I made plans to see Kevin and Melissa the next night.

They have an apartment overlooking the Black River on La Crosse's North Side. Copeland Park, one of two riverside parks in La Crosse, is not far away. That park is home to The Lumberyard, the home stadium of the La Crosse Loggers — a collegiate summer wood-bat team in the Northwoods League. Nationals ace Max Scherzer played for the Loggers while at the University of Missouri. I like to say that Scherzer and I have a special connection despite never meeting. He's a St. Louis native. I used to live in St. Louis. I'm a La Crosse native. He used to play in La Crosse. We're also both born on July 27th.

When Patti and I arrived at the Kadrmas apartment, we were immediately offered a beverage, which we graciously accepted. We then sat on their balcony and talked as the dark water of the river rushed by below. Fireworks soon shot off downstream.

"The Loggers game is over," Kevin explained.

We couldn't really hear the booms, but the light show, even from a distance, was spectacular. When we went back inside, Patti and I told Kevin and Melissa of our 2018 travel idea. Like many, they told us they were jealous we were able to do that.

"Oh, hey," Kevin suddenly exclaimed. "There's this guy you have to meet. He went to every Yankees game a few years ago."

The guy was Steve Melia. He got to know Kevin and Melissa through Legal-Shield, a pre-paid multi-level marketing legal service. He wrote a book called *162* that chronicled his journey to all 162 Yankees games in 2011. Kevin just happened to have that book in his apartment. He found it and handed it to me.

Steve got the idea of attending every Yankees game after watching YES Network's reality show, "The Ultimate Road Trip." Four Yankees fans competed for tickets to all 162 Yankees game in the 2007 season. He was living in Wilmington, North Carolina and never actually watched the show because YES Network wasn't part of his cable package. He would see advertisements for it watching games online and on MLB Network, however, and his interest was piqued. Steve already traveled quite a bit for LegalShield and thought, "I could do that." He got to know one of the contestants, "Bald" Vinny Milano, and made his plans. He did most of that trip solo and joked that it was his "mid-life crisis tour."

Seven years later, he had his girlfriend, Marybeth Longona, along for the ride and the two came up with a charity mission. After the Yankees acquired slugger Giancarlo Stanton to pair with Aaron Judge, Steve knew the Yankees would hit a lot of home runs in 2018.

"I think you can tell how special something is to you if you can remember exactly where you were when you heard the news. And I can remember exactly where I was, at an airport, when I checked my phone and saw the news. I was like, 'You're not going to believe this. We got Stanton,'" Steve said. "I was super excited. That lineup is stacked."

Steve set up a PledgeMe account to ask people to commit to donating a small amount of money for every home run hit by the Yankees. They wound up setting an MLB record with 267 home runs hit Steve's "162 Experience" raised more than $23,000 for four separate charities – Ed Randall's Fans for the Cure, the National Fallen Firefighters Foundation, the Memorial Sloan Kettering Cancer Center, and Give Orphans Hope. The last one really tied into our mission of helping foster children.

When Kevin first told me of Steve's 2011 trip, it didn't really sink in with me at the time because Patti and I were still in the early stages of planning our own baseball trip. Kevin thought I just blew him off. But a few months later, I asked Kevin for Steve's number. The trip was planned out, and we were already in Florida for Spring Training. I called Steve because I wanted to know if Steve was in Tampa for the Yankees games. I got his voicemail. He called me back a few hours later and said he was not in Florida. His trip would not include Spring Training games. He had enough on his plate with every 2018 regular-season game.

We made plans to meet in April when Patti and I would be New York to see the Yankees. Patti and I would interview them for the Home Run On Wheels podcast and they'd speak with us for the 162 Experience podcast.

"The first trip was great, so seven years later, we're back in action," Steve told us in Jersey City.

Steve and Marybeth drove out to New York City's unofficial borough to meet us at the RV, which was at Liberty Harbor RV Park. Steve, who was pushing 50, is about 6-foot-2 and has short salt-and-pepper hair with perpetual day-old stubble on his face. Marybeth is about ten years younger and nearly a foot shorter than Steve. Her bubbly personality lent itself well to being the marketing director for the 162 Crew. After exchanging pleasantries with Steve and Marybeth, we recorded our interviews from inside the RV. Once each podcast was recorded, we took some photos outside in front of the RV's Home Run On Wheels logo.

"Hanging out with you guys, even just for the first few minutes, is very surreal because we know you're experiencing the same kind of things in a little bit of a different way."

The four of us sat at the dinette in the RV. In addition to our microphones on the table, there was my daily baseball calendar. Each day of the year had either a baseball fact or quote. The day we met, the calendar was turned to a quote from Dale Berra, who was asked to compare his MLB career to that of his father, Yogi.

"Our similarities are different," Steve read the quote aloud. It was very applicable to our respective baseball trips.

"It's a lot of baseball," Marybeth said when I asked how they were able to attend all 162 games. Most beat writers even take a day off here or there when the team is on the road. Players regularly get days off. Only seven MLB players appeared in all 162 games during the 2018 season.

"It's a grind," Marybeth added. "But it gives us a reality check of what the players go through. It's every day and we're doing the podcast along with it. It blows my mind, going to all these games and seeing what we're going through and thinking about what the players go through.

"We told our families that during the 2018 baseball season, nobody was allowed to get married and nobody was allowed to die."

The funny thing was Patti and I had just booked a flight from Toronto to St. Louis to attend a May wedding for our friends, Greg and Emily.

Because our trip was not quite as intense as the 162 Crew, Patti and I were able to enjoy a few more city experiences than they could on their travels. We could take a day or two off from a game to go explore. That's what we did in New York City after our podcast interview was over. Steve offered to drive us into the Bronx from Jersey City. We gladly accepted. After seeing how long it took to get from the RV Park to the stadium, we were convinced the subway was the best mode of transportation into the Bronx. Yankee Stadium is just 20 miles from Liberty Harbor RV Park. An hour-and-a-half later, we were in the Bronx. Patti and I were going to a game the next day and told Steve and Marybeth we'd see them tomorrow. We thanked them for the ride and then parted ways. They went inside the ballpark while Patti and I headed to the subway platform. We had plans to go have dinner in

Chinatown and then go to Rockefeller Plaza. We had purchased the New York City Pass, which included the Top of the Rock. We also visited the Empire State Building, Central Park, the Met, and 9/11 Memorial and Museum while in New York.

"It seems like you guys have a lot more freedom than us to do other stuff," Steve remarked. "I was looking at all your pictures on Facebook from Philadelphia and thought, 'Man, that stuff looks like so much fun.' But when you're doing a game every day, you get tired. One of the things about doing all 162 is that we're committed to not missing a game. If we miss one game, it's over."

"Don't get sick," I interjected.

"One of my tricks is to fly out with the first flight of the day," Steve continued. "The reason being is that at least the plane is in station so it doesn't have to wait for another flight to come in. At least you're first out and you don't have to worry about delays. A lot of the time, we're up at 3:30 in the morning to catch a 6 a.m. flight. Then you get back to the Bronx or the hotel and it's like 11 and you just want to sleep before the game because you're so exhausted."

"Have you ever fallen asleep during a game?" Patti jokingly asked. Marybeth immediately turned red and pointed to herself. She pulled her blonde hair off her shoulders to cover her face. We were all quickly engulfed in laughter. Steve, who moonlights as a comedian, took the attention away from Marybeth by sharing an anecdote about a different baseball napper.

"There was this really weird situation where this dude passed out in the section next to us," Steve began. "His buddies start taking French fries and put them on his head. Then they made a Yankees symbol on his back. The more they do it, the more people were paying attention. Security comes over and they're taking pictures."

"We thought security was going to make them shut it down," Marybeth added.

"Before you know it, one guy put a beer can on the guy, another added a bottle, and they've got this tower, like, three feet high of stuff on this guy's head."

"He didn't move at all?" I asked.

"No. He was passed out," Marybeth answered. "It was like something I had never seen."

"I'm kind of old school, like, 'Pay attention to the game,' but this was so funny and everybody was watching it," Steve said. "The very next day, she fell asleep, and just as a joke, I put my glove and a beer on top of her head and took a picture."

Baseball can be slow at times, but the moral of the story is stay awake at baseball games.

"We're Yankees fans and we're only going to Yankees games, I can't imagine what you guys are doing and going to games where you don't know either team very well," Steve said. "That would be harder for me."

We took the subway to Yankee Stadium the next day and got some awesome news while on the train. I received an email telling me the Milwaukee Brewers donated 50 tickets to Anu Family Services for the June 21st game against the St. Louis Cardinals. I literally began jumping for joy. I was doing my happy dance on the subway. A couple people looked at me funny but then I told them why I was so happy and some more cards were handed out. One woman told me not to worry about any strange looks because people who regularly ride New York City subways have seen a lot of weird things.

Our seats to see the Bronx Bombers take on the Twins were in Section 223. We thought we'd be near Steve and Marybeth, but one of their friends hooked them up with field-level seats. A couple of texts were exchanged, and we eventually made our way down to their section. We took our time to get there. We still had to go on our stadium exploration. The Yankees do a wonderful job of paying tribute to the franchise greats. As soon as you enter through Gate 6, you are greeted with giant banners of the Yankees Hall of Famers. It adds to the mystique of Yankee Stadium feeling like an old stadium instead of one that opened in 2009. If you don't want to wait in line, you probably don't want to enter at Gate 6 because that is where the sea of people assembles after leaving the subway.

I wish I had been to the old Yankee Stadium to have some comparison baseline. There are aspects of "The House That Ruth Built" in the current venue, most notably Monument Park. The plaque-lined museum was relocated to the new venue when it opened. Unfortunately, we weren't able to see any of the plaques there because the center-field gallery closes after the first pitch is thrown and is then only accessible to those with a special ticket.

That was just one disappointing aspect of the stadium, where the Yankees cruised to a 7-4 win over the Twins on a damp and cold, foggy night.

"I don't care for when there's a lot of concrete because it feels closed in," she said. "When the concourses are opened up, I like an open feel. I can see the ball game going on when I'm out in the concourse. It doesn't have to be everywhere, but at least from some places when you're grabbing something to eat or exploring, you hear something going on, you can run over to see."

That was one aspect of Fenway Park we really did like, especially down the baselines. Wherever we were, we could still see the field as we walked around. Whether we were in our seats in the left-field corner by the Green Monster or by Pesky's Pole — named for former Red Sox infielder Johnny Pesky, a left-hander who hit just 17 home runs over ten MLB seasons — there were no bad views at Fenway.

But even with all that concrete, emerging from the tunnel and seeing the field for the first time is special. The green grass still vivid through the fog with off-setting diagonal stripes from the mower running from the foul lines to the outfield wall. The barking of vendors shilling beer, soda, water, popcorn, hot dogs and — on this night — hot cocoa echoes through the stadium. Though it wasn't the "old" Yankee Stadium, it still felt classic — and that's probably what they were going for with the closed concourses. You're forced to watch the game from your seats and not from an outfield lounge.

The Yankee Stadium crowd began to thin by the start of the eighth inning, so we were able to sit with Steve and Marybeth, along with a couple of new friends they had made during the penultimate stanza. The people with whom Steve and Marybeth had met were mystified by their trip. Steve then told them what Patti and I were doing and those some people began grilling us with questions. We appreciated Steve's introductions and were more than happy to answer every question. Multiple cards were handed out and some photos were taken.

"How are you able to do this?" "What's your favorite stadium so far?" "What do you think of Yankee Stadium?" "Where are you going next?" "Where are you going to end?" "How long is it going to take?"

Steve and Marybeth had fielded similar questions and even some of their friends and family thought they were crazy to attend every Yankees game in a single season. Steve's family really thought he was nuts in 2011 when he did it the first time, but he did so with their support.

"It really is crazy if you think about it," Steve said. "I mean, we rented out our house for the whole year. We had to sell a lot of our stuff just because when you start weighing, do we keep it or do we sell it, put it in storage — it's a lifestyle change."

"It is," I added. "We went through the same thing."

Downsizing can be good (*Downsizing* was also the name of a movie Patti and I watched one night in the RV). Though we did rack up a number of souvenir stadium cups to go with our lapel pins. Before we left Yankee Stadium, Steve offered some helpful advice.

"Remember to enjoy it," he began. "I'm always so focused on being there on time, we've got to get the tickets, and get hotels and all this other stuff. You're doing this for fun. What are you stressing yourself out about? I have to constantly remind myself of that."

We followed the 162 Crew the rest of the season and were thankful my friend Kevin had helped to connect us.

· · · · ·

When Perform Media launched the Omnisport U.S. news desk in December of 2014, the entire 15-person team was based in Charlotte. We were holed up in a conference room at the Sporting News offices for the first six months before finally getting desks. It was a makeshift staff hastily assembled. I was one of the few people with years of experience hired. After a couple of years, the staff began to take on a different look. One guy was fired, a couple of new people were hired, two other guys moved away but remained with the company. One of those guys is Joe Rodgers, who moved to Cleveland after his wife got a new job. Joe was an All-American swimmer at Oakland University in Michigan and his college roommate, Alec joined the Omnisport news desk a few weeks after I did. Alec had since relocated to Chicago to attend grad school at DePaul but was still part of the staff.

Having Alec in Chicago and Joe in Cleveland gave us the capability to cover events, like Cleveland Cavaliers games while LeBron James was still there, the Cubs in the 2016 World Series, PGA Tour events, the winless Cleveland Browns in 2017, etc. We weren't able to connect with Alec when we got to Chicago over Father's Day weekend, but we did hook up with Joe, who I had not seen in almost a year. He was joining us for a game at Progressive Field on May 29th and we were eager to hang out with him.

I found a pretty good deal on tickets behind home plate. We were in the back of Field Box 152, just a shade toward first base. I was shocked to get such good seats for $35 apiece. I told Joe a couple weeks earlier where we were sitting and that there were a pair of seats available next to ours. I was hoping his wife, Alyssa, could join us.

Like me, Joe left Perform to pursue a new venture. He joined a startup sports gambling website called Bet Chicago. Joe worked from home in Cleveland, handicapping odds for Chicago teams and events. Because the Indians were playing the White Sox, he could use our game to do something on Chicago's struggling American League team. It was a Tuesday game with a 6 p.m. start, so Joe would head to the stadium as soon as his work day was done. When we got to the park, Joe told me he got a last-minute ticket in the 500 level for $5. Alyssa was unable to attend. Joe missed the first pitch and watched the remainder of the first inning from his upper-deck seat. He came down to join us in the second inning. Thankfully the Progressive Field ushers were lax.

Patti and I had already gotten our MLB Passport stamped but were waiting on Joe before we explored the stadium. He had been there before, so we picked his brain a bit for our stadium review. When we left our seats, we weren't worried about missing an opportunity to get a foul ball. The sections behind home plate are completely covered by netting that runs from the press box down to the vertical net at the backstop. One foul ball landed on the net directly above us and rolled harmlessly back to the field. A ball boy retrieved it and tossed it to a young child before re-entering the home dugout.

Progressive Field is one of the few MLB stadiums to allow field-level viewing at no charge. When I say field level, I mean just that. The Indians lets fans watch a full inning from an old bullpen on the other side of the right-field wall. It's a no-frills experience with the only "seats" being the bench on which relief pitchers used to sit. The bullpen phone is still mounted to the wall above the bench. We discovered this perk by accident.

None of us had eaten before getting to the stadium. Joe suggested we head to the Right Field District. This is an open area with a plethora of eating and drinking options. The district is divided into different "neighborhoods" with names shared by actual Cleveland barrios. The Corner Bar has three bars with a total of 40 beers on tap, several of them local brews, and a firepit on the roof deck. Its name is an homage to the endearing nickname given to the old Tiger Stadium, which stood at the corner of Michigan and Trumbull avenues from 1912 to 2009. The Tigers had moved into Comerica Park in 2000.

We explored our options, each of us getting food from a different place. The food at Progressive Field is among the best in baseball and is relatively affordable. You pay ballpark prices but get hefty portions. Patti got a "build-your-own" burger and paid $15 for the sandwich that was served with a ton of fries. My grilled cheese sandwich stuffed with bacon and macaroni was quite filling.

As Joe went to the center-field area to eat his sandwich and get a photo, Patti and I ate while standing at a high-top table just in front of the Corner Bar. We weren't there long.

"Are you two waiting to go to the bullpen?" a female usher asked.

"Excuse me?" I said.

"Are you waiting to watch the game from the bullpen?" the middle-aged woman asked again, slightly rephrasing her question.

"Um, sure," we replied.

She realized our confusion and explained that groups of 20 can watch one inning from the bullpen on a first-come, first-served basis. The sixth inning had just started and there was nobody currently in line. We were first in line for the seventh. I called Joe. No answer. I texted.

"We're gonna go in the field view bullpen area. Join us," I wrote.

"OK," came the reply.

Six minutes later, Joe sent this, "Where? I'm by the Sox bullpen."

I replied with a call. This time he answered. He was by the actual bullpens in right-center. The bullpen viewing area was created after the Indians remodeled the outfield area and added stacked bullpens. The former visitors' bullpen was then available for fans. I told Joe to walk toward the right-field corner. A couple minutes later, he was in line with us. Fortunately, we told the usher we had a third person with us and she included him in her count.

Indians second baseman Jason Kipnis grounded out to end a scoreless sixth inning. We were up. Here we go. The sixth-inning group was vacating the area. A stout black man, about 60 years old was the usher at the bottom of the steps. Once the last fan left the bullpen and was at the top of the steps, he motioned to us to come down.

White Sox DH Matt Skole walked to lead off the seventh. Shortstop Tim Anderson then looked at ball one. The second pitch was a 91-mph fastball right down the middle. Smack. It was coming right at us. Before Anderson's line drive could hit the wall, it landed with a pop inside the glove of Indians right fielder Greg Allen. Adam Engel and Trayce Thompson each struck out to end the top half of the seventh. Time to stretch.

I had never before sung *Take Me Out to the Ballgame* from a bullpen. Patti then took a photo of me and Joe with the field behind us. I was wearing an orange Children's Hope Alliance T-shirt. Joe had on a red Indians shirt, even though he's a Royals fan.

Cleveland catcher Roberto Perez led off the bottom of the seventh with a single to center field. Allen and shortstop Francisco Lindor followed with singles to right. The bases were loaded for left fielder Michael Brantley, who slapped a grounder to the left side. It found a hole and Perez scored to give Cleveland a 6-1 lead. Kipnis homered in the eighth and the White Sox added a pair of runs in the top of the ninth to make it a 7-3 final. The solo shot by Kipnis was the third home run hit by the Indians that day. Cleveland eventually won the American League Central but was ousted by the Astros in the divisional round of the playoffs.

. . . . .

As we did when we took Holmes to a Reds game on June 5th, we again found free street parking on Freedom Way just a block from the stadium.

"You guys got lucky," Kirsten Pohlman told me.

"I know," I replied with a grin.

"Winning," Patti added.

The Pohlmans had just arrived in Cincinnati and were the first of our friends to stay with us in the RV. Kirsten, Tricia and 8-year-old Finnegan joined us on June 8th to see the Cardinals take on the Reds at Great American Ball Park. While Finnegan had been to some minor-league games around Nashville, this was his first Major League Baseball game. He loved it.

To see the excitement on his face, being at his first MLB game, is exactly the type of experience we wanted to create for other kids while on our journey. It's awesome to see that joy on a kid's face. While Finn had played Little League, it was clear he had caught the baseball bug.

When we were at the park a couple days earlier with Holmes, we had to walk around to the right-field corner to enter the stadium. This time we used the Reds Hall of Fame entrance directly in front of us. In front of the gate is a statue of Hall of Fame catcher, Johnny Bench, his bronze likeness popping up from behind the plate to throw the ball either back to the pitcher or down to second base.

Once inside the stadium, we located our seats in Section 422 above home plate. From there, we had a great view of the Ohio River despite an overcast day. Rain was in the forecast, but we were hoping it would hold off. We had yet to have a rain delay on our trip, and we almost made it through this one. A light drizzle began in the sixth inning, but the heavens opened up in the middle of the ninth inning with the Cardinals holding a 6-4 lead.

The game was stopped and our group huddled with others under some cover behind the section. Great American Ball Park has spacious concourses, but the upper deck is largely uncovered. Like most people up there, we remained close to the closed concession stands where was an overhang to keep us dry. As the rain began to dissipate, the remaining fans returned to their seats. Tricia and Patti used paper towels to dry our seats.

"Hey, Mom, there's nobody down there, can we move down?" Finnegan asked, looking up at Tricia with blue eyes.

"Um," Tricia began, looking toward me and Patti for some approval.

"Sure," Kirsten jumped in.

The decision was made. Finnegan was right. Most of the people sitting behind home plate had vacated their seats and did not return. The stairs to the main concourse weren't far from us. Others had also made the decision to snag a better seat. Finnegan rushed down the stairs as we struggled to keep up with the energetic 8-year-old. When we reached the concourse, he sprinted to a row of open seats directly behind home plate. We were nine rows up. It was the bottom of the ninth inning, so the ushers didn't stop anyone from moving into the open seats.

The delay had lasted 36 minutes. When the tarp was removed, Cardinals reliever, Bud Norris, trotted out to the mound. Scott Schebler led off with a double to center field. Norris then struck out Tucker Barnhart, but Joey Votto knocked in Schebler with a line-drive single to center. Norris struck out Scooter Gennett and the Reds were down to their final out.

But then Norris gave up back-to-back singles to Eugenio Suarez and Jesse Winker and the game was tied. Norris had blown his second save opportunity in 14 chances and we were heading to extra innings. It was just the second extra-innings game of the season for us, but the first one we watched to the end. We didn't stick around to see the Mets beat the Nationals in 12 innings on that frigid April night in Washington.

Marcell Ozuna drew a one-out walk in the top of the 10th and Yadier Molina moved him to third with a single to right field. Jedd Gyorki followed with a single of his own and the Cardinals had regained the lead. It held as Brandon Dixon, who entered the game in the ninth as a pinch-runner for Votto, struck out with two runners on to end the game.

The Reds fell to a dismal 22-42 on the season and the home teams were now 4-10 on our trip.

We had never been to Great American Ball Park, or Cincinnati for that matter, before 2018. I had been in the Cincinnati area — with stops in Florence, Kentucky, and Mason, Ohio — but had never visited the city itself. We liked what we saw in Ohio's Queen City, though we questioned that nickname. The origin of the moniker is a poem that described the Ohio River port, which was the largest inland city in the United States at the time and the "Queen of the West." We lived in Charlotte for over three years and hold that city to be America's true Queen City because it had the nickname 100 years earlier and was named for an actual queen. Charlotte is named for the Queen Regent of England in the 1750s — Queen Charlotte Mecklenburg Strelitz of Germany, wife to England's King George III.

"It was actually named for a queen, so that, to me, just gives it the crown," Patti said with her pun evoking laughter from me.

What Cincinnati does have that Charlotte lacks is a zoo. We visited the large zoo, which doubles as a botanical garden with various flora throughout the park with the Pohlmans on Saturday. The first time I met Tricia was during a 2012 visit to her hometown of Nebraska City, Nebraska. The small town, which was the first to celebrate Arbor Day, is just south of Omaha. We also went with the Pohlmans to the Omaha Zoo that weekend, though I was surprised by the $19 admission cost. Patti and I had been spoiled living in St. Louis with its free zoo in Forest Park, but we paid $17 each to enter the zoo in Cincinnati on June 9th.

I was the first to shower in the RV that morning, and as I waited for the ladies to finish getting ready, I noticed Kirsten and Finnegan were not there. Several minutes later, I see the two of them walk back to the RV holding their gloves and a baseball. Kirsten walked with his son to a nearby park to play catch. I immediately thought of the kids who don't have a dad to play catch with them, and hopefully we inspired people along the way to get involved by fostering, adopting, or volunteering at a foster care or adoption agency.

We were shocked by the Cincinnati zoo's massive size, and while we missed the famous baby hippopotamus, Fiona, we did see a baby bonobo breast-feeding and were completely entertained by a family of gorillas. Two young gorilla sisters were having fun wrestling. One would swing from a vine and land on the other with leaping body drops that would make professional wrestlers proud. We spent about four hours at the zoo before heading downtown to do some more sight-seeing and we had the perfect spot in mind to maximize our views.

The Carew Tower is the second-tallest building in Cincinnati but is the highest point in the city because of its elevated location. The 49-story Carew Tower, built in 1930, has a rooftop observation deck that costs just $4 for adults. From there you can see clearly how much the Ohio River zigs and zags to create to Ohio-Kentucky border. You can also glance right into Great American Ball Park, where the Cardinals and Reds were playing under the afternoon sun. The Cardinals scored five runs in the first three innings en route to a 6-4 victory. The Reds loss dropped the home teams to 4-10 through our first 13 stadiums.

Shops and restaurants occupy the first two floors of the art deco building, which is situated right next to Cincinnati's Fountain Square. The plaza gets its name from the giant water feature in its center. The Tyler Davidson Fountain, also known as The Genius of Water, was dedicated in 1871 and renovated in 2006. The 43-foot-tall bronze sculpture sits on a granite base with the words, "To the people of Cincinnati" inscribed on the foundation. A female figure with arms outstretched rains water down on the ornate figures below before falling into the pedestal's basin.

With our tummies rumbling around 5:30 p.m., we left downtown to hit up another Cincinnati landmark for dinner. Rhinegeist Brewery is the coolest craft brewery I've ever seen and is just a block away from a vast farmers' market in the historic Over-The-Rhine neighborhood. The brewery is kid-friendly with pinball machines, cornhole, a foosball table, and several board games. Kirsten and Finnegan played a competitive game of foosball while I floundered, attempting to conquer a Game of Thrones pinball machine. The brewery does switch to a 21-and-up establishment at 9 p.m. A popular spot for wedding receptions, the brewery's huge building houses a full-sized dinosaur. The Galeamopus fossil, unveiled in May of 2018, was dug up in Montana by the University of Cincinnati and is on loan from the Cincinnati Museum Center.

The Pohlmans were leaving Cincinnati on Sunday, but we all went out for breakfast first. I found a well-reviewed place called **Sugar n' Spice** six miles from the RV park. Billed as the "Best Breakfast in Cincinnati," the restaurant is in a pink building with a statue of a pig balancing a stack of pancakes on its snout. The base of the statue has more pigs encircling the larger swine like they're on a carousel.

There was a wait, popular place on a Sunday morning. We chatted on the benches outside for about 20 minutes before being seated in a corner table. Cartoonish drawings decorated the walls, which also had several shelves stocked with rubber ducks. There were probably a thousand of them stacked neatly. After we ordered, the owner came over to the table and inquired about our whereabouts. We simply told them our states of origin, Wisconsin, Illinois and Nebraska — and that the Pohlmans had driven up from Nashville to attend a Reds game with us. He told a couple of kid-friendly jokes for Finnegan's amusement and then pulled out a tub of more rubber duckies. It was an assorted lot with different colors and costumes. Patti and I snagged a purple duck wearing a Sugar n' Spice apron. That little duck still sits on the dash of my car.

Breakfast was indeed fabulous and Patti was introduced to goetta, a German-style sausage mush. The Pohlmans were heading home but not before a stop at the Newport Aquarium on the Kentucky side of the Ohio River. Patti wanted to get her nails done, and I eventually followed the Pohlmans to the aquarium. We went back to the RV first to let Holmes out, so I arrived at the aquarium well after the Pohlmans. Patti and I were both getting a little "me time" as I had my own Shark Week-end day.

"Everybody needs a little time away, I heard they say," Patti told me, using lyrics from the Chicago song, *Hard to Say I'm Sorry*.

The Newport Aquarium is bigger than I expected, housing thousands of creatures from all across the globe in a million gallons of water. Several small fish fill multiple aquariums in the first room. They fish are identified by placards that have photos and place of origin. One yellow and brown-striped fish got my attention because it is probably the laziest name given to any species, Stripey. They put a lot of thought into that one.

The Ring of Fire has various octopi; the Amazon has marine life from the giant South American river; Unbridled Fun is a collection of seahorses. There are penguins, frogs, rays, lizards, and eels. But the two main attractions are the sharks and the alligators.

Newport has a pair of albino gators named Snowflake and Snowball, each roughly six feet long. Their habitat is an indoor pond, well-lit, but also one that protects the sensitive white gators from ultraviolet rays. A boardwalk is a few feet above the pond, allowing visitors to see the gators no matter where they may be. In the next room was Mighty Mike, a 14-foot alligator that was the biggest gator outside of Florida. He was on a five-year loan from Florida's Crocodilian Conservation Center but was returned in September of 2018.

There are three places to see sharks — Shark Central, which has several smaller sharks and even a touch tank; the Shark Bridge, an enclosed 75-foot V-shaped rope bridge above the multiple tanks that hold the larger species; and Surrounded by Sharks, a seamless, underwater glass tunnel through a giant tank that holds various sharks and rays and loggerhead sea turtles. I was among the many visitors who stopped to take pictures of the hammerhead shark, the five-foot reef sharks, six-foot sandbar sharks, and the ten-foot nurse and sand tiger sharks. Sharks are fascinating creatures, and seeing them up close is a pretty cool experience. It's also the closest encounter I ever want to have with a shark.

Once Patti came back to meet me in Newport, her nails looked fabulous and we decided to walk across the Purple People Bridge, which hosts weekly events. This is another must when visiting Cincinnati, and you should definitely stop in the middle of the bridge so you can stand in two states at the same time. The Kentucky side has a massive riverfront shopping entertainment center chock full of restaurants and the aquarium. There was a festival on Kentucky's riverfront boardwalk. Live music was provided by a band with a lead singer who wanted to ensure everyone within earshot knew they were playing music by The Beatles.

"And that was The Beatles," he yelled after every song.

Prior to the Pohlmans arrival, Patti and I were able to see other areas of Cincinnati. We were impressed by the multitude of murals across the multicultural city influenced primarily by Germans. We ventured into the Over-the-Rhine neighborhood, an historic German district that has several murals. We ate dinner at The Eagle, famous for its fried chicken, and it lived up to the hype. There was a late lunch another day with Michelle Myers, who attended Limestone High School with Patti and now lives in Cincinnati. Patti had not seen Michelle in nearly 20 years and they were able to connect thanks to Facebook — and the meddling of Michelle's mother, Kay. Michelle does not have a Facebook account, but Kay does and acted as the mediator between Michelle and Patti before phone numbers were exchanged. Patti and Michelle were able to catch up and relive old memories during our meal. I jumped in now and again when Michelle, a thin woman with long, dark hair, inquired about our relationship, how'd we meet, how long have we been married, and the such. She wasn't much of a baseball fan, so there weren't many questions about our trip.

We had spent a week in Cincinnati, but it was time to head north where we'd meet up with Gordie the Unicorn. From there, it was onto Chicago to see the White Sox and Cubs and some more friends and family.

· · · · ·

As we went through Hell to get from Michigan to Illinois, pausing in Indiana to stop my car horn's constant beep and encountering traffic around Chicago, Gerry and Nancy Wright patiently waited for us in Yorkville, Illinois. We told them we were hoping to get their around 1 but would call when we had a more definitive time. They took 1 p.m. as gospel and Gerry called as we crossed the Indiana border into Illinois.

"Where are you guys?" he asked Patti, who explained our detour to Hell and the delays.

Patti's parents had arrived at the RV park a couple hours before us. Gerry asked if we had bug spray, warning us that the riverside campground was full of mosquitoes. Gerry and Nancy, both in their late 70s, had lunch at a Yorkville diner and walked around the quaint downtown to kill some time during their wait. The park was about an hour southwest of downtown Chicago and my in-laws followed us in once we finally arrived around 4.

It was a Friday and I had a DJ gig the next day in the town of Sycamore. I needed to pick up some speakers rented for me at a Guitar Center before they closed. I hurried to get the car off and the RV connections hooked up. It was hot and humid, so electricity to run the air conditioning was the top priority. Pulling out the hoses and connecting them had become routine by now, and within 15 minutes, I was en route to the Guitar Center in Oswego, about 20 miles away.

Gerry and Nancy spent the night in the RV; we gave them the bedroom while Patti and I climbed into the bed above the cab. It didn't feel right to ask two people in their late 70s to climb a ladder to get into bed.

I was up early the next morning for my gig, which was the company party for Ideal Industries. The company manufactures telecommunications parts, and I got a kick a few days later when the Ideal logo popped up on the Wrigley Field videoboard. The company was a Cubs sponsor and I had no idea. Had I known, I probably would have told more people about our trip during the five-hour event.

While I was playing music and MCing the company picnic, Patti spent the day with her parents and sisters, Joy and Veronica, who drove up from Peoria. Other than going out for lunch in Yorkville, the five didn't leave the RV. Patti's parents were gone by the time I returned and Joy and Veronica left shortly thereafter. It was Father's Day weekend, and we were happy Patti got to spend some time with her dad. I'd be seeing my dad in a few days.

We spent Father's Day itself at Guaranteed Rate Field, home of the Chicago White Sox. Patti's cousins, Helen and Margery, along with Helen's boyfriend, Rob, were joining us. We met at a Panera in Oswego and piled into Helen's car.

Getting to Guaranteed Rate Field, or "New Comiskey" as locals still call it, is pretty easy. It's right off the I-90/94 freeway on Chicago's south side and parking is ample. Street parking is free on Sundays, so that filled up rather quickly. We parked in one of the adjacent lots where tailgating was in full force an hour before first pitch. The White Sox are one of the few MLB teams that still allow tailgating in their lots.

Neither Helen, Margery, nor Rob had ever been to a big-league baseball game before. They may have all been in their 40s, but we were taking some big kids to their first MLB game.

"I can't believe the lushness of the green grass," Helen said as she walked through the concourse. The White Sox grounds crew was on the field, putting the final touches on the turf before the game began. The outfield grass had broad, off-setting stripes of dark and light green, depending on how the mower's blades and rollers were set.

The White Sox were playing the Tigers and both teams were well-represented as we walked to our seats in the right-field corner. Both teams were under .500, but nearly 27,000 people braved the heat. Some kids were cooling off in the "Old Comiskey" shower behind the center-field wall.

"Everybody's having fun," Helen said as she soaked it all in.

As Patti, Helen, and Margery went to the team store to get our stadium lapel pin, Rob and I went to claim that game's giveaway. The White Sox ran a father-daughter day promotion and were giving away black and pink caps at a bar area on the second level. Rob and I grabbed some beverages and hopped in line. It moved rather quickly and we left with a pair of Sox caps that were given to the hatless Helen and Margery. Rob came with his own White Sox cap and Patti and I were donning our Children's Hope Alliance hats.

The Tigers jumped out to a 2-0 lead on Nicholas Castellanos' two-run homer to left-center in the first inning. The White Sox answered with Matt Davidson's solo blast in the bottom of the second. I had previously seen Davidson play for the Charlotte Knights, the Sox's Triple-A affiliate. I even had a Matt Davidson *Star Wars* bobblehead sitting on my desk at work.

Davidson's home run set off fireworks from Guaranteed Rate Field's "Exploding Scoreboard." The fireworks are shot from seven towers that rise more than 100 feet behind the center-field Jumbotron. Each tower holds pinwheels that spin as the explosions commence.

The Tigers added another run in the fourth inning when a single from shortstop, Jose Iglesias, knocked in second baseman Niko Goodrum. By then we had already begun our stadium walkabout.

There is no mistaking Patti, Helen and Margery as relatives. Helen and my wife share enough physical traits, they have been mistaken as sisters. The three cousins posed for a photo between a couple of statues in the outfield concourse. I took another picture of Rob and Helen, who both made weird faces as I snapped the photo using Helen's phone. They had goosed each other, resulting in the funny expressions. I asked if they wanted me to take another, but they were pleased with the humorous shot.

We had walked up to the upper deck and seen the statues and tributes to the club's 12 retired numbers.

Guaranteed Rate Field has some of the best food we encountered at MLB parks. Patti fell in love with elote, Mexican street corn that was grilled to perfection. My pork tamales were also delicious. By the time the seventh inning rolled around, we needed an escape from the heat. Just beneath us was the stadium's Craft Kave, an air-conditioned bar area that served up myriad local and regional beers. Large field-level windows allowed patrons to still watch the game with a bullpen view. The beer was secondary; it was the AC that called us there to watch the Tigers wrap up their 3-1 victory. Head shots of each member of the 2018 club adorned the grey wall just inside the double-door entryway. Side-by-side logos honoring the club's 100th anniversary as a charter member of the American League in 1901 hang next to the photos.

One thing that is disappointing about Guaranteed Rate Field is the missed opportunity to create an amazing view beyond the center-field wall. White

Sox fans told us the architects were "too loyal" to old Comiskey Park that faced away from downtown Chicago. The current stadium, with an open design, lends itself well to having the city's iconic skyline as the backdrop behind the outfield wall. Instead, there isn't anything to catch your eyes over the score-board, like the Clemente Bridge and the Pittsburgh skyline at PNC Park or the Gateway Arch in St. Louis.

The game ended just after 4 p.m. This was our 15th stadium, meaning we were officially halfway through. The home teams were just 5-11 and the White Sox had fallen to 24-46.

Before leaving Chicago, we had dinner at a Vietnamese restaurant in the Hyde Park neighborhood. Then it was back to our car, still parked at the Panera in Oswego. Helen, Rob, and Marge came out to see the RV before heading home.

"I could never live in here for months on end," Helen remarked. "I'd get claustrophobic."

"Yeah, there's no place to get away from anybody," Margery chimed in. Patti and I just looked at each other and laughed. We did get on each other's nerves during our trip, but our relationship made it through unscathed.

· · · · ·

Jason Stevens was one of the most loyal followers of the Home Run On Wheels road trip. I heard from my high school classmate, who grew up a Cardinals fan despite being from Wisconsin, on a regular basis as we traveled from city to city. He lives in Chicago, where he works as a finance director, and was eager to meet up while we were in the area. He wasn't able to get out to the White Sox game on Father's Day or the Cubs game at Wrigley Field on June 19th but did join me for a Frontier League game between the Joliet Slammers and Windy City Thunderbolts the next evening in Crestwood.

He came straight from the office for the game, which began at 6. I was at the Standard Bank Stadium around 5 to do a couple of interviews for the pod-cast. With the recording equipment back in the car, I waited for Jason's arrival just before the first pitch.

I was comped two tickets and we took a couple of seats down the first-base line. Jason bought us a couple of beers and we chatted about baseball, the RV trip, and our high school days. We were teammates on our high school football and baseball teams. Jason was the better athlete and a shade under 6 feet tall. He played basketball in the winter while I wrestled. While I've added about 60 pounds since high school, when I wrestled at 130 pounds as a senior, Jason has remained fit. He hikes and is an avid runner. He and Patti ran the same Chicago marathon in the fall of 2013.

The Slammers got off to a 1-0 lead in the top of the first on Travis Bolin's RBI single to left. Danny Zardon, a 2016 draft pick of the Phillies, scored on the play.

As we discussed the podcast, Jason said he preferred hearing about the RV trip more than interviews with ball players.

"I can get those anywhere," he said before suggesting that we focus on our experiences traveling the country. We took his advice, though there was another player interview. This one Jason didn't mind because it was with Wisconsin native, Jeren Kendall, a Dodgers prospect from our region.

"I appreciated the Western Wisconsin banter," he told me in August.

The Slammers added another run in the third when London Landley singled and then scored on Zardon's sacrifice fly.

Jason got another round of beers and we talked about the route we were taking on the trip.

"You've got to go to Yellowstone," he demanded, joking that he'd hurt me if we didn't. I told him that was the plan and that we had already been to a pair of national parks in Maine and Ohio.

Both teams score in the fifth inning as the Slammers take a 3-1 lead. Lindley, a 2015 draft pick of the Rangers, scored on an error in the top of the inning. Windy City's Blair Beck scored in the bottom of the inning on a double by Jonathan McCray, who reached Triple A in 2017 with in the Royals organization.

We got another round from the stand behind us before the seventh-inning stretch. Joliet's Justin Garcia, a 2015 pick of the Astros, slapped a two-run single in the eighth to cap the scoring.

This was one of the more casual nights I had at a ballpark. I did have to write a story for my own website on the teams' day-night, home-and-home doubleheader, and edit the audio for the podcast, but I wasn't obligated to explore the park for a stadium review. I just sat with a friend and talked while watching the game.

The next day, Patti and I packed up and headed to Milwaukee to see the Brewers and Cardinals play at Miller Park. The Brewers donated 50 tickets to

Anu Family Services for the June 21st game and we were also going to games on June 23rd and July 4th.

"Tell Patti I said, 'Go Cardinals,'" Jason said before we hugged outside the stadium.

"Sure," I replied without any intention of relaying the message. "It was good to see you, man. Thanks for the advice."

"No problem. Have fun and be careful," he said before adding, "Remember, go to Yellowstone."

· · · · ·

I had another mini-high school reunion the next night. Aquinas classmates Eric Petzold, Nick Hotchkiss and Kevin Kadrmas were all attending the same Cardinals-Brewers game we were seeing.

We got together with Kevin and his wife and parents before the game. Patti and I followed them to Miller Park and said hi to Eric and Nick, who had brought with him his new fiancée. Eric's blond hair was now a solid grey but still thick. Nick hadn't aged much since high school, though he now had a dark goatee and his hair was buzzed high and tight. He had a Brewers cap with him, but it sat on an empty seat beside him as the trio enjoyed a pregame meal at Miller Park's TGI Friday's.

We didn't say much more than hello to Eric and Nick before we head up to Section 422 to meet Mark Roesler and the group from Anu Family Services. We were hoping to see them after the game, but they headed back to La Crosse immediately afterward. Kevin's family had a hotel in the Milwaukee area, so he and Melissa asked us to go out for a nightcap. Kevin used to live in Milwaukee and wanted to take us to one of his old haunts.

Steve's on Bluemound is a neighborhood sports bar. Packers, Bucks, Badgers, and Brewers signs hang on the wall next to neon beer signs. Three flat screen TVs are behind the long wooden bar, above several tap handles. We took a seat at a round, high-top table next to the bar and ordered some drinks. It was a Thursday night, so there weren't many people inside the bar at 11 p.m. Those there were all wearing baseball attire. Patti was the only one in a Cardinals jersey.

Kevin asked how our meeting went with Steve Melia and Marybeth Longona in New York. I told him we enjoyed meeting them and thanked him for helping to set that up.

"You guys staying through the weekend?" I then asked. "You know we're going to Saturday's game, too, right?"

"Nah, we're leaving tomorrow morning," Kevin replied.

After two rounds, it was time to go.

"We'll be in La Crosse for a couple days after the Fourth of July," I reminded Kevin.

"Cool. Let's get together again," he said.

We did.

Patti and I ended our two-week stay in the Milwaukee area on July 5th and headed west. We were spending two days with my grandparents in Bangor, just outside of La Crosse, before heading up to the Twin Cities. The same storm that soaked us in Milwaukee on July 4th also washed out the fireworks celebration that night in La Crosse. The Independence Day celebration had been pushed to the next night. Kevin suggested we join him at Riverside Park to watch the show. I asked my grandma if that would be fine.

"Sure, Ronnie," she replied. "Go see your friends. Take the spare key with you."

My Grandma Clements is one of the few people who still calls me Ronnie. I don't mind.

After having dinner at my grandparents' home, Patti and I met Kevin at his apartment complex. Melissa volunteered to help out the Coast Guard Auxiliary keep boat traffic away from the area in front of the park. People used to be able to park their boats anywhere on Mississippi River but that changed years earlier when a boat was set on fire and sunk after a burning fireworks capsule fell onto it. The boats now had to be out of harm's way.

It was an impressive display, one of the best fireworks shows we had seen.

"They always do a great job," Kevin said after Patti commented how much she enjoyed the show. Shortly after the last boom, the boats began to disperse and we waited for the boat Melissa was on to come to shore. We watched as the small crew tied it to the dock and disembarked.

As we walked through the park, music from the stage where country singer, Chris Lane, was performing filled the air.

"He just played Summerfest in Milwaukee," I said of Lane, recalling his name on the list of July 4th performers.

The four of us went to a nearby rooftop bar overlooking the river and had just one drink before leaving. It had been a long day for all of us and it was a "school night."

My aunts, Debbie and Shelly, came out to their parents' house the next day to see the RV.

Debbie's reaction was, "Wow." Shelly, who is only four years older than me and is more like a big sister than an aunt, was surprised by the storage space as she got the tour with her husband Mike. They had just returned from a trip of their own to celebrate their 30th wedding anniversary. Mike and Shelly made a late-afternoon visit before returning to the farm they run. It's the same farm my grandparents ran for decades and the one on which I grew up.

My dad relied on his parents to help raise me and Faith. Our biological mother had abandoned us when we were toddlers. My dad remarried when I was 7 but divorced when I was 13. My grandmother, his mother, has always been the one constant maternal figure in my life. I was grateful to still have her and all of my grandparents in my 40s. When she had a heart attack in October, I thought our family was losing its matriarch. She pulled through and we were back at their house for Thanksgiving dinner in November.

· · · · ·

My cousin Samantha got married on September 22nd, 2012. Samantha is the oldest of my aunt Shelly's three children and the only girl. I wanted to attend Samantha's wedding, but Patti also wanted me to go with her to her cousin's wedding on the same day.

Her cousin Shelley married Santiago Garcia in Peoria. Patti and I had met in March and this was my first opportunity to meet her extended family. I sent my regrets to Samantha and her groom, Nick, and went with Patti to the Wright-Garcia ceremony.

Both September 22nd weddings were held at Catholic churches. The church in Peoria had a predominantly Mexican congregation, and the wedding reception was full of Hispanic music and Mexican dances. It was a good time and even Patti's parents were dancing to songs they had never before heard.

Shelley, the sister of Helen and Margery, grew up in Peoria but now lived in Marshfield, Wisconsin, about three hours east of Minneapolis. The Garcias agreed to join us at Target Field to see the Twins play the Orioles on July 8th.

Patti and I were in the middle of the best stretch of our trip. We had gotten kids to games in Detroit on June 13th, Milwaukee on June 21st, and had things lined up for the Orioles-Twins game on July 7th and a July 11th game between the Diamondbacks and Rockies in Denver. As our mission gained momentum, we were also able to spend time with family.

We met Santi and Shelley at the Mall of America and took the light-rail to Target Field. We talked about the trip and our visit to Paisley Park earlier that day. Santi asked about our favorite stadium so far (PNC Park) and what we thought of both Miller Park and Target Field. Shelley asked how it went with the kids from Family Alternatives the previous day.

"Great," Patti answered. "I think everyone had a good time."

While we were in the 300 level for the Saturday game, our Sunday tickets placed us in Section 121. The seats were up the third-base line, perpendicular to where the infield grass meets the outfield. We were in prime foul ball territory. A few balls came close, but none landed in our section. My quest for a baseball was still fruitless.

Santiago had never been to a Major League game before and wanted to see more of the stadium. Patti and I did some exploring a day earlier but most of that was outside the ballpark. We hadn't experienced many of the amenities inside Target Field and were more than happy to walk around with Shelley and Santiago. Our seats were right in the sun and none of us had any sunscreen. Truth be told, that was the primary reason for abandoning our seats in the fifth inning.

We eventually found ourselves in Bat & Barrel restaurant and bar on the club level in the right-field corner. Most of the televisions above the bar were showing the Twins game. Patti and I visited Bat & Barrel the previous day and a couple TVs were set to soccer. Small groups were gathered in front of them to see Croatia play Russia in the World Cup.

"Why are you guys watching soccer at a baseball game?" I asked.

"It's the World Cup," a tall woman with dark, shoulder-length hair answered.

"Yeah, but the U.S. isn't in it," I said.

"We don't care," she said while getting moral support from her friends with a few, "Yeahs."

We razzed each other, all in good fun. I actually kept my eye on the game, too, and the soccer fans went nuts when Croatia upset Russia on penalty kicks.

If there was any soccer on during the Sunday game, we didn't notice.

The wall outside the restaurant entrance is truly something unique. Red, white, and blue bat handles stick out of the wall to form the MLB logo of a player with bat raised, waiting to strike the oncoming ball. Though the logo isn't modeled after any one player, Minnesota fans like to believe it is the silhouette of Twins Hall of Famer Harmon Killebrew.

Our foursome walked out to the balcony and grabbed a table. A server came over and we placed an order for some food and drinks. As we waited, the first two Baltimore hitters grounded out. Manny Machado then doubled before Mark Trumbo drew a five-pitch walk. The Orioles were kept scoreless, however, when Chris Davis struck out to end the inning. Minnesota held a 2-0 lead, but the game was about to get blown open.

Our food arrived, nothing special, just some light finger snacks. Brian Dozier, who would join Machado with the Dodgers three weeks later, doubled to lead off the bottom of the sixth.

That brought up Twins third baseman Eduardo Escobar, who blasted a home run to right-center that struck a white 2018 Chevy Malibu parked under a stairwell in the concourse. The car was there as an advertisement for a local auto dealership. I figured that if a player hit the car, some fan would win the car. Escobar's two-run shot nailed the car just above the front passenger-side wheel well. We'd seen the promotion run at other stadiums but had never actually witnessed a baseball hit the promotional vehicle. There was no such promotion at Target Field, though I found a Twins employee who works in the front office to suggest and encourage it. Escobar's homer left a small dent in the car and was part of an eight-run sixth inning that cemented Minnesota's 10-1 victory.

Santi and I wanted to get a closer look, so we left the right-field Bat & Barrel restaurant and made our way to the concourse. I snapped a photo of the dented vehicle and tweeted it out. The Twins replied from their official account with one word, "Oops."

. . . . .

Patti was a contract employee for Wells Fargo when we began our trip. She got hired as a full-time employee with benefits in May of 2018, two months into our journey. The man who promoted her transitioned to a different department a couple weeks later with a promotion of his own. Patti's new "boss" was a man named Scott Casey. She had never met Scott and had very little interaction with him prior to May. When she found out Scott lives in Denver, arrangements were made to finally meet in person.

We were leaving Denver on Saturday, July 14th, so Patti and Scott decided to meet for lunch on Friday. The spouses went with.

Scott picked a restaurant in the downtown 16th Street Mall, which is an open-air district with a trolley that runs between the east-west bound lanes of the thoroughfare. Between tourists and office workers grabbing lunch, foot traffic was heavy on a gorgeous summer weekday. Scott and his wife, Kim, met us at Appaloosa Grill, where we took advantage of the perfect weather by sitting outside.

There wasn't much shop discussed. Instead, we all got to know each other. We found out Kim works at one of Colorado's largest marijuana dispensaries as its public relations officer. We also learned that Scott played football at Lakeland College in Wisconsin before a knee injury ended his playing career.

Scott asked me about my sports journalism career, and they had a ton of questions about our trip. We had questions for them, too, as we tried to figure out what we were going to do after lunch. They suggested we head out to Red Rocks, the park with an amphitheatre famous for its near-perfect acoustics. We had done that the night before. After our Friday lunch, Patti and I roamed around downtown Denver for a bit before heading back to the RV to prepare for the next day's departure.

Red Rocks was only about 15 minutes from our RV park in West Denver. The area is stunning with giant rust-colored boulders that jut up from the terrain. Hiking trails wind through the park around the concert venue. We didn't realize there was a show that night, but the parking lots were filling up rather quickly as we arrived. We told one lot attendant we weren't going to the concert but rather hiking with our dog and did not have to pay to park.

Holmes loves trails and transformed into his mountain goat alter ego. I learned my lesson from Cuyahoga Valley National Park and kept him on the leash. While the hiking trails had just a few people on them, a line of cars filled the road and the foot traffic around the amphitheatre was heavy.

As we hiked, music from the concert stage permeated the air. Moe, a band with which we were not familiar, was the headliner but had not yet begun playing. The opener was a group called Pigeons Playing Ping Pong. We learned of that band over Memorial Day weekend when we saw a guy wearing a Pigeons Playing Ping Pong T-shirt while at the LionFire Music Festival in Slippery Rock, Pennsylvania. We had never heard of the band before then, and now here they were, opening a show at Red Rocks. It was quite the coincidence.

When our hike was over, we headed back to the car — going against the wave of people walking toward the venue entrance. A few folks stopped to give Holmes a quick pat on the head. The route back to the car took a bit longer than it should have. I led us to the wrong one, so we backtracked and hiked uphill to the correct lot. We walked past a trio of people drinking beers outside of their vehicle.

"Where's ours?" I joked.

"Oh, you want one? Here," one of the two women replied before handing us each a can.

"Oh, wow. Thanks. I was just joking," I said.

"No problem," she responded and then we introduced ourselves. The woman who handed us the beers was from Wisconsin — small world. After a few minutes of chit-chat, we thanked them again and were on our way as they headed in the opposite direction toward the amphitheatre.

There was water for Holmes in the car, and he took a healthy drink before we took off. We told each other that we had to see a show at Red Rocks in the near future.

We got some burgers and ice cream at a small restaurant in the nearby town of Morrison. The place had outdoor seating and Holmes was able to meet a few fellow canines there with their respective humans. The restaurant owner came out to give a hot dog to each pooch.

I had a bit of a panic Friday afternoon. We were leaving the next day and I realized the tilt pin for our tow dolly had somehow been lost. We spent the evening on a mission to find a replacement. It took us a few stops before we found one at a hardware store. With the task complete, we looked for a place to have dinner and settled on a microbrewery that served its own pizza. We ordered a pie and each got a flight. A large party was seated next to us. I heard one of them mention San Antonio, where I was born and my brother lives. The group was indeed from San Antonio and was in Denver for a wedding. The patriarch was a man named Tom White, a white-haired man in his mid-50s. He asked where we were from, always the opening for me to explain our trip. His blue eyes lit up. He and his wife had two adult bio-kids but also adopted three children from the foster system, including 9-year-old twins. The other child was 13 years old and Tom explained that he and his wife were empty-nesters who didn't mind starting over. It was awesome to meet someone like that who opened their home and their heart to kids in need.

. . . . .

After leaving Denver, we spent the All-Star break at Yellowstone National Park and then stopped in Missoula, Montana for one night. I actually watched the All-Star Game itself at a microbrewery in Missoula. The next night was spent in gorgeous Coeur d'Alene, Idaho before we drove across Washington state to the Seattle area. We were going to stay with my cousin, Camoren, and his family in Port Orchard on the Kitsap Peninsula. My Uncle Bruce and Aunt Deb, Camoren's parents, live in nearby Olalla. Camoren and his wife, Gillian, have two daughters — 6-year-old Lyndee and 2-year-old Miura. My last visit to the Seattle area was before Lyndee was born, so I was excited to meet both of my little cousins.

One of the cities through which we drove was Butte, Montana, which has a 90-foot statue called "Our Lady of the Rockies" atop one of the surrounding mountains. The statue, which is redolent of the Christ the Redeemer statue in Rio de Janeiro, is the fourth-tallest statue in the United States. What are the other three? Birth of the New World in Puerto Rico, The Statue of Liberty in New York, and the Pegasus and Dragon in Florida.

While the trek through the Pacific Northwest is gorgeous, the winding route provides very little cell service. This was an issue for Patti, who spent most of our multi-hour drives sitting in the back of the RV working. Without any cell service, she can't turn on her iPhone's Wi-Fi hotspot. She had to schedule conference calls around our travel when she knew service would be spotty and plan for offline tasks like project plans or presentations.

We stopped at one I-90 rest area in Montana because she had service and had to run a call. That proved to be a fortuitous stop. After I took Holmes out for a stroll, I ventured into the national forest to check out the small campground located next to the rest stop. The Sloway campground in the Lolo National Forest overlooks the zigzagging Clark Fork River. I walked to the edge of the steep slope to catch a glimpse of the river. As I looked down, I noticed a $20 bill at my feet. My walk around the campground paid off, literally. That $20 could have paid for two nights at the campground. National forest campgrounds are very inexpensive but provide few amenities.

We made another unscheduled stop the next day just east of Seattle. I realized we would be driving right past Snoqualmie Falls. If you've ever seen the opening credits for the television show, *Twin Peaks*, you have seen Snoqualmie Falls. The 268-foot waterfall wasn't something we wanted to pass up, so we again ignored the famous advice given by TLC and chased that waterfall.

"We watch *Twins Peaks*, so we made a detour to see Snoqualmie Falls," I texted Gillian to let her know we'd be arriving late.

I had originally told her we'd be there around 6. The estimate was now 7, but had I known how bad traffic on Interstate 5 north of Tacoma would have been, I would have told her 8.

Snoqualmie Falls is beautiful, appearing to be a pair of side-by-side curtain falls because of a boulder centered at its brink. The water drops into a circular basin surrounded by a lush forest. A two-acre park is next to the waterfall, which is harnessed by a nearby hydroelectric plant to generate power for the neighboring communities. The park includes a pair of observation decks and a gift shop located inside the hotel atop the falls. That hotel is the Salish Lodge, which is a popular event venue and doubles at the Great Northern Hotel on the television series. Patti and I perused the gift shop before getting back on the road.

We were only about a mile away from the waterfall when I pulled the RV over. We had officially driven 10,000 miles. I snapped another photo of the odometer and then put the rig back in gear. We got to Camoren's house in Port Orchard around 7:30.

Camoren's house is down a long dirt driveway lined by evergreen trees. He and my Uncle Bruce spent the weekend prior trimming the trees to ensure there was enough clearance for the RV to pass. I told Camoren we needed 13 feet. The driveway comes to a fork after a couple hundred yards. To the right is one house, to the left my cousin's. It's a nice place with three bedrooms upstairs, a big living room, and spacious kitchen with separate dining room on the ground level and a game room with a bathroom and laundry room down a small flight of stairs. It's a sunken space but not exactly a basement. There's a big back yard with no fence, just woods. We pulled into the front of the house, where a trampoline and swing set were next to the tree line. Camoren suggested I turn around so I didn't have to back up when we left four days later.

Turning around in front of the house wasn't possible. So I backed out the same way I came in, snapping a few branches my cousin and uncle had missed. I got to the fork, drove a tad up the neighbor's drive while brushing a few tree limbs, and then backed in. Using Camoren as my human "backup Cam," I slowly backed into the designated spot in front of the garage.

Because the girls had their own bedrooms, Patti and I chose to sleep in the RV during our stay. We plugged into the house electricity and Camoren ran a hose to the rig, so we could brush our teeth and the like. We would shower inside the house.

While Miura was shy and distant the whole time, Lyndee was very curious about the RV and latched onto me immediately.

"She was a big Ron Clements fan," Patti joked.

"She's only 6 years old, but I think she's the president of the Ron Clements fan club," I replied.

"President and only member?"

"Oh, come on!"

Lyndee, whose blonde hair was usually pulled back in a pony tail, was also a big Patti fan and hung out in the RV on Friday while Patti was working. She sat on the bed behind Patti's workspace and looked out the window, telling Patti she'd watch the driveway. Patti got a reprieve when Gillian and I left with the girls to have lunch on the Port Orchard waterfront. Across the Sinclair Inlet of the Puget Sound from Amy's on the Bay is the Bremerton Navy base where Camoren works as a welder. He's been working there since he was 19 while still living at home. When he left his parents' home several years later, he had purchased the house in Port Orchard and moved in. He was 39 at the time of our visit and had created a wonderful life for himself and his lovely family.

Cam's dad, my uncle, worked at the same base while serving in the Navy. Now retired, the former Senior Chief still works there as a civilian contractor. Bruce came out to see us Friday night. Well, he probably came out to see his two granddaughters, but I'm telling the story. Bruce looks a lot like my dad. They have the same prominent Clements nose, short salt-and-pepper hair (though my dad's is whiter), well-groomed goatee, and broad shoulders. Bruce has a calm demeanor with a soft, yet authoritative voice. My grandparents had nine children with three boys born in succession and just four years apart. Bruce was between Bernie and Brian and the most gifted athlete of the three. A naturally strong farm boy, Bruce was an all-conference linebacker in high school, and even now at 62, was still in excellent shape.

Bruce spent a couple hours visiting on Friday, and it was time I cherished. He's always been a kind man and I looked forward to seeing him on Sunday. He was going to the game with us, as were Gillian's parents, Jim and Tish. Gillian had already purchased seven tickets for the group.

We wanted to get kids to a game in Seattle and I reached out to a pair of foster care institutions based on recommendations from CASA. The two non-profits were Treehouse and the Mockingbird Society. I contacted both organizations three weeks prior to our Seattle stop. That wasn't enough notice for

Treehouse to arrange for families to attend a Mariners game. The Mocking-bird Society was out because it had a scheduled event with Pearl Jam that weekend. The Seattle rock band was doing several promotional events leading up to their charity "Home Shows" at Safeco Field in August.

"Very well," I said, knowing we couldn't compete with Pearl Jam.

Patti and I were up early Saturday morning. We had a 5K to run at Safeco Field and it took about an hour to get from the Kitsap Peninsula to downtown Seattle. We waited for the ferry from Southworth to Fauntleroy at sunrise. The water was calm and acted as a mirror when the golden sun appeared on the horizon. The long reflection rippled as the ferry arrived.

Once across, I drove the Scion north to Safeco Field. We wore the Home Run On Wheels T-shirts I had printed and shipped to my grandparents' house in Wisconsin. Mine was a light grey while Patti's was solid white. Each had a small Home Run On Wheels logo on the left breast and a larger red logo on the back. A few folks asked us about it, which was our intention. Everything was about raising awareness of the needs of children in the foster system. We chose to run this particular 5K because its intention was to raise awareness of domestic violence. Many children enter the foster system because of abuse in the home. This was one way to tie our mission into that of the race.

The Refuse to Abuse 5K at Safeco Field was Saturday, July 21st. The race raised funds to benefit the Washington State Coalition Against Domestic Violence and its statewide violence prevention and education work.

The starting point was just outside the Safeco Field parking garage and the course began with a loop of the stadium. We then entered the ballpark via the right-field gate and ran, with brief periods of walking, through every level of the stadium. The route took us through the club level and back out to the garage before re-entering on the suite level. We were directed to the top level of Safeco Field and then it was downhill from there, running down the ramps to the bowels of the stadium before running out onto the warning track in center field. A lap around the field was all that remained before the finish line.

Mariners manager Scott Servais got the race started and then was at the finish line to greet runners as they crossed. I grabbed a few moments to chat with him and told him what we were doing. He was impressed. When I told him I was from La Crosse, Servais told me his parents attended the same high school I did. A sweaty brunette woman interrupted our talk by asking if she could get a photo with the Seattle skipper. He obliged and our conversation was over.

I completed the 5K in 33 minutes and 24 seconds, a time with which I was content because I had not done any sort of distance running since my honorable discharge from the Marine Corps 17 years earlier. I wasn't exactly feeling the proverbial "runner's high" afterward. Several people asked, "Wasn't that great?" I was just like, "Um, nope." But it was for a good cause.

We mingled for a bit, telling a few folks about our trip, and then strolled through downtown Seattle for an hour. CenturyLink Field, home to the NFL's Seahawks and the Seattle Sounders of MLS, is next door. The area was abuzz with vendors, buskers, sports fans, and 5K participants all crowding the streets. The Sounders were set to kick off against the Vancouver Whitecaps and the Mariners played the White Sox later that night. Grabbing last-minute tickets to the Sounders game was tempting, but we were wearing our running gear and had plans with Patti's cousins.

· · · · ·

Floyd Wright joined the Navy on March 2nd, 1948, less than two months after his 18th birthday. He wanted to join sooner, but his mother wouldn't sign off. He was the youngest of nine children and his mother didn't want to lose him to another war. Floyd has several nieces and nephews, one of whom is Gerry Wright, Patti's father. Floyd felt called to military service following World War II and made the Navy a career, retiring in 1970. His last duty station was Naval Air Station Whidbey Island and started his family with his wife, Dorothy. Uncle Floyd, who turned 90 in 2019, moved back to Illinois after Dorothy died and lives near Gillespie. His two daughters still reside in the Seattle area. Patti had not seen Jackie or Ruth in years and was anxious to spend some time with them.

We met Ruth and her husband, Craig, at Pike Place Market and walked to a waterfront restaurant called The Crab Pot for lunch. Seattle may have a reputation for constant rain, but it didn't rain once in the four days we spent there. July 21st was a particularly gorgeous day and the four of us sat outside. As much as they had questions for us, we had questions for them. I was especially curious to know about Craig's job as a corrections officer. I asked the same dumb questions he's probably fielded a thousand times, what do you think of television shows like *Oz* and *Prison Break*? "Do you like *The Shawshank Redemption*?" He answered the questions in stride and without disdain.

Craig, a well-built man with greying hair who stands about six feet, two inches, had to leave after lunch. It was Saturday, but he had to work. We were tasked with taking Ruth home after she showed us around Seattle. We wanted to go up in the Space Needle, but it was under renovation and not all of it was open to the public. We decided to visit another time when we could get the full experience. Instead, Ruth took us to the Columbia Center Tower, which is more than 400 feet taller than the Space Needle.

"You can't see the Space Needle from the Space Needle," the young blond gentleman working the elevator told us.

The Columbia Tower is the tallest building in Seattle and the views from the Sky View Observatory are impressive. We could see the tops of the Olympic Mountains in the west beyond the sound. The snow-capped peak of Mt. Rainier to the east appeared to float above the clouds. Rainier dominates the skyline from just about every vantage point in the city. We wished we could have had the time to visit both national parks, on the Olympic Peninsula and at Rainier.

We could look down into both Safeco Field and CenturyLink Field, where the Sounders game was still going. The Sounders got a pair of goals from Nicolas Lodeiro in a 2-0 win over the Whitecaps.

Upon leaving Columbia Center, we returned to Pike Market. I wanted to get a coffee from the original Starbucks location. The line was out the door and wrapped around the block. I had been there before and getting a Caffè Mocha wasn't that important.

Ruth lived just north of Seattle but had one more thing to show us before we took her home. She introduced us to an unexpected and lesser-known attraction: the Ballard Locks. Here, boats line up to travel from the salt water of the Puget Sound to the fresh water of Salmon Bay and Lake Washington Ship Canal. We got to see several vessels, large and small, "lock through." It is truly an amazing feat of engineering, especially with a difference in water levels of several feet. Salmon also assemble in the fish ladder and spend time adapting to the fresh water after traveling from the ocean. From here they would swim upstream to spawn. Of course, all of those salmon make good dinner for seals and bears along the way. There was one seal on the saltwater side of the locks fishing to his heart's content. We watched his head repeatedly appear and then disappear beneath the liquid surface as we walked along the waterfront.

Ruth was prepared for our visit to her home with some snacks she had prepared. She set everything on the table and we were joined by her 26-year-old daughter, Marie. Ruth's older sister, Jackie, popped in to say hello but was on her way to see Sheryl Crow perform at a winery. We got to meet one of Ruth's two sons, Collin, as we were leaving. Collin briefly stopped by to pick up a change of clothes before joining his twin, Kyle, at a friend's birthday party. The two boys attended the University of Washington.

To quote Ice Cube, it was a good day. Sunday was back to baseball, however. The All-Star break was over and we were ready to see a game at our 20th stadium.

· · · · ·

I love high-fives. It doesn't matter if I've known you for five years or five seconds, if you walk by me, you might get a high-five. The first time Gillian saw me give someone a high-five at the ferry terminal in Bremerton, she asked, "Do you know him?"

"Nope," I said. "Just wanted to high-five him. He's wearing a Mariners jersey. Probably going to the same place we are."

The ferry from Bremerton drops passengers off right in downtown Seattle, one mile north of Safeco Field. We could have taken a cab or a rickshaw ride to the stadium, but our group of seven walked it. Jim and Tish were each 71 years old and have bad knees but made the walk without complaint. They are no longer married but remained friends and both moved from Michigan to Washington to be closer to their granddaughters.

There were more high-fives on the mile walk to the park. We passed a bar that said it was Seattle's oldest. I suggested we pop in there after the game for a drink. I've got a thing for historic bars and a life goal is to visit the oldest bar in every state. So far only Florida, Georgia, South Carolina, and North Carolina have made the cut.

We entered Safeco Field though the home-plate gate and walked under the giant Chihuly-like baseball chandelier. The chandelier is made of 1,000 translucent bats molded of resin and mounted on brushed aluminum spiraling forms. The floor of the rotunda is painted with a mixture of seafoam greens and blues to suggest a churning sea. Seeing the elaborate fixture lit up at night would have been great, but it was not illuminated for a 1 p.m. game.

In the concourse, there were more high-fives with people I didn't know. I was just a random guy walking down the concourse at a baseball stadium giving high-fives to strangers. Gillian was just laughing at me by this point.

"It was really funny," Patti said. "I wish I would have had a camera on you. Maybe this will be an assignment going forward, to follow you with a camera to film people's reactions. Some of them are like, 'Hey!' and will be gung-ho and high-five you. Others will high-five hesitantly and then turn around to look back at you like, 'What's that about?'"

"I've been left hanging a lot," I interjected.

"Some people are either not paying attention, or like, 'What are you doing?'" Patti said. "They're suspicious."

"I wish we would have had a YouTube channel," I said. "That's something my dad suggested."

"We can only do so many things," Patti said. "There was a learning curve."

True enough.

Gillian told us we had to get the garlic fries at the stadium. Garlic fries are a staple of every MLB stadium along the West Coast. While Safeco Field's garlic fries didn't quite live up to the lofty expectations, they were still tasty. The concession stands should probably hand out mints with each order, but we'd rather suffer the consequences of garlic breath than have a small leg in our teeth. Let me explain. A favorite treat popular with the Asian fans is toasted grasshoppers. Neither of us were brave enough to try a crunchy arthropod.

We saw the Mariners cruise to an 8-2 victory thanks to a pair of home runs by first baseman Ryon Healy. After an 0-5 start, the home teams had now won five straight and were 12-12 on our trip.

Following Sunday's game, we stopped the nearby Pyramid Brewing Company for a drink before getting back on the ferry to head across the sound. It was amusing to get Tish's opinion on the game. She grew up in England and doesn't really care much about baseball.

As Camoren and Gillian went back to their place, Patti and I headed to my uncle's house. We had barely seen Deb and wanted to spend some time visiting her and Bruce. We also wanted to speak with them about their experiences during the 17 years they spent as foster parents.

· · · · ·

Camoren was 17 years old when my Uncle Bruce and Aunt Deb began fostering other children. They were about to be empty-nesters and wanted to fill a void they had felt for years. Their daughter Darcy, who was 11 months older than Camoren, died at the age of 12 in a car accident caused by a drunk driver.

Camoren knew his parents dealt with that grief for years and signed off on bringing kids into the home. He had just two rules: none of the kids could be older than him and he wouldn't babysit. Because he was 17 and about to begin his senior year of high school, the first rule wasn't an issue.

"I think he enjoyed having kids around," Bruce said of Cam. "One of the most rewarding things about fostering and taking children into your house is the memories you build with them and you remember the good things. We had a lot of them."

They came close to adopting one girl but that didn't come to pass. The average stay for kids in their home was about 18 months, but they had a pair of children for two years. Bruce and Deb were even allowed to help choose the family those siblings ultimately went to.

"I learned a lot about myself, like the patience I had, and you learn so much from children," Deb said. "You get children you don't know and you're supposed to treat them like your own, but you truly can't because you have all these rules. You just do the best you can. We started out with the state for three years and then went to this private foster care agency, and it is Christian-based, in 2000 and we were with them for almost 15 years… I'll even give people the phone number of my old agency. We had a great agency, Community and Family Services. The best part was you could call them whenever, around the clock. They had super support."

Bruce knows that made a positive difference in kids' lives. He recalled seeing a boy they fostered at a grocery store and the boy ran up to him to give him a hug.

"I know they learned how a family should be," Deb said. "They learned there are rules and there are consequences. There's time to eat and there's time to play and what it's really like to have both a mom and dad, although we wouldn't allow children to call us Mom and Dad. We were Miss Deb and Mr. Bruce. A lot of them wanted to call Bruce, 'Daddy,' but we wouldn't let them do that."

Deb said she gets "up on her soapbox" and still tries to recruit people to be foster parents, even though she and Bruce stopped as they both reached their 60s.

"There's such a huge need," Deb said. "If you're thinking about it, please do it."

It's not easy, however. The system can be frustrating and Deb said foster parents should have a larger voice when it comes to the welfare of the children because they are the ones with the children every day. While the ultimate goal may be to return children to their biological families, bio-parents sometimes have "all the rights" despite having their kids removed from the home.

"The kids come first," Deb said. "The court-ordered visits were tough. We saw the same issues over and over, and we'd have to start from scratch when they came back. We had one boy who would go see his biological parents and he'd come back with lice every week. Every flipping time. I told the social worker every time to check the home because I know they don't want lice in their facility. Sometimes I just had to put my foot down. One of the failures of the foster system is that the best intentions don't always come to be," Bruce said before citing drug use in the home as one of the "evils" that result in children being returned to foster care.

"In many cases, you know the child is not going back to the parents," Bruce added. "It's a lost hope and putting the child through it, even if the child is fast-tracked to adoption, it still takes way too long."

Even with all the frustrations that go with being a foster parent, when I asked them if they would do it all over again, Bruce said without hesitation, "Absolutely."

· · · · ·

We made a point to spend at least one night in every state through which we passed. We had never before been to Oregon and scheduled an overnight stop near Portland. We used Harvest Hosts and found a winery 30 miles west of Portland. The winery even had water and electric hookups for us and plenty of room for Holmes to run around. We did a tasting before the Plum Hill Vineyards tasting room closed at 5. We had a bit of time to kill before heading into downtown Portland for dinner. The people inside were definitely interested in the RV, seeing the Children's Hope Alliance and Home Run On Wheels logos through the windows. We answered their questions and handed out a few cards. But I was anxious to leave. We were meeting my sister and her family in Portland.

Danielle texted me the previous Thursday to let me know her husband had a work conference and they would be in Portland when we passed through. Danielle asked if we wanted to go with them to see Multnomah Falls on the other side of Portland, but we were arriving too late. Dinner it was. We'd met at 7. It was 8:30 before my sister arrived with her family. Shivum had landed a job interview while at the conference and had to shop for a suit to wear. Patti and I brought a bottle of wine from Plum Hill to share with Danielle and Shivum but polished it off ourselves as we sat on a riverfront bench and waited.

Several restaurants and hotels line the boardwalk along the Willamette River. We chose Il Terrazo, a quaint Italian place that had outdoor seating.

Shivum and Danielle apologized for being so late, to which I replied, "No biggie. Happy to see you."

My nephew Yogi was four and niece Aria was almost two. Both had been to our 2017 wedding but neither remembered. When I showed Yogi a picture of him with my other nephew, Brock, he went from shy and quiet to energetic and talkative in seconds. Aria had no such shyness and quickly warmed to both me and Patti. She also got up from her seat several times to run around the sidewalk in front of our table. Fortunately the joggers were alert. Danielle reeled her in each time. This was a pleasant surprise and didn't want the night to end. Unfortunately it had to. Shiv, who has his own medical practice in rural Texas, had his interview the next day. Patti and I had a long day of driving ahead of us. It was seven hours to Kamp Klamath on the north end of the Redwood National and State Parks. Rampant forest fires in Southwestern Oregon and Northern California made the drive even longer.

We were able to spend some more time with my sister's family before leaving Texas. They couldn't come to Arlington to join us for a Rangers game on September 4th, so we went to them. The two-hour drive from Dallas to Olney was a bit out of the way for us, but we had never been out to my sister's house. They had also still not seen the RV. Olney is rural community of 3,300 people in North Central Texas. There was plenty of room to park the RV in front of their house, which is on the outskirts of town. Danielle had lunch ready for us and I was able to play with my nephew and niece for over an hour. It easily could have been longer. A 4-year-old boy and nearly 2-year-old girl have a lot of energy. I learned something about my nephew, Yogi. He's pretty competitive and got upset when I won the third game of Sorry, even though he had won the first two. Shivum got home just as we were about to leave, so we stuck around a bit to chat with him and give him the grand RV tour. Because we had an eight-hour drive ahead of us, we couldn't visit all day, as much as we would have loved to. We only had a couple of hours, and by 2 p.m., were back on the road and bound for Kansas City.

· · · · ·

I wasn't sure if we were going to make it to the Harris household in Peoria, Arizona. As we entered the Phoenix area, so, too, did a violent dust storm that significantly reduced visibility on Interstate 10. The Highway 101 exit is an overpass above the freeway and the winds were such, I was fearful we might topple, despite the weight of the RV. I took things slow and we drove to the home of Peggy Harris in Glendale. Though we were staying with Chris and Katie Harris in Peoria, Peggy was Chris's aunt and had a spot on the side of her house for the RV. We were grateful to not have to pay to park the RV somewhere. We were taking the vehicle to the Camping World in Avondale the next day, but this night it would be at Aunt Peggy's.

We could not show Chris and Katie Harris enough gratitude. They put us up for ten days while we waited for the Diamondbacks to complete a nine-game road trip. Their 19-year-old son, Logan, even gave up his room for us, sharing a room with his 12-year-old brother, Jonah, instead.

Patti grew up with Katie, and even after Katie's family moved to California, the two continued to write letters to each other. Patti shared one of those letters with me when a 10-year-old Katie was swooning over "dreamy" Michael Jackson. They had lost touch through high school and college but were able to reconnect as adults thanks to Facebook. Chris and Katie flew to St. Louis for our wedding and now it was our turn to visit them.

We arrived in Phoenix on a Monday evening, and Chris was waiting for us at his aunt's house. He led us to his place, and other than our day trip to the Grand Canyon and the Diamondbacks game on August 21st, we barely left the Harris home. I did drive down to the RV in Avondale a couple of times to check on the lack of progress. I should have been working on this book during our time in Arizona but instead I was lured by Logan's PlayStation 4 and took just three days to beat *Diablo III*.

Our only weekend in Phoenix was jam-packed and Chris and Katie put me to work. Katie's birthday is August 16th. That was a Thursday in 2018, but there was a birthday party planned for Saturday. We did go out to eat with Chris and Katie on Thursday at a restaurant called the Angry Crab Shack. The no-frills restaurant is one of Katie's favorite places. Patti's birthday was August 11th and I had purchased her a spa day at a resort in Scottsdale. While she spent most of the day being pampered, Chris was grilling meat for his carne asada street tacos. The meat had to be shredded. That's where I came in. Any idea how much meat it takes to feed 20-30 people? A lot. I spent a few hours cutting and shredding. When my forearms would get sore, Katie took a break from her setup activities and relieved me. And then we'd switch. And so on. Katie was worried Chris didn't have enough meat, so she had Patti pick up some chicken on the way back to their house. That got grilled as well. Nobody went hungry that night and Chris made some pretty damn good street tacos.

Patti and I stayed up too late, drank too much, and woke up too early for our trip to the Grand Canyon the next day. But at least it was a nice, sunny day and not too hot. Most days the temperature was over 100 degrees (but it's a dry heat). There were also two days of heavy rain, which was unexpected. It didn't rain once while we were in Seattle but twice in a week in the desert.

There is a third Harris child, 8-year-old Grace, and she is a character. We didn't see much of Logan between his job and college classes, and Jonah spent a lot of time in his room on his gaming console, but Grace was always up for chatting. When her parents asked if she wanted to go to a Diamondbacks game with us, a "Yes" was delivered with enthusiasm and without hesitation. Jonah would join us at Chase Field as well.

We had six seats in Section 130 down the third-base line. Again, prime foul-ball territory, but again, I left empty-handed. One ball did land a few rows in front of us.

There was a decent crowd for a Tuesday with the lower bowl nearly full. The upper deck was sparely populated, and the PetSmart Patio in left field was empty. That section is always full on Sunday and Monday home games when dogs are allowed inside Chase Field as part of the team's Dog Days of Summer promotion. The pool behind the outfield wall in right-center was also empty. The pool deck is reserved for groups only, so that wasn't an amenity we were able to enjoy.

Though it was over 100 degrees outside when the game began, it was a cool 70 degrees inside. Chase Field has a state-of-the-art air-conditioning system with the AC units housed in a separate building. The cool air is then pumped into the stadium, which was the first to have a retractable roof and a natural grass field. The roof can open and close in four minutes while the roofs at Miller Park and Safeco Field take about ten minutes. Because of its layout, Chase Field reminded me a lot of Miller Park. But the seating was cramped with narrow rows that made it feel like we were sitting at ancient Fenway Park. For a stadium that was only 20 years old, we expected a bit more leg room.

If someone in the middle seats had to get out, there was no moving your legs to the side, everyone had to stand up. I was seated on the end, and as I stood to let someone out, I noticed a man walking up the stairs wearing an East Carolina shirt.

"Go Pirates," I said. He returned with a, "Yeah."

When he returned from the concourse, he stopped at our row and handed me a Coors Light.

"Always nice to see a fellow Pirate," he said.

"Oh, thanks, man," I replied.

His name is Zach Baker and he played football at East Carolina during the same time I covered the team. I remembered him as a 6-foot-2, 210-pound safety who was invited to Steelers training camp in 2006. His hair was shorter now and I didn't initially recognize him, but we had actually been Facebook friends for years. Seeing another East Carolina graduate in Arizona, and someone I knew, was the last thing I expected.

The Diamondbacks beat the Angels on a walk-off error and the home teams improved to 17-14. Grace posed for a photo with Arizona's mascot, D. Baxter the Bobcat, following the game.

Patti and I had taken our notes and were ready to record the next podcast episode Wednesday night. We spoke of the kids' zone located on the upper concourse. While most stadiums have their kids' zone on the main concourse, the less expensive seats are higher and maybe that's why the Diamondbacks chose the upper concourse for the kids' zone location.

We didn't make it to La Terraza restaurant near Section 300 above right field. Just beneath La Terraza on the Diamond level is The Draft Room, where I did go to retrieve some drinks for me and Patti. The Draft Room had a large selection of local beers. I got a couple of lagers and headed back down to our seats.

Chase Field has a large variety of food and drink options and it's not that expensive, except for the carne asada dog. The 18-inch hot dog topped with fries, queso blanco, carne asada, pico de gallo, and guacamole and served on an elongated telera hot dog bun will set you back $28. I really wanted to get one after I saw someone walk by holding one. Then I saw the price and then decided against it. Patti got a soda in a souvenir cup for $7, though it did not include a refill like we saw elsewhere.

Two interesting exhibits we saw at Chase Field were the wall of autographed baseballs and the 20th Anniversary Experience. The baseball wall includes a key to help visitors locate and identify the signatures of various players and managers on the wall. The 20th Anniversary Experience was an exhibit that paid tribute to the team's short history, including Arizona's 2001 World Series championship with Curt Schilling, Hall of Famer Randy Johnson and slugger Luis Gonzalez.

Chase Field and Comerica Park are the only two MLB stadiums with a keyhole — a 50-foot strip of infield dirt that runs from the pitcher's mound to the batter's circle. It's a throwback feature that gives each stadium a bit of a retro feel. All in all, it was a fairly positive review, despite the tight seating.

Patti is among the many who believe baseball should be played outside, but she was thankful to be inside with air conditioning instead of roasting under the sun with 100-degree temperatures. We will eventually see a game at Chase Field early in the season when the roof is open. The experience at a stadium is much different with the roof open as opposed to when the roof is closed.

Including the permanently roofed Tropicana Field, there are seven MLB stadiums with roofs. The other six have retractable roofs. We were lucky to see games in 2018 at Marlins Park, Rogers Centre, Miller Park and Safeco Field with the roofs open. Because of the August heat on our trips to Phoenix and Houston, the roofs were closed at Chase Field and Minute Maid Park, respectively. We were OK with that.

Before leaving the Phoenix area, we were able to see my stepbrother and his new wife. Leif Abrahamson is the youngest son of my dad's wife, Kristin. Leif had lived in Hawaii, where he met Jacqui and the two were married in June of 2018, just before leaving the South Pacific for the Arizona desert. With his long, blonde hair, lanky frame, and casual attire, Leif very much looked like someone who enjoyed surfing the Hawaiian waves. But he and Jacqui, both teachers, acclimated well to their new sandy surroundings.

Chris and Katie joined us on a Friday evening when we met Leif and Jacqui at a Mexican restaurant in Goodyear. I had never met Jacqui and hadn't seen Leif in a decade and was grateful we were able to connect.

While the RV sat at Camping World in Avondale for more than a week, nothing was repaired. It was a waste of time and effort to take it there. Annoyed, we picked up the RV — got the tow dolly still at Peggy's house — and drove east the morning of August 23rd.

Houston was our next stadium, but we took a few days to get there.

· · · · ·

It's usually a six-hour drive from Phoenix to the New Mexico-Texas border. We used Harvest Hosts and made arrangements to spend the night at a winery outside Anthony, New Mexico.

The drive took nearly eight hours.

After stopping in Eloy, Arizona to fuel up, our progress was halted by a fatal car accident on Interstate 10. A Cadillac had slammed into the back of a semitrailer. We could see the wreck about a quarter of a mile in front of us — and less than a mile from where we had just stopped to get gas. There was a frontage road about 50 feet to our right. Had we known about the accident, we would have taken it instead of getting on the Interstate. Emergency vehicles were still arriving on the scene, a few firetrucks squeezed by as we joined the line of vehicles on the shoulder. A helicopter landed on the freeway and took off about 15 minutes later. This was a bad one. And we could do nothing but wait. A family in a vehicle next to us was on its way to a wedding. They were probably going to be late.

We had hoped to arrive at the winery before 6, but it was 7:30 before we met David Fisher at Sombra Antigua. He and his wife owned the winery and lived in a house right behind it. He understood our delay and was very accommodating. When we finally got the RV set up and let Holmes out, I called our new friend, Lance Williams, to ask if he could meet us for dinner. Lance was the hiker we met by Old Faithful in Yellowstone and then ran into again in Mammoth Springs Village. I told him two days earlier we were going to stop in the area and we had planned to meet. Thankfully our travel delay didn't change anything and he came out to a restaurant on the Texas side of the border to see us. Anthony is a city split between two states — half in New Mexico and half in Texas. We met at El Camaron Pelao, which roughly translated means the Naked Shrimp. School was back in session and we asked Lance, the science teacher, how things were going. He inquired about our trip, particularly the West-coast swing. We had just four stadiums remaining and could see the light at the end of the tunnel.

One our longest days of driving followed, a 600-mile trek across West Texas from El Paso to Austin. Because we were on a baseball trip, we had to take a Texas detour to see the bats in Austin. OK, different kind of bats but still a must-see. Every night, just after sunset in Austin, 1.5 million bats emerge from the Congress Avenue Bridge. It's pretty awesome as the waves of bats blacken the twilight sky over the Colorado River. It's a different Colorado River than the one that winds through the Grand Canyon.

After seeing the bats in Austin, we spent two days exploring San Antonio before making our way south to Houston. We'd see two Astros games at Minute Maid Park and had family with us for both. Patti's cousin, Caressa Hensley, her fiancé, Tim Arredondo, and their infant son, Gabriel, lived in the Houston suburb of Pasadena. Caressa and Tim had left Peoria about a year earlier when Tim got a new job. Gabriel was just four months old but was at his first MLB game as we sat in Section 317 above home plate. Gabriel didn't last long and they left after four innings, but it still counts as his first game. Even though they had baby head phones for Gabriel, things were bit too loud for him. It was also quite warm. Though Minute Maid Park has air conditioning, it did little to cool the upper levels. Heat rises, right? Despite many efforts to get him to stop, Gabriel wouldn't stop crying, so Caressa and Tim decided to take him home. When they left, Patti and I set out on our usual stadium exploration.

The Phillips 66 Home Run Pump behind center field tracks the number of homers hit by the Astros at Minute Maid Park since its opening in 2000. Also in the outfield concourse are several murals celebrating the team's 56-year history and the franchise's great players, like Nolan Ryan, Craig Biggio, and Jose Altuve.

The seventh-inning stretch in Houston is fun. Following the playing of "Take Me Out to the Ballgame," fans sing along to the Lone Star state anthem, "Deep in the Heart of Texas" (Clap, clap, clap, clap). We used that song during one of the podcast episodes we recorded while in Texas.

Baseballs hitting the low-hanging catwalk at Tropicana Field isn't a rare occurrence. The catwalk, which obstructs scoreboard views from those in the upper deck, gets hit often and the Rays even have ground rules in place for when that happens. We were not expecting to see a ball hit the rafters at Minute Maid Park, but that's what happened on August 28th. Oakland outfielder Stephen Piscotty hit a ball down the left-field line so high that it never landed.

Astros left fielder Marwin Gonzalez drifted toward the line while tracking the ball. By the time he reached the wall in foul territory, a halted Gonzalez was still looking toward the roof and shrugged his shoulders. Piscotty's towering eighth-inning blast got caught in the V-joint connecting the stadium's support beams. The smash was ruled a foul ball and Piscotty grounded out to third three pitches later.

The game was tied 3-3 entering the ninth inning, but the A's got an RBI ground-rule double from Nick Martini in the top of the inning and held on for a 4-3 victory. A's reliever, Blake Treinen, retired the side in order, striking out Astros designated hitter, Yuli Gurriel, to end the game.

After visiting the Johnson Space Center in Houston on September 1st, my brother, Ben, and his girlfriend, Bailey, joined us for Dog Day at Minute Maid Park the next day.

It was the first time we were meeting Bailey, who started seeing Ben a year earlier. She was considerably younger than my brother, but we could tell they made each other happy. The four of us went out to grab a late lunch before heading to the stadium. Just as we sat down, my dad called me, knowing that I was with Ben. My brother is notoriously bad at returning phone calls, so this was a way for our dad to get him on the phone. They talked for a good 20 minutes as our food arrived and Ben was able to end the call.

Our seats in the left-field corner provided a good vantage point to see Minute Maid Park's "steam" train. The replica 1860s locomotive engine, with a coal-tender car full of gigantic fake oranges in tow, runs from center to left field along an 800-foot long set of tracks. The black train with red trim moves about 2 miles per hour and takes about a minute to go from end to end. Its run begins just as the final notes of the national anthem are either sung or played. It also goes into motion following Astros home runs and victories. Faux steam emits from the black stack and conductor "Bobby Dynamite" blows the whistle from inside the engine's cab.

Ben and Bailey spent the night in the RV, sleeping on the pullout sofa. They didn't want us to go through the hassle of lowering the mattress above the cab. I didn't put it down the next morning to show them before we left but almost immediately regretted it. The bed would not go back up.

I called the Thor customer service line, but the quickest they could get someone out was 90 minutes. We had to check out in less than an hour. Ben got curious, though, and ducked to open the small cabinets above the dash. In the cubby above the steering wheel is an electrical box. Ben noticed a wire had come loose. He reconnected it, and voila, the mattress returned to its spot against the ceiling. I hung up with customer service and was thankful my brother, and his inquisitive mind, saved the day.

. . . . .

We felt very welcome at Globe Life Park, quite literally. The Texas Rangers were the only Major League Baseball team to recognize Home Run On Wheels on their stadium message board. We were included among the visiting groups and our group consisted of me, Patti, my mom Karen, her husband Marc, and their friends Pete and Lynne.

My sister, Danielle, and her husband, Shivum, were originally supposed to join us, but they couldn't make it, so Pete and Lynne took their spots. We also thought we would be getting some more kids to a game in Arlington, but we got some bad news on August 6th. Though Eckerd told us in March they were committed to getting children to a Rangers game during our time in Arlington, I received an email with some bad news.

Eckerd had what its chief development officer said was a "significant leadership transition in Houston" and no longer had the "bandwidth" to handle our project.

"We are really are focused on excellence in service delivery and mission," the email from Margaret Adams said. "Please accept our apologies and know we are rooting for Home Run on Wheels!"

"Certainly disappointing news, but thanks for letting me know," I replied, upset and wondering now if we could somehow make it work with another organization. Time was against us. Danielle recommended one agency in Fort Worth and I contacted them, but there just wasn't enough time to coordinate with families to get them to a Rangers game on September 4th. We had been looking forward to Arlington all season, believing we would have kids there with us, but we couldn't dwell on our discontent. We were still going with our small group of six people and knew St. Louis was still a possibility to end the trip on a high note.

Because the Rangers stumbled to a 67-95 record to finish last in the AL West, the rather large Globe Life Park felt rather cavernous as we watched the Rangers beat the Angels. A crowd of just 17,625 was in attendance at a ballpark that seats nearly 50,000.

I was able to acquire six tickets at a significant discount thanks to some advice I received in Denver. An Army veteran at Jagged Mountain Craft Brewery, just a couple of blocks from Coors Field, told me about VetTix.org. The site offers free tickets to veterans and discounted tickets through FNGTickets.com. We could have saved some money had I known about this prior to mid-July. I wasn't able to score any free tickets using VetTix but did get our six tickets in Section 37 for a grand total of $73. These were field-level tickets with a face value of $65 apiece. I was grateful to that man in Denver. My mom offered to reimburse us for her two tickets, but I declined and said it was our thanks for allowing us to stay at her house for free. I did accept cash from Pete and Lynne, however.

We arrived at the stadium about 45 minutes before the first pitch. Lynne recently had foot surgery, so we hopped on one of the golf carts that take fans from the convention-center parking lot to the main gate across the street from the Texas Live! complex. These golf carts aren't free, charging up to $10 per person. We talked them down to $20 for the group.

Once inside, it was dinner time. While Karen, Marc, Pete, and Lynne opted for the traditional ballpark fare of hot dogs and nachos, Patti and I were on a mission to find the MVT Dog: the Most Valuable Tamale Dog. This is a culinary monstrosity meant to feed four people. A 24-inch hot dog, wrapped in a tamale "bun" is then topped with chili, nacho cheese, and sliced jalapeño peppers. Patti and I carried the huge hot dog to the nearby tables that are decorated to resemble baseballs with mock bats acting as legs. The tables are in a covered courtyard that provides a view of the action from behind home plate. I tried to get a home plate photo at every stadium. I also wanted to snap a photo of the game's first pitch, so I asked the usher if I could stand with her until Mike Minor offered his first delivery to David Fletcher. She obliged and we chatted about our trip. Standing next to us were two of the Rangers "Six Shooters" squad, Cassidy and Fatima. They overheard details about our trip and that Globe Life Park was the last remaining stadium Patti had yet to visit. She had now been to all 30 MLB stadiums over her lifetime. I asked for some sort of recognition for Patti, maybe as a participant for one of the between-inning games. The two "Six Shooters" instead rewarded her with the "Fan of the Game" swag bag filled with a soft-sided backpack cooler, a couple bobbleheads, a shirt, and some baseball cards. The pièce de résistance was a "House Banister" bobblehead with former Rangers manager Jeff Banister sitting on the Iron Throne.

With photo taken and swag bag received, we headed to our seats to join the rest of our party with our monstrous hot dog and Patti's gifts. Before we got there, however, we stopped at guest services to get our MLB passport stamped. We took the leather-bound book with us to every stadium, except one, to get a stamp on the page of the coinciding ballpark. We actually forgot to take the passport book with us to Yankee Stadium, but a member of guest services stamped a small piece of paper with the date — April 25th — and we affixed it to the designated space with some good old-fashioned Scotch tape.

When we told the three Rangers employees there about our trip, the team's senior director of customer service, Donnie Pordash, asked where we were sitting. When I told him Section 37 thanks to VetTix, he said, "Oh, I was going to upgrade your seats, but I can't do any better than that."

I emailed Donnie the next week to thank him and he replied with an appreciative phone call. It was the only time during the regular season someone from a team took the time to recognize our visit.

We couldn't finish the MVT dog but did put a pretty good dent in it. We offered some to my mom, Marc, Pete and Lynne but had no takers. The usher and primary vendor in our section — both named Doug — razzed us a bit about not being able to polish off the MVT dog. My email to Donnie also included a "special shout out" to the Dougs. While nobody wanted to share our MVT Dog, everyone was impressed with Patti's goodie bag.

The Rangers have a message board to acknowledge birthdays, anniversaries, and visiting groups. Home Run On Wheels was in the latter category, though we almost missed seeing it on the vertical screen in center field. I thought the group recognition was after the fourth inning, and when it wasn't, I hastily searched the team website and believed we'd be on the message board between the seventh and eighth innings. Patti and I decided to explore the ballpark. When we got to the upper deck in the right-field corner, where the Rangers had a construction observation deck for their new stadium right next door, the fifth inning was ending. The public address announcer's voice bellowed through the stadium speakers, directing people to the message board for a list of the night's visiting groups.

"Oh, crap, that's us," I shouted to Patti, and I sprinted to the nearest section. Patti, wearing her high-heeled baseball shoes, followed, though not at such a brisk pace. I set down my beverage, as not to spill, but Patti scooped it up as she passed by. From the passageway, I couldn't quite see the message board flanked by a pair of illuminated Coca-Cola bottles. I moved left, zig-zagging through the largely empty section until I could clearly see the screen. There we were, "Home Run On Wheels" scrolling vertically. I tried to get a photo, but the digital words were to blurry to make out on my phone. But we saw it and our guests that night saw it. The Rangers, and every other MLB team, usually charge for such messaging, but ours was gratis. I had set it up a few weeks ahead of time when I still thought we were going to the game with a group of kids. The Rangers agreed to add our group at no cost because we were on a charity venture. Of all the MLB teams with which we interacted, the Rangers were perhaps the most accommodating. The Tigers, Pirates, and Marlins were pretty good, too.

Globe Life Park was also the only stadium where we made an appearance on the Jumbotron, though we could have made a scoreboard appearance at Nationals Park and not known it. After seeing Home Run On Wheels on the message board, we took the elevator down to main concourse level. We rode with two friendly food service employees, one of whom had worked at the stadium since it opened in 1994. We walked past the closed Rangers Hall of Fame, which was undergoing renovations to transform into an interactive exhibit for the team's new home. We made our way past the Nolan Ryan statue and found ourselves behind the left-field bleachers when a high-tempo country song began to play. The Rangers were doing the "Dance Cam," so we decided to be goofy and bounce around to the beat. A cameraman spotted us, and boom, we were on the big screen dancing like idiots for the entire stadium. My mom said she was laughing too hard to get her phone out to take a picture.

"That's probably a good thing," Patti told her, thankful there was no photographical or video evidence of our dancing. There were witnesses, however.

Lynne told us we were on the screen longer than anyone else during the between-innings dance segment. One random woman even recognized us as we were leaving the stadium following the Rangers' 4-2 victory over the Angels and said, "Hey, you guys are good dancers."

I assume she was being nice because being a good dancer is a compliment I have rarely heard.

Our 28th stadium of the season was in the books, and Patti had officially been to every MLB venue. I had one more to go.

"Are you even going to go to the games in Kansas City and St. Louis with me?" I jokingly asked her before we got to Globe Life Park.

"Haha. I kind of have to," she quipped. "But I am really looking forward to it, especially after being to all these other stadiums in such a short span and then coming into Kauffman and Busch with fresh eyes. It will be fun to compare and contrast."

"You have raved about Kauffman Stadium ever since we were in Milwaukee," I told her.

"I haven't raved about it," Patti replied. "What I said was they have a really good tailgating scene. It's kind of cool."

We did have a good time in Kansas City and watched the Royals dispatch the White Sox with a 6-3 victory in front of a sparse crowd on September 11th. The Royals were honoring military service members that night and retired Navy Petty Officer Generald Wilson sang the national anthem. Wilson is my favorite anthem singer after first seeing him at a St. Louis Rams game in 2009. He is a St. Louis native and does the anthem before many events in his hometown, but he's been flown around the country to perform the anthem from New Jersey to California. He sang the national anthem before the NFC championship game in Philadelphia on January 21st, 2018.

Despite the Royals offering free tickets to military families, only 17,613 people were at the game in a gorgeous stadium that seats nearly 38,000. The White Sox and Royals were two of the worst teams in baseball in 2018, so we weren't surprised by the poor fan turnout on a Tuesday night. We also knew the atmosphere would be much different on the other side of the Show-Me State. We were almost done and that fact was beginning to set it.

"It was like, 'Wow, are we really at this stage of the trip?' It's been a whirlwind," Patti recalled. "It's been long. It's been fun."

CHAPTER 14:

ST. LOUIS FINALE

Baseball is embedded into the soul of St. Louis. The Cardinals have been a fixture in the Gateway City since 1892 and their 11 World Series championships have created a diehard fan base that loves Cardinals baseball more than toasted ravioli.

"I don't ever remember a time not being a baseball person," Ryan Fagan, a St. Louis native and the national baseball writer for Sporting News, told me prior to our trip. "Looking back through pictures my folks still have, I always had a little baseball glove or baseball cap or tiny bat in my hand from the time the first pictures were taken. There was no other thing. There was always just baseball. My childhood was my parents and baseball. That's how it worked. My earliest baseball memory, honestly, wasn't at the ballpark. It was listening to the radio with Jack Buck and Mike Shannon calling Cardinals games on KMOX. In my neighborhood, there wasn't a thru-street, it was a loop. My friends and I would literally ride our bikes around the loop and hear the game the whole way around because people had it on sitting outside on their porch.

When you grow up in St. Louis, baseball is ingrained in you. It's in your DNA. Part of the fun of being at the ballpark is, and I still love this, walking out of the tunnel at any ballpark. The first time you can see the field, there's always this little magical moment that takes you back to childhood."

Of all the stadiums we saw in 2018, Busch Stadium was the one we knew the best. We both lived in St. Louis for several years. Patti's 17 years in St. Louis is the reason she became a Cardinals fan after being apathetic toward baseball for most of her childhood near Peoria, Illinois. I had lived in the Gateway City for nearly eight years. We met in St. Louis in 2012 and got married in St. Louis in 2017. Patti used to have a ten-game season ticket package and we have sat in just about every spot at Busch Stadium, from the 400 level to the suites to the bleachers.

"This place has my heart," Patti wrote in our stadium review. "It is where I fell in love with baseball. The atmosphere is part of the reason why."

There are a lot of extras in and around Busch Stadium. Ballpark Village, across from left-center field on Clark Street, houses several restaurants and bars. The AT&T Rooftop, an all-inclusive area, offers views inside Busch Stadium similar to the Wrigley rooftops. Those sitting in the AT&T Rooftop and the adjacent bleacher seats count toward the Busch Stadium admission.

Ballpark Village also includes the Cardinals Hall of Fame with several of the game's all-time great players fêted. You'll see Cardinals greats, like Mark McGwire, Ted Simmons, Willie McGee, Vince Coleman, and Chris Carpenter, as well as Baseball Hall of Famers Lou Brock, Tony LaRussa, Red Schoendienst, Bob Gibson, Rogers Hornsby, Ozzie Smith, Whitey Herzog and Musial.

The downtown view, complete with the Gateway Arch, is rivaled by few other stadiums. The Budweiser Terrace, which was new in 2018, and Bowtie Bar in the "Left Field Porch" are great places for casual fans to hang out. There are cabanas on the terrace, and the Bowtie is the one place that does not stop serving alcohol after the seventh-inning stretch. If a game goes 12 innings, you can still get a beer at the Bowtie Bar in the 12th inning.

Then there are also giant Bobbleheads scattered throughout the stadium, the most popular being the one of future Hall of Famer Yadier Molina. The catcher's likeness is located near the Bowtie Bar.

Most teams say they have the best fans in their respective sports. But for the Cardinals, their fan base is literally branded BFIB, Best Fans In Baseball. Those fans help create a fun environment to see a game with an excellent view of downtown St. Louis and the famous Gateway Arch. Busch Stadium is extremely easy to get to and St. Louis has various bars and restaurants that offer complimentary shuttle rides to the stadium. St. Louis and Milwaukee were the only two cities we noticed that offer this service. The Metrolink light rail will also drop you right off at the third-base gate, known as the Stan Musial Gate because of the large Stan statue there. "Let's meet at the Stan statue," is a phrased uttered often between April and October. Busch Stadium always ranks among the highest in attendance and 2018 was no different with over 3 million fans visiting the stadium.

Derrick Goold, the Cardinals beat reporter for the St. Louis Post-Dispatch, is a Colorado native but has realized how special baseball is to the city of St. Louis fans.

"The city is very much intertwined with baseball," Derrick told me. "When you think back to the lifetime of our grandparents, the Cardinals were the furthest west and furthest south Major League Baseball team. They were for a long time, but they also won titles. In a lot of ways, they were the Yankees of the National League because they have the 11 championships. That gave them both the historic prominence and a geographic prominence as baseball's outpost, essentially. Then they had a megaphone in KMOX to broadcast Cardinals games to the lower 48 states. You could get KMOX anywhere. That spread the word of Cardinals baseball, spread the word of greats, like Stan Musial, Bob Gibson, and Lou Brock and all the Hall of Famers. A few things stand out to me about St. Louis and its fondness and passion for baseball and how it's in the roots and water system of the city," Derrick continued. "No generation for the past 100-plus years without a championship. Since 1910 or so, the Cardinals have also not had a team without a Hall of Famer on it. Albert Pujols left in 2011, so maybe now Yadier Molina is the one who carries that forward. The other thing is you look around the globe and I have a friend who likes to count the hats in group scenes from around the world. If you have a gathering for New Year's at the Eiffel Tower or you see the running of the bulls in Spain, you look at the hats of sports teams and you'll see Yankees hats and Red Sox hats, and you'll see Real Madrid hats or FC Barcelona hats and probably Chelsea hats, maybe some Arsenal hats or Manchester City, but one of the baseball teams that pops up quite a bit is the Cardinals. In a way, that makes the Cardinals a global liaison for what St. Louis represents. If you think about the three things St. Louis is known for, there's the Arch, Anheuser-Busch, and the

Cardinals. I'm not sure how many other towns you'd have baseball in their top three. It's become interwoven into the identity of the city."

Because Busch Stadium was our final ballpark, we wanted to end with a bang and do something special. My efforts began in May.

While in St. Louis for the wedding of our friends, Greg and Emily, I reached out to a few foster care organizations in St. Louis. I heard back from Kim Johnson with the Foster & Adoptive Care Coalition. We spoke and she told me they already had an existing relationship with the Cardinals, so getting kids out to a game in September should be no problem.

Nothing's ever easy. The Cardinals told her that a September request had to be for games played Monday through Thursday. Weekend games would be at a premium because they were against popular opponents as the postseason loomed. Kim was insistent on a weekend game because kids would have returned to school. Her email to the Cardinals brought tears to my eyes.

"I want to make you aware kids in foster care have lots of struggles that go way beyond having a place to call home. They rely heavily on routine and having time to 'digest' stimulating experiences, like coming to a Cardinal Game. Saturdays would provide time for their families to help regulate the kids and prepare them for a successful week at school. By attending a game during the week in the evening, it could cause a them to derail and it may take days or even weeks to recover. Our preferences would be the Saturday games or the Sunday games, if weeknights are our only option, a Thursday would have the least amount of disturbance for their regular schedules. We are extremely grateful for this experience but always need to keep our kids well-being at the top forefront. I hope you understand and can work with us to help bring a once-in-a-lifetime experience for our kids and to raise awareness of kids in foster care."

Over the next few months, neither side budged. I jumped in with some emails to Cardinals public relations and community affairs and had a phone call with Keith Brooks of Cardinals Care — the team's charity. It was frustrating, and we weren't sure if we were going to be able to get some kids to Busch Stadium.

Then we had a breakthrough.

"We got some tickets. Call me," the text message from Kim said.

Wells Fargo donated 20 tickets to the United Way, which then turned those tickets over to the Foster & Adoptive Care Coalition. It was a happy coincidence that Patti works for Well Fargo. The tickets were for the September 14th game against the Dodgers. It was a Friday night, but we were there in Section 363 with some foster families. Patti and I also started a GoFundMe page to take donations from folks willing to help. We raised over $700 and used the funds to buy 30 tickets that we donated to the Foster & Adoptive Care Coalition. Those tickets were for a Sunday afternoon game on September 23rd and the seats were in the left-field bleachers. I wanted some kids to have a chance to get a home-run ball. There were none hit to left field that day, but the Cardinals did hand the Giants a 9-2 defeat. I had also arranged for some caps and other Cardinals paraphernalia to be given to the foster families attending. Those gifts from the Cardinals were in addition to Sunday's winter cap giveaway.

"That's awesome. Any time our kids can have a treat like that is incredible, so we really appreciate it," Katie Corrigan, the director of family development for the Foster & Adoptive Care Coalition, told me when I informed her of our fundraising result.

Katie and Kim met us at their office in Brentwood, just southwest of downtown St. Louis on July 20th. Kim didn't want to be interviewed, though she spearheaded ticket efforts on behalf of the organization. Katie volunteered to be on the podcast and explained what going to a Cardinals game means for foster kids in such a baseball-rich community.

"The stresses these kids are facing are out of this world," she began. "They have the weight of the world on their shoulders. They have a lot of worries. To be like any other typical, normal child at the ballpark and not having that stress and able to be a child is life-changing for them. It's a memory they'll remember forever. A baseball game is something all St. Louis kids can relate to, and to have a positive shared experience is really incredible."

There were 13,000 Missouri children in foster care in 2018, and 1,100 of them were awaiting adoption. The Foster & Adoptive Care Coalition licensed 47 St. Louis-area families in 2018. Missouri has a nine-week training program to help prospective parents learn how to deal with children who might be coming from traumatic backgrounds.

"Any concerns the parents might have with the child's behavior, we know there is always meaning behind that behavior," Katie said. "It's not a child acting out; it's a child not knowing how to ask for help. We work with them to find out what are the best interventions and what we can do proactively instead of reactively."

"Trust has probably been broken along the way and some of these kids don't know how to trust," Patti added.

"A foster parent is a stranger to them, so it is starting at zero and building that trust," Katie continued. "It's also modeling for the parents and there are opportunities for the foster parents to mentor the biological parents. When the kids see that happening, there is going to be trust with the foster parents because they see the foster parent isn't judging or blaming their parents. You're all on one team, working together. Reunification is the goal and that is what's best for the kids. To be with their family."

Katie is a St. Louis native and lifelong Cardinals fan. She shared a story of one of the first baseball games she attended. Willie McGee, who played for the Cardinals from 1982 to 1990 and was the 1985 National League MVP, hit a home run to the upper deck at the old Busch Stadium. A 6-year-old Katie leaped toward a guard rail to catch the ball. Her dad reached out to prevent his daughter from falling onto the field. The ball hit him right in the mouth and was lodged in his teeth.

"In comes security and all kinds of Cardinals helpers, and this woman turned around and grabbed the baseball right out of my dad's mouth," Katie recalled. "We didn't even get the ball. Not such a good ending there, but luckily, he was all right and we made the big screen, so that was fun."

"Did he lose any teeth?" I asked.

"He didn't, believe it or not," Katie answered. "Just a little blood. He shouldn't have worried so much about me and we would have gotten that ball."

When we finally stopped laughing, I told Katie we had yet to get a baseball. There were no foul balls or home runs that found us at Busch Stadium either. But we did get one baseball. An usher between sections 361 and 363 learned of our travels and he called me down from my seat. The usher's name is Jim and he handed me a baseball signed by Cardinals second baseman Kolten Wong.

"Kolten hit this during batting practice today," Jim told me during the September 16th game. "I always try to get a batting practice ball and give it to a fan. What you've done this year is amazing and I wanted you to have this."

I was speechless but was able to stammer a thank you. Jim has been an usher at Busch Stadium for 30 years. He was probably 70 years old, white hair under a red Cardinals cap. His 6-foot frame shortened as he aged. I chatted with Jim between innings and thanked him again before returning to my seat.

While we were going to a few more games and had kids going to a game on September 23rd, the game a week earlier was our "grand finale." It was "Sunday Night Baseball" and we had a group of 25 people joining us. These weren't foster kids but friends and family who wanted to help celebrate the end of our journey.

Mike and Ginny Kempf, whom we saw during Spring Training, were there. Patti's sisters, Joy and Veronica, came down from Peoria, as did cousin Helen and her boyfriend, Rob. Our friends, Pete and Maria Shuleski, came out, as did Charlie Barrale. We had the RV outside Busch Stadium and told people to meet us there to get their tickets. The RV filled up quickly. Our friends Warren Vincent and Wendy Lamar pressed into the bedroom, Veronica and Joy sat with Patti and Charlie at the dinette. Our great friend, Angela Lehmann, on the sofa with Nancy Jackson and Ginny as Mike stood in front of them. I was up front, where our guest of honor was settled in the passenger seat.

Children's Hope Alliance CEO, Celeste Dominguez, flew up from Charlotte to be with us. We weren't sure if she was going to make it out because Hurricane Florence had canceled several flights, but she was determined to be in St. Louis.

"I wanted to be here for this," Celeste told us during our podcast interview in St. Louis. "We started off together. We needed to end this together."

I wasn't able to get any media coverage in St. Louis, but I was interviewed before the September 16th game at Ballpark Village. Todd Thomas, who is known as "That One Guy" during Cardinals games, agreed to talk with me as part of his pregame duties. Todd is a member of the Cardinals promotional team and runs the between-innings games. He also serves as a hype man at Ballpark Village before every home game. His fan interviews are shown on the giant screen at Ballpark Village and on the Jumbotron inside Busch Stadium.

I was wearing my Home Run On Wheels T-shirt and Todd casually walked over to me, pretending I was a stranger even though we've known each other for years.

Charlie, who is close friends with Todd, walked over with us. When the interview was over, we finished the beverages Todd got for us and returned to the RV. Patti went straight back. Charlie and I stopped to enter the stadium. It was Mark McGwire bobblehead night and we wanted to grab the freebie and take it back to the RV so we didn't have to carry it around during the game.

When the bobbleheads were securely inside the RV, the group went in. Pete and Maria were already inside, as were friends Matt and Lori Headley. We were in Section 361, on the edge of the upper deck along the third-base line. The left-field pavilion, as it's called, abuts the upper concourse near the Perficient Perch.

The Perch is a concessions area that presents a wonderful view of the St. Louis skyline. The Gateway Arch is the prominent feature. Patti, Celeste and I posed for a photo with the Arch in the background. We'd use this for the podcast episode. Being so close to the Perch was convenient when we wanted to get food or drinks. After getting the photo with Celeste, Patti and I went to retrieve the hot dog and soda that were included with our tickets.

As we waited in line, we told a couple of our trip and mission and that we were now finally done with Busch Stadium, our 30th park. The concessionaire, a grey-haired black woman about 60 years old, heard us. Turns out she was a foster parent for 30 years and wound up adopting four children. She added an additional hot dog to our order and told us to have a "blessed day."

314

We met people from all walks of life who had some connection to foster care — whether they were foster parents like this woman or my aunt and uncle, grew up in the foster system, like a waitress named Torri we had in Dallas, or had a relative who fostered. Torri told us she had treats, like the occasional manicure, but was never able to attend a professional sporting event.

"These are kids that don't get to do this," Celeste said. "They've never seen a field. We talked about that when we first began. They've never been to a game. They cannot envision what a stadium looks like. For those foster parents to have this resource and be able do that with the children, that itself is really cool. I'm betting we're going to find a number of years from now that somebody became a foster parent or became an adoptive parent because they learned about it through this venture."

"I certainly hope so," Patti replied. "Hopefully we planted that seed and made that seed grow."

·　·　·　·　·

We took Holmes to the vet on September 20th. Patti's suspicion of cancer was confirmed and he'd undergo his first treatment four days later. The chemotherapy was expensive. The first treatment set us back $900 with subsequent visits costing anywhere between $170 and $600. Even though we stayed with Veronica rent-free while the RV was being serviced, we weren't exactly able to save any money.

Patti and I had tickets to see the Brewers and Cardinals play at Busch Stadium on September 24th and 25th. Because he had his first treatment on September 24th, Patti stayed with him. We were staying with the Shuleskis for a few days, and Pete took Patti's spot for the Monday night game.

I sat next to a father and son from Wisconsin. The son was a freshman at Saint Louis University and Dad came down to check on him while taking advantage of the Brewers being in town. I told them about our trip and why Patti wasn't there with me. A couple in front of us had just gone through a similar situation with their dog and empathized. The woman then asked about our trip, which I explained, and handed cards to her and the father-son duo.

"With all of this, with these distractions, you did go to the game and I know that you were still able to spread the word about our mission with Children's Hope Alliance and all the organizations across the country," Patti said. "We didn't forget about the needs of kids in the foster system and getting them the help they need. I know you were still telling people about that message, even at the end."

Ryan Braun's solo homer to left helped propel the Brewers to a 6-4 win. Pete and I were seated in Section 157 with a direct view of third base. I wanted to get a picture of Braun rounding third, but my phone's camera had a delay. It worked out for the better. Instead of getting Braun's foot on the bag, I caught him in mid-air, high-fiving third-base coach, Ed Sedar.

Holmes showed immediate improvement, so Patti joined me the next night while Maria kept an eye on Holmes. We were sitting three rows from the field in the right-field corner. The Cardinals were out of the playoff hunt, so tickets were pretty cheap on third-party sites. I paid $27 a pop for these seats on VividSeats.

The Brewers jumped out to a 2-0 lead on homers from Jesus Aguilar and Braun, who again launched a shot to left field and high-fived Sedar at third base. I looked around to find other Brewers fans near me. There were a few. The Brewers had a four-run fourth, making the Cardinals faithful uneasy. Midway through Milwaukee's 12-4 trouncing of the Redbirds, Patti got a text from Maria.

"Holmes report. All is well," the text from Maria said. "He slept soundly on the couch all evening. I just got him up to go pee, which he did for a long time. Then he came right back in and drank a bunch of water. He is resting again."

"Thank you," Patti replied before relaying the information on to me.

Having the energy to jump up on the couch was a big deal. Over the previous three weeks, he didn't have much strength in his back legs. This was a good sign.

Christian Yelich, who tripled in the fourth, homered in the ninth inning. I joined the chorus of "MVP" chants from the smattering of Brewers fans in attendance. Yelich finished the season with a .326 batting average to lead the National League, and his 36 home runs and 110 RBI were second in the NL. Yelich, who was indeed named the 2018 NL MVP, scored both runs the next day in a 2-1 Brewers win as they completed a three-game sweep and clinched a postseason berth. They would later clinch the NL Central at Wrigley Field in a one-game playoff against the Cubs.

· · · · ·

When we first moved to Charlotte in December of 2014, people would often ask us how we liked the Queen City. Our reply was always the same, "We like Charlotte. We loved St. Louis." And still do.

The Gateway City is a great place to live. It is easy to navigate with three Interstate highways and two beltways. There is also plenty to do without having to spend a dime. The city, or its suburbs, almost always has some sort of free festival to attend. When we were there, the Webster Groves Jazz Festival was going on and we enjoyed some free music while hanging out with our friends Angela, Bill, Henry and Wendy.

Because of a trust that was set up when St. Louis hosted the 1904 World's Fair and Olympic Games, nearly everything inside Forest Park is free. Forest Park is a giant green space, larger than Central Park in New York City. The park is home to the world-class St. Louis Zoo, the St. Louis Art Museum, the Missouri History Museum, and a large greenhouse called the Jewel Box, which is popular for weddings and photographers. Unless you are reserving the Jewel Box for a wedding, it is free to visit. The zoo and museums also do not have admission fees. Parking at the zoo has a minimal price, but ample street parking can be found in the park.

Thee Great Forest Park Balloon Race and pre-night "glow" were also held while we were in town. This balloon glow is also another park event that costs nothing to attend.

Then there is the Gateway Arch, officially known as the Jefferson National Expansion Memorial. It is the iconic symbol of St. Louis. The Arch has a free museum at its base and taking the elevator to the top costs just $13.

City Museum, located in downtown St. Louis, is not free but is a blast. It is essentially an indoor amusement park and fun for kids and adults.

St. Louis may get a bad rap because of crime that can be found at any major city, but it is one of the best places we have ever lived and consider it our second home.

CHAPTER 15:

RANKING THE STADIUMS

After seeing every MLB stadium in one season, you would expect that we'd rate them. That we did. We published complete stadium reviews at Home-RunOnWheels.com while on the trip. We also posted our final stadium rankings on our home page.

Outside of one or two stadiums, we really enjoyed our experiences at every MLB ballpark. It's easy to do when you spent over six months on the road to see baseball games. We saw a total of 40 regular-season games with the home teams going 22-18. That was a pretty good turnaround, considering the home teams were 0-5 through our first five games and were 2-8 by the time we left Canada. Only the Phillies (over the Pirates) and Yankees (over the Twins) had won while at home over the first third of our journey. Even the Red Sox lost to the Rays while we were at Fenway. We saw the Red Sox beat the Rays in St. Petersburg on Easter Sunday. The Red Sox won again in Toronto on Mother's Day, but that was the last time we saw the eventual World Series champions in person.

After traveling to all 30 MLB stadiums in a single season, here are our final stadium rankings:

1. **PNC Park in Pittsburgh**

   PNC Park lives up to the hype. Before we arrived in Pittsburgh, we had been told by several people that PNC Park was one of the best stadiums in baseball — if not the best. We obviously agreed. We're thankful to Joann for showing us the ins and outs of the stadium (refer back to the Spring Training chapter). The views from the stadium are phenomenal with the city's downtown and the Roberto Clemente Bridge as the backdrop beyond the outfield wall. The Clemente Bridge spans the Allegheny River and the waterfront near the stadium has a well-manicured park that is perfect as a spot to hang out before or after the game. PNC Park, built in 2001, is an intimate venue that offers all the perks of a modern stadium while maintaining a class ballpark feel.

2. **Petco Park in San Diego**

   Petco Park instantly became one of our favorite stadiums. It is one of the easiest stadiums to get to with a wonderful public transportation system, including a trolley that takes you right to the gates. We went to a pair of games at Petco Park, sitting in a different area each time. We sat in Section 205, just above the home dugout, on August 10th and then had outfield seats in Section 129 the next day. The Park at the Park, an open lawn on a small hill behind center field, and the old Western Metal Supply Co. building are two of the main features of Petco Park. The Park at the Park is an ideal spot for casual fans who might want to picnic with their friends or family and check in on the game. It also contains a giant statue of "Mr. Padre," Tony Gwynn, and has a small Wiffle ball field for kids. The Western Metal Supply Co. building was an original structure of downtown San Diego that the Padres incorporated into the stadium when it was built in 2004. The structure now houses the main team store, as well as the Breitbard San Diego Sports Hall of Fame and the Padres Hall of Fame (see Chapter 7). Go to the top of the building for several bars and restaurants. Each provides either rooftop and balcony views of the field.

3. Fenway Park in Boston

Like PNC Park, Fenway lived up to expectations. While baseball's oldest stadium, Fenway offers modern amenities like charging stations and outlets at every turn. Boston's T train system is the best way to get to Fenway because traffic is horrendous. Fenway has one of the best atmospheres in all of baseball, inside or outside of the stadium. Thanks to some eateries and bars embedded into the exterior of the iconic Green Monster, you can even enjoy being "inside" Fenway Park without actually being inside Fenway Park. Though the seats are tight and some sections have obstructed views, it's an awesome spot to see a game. There is definitely a nostalgic effect at Fenway, and the Red Sox add to that by incorporating the team's storied history into the stadium. A stroll through Fenway also allows the visitor to take a step back in time to admire the franchise's historical roots. Add in the fact that Boston fans are among the most passionate in the country, and it equals a glorious day at the park.

4. Oriole Park at Camden Yards in Baltimore

Oriole Park at Camden Yards is one of the fabled parks we both looked forward to visiting. When speaking to various people about our trip during Spring Training, many said this was one of their favorite parks, if not the favorite. The Orioles took an old train station and transformed the area in 1992 into a baseball stadium that became the model for nearly every new MLB stadium that has followed. We saw several aspects of Camden Yards at other stadiums, most notably Progressive Field and SunTrust Park. Do yourself a favor and walk around Camden Yards on your first visit there. It was our first time there and we left our seats on the lower level and headed to the upper decks to get another perspective. On our way down the center-field steps, we got a great bird's-eye view of the team's statue garden. We made our way down and snapped some photos of the figures of former manager Earl Weaver, and Orioles greats Cal Ripken, Jr., Eddie Murray, Frank Robinson, Brooks Robinson and Jim Palmer. As mentioned above, the Orioles converted the former Camden train station into their team offices. The elongated building, one of the longest in the world, is also home to the team store and Dempsey's Brew Pub & Restaurant. Just a few blocks away is also the Babe Ruth Birthplace Museum. There is a lot of baseball to see in Baltimore and not all of it is on the field at Oriole Park.

321

5. Busch Stadium in St. Louis

As mentioned in the St. Louis chapter, the Busch Stadium view of the Gateway Arch and Mississippi River is among the best in among the best views in all of baseball. It's an easily accessible downtown stadium with wonderful fans and a perennially competitive team. The Cardinals are one of baseball's flagship franchises with a history rich with iconic players. Cardinals fans are quick to remind you about the team's 11 World Series championships.

6. Coors Field in Denver

Coors Field has the best view in all of baseball. We were fortunate enough to watch sunset over the Rocky Mountains from the Mile High Purple Row. As I said in the Rocky Mountain High chapter, there are several things to love about Coors Field, beginning with the view of downtown Denver behind home plate and the mountain views. The batter's eye area behind the center-field wall might be the most beautiful in all of baseball. It is perfectly Colorado with several evergreen trees, fountains, a small waterfall cascading over the many rocks situated in the section that bleeds into the bullpens.

7. Comerica Park in Detroit

Even before we entered Comerica Park, we were impressed. The stadium has some of the most decorative gates in Major League Baseball. The main gate is flanked by two giant bats and four prowling tigers. In front of the gate is another giant tiger statue, which is a popular photo spot for visitors. Driving into Detroit is simple and there are plenty of parking garages near Comerica Park's downtown location. Comerica Park also has an ornate Tigers carousel and that baseball Ferris wheel. As mentioned earlier in the book, Comerica Park also does a fabulous job of commemorating the franchise's storied history.

8. SunTrust Park in Atlanta

SunTrust Park is a very affordable venue and even has "bottomless" options at the concessions. A must-see area of SunTrust Park is Monument Garden, which pays tribute to the team's numerous Hall of Famers. One in particular stands out with a giant statue of Hank Aaron and a video that shows his 715th career home run to pass Babe Ruth in 1974. "Hammerin' Hank" retired as baseball's home run king with 755 homers and that number is commemorated behind his statue. Flanking the number 755 are the team's retired numbers — including Aaron's 44. The Monument Garden area also has images of the team's other iconic players and a row of bats and gloves to symbolize each Hall of Fame player who has donned a Braves uniform. The championship banner from 1995 — the team's only title since it moved to Atlanta from Milwaukee in 1966 — is also proudly displayed. What the Braves did was create a modern stadium that still reveres the franchise's nearly 150-year history.

9. Kauffman Stadium in Kansas City

Seeing Kauffman Stadium in 2015 when the Royals won the World Series would have been great. Unfortunately we saw the basement dwellers in the American League Central play host to the almost equally bad Chicago White Sox. Despite the terrible teams squaring off, there was a decent crowd at Kauffman Stadium for a Tuesday. It was September 11th, and the Royals invited several military families to the game in honor of their service on the anniversary of one of the country's worst tragedies. The fans were engaged, kids were enjoying the various amenities offered, and it helped that the Royals handed the White Sox a 6-3 defeat. Kauffman Stadium has one of the coolest outfield backdrops you'll see anywhere. The spectacular fountains shoot water spouts between every inning and during pitching changes. The fountains are a nod to Kansas City's reputation as America's "City of Fountains." They also spring into action for pregame festivities and following home runs and Royals victories. Behind the giant crowned scoreboard is an awesome kids' zone filled with a small baseball field, batting cage, pitching area to test the children's arm strength, and a "Royal" carousel.

10. Target Field in Minneapolis

Target Field is one of the easier stadiums to navigate and it helps that the light rail takes you right there. As I said in the Twin Cities chapter, we were there on gorgeous July days to see a pair of games inside a wonderful stadium. We saw the Twins win twice, which helped create a brilliant atmosphere in which to experience baseball games as the energetic fans were loud from start to finish.

11. AT&T Park in San Francisco

The geography that makes San Francisco appealing also makes getting there challenging. Whether you drive or take a ferry, plan at least an hour to get to AT&T Park. On a clear day, AT&T Park offers a gorgeous view of the San Francisco Bay and surrounding area. Unfortunately for us, the ever-present summer fog hindered our view on the July 27th game. AT&T Park is still a beautiful venue with passionate fans and plenty of amenities to keep kids of all ages entertained. Our biggest beef with AT&T Park is its cost. This is the most expensive stadium in all of baseball. Everything costs more — tickets, parking and concessions. The stadium is kid-friendly but not family friendly. One other tip is to dress warm if you go in July.

12. Progressive Field in Cleveland

Cleveland does indeed rock. We really enjoyed Progressive Field, despite a lack of any exceptional food options. As mentioned earlier, the statues are a nice touch and the bullpen viewing area is very cool. Getting into downtown Cleveland was a breeze — even driving into town at 6 on a Tuesday. We noticed plenty of street parking and lots as we got closer to the stadium. We kind of did it the hard way — parking blocks away to park for free. Concession prices are reasonable and we definitely feel like we got our money's worth at Progressive Field.

13. Citizens Bank Park in Philadelphia

From the outfield Harry the K's restaurant, which does not require special admission to enter, to the plethora of eateries and passionate fans, Citizens Bank Park is fantastic. Philadelphia fans have a longstanding reputation of being enthusiastic and we did not experience anything different. They were engaged, yet respectful, unlike the reputation Philadelphia fans have acquired over the years. Outside of the chilly temperature for an April 20th game, we thoroughly enjoyed our visit to Citizens Bank Park and the City of Brotherly Love. Citizens Bank Park offers an excellent variety of food, including several of the local favorites. The Yard kids' zone is also another perk of Citizens Bank Park and has its own concession stand with ice cream and cotton candy.

14. Miller Park in Milwaukee

Miller Park is one of most uniquely designed stadiums in baseball. The radial geometry retractable roof, considered a technological wonder when the stadium was built in 2001, opens like a fan to expose the diamond and was the first of its kind anywhere. Miller Park can be a blast, as mentioned in the Milwaukee chapter, but the stadium does have a different feel to it when the roof is closed. It creates a cavernous environment that is really not conducive for a great fan experience.

15. Great American Ball Park in Cincinnati

As stated earlier in the book, the Reds do a great job of paying homage to the team's history. Unfortunately for Reds fans in 2018, their team just wasn't very good and that created a stale environment. The Reds lost each game we saw in Cincinnati, but it is a great place to see a Major League Baseball game without spending a lot of money. The Kroger Fan Zone is also one of the excellent amenities GABP has to offer.

16. Dodger Stadium in Los Angeles

Dodger Stadium sits high on a hill and the parking lot affords excellent views of downtown Los Angeles, especially when the skyline is all lit up at night. There is essentially one way in and one way out. It stinks. As for the stadium itself, while antiquated, Dodger Stadium is fun but expensive. Despite the age and some inconveniences, it's still a great place to see a baseball game. Most seats have a good view of the field and there are some places in the outfield from which you can see the game as well.

17. Guaranteed Rate Field in Chicago

Guaranteed Rate Field may have a terrible logo to be placed on a baseball stadium with a red downward arrow, but the stadium itself isn't bad. It's not one of MLB's great stadiums, but the home of the Chicago White Sox has excellent food, wonderful tributes to the franchise's history, and some interesting attributes we enjoyed. One of those unique extras is an operational shower from the Old Comiskey Park that has found a new home in the left-center field concourse. Some fans took advantage of that shower to cool off on Father's Day with the temperature above 90. While Guaranteed Rate Field has an outstanding tailgating scene, the stadium is sort of a sterile environment to watch a game. It didn't help that the 2018 club wasn't very good.

18. Minute Maid Park in Houston

Minute Maid Park did not have the electric atmosphere I expected it to have. The September series against the A's was huge, but fans appeared to just be going through the motions in what wound up a 4-3 A's win. That's not to say the fans aren't into the game. They are, but there wasn't the consistent fan interaction I had anticipated. The same could be said for Houston's 4-2 win over the Angels on Dog Day. The tight concourses are made even tighter because of escalators in the middle of the concourse walkway, which is a terribly flawed design. Minute Maid Park probably has a different atmosphere with the roof open, though we were glad it was closed with 100-degree temperatures outside.

19. Angel Stadium in Anaheim

Angel Stadium is a breeze to get to. We stayed at an RV park within walking distance of the Big A, but the stadium is located right next to Anaheim's train station, the ARTIC. Angel Stadium is also affordable, especially when compared to Dodger Stadium or AT&T Park. While Angel Stadium may not be the provide the best atmosphere to see a game, the rock waterfall, known as the California Spectacular, should be a must-see on anyone's baseball bucket list. Flowing water cascades over boulders stacked to form a capital A to the left of the batter's eye. When the Angels hit a home run – as Andrelton Simmons and Eric Young Jr. did on August 6th, 2018 – or the home team wins, flames shoot on either side of the A to fill the center void with light. Ivy climbs either side of the mini-mountain and flag poles sprout from a faux grassy knoll to the left of the formation, which was unveiled in 1998.

20. Safeco Field in Seattle

Because we did a 5K at Safeco Field, we probably saw more of it than any other stadium, albeit briefly. It's a tough stadium to get to because Seattle is a difficult city to navigate. It is in a neat location near the water, but home plate faces away from the Sound. As you gaze beyond the outfield wall, you see CenturyLink Field, where the Seahawks play, and downtown Seattle, not the

Puget Sound. Safeco Field is nice. That's how I would sum it up: nice. There is nothing particularly exceptional about the stadium, but it is a good place to see a game. We were lucky that the roof was open on a clear, sunny day.

21. Rogers Centre in Toronto

We were fortunate enough to see Rogers Centre with the roof open on Mother's Day. It was a packed house against the Red Sox, which meant we got to see the passion of Blue Jays fans in person. As Canada's only MLB team, the Blue Jays have wonderful support. But there just seemed to be something lacking at Rogers Centre to get a higher mark. The artificial turf doesn't help when every other retractable roof stadium has grass. There is not much "extra" within the stadium itself, unless you count the hotel.

22. Wrigley Field in Chicago

Wrigley Field is one of the most iconic stadiums in all of Major League Baseball and every fan should see it at least once. That doesn't mean it's a great stadium. The area around Wrigley Field, Wrigleyville, is amazing and is one of the best sports areas anywhere in the country. But the stadium itself kind of sucks. Cubs owner, Tom Ricketts, has placed more of an effort to build up the area around Wrigley than he has on fan amenities inside the stadium. Going to a game at Wrigley is a blast, but you go for the mystique, not for the amenities.

23. Yankee Stadium in New York City (Bronx)

We wish we had been to the old Yankee Stadium before visiting the current venue so we had a comparison baseline. That said, Yankee Stadium does a nice job of combining the old with the new and using aspects of the former stadium in the current building. As soon as you walk into the stadium through Gate 6, you are greeted with giant banners of the Yankees Hall of Famers. It adds to the mystique of Yankee Stadium feeling like an old stadium instead of one that opened in 2009. To get there, take the subway. You do not want to drive to Yankee Stadium. It is an arduous process to simply get to the stadium by car and then the parking is a nightmare in the residential Bronx neighborhood. From tickets to parking to the concessions prices, everything about Yankee Stadium is expensive. Yankee Stadium does a really good job of blending the old with the new and that is best epitomized with Monument Park. Unfortunately, you can only gain entrance to the plaque-laden museum before the game. Once the first pitch is thrown, that area is shut down except to those with a special section ticket.

24. Globe Life Park in Arlington

While it's understandable why the Rangers are getting a new stadium — an open-air venue in the mid-summer Texas heat can be unbearable — it is kind of a shame Globe Life Park will be shuttered. It is actually a pretty nice stadium, and when we were there on September 4th, it was a cool 85 degrees with a nice breeze. Globe Life Park has several nice features, but attendance was not great in 2018. We were there to see a last-place team playing the team directly above them in the American League West standings in a half-filled stadium. Some fans were really into the game, but it was largely a stale environment.

25. Chase Field in Phoenix

The roof was obviously closed for an August game in Phoenix. Chase Field doesn't have a lot in terms of extras, but one neat thing about our visit was the 20th Anniversary Experience. From Luis Gonzalez and Randy Johnson to Paul Goldschmidt and Zack Greinke, the Diamondbacks have had some pretty good players over their brief history. Johnson and Curt Schilling were the 1-2 punch that led Arizona to a World Series championship in 2001. The 20th Anniversary Experience walks visitors through the last 20 years and does a nice job of paying tribute to that 2001 championship team and Hall of Famers who have donned a Diamondbacks jersey.

26. Marlins Park in Miami

Baseball is best experienced outside, especially on Opening Day, and the roof was open on March 29th. As mentioned in the Opening Day chapter, we appreciated Marlins Park as we explored it and ate some of the best food you'll find at any MLB park. It's not the easiest stadium to reach and public transportation to the stadium is not ideal. The Marlins do at least try to create a fun environment, but fans help create a great baseball atmosphere. It's the crowd Marlins Park lacks to make it great.

27. Oakland Coliseum

The Oakland Athletics need a new stadium. The Coliseum is definitely not aesthetically pleasing but does have a certain charm considering the team has played there for more than 50 years. But there just isn't much to the Coliseum. There are plenty of tributes to the team's history and Hall of Fame players, like Dennis Eckersley, Rollie Fingers, Reggie Jackson, Jim "Catfish" Hunter and Rickey Henderson — after whom the field is named. The A's were sort of in limbo in 2018 with stadium renovations because they knew they're getting a new one. It is necessary and despite that charm, it likely won't be missed by many.

28. Nationals Park in Washington

Because of the everlasting construction, getting to Nationals Park isn't exactly easy. As I wrote in the Dog Days chapter, the Metro is the best option and street parking is free on Sundays. Parking near the stadium is downright expensive with prices ranging between $35 and $50. While ticket prices are reasonable, the Nationals should be ashamed of what they charge at the concession stands and for parking. Other than the Bullpen, which is outside of the stadium and is a popular pre-game hangout, Nationals Park doesn't have any great amenities.

29. Tropicana Field in St. Petersburg

We weren't inside Tropicana Field for ten minutes when Patti remarked, "This feels like a hockey arena." Honestly, we did not have high hopes for baseball's only permanently roofed stadium. Baseball should be played outside, or at least with the option to. One benefit though is that it did have an intimate feel and there aren't many bad views inside the stadium. The few Rays fans there were engaged in the game, bringing out their Rays-themed cowbells from time to time. The Trop suffers from the same issue as Marlins Park: not enough fans to make it a fun environment to watch baseball. The parking lots around The Trop do allow tailgating and that's encouraged. The Budweiser Porch in right-center field is a good spot to watch the game while enjoying a drink and eating from one of the many adjacent concessions stands. The Rays touch tank is a unique and popular extra. While The Trop may have a certain charm for some, it's easy to understand why it's regarded as one of the least-favored MLB stadiums. The Trop may not be a great place to watch a baseball game, especially with its ghastly catwalk, but you can see MLB players compete without breaking the bank.

30. Citi Field in New York City (Queens)

As much as something can be in the middle of nowhere in New York City, Citi Field is in the middle of nowhere. There is nothing around the stadium, aside from Flushing Meadows across the freeway and some chopshops beyond the right-field parking lot. Parking is very expensive and traffic is a nightmare. Take the 7-line on the subway if you must see a Mets game at Citi Field. If you like hearing and seeing airplanes go over frequently, Citi Field is the place with LaGuardia Airport in close proximity. The constant jet traffic is quite distracting when trying to watch a baseball game. Citi Field is a bland stadium with few amenities. Only the passion of Mets fans gives it any redeemable value.

CHAPTER 16:

THE POSTSEASON

Before we began our trip, Marc Lancaster said the games would eventually run together. He was right. Over the course of 40 games in 30 stadiums, we had to take a minute to properly recall a certain game in a given city. Marc did correctly predict that we would also have some distinct memories, unrelated to the games themselves.

"It's mostly going to be about, 'Oh, man, I had the most ridiculous concession item at this park,' or, 'We saw this crazy thing happen,' or 'We got this great giveaway at this park.' It's more about the experience around the game, something MLB has learned from the minors the last 20 or 30 years and really upped its game there."

Ridiculous concession item? The MVT Dog in Arlington.

Crazy things that happened? Meeting a unicorn and seeing a kid at his first MLB game catch a home run ball.

Great giveaway? Patti's goodie bag from the Rangers.

Check, check, and check.

Marc also advised we see what every park is known for and that is something we tried to do. We didn't hit every unique aspect of each stadium but saw as much as we could.

We saw Miami's colorful home run sculpture in its final season inside Marlins Park. We touched the cownose rays at Tropicana Field. We ate crab cakes in Baltimore, cheesesteaks in Philadelphia, lobster rolls in Boston, brats in Milwaukee, and Dodger Dogs in Los Angeles. We experienced the historic mystique of Fenway Park and the Green Monster and Wrigley Field, where we saw the Cubs "Fly the W" after beating the Dodgers. We watched Miller Park's famous racing sausages, who have inspired the Presidents Race in Washington and giant hot dog races in Cleveland and Kansas City, among many other races around MLB and minor-league parks. We rode the Ferris wheel at Comerica Park, soaked up the gorgeous views of the Pittsburgh at PNC Park, and played a game of pool inside the Western Metal Supply Co. building at Petco Park in San Diego. We also tried to see every statue there was at each MLB stadium (see Chapter 4).

Patti picked up an atlas before we left Charlotte and traced our 15,000-mile route using a highlighter on the national map and the maps of each state through which we drove.

"It's fun to look at where we've been," Patti said. "My mom and dad always had an atlas whenever we took a road trip. I loved having an atlas and plotting out the trip and then seeing where we've gone on that big map."

But our trip reached its conclusion with our final game on September 25th to see the Brewers beat the Cardinals at Busch Stadium, where the Gateway Arch serves as an inimitable backdrop. The Brewers clinched a postseason berth at Busch Stadium the next day and we would watch the playoffs on television. Had the Brewers and Cardinals both made the playoffs as wild-card teams, we decided we would attend the wild-card game in Milwaukee. But the Rockies bounced the Cardinals from contention a few days later and the 2018 season needed two extra games to decide who would win the National League Central and West divisions and who would be the NL wild-card teams. The Dodgers and Rockies played in a Game 163 at Dodger Stadium while the Brewers and Cubs did the same at Wrigley.

The Dodgers won to set up a NL Division Series with the Braves. The Brewers claimed the NL Central crown with a 3-1 victory on October 1st. That meant the Brewers had homefield advantage through the NL playoffs while the Cubs and Rockies met at Wrigley the next day in the NL wild-card game.

The Cubs had two chances at home to advance in the postseason and lost both times. The Rockies ended Chicago's hopes of going back to the World Series with a 2-1 win that set up a showdown with the Brewers.

Milwaukee, blessed with a deep bullpen and potent offense, swept the Rockies in three games while the Dodgers dispatched the Braves in four. Atlanta's lone win was bolstered by Ronald Acuna's second-inning grand slam in Game 3 of the series. Chalk held on the American League side as the Red Sox and Astros easily cruised past the Yankees and Indians respectively.

The Red Sox and Astros each won over 100 games, with Boston boasting an MLB-best 108 wins in 2018. Most people were expecting an epic American League Championship Series, but they didn't get it. After dropping Game 1 at Fenway Park, the Red Sox won four straight, holding the defending World Series champs to just 12 runs over those four games, to advance to the World Series for the fourth time in 15 years.

I was obviously more excited about the National League Championship Series because my Brewers had homefield advantage by virtue of their 96 regular-season wins (including the Game 163 victory). We had seen the Brewers take on the Dodgers earlier that season in Los Angeles and it was a great game with Yasmani Grandal's walk-off homer in the bottom of the 10th to give the Dodgers a 6-4 win. The Brewers had the top of the order up in the top of the ninth and Lorenzo Cain needed just a home run to complete the cycle. Cain flew out to the warning track and the Brewers were held scoreless in the inning. Grandal wound up signing a one-year contract with the Brewers on January 14th, 2019.

We saw the Brewers a total of seven times in 2018 and they went 5-2 in those games. I thought the season was going to have a special ending with the Brewers going to their second World Series. It didn't happen as the Dodgers won an epic seven-game series to head back to the World Series for the second straight year. It probably wouldn't have mattered which team played the Red Sox, who easily dispatched the Dodgers in five games to claim the franchise's ninth World Series crown.

Baseball season was officially over and we created memories to last a lifetime — not just for us, but for the 300 people who received tickets to attend games in Miami, Greensboro, Durham, Detroit, Milwaukee, Minneapolis, Denver and St. Louis as part of our mission. Our next trip was on hold until Holmes was finished with his chemo protocol. He responded extremely well, and within a month, was back to his old self. You wouldn't even know there had been anything wrong with him. We also had to wait for the RV repairs to be completed and that took six months — but that time also allowed us to spend time with family.

We were with Patti's parents for a couple weeks, then stayed with her sister, Veronica, until we could finally pick up the RV. While staying with my sister-in-law for over three months was not ideal, at least we didn't have to pay for RV storage or to winterize it. That was a bit of a silver lining.

We visited my Grandma and Grandpa Clements for Thanksgiving — two weeks after they celebrated their 69th wedding anniversary, and saw my other grandparents while in Wisconsin.

We caught up on several of the television shows we missed while traveling and I focused on writing this book and even picked up a couple of freelance gigs. We became Florida residents while on our MLB trip and had absentee ballots sent to us for the 2018 election. We received them at Veronica's house in late October and mailed them back on November 1st. We then headed to Florida for a week in December to spend time with my sons, RJ and David. We were able to celebrate, not only Christmas in Orlando, but David's 21st birthday. I told the Magic he was celebrating his birthday and we got our seats upgraded. We moved from our seats in the mezzanine level to seats nine rows from the court. But that wasn't all. David got to be on the court with the "Blue Crew" during a third-quarter time out and even shot the T-shirt cannon. David, who towers over me at 6-foot-1, said it was an experience he'll never forget.

We did take Holmes on another road trip, a week-long stay in Mobile, Alabama while I covered the 2019 Senior Bowl. We drove my car.

As the new year approached, we knew we were going to take another RV voyage – most likely that Route 66 tour – but had no plans to remove the vehicle wrap with the Children's Hope Alliance and Home Run On Wheels logos.

The Home Run On Wheels MLB journey may be over, but the mission continues.